THE SEVENTEENTH CENTURY IN FRANCE

BY
JACQUES BOULENGER

CAPRICORN BOOKS

NEW YORK

CONTENTS

CHAPTER   PAGE

   I. THE YOUTH OF LOUIS XIII   1

  II. RICHELIEU   30

 III. THE PREPONDERANCE OF FRANCE (1630–1643)   62

 IV. THE KINGDOM UNDER LOUIS XIII   88

  V. THE BEGINNINGS OF SOCIETY AND OF CLASSIC LITERATURE   112

 VI. THE FRONDE AND MAZARIN   136

VII. THE " ROI-SOLEIL "   172

VIII. THE GLORIOUS YEARS, 1661–1678   209

 IX. DECLINE   235

  X. RELIGIOUS MATTERS   259

 XI. SUNSET   285

 XII. THE KINGDOM UNDER LOUIS XIV   320

XIII. THE GREAT AGE   359

    INDEX   397

CHAPTER I

THE YOUTH OF LOUIS XIII

I. Marie and Leonora. II. The States-General. III. The Concini.
IV. Luynes. V. The advent of Richelieu.

I

ON May 14, 1610, Queen Marie de' Medici was conversing with Mme. de Montpensier in her "cabinet" in the Louvre, when the sound of some unwonted disturbance fell upon her ears.

"As the noise increased in the most extraordinary way," Marie herself tells us later, "I sent Mme. de Montpensier to find out what it meant, and I began to fear some accident had befallen my son, and that he was dead. My alarm increased when I saw Mme. de Montpensier suddenly close the door and turn round to me, her face blanched with terror—for she had seen the King lying dead. And to all my agonized questions as to my son's fate she would give no satisfactory reply, but contented herself with telling me: 'Your son is not dead.' I determined to see what was causing all this confusion for myself; I opened the door of my cabinet, and just as I was coming out of my room I beheld, besides the persons already there, over two hundred naked swords coming in, and M. de Praslin, one of the four Captains of the Guard, turned to me and cried: 'Oh, Madame! We are lost!' And just at that moment I saw the King laid upon his bed. . . ."

Accession of Louis XIII.

She adds that she very nearly fainted. It is possible: but the murder of her husband made her mistress of his kingdom, and that fact, apparently, prevented her from fainting outright.

Not, indeed, that she was ambitious, or that she had any taste for politics. When on a former occasion the King had

1

desired to give her a place at his Council-board, she had betrayed such evident signs of boredom, and given proof of so wonderful an incapacity for business, that he had promptly sent her back to her ladies.

Character of Marie de' Medici.

But though Marie had no wish to direct the policy of the kingdom, she had a keen desire to control its treasury. That economy—almost amounting to avarice—which was perhaps the most valuable of all Henri IV's virtues as a monarch, was not his most agreeable quality as a husband. The Queen's chief thought, when she heard of his death, was that now she would be able to spend as freely as she chose. The interests of France were a very secondary consideration. A grossly stupid lady was this Marie de' Medici !

Looking at her official portraits, by Rubens or Porbus, and, above all, seeing her as engraved by Guillaume Dupré : obese, sensual, the low forehead shaded by frizzled fair hair, the prominent short-sighted eyes, the red and white complexion of a fat overfed woman—we are reminded of Saint-Simon's verdict : " Imperious, jealous, stupid to a degree, ruled at all times by the dregs of the Court and of the people she had brought with her from Italy, she was the cause of wretchedness to Henri IV, to her son, and to herself as well, though she might have been the happiest woman in Europe merely at the cost of abstaining from giving way to her temper and her servants." As to her giving way to her servants, nothing seems less certain, but undoubtedly she gave way to her temper, and it was anything but a good one.

" You are self-willed," Henri IV told her, " not to say obstinate !" She had fits of rage which upset her to the extent of making her ill. Obtuse, lazy, brutal, irresolute, " spiteful both by her natural temper and thanks to the impelling influence of others," it was this foreigner—she talked vile French till her last hour, saying *soucré* for *sucré* and *i fa cho* for *il fait chaud*— this " fat she-banker " who was to take the place of Henri IV in the Kingdom of France.

She had no affection for her eldest son, and hardly ever went to see him at the Château of Saint-Germain, where her own children and those of the King's favourites were all brought up, pell-mell. In the year 1610, Louis XIII was a little boy of nine, self-willed and mischievous, subject to violent fits of blind fury, who spent his days playing at soldiers, and whose governors—following the custom of those times—did not spare the rod, when, as frequently happened, the child proved "stubborn." Marie is said to have preferred her second son, Gaston d'Orléans. But she probably never felt deep affection for any one except for her tirewoman, Leonora Dori, otherwise Leonora Galigaï.

Leonora was the daughter of the Queen's nurse, and the friend of her childish days. When Marie came to France, she **Leonora** forced her on the Court, though not without some **Galigaï.** difficulty, for the King was by no means attracted by the dry, dusky, sly-faced little woman, who began by compromising herself in the most outrageous manner with a good-looking Italian, another of Marie's followers, known as "the Sieur Conchine." Though born himself of a good Florentine family, Concino Concini did not hesitate, in 1601, to marry the Queen's humble waiting-woman, and he had no reason to regret his action. Soon, in fact, it became evident that the wily Leonora ruled the Queen's mind entirely, and that the King was powerless to prevent it. The Bedchamber Woman had a right to be lodged within the palace, just above the rooms occupied by her mistress, and had constant access to her person, so every evening Leonora went down to the Queen's apartments, and when, a few years later, she fell into a state of infirmity which prevented her from leaving her own rooms, Marie de' Medici went up to her.

After 1610, and the death of the King, the friendship between the two women became closer than ever. Leonora, so Tallemant tells us, was "very eccentric": "being an unhealthy woman"—she suffered from some nervous complaint—"she fancied she had been bewitched, and in her fear of spells, she always went about veiled, so, she declared, as to avoid *gli guardatori*." She habitually consulted astrologers, and kept a Jewish doctor, Montalto, about her person, by the Pope's special permission. She lived, indeed, quite out of the world, and knew nothing of the ways of society : shut up in her apartment, which consisted of three rooms, so much afraid of the evil eye that she would receive no visitors save her men of business and a certain dubious Neapolitan abbé of the name of Andrea di Lizza, who acted as her factotum and played her airs on the guitar, she spent her days tormenting her servants, stringing beads, and compounding magic philtres. But so great was the influence this half-cracked being wielded over Marie de' Medici that many citizens of Paris believed the Queen to be either infatuated with her or bewitched by her. " Her Majesty dotes on Leonora in the most extraordinary way, it is as if she were in love with her," wrote the Florentine Ambassador in June, 1610. In all questions of place, of pensions, or business of any kind, " Madame la Maréchale " used her influence, and invariably intervened. As will be readily believed, she never forgot her own financial interests nor her husband's, and he, indeed, would not have allowed her to forget them. Immediately after the King's death, she had the Marquisate of Ancre in Picardy conferred upon him, and had him appointed First Gentleman of the Bedchamber, Marshal of France, and Governor of Roye, Péronne, and Montdidier. Absorbed as they were in the business of amassing money, neither she nor Concino meddled in general politics until the year 1615. The Regent governed according to the advice given her by her aged ministers, who were agreed on one point only, that she would do well to wait and let things take their course ; by Father Coton, the King's confessor ; by the Nuncio, who had a seat at the Council-board ; and even by the Spanish Ambassador ; as to her Council, she only consulted it as a matter of form. Thus was France governed.

On the very morrow of the death of Henri IV, the Prince de Condé began to talk of forming the " great " nobles into a **Intrigues of the** league, with the object of restricting the Regent's **Great Nobles.** power. These " great " nobles, who were really quite distinct from the rest of the nobility, consisted of the Princes of the Blood, in the first place ; of the royal bastards ; of the " foreign " princes, such as Nevers, Bouillon, and others ; and finally of certain Governors of Provinces, who were sovereigns of a kind, like the Montmorencys, the Lesdiguières, and the d'Épernons. Each of these nobles, successors of the great feudal vassals, was surrounded by a whole body of men attached to his house, and devoted to it, who were, in a sense, his subjects first, and the subjects of the King afterwards. These were his "servants," they "belonged" to him, they were "his": first, a crowd of cousins and poor relations, small squires and gentlemen who were lodged in his house, who fed at his table, rode his horses, handled his hounds, and formed his noisy escort wherever he went, thus doing him honour, and affording lively proof of the power and grandeur of his house; then the servants, properly so called, in immense numbers, footmen, cellarmen, cooks, runners, coachmen, lackeys, engaged without any close scrutiny into character, and more or less ill-paid, who slept in odd corners, and lived as best they could, but were protected, like the rest, by the master whose livery they wore, and grew grey and died under his roof; and finally there were the pensioners of every sort—hired bravoes, chaplains, almoners, physicians, or men of letters, whose duty it was to laud their patron's virtues in verse and prose, write his love-letters for him, and supply his wit. When such a man as Condé or Lesdiguières revolted, every soul who "belonged" to him, from the humblest page to the officers for whom he had procured posts in his Government, his gentlemen and his lackeys, followed in his train and consequently revolted with him. All he had to do, to provide himself with an army like the King's, was to raise a few thousand fighting men. And if, that done, he chanced to win a battle, the monarchy was in actual peril.

Naturally, the weaker the monarch grew, the stronger the great nobles became. Theoretically—for practically things were very different—there was no limit to the King's authority, at this period, save his "good pleasure," and he owed no account of his actions to any one. Thus any revolt against the King on any pretext whatever was a crime. But when the King happened to be a minor, and a Regent exercised authority in his name, there was a feeling that the moral duty of obedience was much less pressing. The decisions of a Regent might very fairly be considered open to discussion: was it so very certain that she was ruling in the best interests of the King her son? As a consequence, rebellion became a much less definite and also a far more tempting form of crime. It is for this reason that seditions were of such frequent occurrence under Marie de' Medici and, later, under Anne of Austria. And it will be noted invariably that the insurgents carefully pointed out that they were not rebelling against the King, but against the Regent or her Ministers, and that they claimed, just as much as the partisans of the legitimate Government, to be fighting in the name of the King, and in his " true interests."

II

Harassed by the great nobles from the very outset of her Regency, Marie de' Medici was not in a position to think of carrying out the ambitious plans formed by Henri IV. Sully himself realized this, and advised her to disband the greater part of the army collected in Champagne, at great expense, in view of the approaching war with Spain.

But in any case the Juliers business had to be settled first : in the course of August and September, 1610, the Duchy was taken, without any difficulty, from the Emperor Rudolph. But " this expedition was the last concession made to the past." Marie de' Medici, urged on by the foreign priests and aged men who were her counsellors, laboured—as was indeed her wisest course—from that time forward, to release herself from Protestant alliances and draw closer to Spain. Thus all the designs of the preceding reign were overthrown.

The Queen had kept Henri IV's ministers, Sillery, Jeannin, Villeroy, and Sully. But between the three first-named—they were very old, and generally known as the " three greybeards "—there was little agreement, save in a desire to do their utmost to keep all business out of the hands of the fourth. For everybody hated old Sully, with his bald head and his snarling temper, who never ceased grumbling in his great beard, worked ostentatiously all day long in his study at the Arsenal, sitting under the portraits of Luther and Calvin, and watched over the finances with a vigilance that was most disagreeable. The Queen herself, though she realized his usefulness, could not forgive the scant ceremony with which, in the late King's time, he had invariably cut down her expenses and refused her pocket-money. And further, Sully had two

6

great faults. He was a Huguenot, and his person recalled memories of the late Government. Thus he soon perceived that if he insisted on retaining his post as Superintendent " it might bring some misfortune upon him " ; he prudently handed in his resignation (January 26, 1611), and departed to live in his various country houses, at one of which he died in 1641, having looked on furiously while his successors ruined his work, and with bitterness in his heart having seen Richelieu build it up again.

His disgrace caused great dissatisfaction among tne Protestants, already alarmed by the negotiations with Spain. They called a regular Assembly at Saumur, and drew up some imperiously worded " Memorials " ; when the King's Commissaries called on them to disperse, they declared they would do nothing of the sort until they had received the Regent's replies to their demands. Then Marie de' Medici resorted to the expedient which was always her chief method of government : she bought over (at a heavy price) one of the chief leaders of the party, the Duc de Bouillon, and to such good purpose did Bouillon exert himself that the Assembly gave in. All fear of trouble from the Huguenot party being thus removed, the Regent published the treaty she had signed a few months previously with Spain (April, 1611), which provided for those astonishing unions, the marriages of the grandchildren of Philip II with the children of Henri IV. The contracts of marriage between the King of France and the Infanta Anne of Austria, and between the King of Spain and the sister of Louis XIII, were duly signed in August, 1612.

Thus all warlike projects were at an end : and the contents of the war-chest, so laboriously amassed during the late King's reign, became available at last. This treasure, on the morrow of Sully's retirement, amounted to some six millions of *livres*, packed into hundreds of bags and coffers and kegs, which were shut up in the treasure tower of the Bastille. To reach them, the Lieutenant of the fortress had to unlock one door, behind which was another, with three locks, the keys of which were kept by the Queen, the Treasurer, and a Treasury official, respectively. But even such precautions as these did not suffice to protect the precious hoard. The Regent only contrived to maintain her position by dint of largess and pensions; the moment the shower of gold relaxed, princes and great nobles were stirred by an indignation, the fierceness of which drove them to instant and public denunciation of the disorders in the State.

So it came about that in 1614, Condé—having first of all entrenched himself at Mézières, in the company of Vendôme, **Condé's** Longueville, Bouillon, and Mayenne—published a **Manifesto.** manifesto which insidiously deplored the fact that the population was ground down by taxation, the nobility impoverished, and justice hard to obtain, and in which, says Richelieu, "the best of all was that he complained of the profusion and extravagance with which the King's money was being spent, as if it were not he and his who had received it." The necessity for soothing the indignation of the first Prince of the Blood and his adherents, supported as they were by all the Huguenots, was evident; and as the Queen's counsellors were determined to avoid war, the only resource left them was to try the usual remedy: pensions. This succeeded very well: by the treaty of Sainte-Menehould (May 15, 1614), Condé received 450,000 *livres*, Longueville 100,000, Mayenne 300,000, and the others in due proportion, not to speak of Governments and other favours, in consideration of which the Princes made peace with the Court, which, as the reader will perceive, still had at its disposal a fair number of the bags of money M. de Sully had so carefully laid by.

But the Regent had allowed herself to be coerced into giving a dangerous promise—that of summoning the States-**Convocation of** General. The Princes were convinced that after **the States-** the service they had rendered to the kingdom, **General** after the issue of their manifesto, in fact, the country could hardly fail to prove its gratitude by electing deputies who would support them in their opposition to the Government. But the Court instantly invented "official candidature" in all its perfection. It then proceeded to arrange a journey all through the provinces for the young King: this was one long triumph. Thanks to these precautions, the majority of the elected deputies were hostile to the Princes. So much so that the Regent determined to convoke the

THE YOUTH OF LOUIS XIII

Assembly, not at Sens, as she had at first intended, but in Paris, and in that city the States-General were inaugurated on October 26, 1614, after a procession and a solemn Mass at Notre-Dame.

Of course they only represented the upper classes of the nation. The "common people," and even the middle-class population of shopkeepers and the like, were not represented at all, and the deputies of the "Third Estate," in this year 1610, would probably have been sorely offended at the idea of having to protect the interests of the "riff-raff." Almost all these Third Estate deputies were connected with the magistracy : out of their whole number (192), there were only seventy-six who could not claim a right to the title of *Messire* or *noble homme* ; 156 were judicial or financial officials, 15 were mayors or aldermen, a few were lawyers, two or three were plain burghers, and three, at the outside, were merchants. Thus instead of representing the interests of the majority of Frenchmen, they stood for those of the parliamentary and middle-class patriciate which had set itself up within the kingdom and had developed proportionately to the gradual establishment of a recognized traffic in offices.

To grow rich, then purchase one of the innumerable " offices " which lack of money was perpetually forcing the sovereign to create, and thus to attain a rank that could be transmitted to posterity—such were the means by which families made their way upwards in the seventeenth century. An official who owned a large fortune would contrive to buy some great office, civil or even military ; this gave him a title, and enabled him to marry his daughter to some prominent gentleman : and in this way the descendant of the Potier family became Duc de Gesvres, Mlle. Séguier was transformed into the Duchesse de Verneuil, Mlle. de Mesmes became Duchesse d'Elbeuf, Mlle. Guyonne Ruellend, the daughter of a dishonest but exceedingly wealthy financier, Duchesse de Brissac, and Mlle. de la Porte, whose father was a lawyer, Duchesse de Richelieu. Middle-class folk such as these were duly turned into authentic lords and ladies, and believed they had as much right to look down on the low condition from which they themselves had risen as any member of the ancient aristocracy. The nobles themselves, ruined by the cost of living, which was perpetually increasing, whereas the income from their estates stood still, or dwindled, were forced to marry rich wives to exist at all. A family which had lived in affluence in the sixteenth century, found itself in difficulties in the seventeenth, with the very same fortune : its judiciary and financial rights had been suppressed, any attempt at trade or labour involved forfeiture of position—how then were its pecuniary resources to be increased, save by marriage ? Only two means of subsistence were open to a gentleman of small fortune : marriage, or the King's bounty. In the provinces, more especially, the sovereign's bounty was apt to be slow in its coming, and consequently the old nobility often married into the families of rich plebeians. But it continued to be none the less jealous of the privileges conferred by birth, and the feelings it entertained, as a class, with regard to that of its fathers-in-law may be easily guessed.

Thus immediately after the opening of the States-General in 1614, the deputies of the Nobility tried to strike a blow at those **Suppression of** of the Third Estate by demanding the suppres-**the "Paulette."** sion of the *paulette*. Every official, judicial or financial, who paid this tax—invented by Sully in 1604, and named after the financier Paulet, the first man who farmed it—owned his office outright, so that it did not fall in to the King at its holder's death : so long as the annual fees were paid, his heirs could dispose of it as they chose. To demand the suppression of the *paulette* therefore involved an attempt to suppress hereditary offices, a severe blow to the lawyers who represented the Third Estate. They retaliated, very cleverly, by a demand for the suppression of all pensions : " You are requested, Sire, to abolish the *paulette*," said Savaron, the spokesman of the Third Estate, who made an exceedingly good speech on this occasion, " that is to say, to deprive your coffers of the 1,600,000 *livres* your officers pay into them every year, but there is no mention of any suppression of the excessive outlay on pensions . . . 5,660,000 *livres* ! " The Nobility, unable to retort, declared it had been insulted, and demanded satisfaction. Thereupon the Clergy intervened, and sent a delegate to the Third Estate—a young bishop, already well known for his tact and activity, Armand du Plessis de Richelieu

THE YOUTH OF LOUIS XIII

by name. Savaron made a most spirited explanation, declaring he had not intended to give offence to the Nobility, "either in will or deed," but that for the rest, he had carried arms for five years before he had begun to serve the King in his courts of law, and was therefore in a position to give satisfaction to anybody. In the end, the matter was settled. As a sop to the malcontents, the suppression of the *paulette* was set down in the Memorials of the Assembly—but the question was never seriously discussed again.

Hardly had the Third Estate emerged from this conflict with the Nobility, before it entered on a struggle with the Clergy. It had headed its Memorials with a clause couched in the following terms, which it desired might be accepted as "a fundamental law of the State":

The Third Estate and the Clergy.

". . . That as he [the King] is recognized to be sovereign in his State, holding his crown from God alone, there is no power on earth, whether spiritual or temporal, which has the smallest right over his kingdom. . . . That the contrary opinion, to wit, that it can be lawful to kill or depose our Kings . . . is impious, detestable, contrary to the establishment of the State of France, which is directly dependent on God alone. . . ."

Now this article, which strikes us as inspired by the most absolute good sense, aimed at nothing less than the high-handed solution, by one of its political consequences, of a quarrel that had been maintained in France for several centuries—the dispute between the Gallicans and the Ultramontanes. Since the days of the League and the intervention of Rome in France, the question for all who were not professional theologians had been embodied in the following proposition: "Has the Pope the right, or not, to exercise any control over the crown of the Most Christian King? If the King becomes a heretic, can the Pope depose him? And if the reply to these two questions is in the affirmative, does it not follow that any Frenchman who is a good Catholic may kill the King whom the Pope has condemned, or even disapproved, just as Jacques Clément killed Henri III, and Ravaillac killed Henri IV?" The extreme Ultramontanes, the Jesuits themselves, certainly did all they could to avoid any acceptance of this ultimate outcome of the

11

argument, and disavowed those who, like Father Mariana, proclaimed it (1610). But in the mind of the populace and the simpler folk, it remained the logical consequence of the principles set forth. So much so that, in 1614, many people were convinced the Ultramontane priests had banded themselves together and used the arm of Ravaillac to murder Henri IV: when the murderer had been put to death, the instrument only had been destroyed, the accomplices had escaped punishment : these accomplices now surrounded the Queen, and were pressing the Spanish alliance upon her : there was no certainty, indeed, that Marie herself had not been implicated in the plot ! . . . And, to the more enlightened Frenchmen, Gallicanism was still a traditional doctrine, in favour of which Parliament and the Sorbonne, amidst a war of decrees issued on both sides, had both been struggling for centuries against Rome. So that, on the whole, the Third Estate, when it inserted the clause dealing with the divine right of the French Kings, simply gave expression to a national feeling. But it was not able to defend it.

When the Clergy, which contained a great proportion of Ultramontanes, first heard of the motion in the Chamber of the Third Estate, it fell into " an extraordinary state of agitation and depression." But among its members were many young and gifted prelates, such as Richelieu, who gathered round the celebrated Cardinal du Perron : and several of these, the Archbishop of Aix, the Bishop of Montpellier, and others, went and suggested to the Third Estate, " with silken words," that if by chance there should happen to be any clauses that might affect religious matters in their Memorials, it would be as well to consult the Clergy on the subject. . . . The gentlemen of the Third Estate made as though they did not understand. Then Du Perron himself intervened. On January 21, 1615, he proceeded in person to the Chamber of the Third Estate, attended by an imposing escort of bishops and noblemen, and there pronounced a brilliant and glowing speech, which lasted for three hours. The Third Estate was flattered, but still it did not give way : and Parliament renewed its condemnation of the Ultramontane teachings, while the Prince de Condé, with due regard for his own popularity, read out a long memorandum against regicide to the King's Council. In the end, the Court,

12

which was swayed by the Ultramontane party, discovered a way of giving satisfaction alike to Clergy and to Third Estate: it informed the Third Estate that there was no further necessity for inscribing the clause in the Memorial, because the King considered it already "presented and received." And this done, its one desire was to close the sittings of these troublesome States-General. On February 24, when the Third Estate tried to meet as usual, the members found the door of their "Chamber" locked in their faces. Thus did the Regent trick the States-General of the year 1614. Each of the three Orders that composed it had striven to defend its own interests only, and Bassompierre describes it quite adequately in these careless terms: "The year 1614 began with the debate about the article of the Third Estate, which made some little stir in the States-General: it was patched up at last. Then came the carnival, in the course of which M. le Prince gave a fine ballet, and the morning after that the States came to an end."

To give some satisfaction to public opinion, which appeared very hostile to hereditary right in the various offices, the Court had issued a somewhat vague announcement of its intention to suppress the *paulette*. The Paris Parliament, like all its fellows, would have been affected by this measure. For this reason, and by way of reprisal, it began to oppose it. It assembled, in spite of the Queen's command to the contrary, and proceeded, on May 22, 1615, to lay its solemn remonstrances before her, complaining of the existing confusion in the finances, of the favour shown to foreigners (the Concini and the Nuncio), and of the Ultramontane tendencies of the Court. But the Queen having spoken very firmly in reply, it apologized forthwith: the members did not as yet pride themselves on the possession of that Roman heroism which was to be fashionable in the days of the Fronde.

Then Condé, always ready to seize every opportunity for "embroiling matters," took up the business on his own account.

Marriage of Louis XIII and Anne of Austria, 1615. With much noise and bustle he sent forth a manifesto in which he, too, reproduced all the most popular grievances: and, with the aid of Princes and Protestants, he proceeded to raise an army. Thus, it was under the protection of the royal troops

13

that Elisabeth of France was conducted to the Spanish frontier, and the fair-haired Anne of Austria was brought back to Bordeaux, where she was married to the King on November 28, 1615. The enemies of the Government lacked resolution, and the Court had an army at its command. But the Queen, sluggish and undecided by nature, and prompted, too, by her aged ministers and her very prudent Italian counsellors, preferred negotiation to battle. Three months' parley ended, at last, in the peace of Loudun (May, 1616). According to the published articles of this glorious treaty, the Princes affirmed that their only care had been the general interests of the country, and they secured a refusal to recognize the Council of Trent in France (this was to please the Gallican party), and the dismissal of the Maréchal d'Ancre, who was universally detested, from his post as Governor of the citadel of Amiens : but by certain secret clauses they cheerfully accepted a sum of something over six millions of *livres*. It will be seen, therefore, that they had " worked " even more successfully than in 1614 : the peace of Sainte-Menehould had not brought them in more than half that sum.

II

Then Condé, defender of the people, went back to Paris, where he was hailed with loud acclamations. He had hardly passed his twenty-eighth year. Brutal and rapacious, prompt in his decisions, but uncertain in his plans, he was nevertheless by no means devoid of charm, and his wife—the beautiful Charlotte de Montmorency, for whose favours Henri IV had sued in vain, and who, when she first saw the royal greybeard, frankly exclaimed, " Jésus ! How mad he is ! "—was still more attractive, and won many hearts for her husband. But just at that moment the whole of Paris was singing the praises of M. le Prince : was he not the sworn enemy of the Maréchal d'Ancre, whom all France hated as it was one day to hate another Italian, the favourite of another Queen : Cardinal Mazarin ?

As a matter of fact, it was not so much Concino as his wife who enjoyed the favour of Marie de' Medici. He, so Fortenay-

Mareuil assures us, " never spoke to the Queen, nor even saw her, except during the hours of public reception," and he did not live within the Louvre, but in a small house close to the Palace gardens. When he desired any special favour, he would write a letter to his wife, beseeching her to support his request. This Leonora frequently refused to do : and in such a case he would go to see her, and, when he had exhausted every gentle argument at his command, he would take her by the throat and draw his dagger, so that the lady, exhausted and terrified, at last planned her own retirement to Italy, to escape from her exacting spouse. On the whole, we are forced to the conclusion that Concini was not absolutely displeasing to Marie de' Medici, though she did frequently treat him ill : but his personal power was chiefly based on the idea of it with which he contrived to inspire others : he may really be described, in short, as a master of " bluff," and this is proved by the fact that it was Leonora, and not her husband, who overthrew the " greybeard " Ministry in 1616.

It was not so much through the Queen-Mother's liberalities as by their own business undertakings that the Concini had
The Concini. grown so rich. Now Sillery, Jeannin, and Villeroy had done their best to thwart their financial enterprises, and circumvent their practice of receiving bribes. For this reason Leonora, when she had succeeded in obtaining their dismissal, desired to fill their places with men who would certainly not behave with similar insolence, and chose Claude Barbin, Guillaume du Vair, Bishop of Lisieux, and Mangot, to whom she shortly afterwards added that young Bishop of Luçon who had distinguished himself so greatly in the States-General, M. de Richelieu. Every one of these men possessed a certain merit. Concini was so struck by his interview with Monseigneur de Luçon, especially, that he declared him capable of giving lessons to " tutti quei barboni.' Notwithstanding this, the real leader of the Ministry was not Richelieu, but Claude Barbin, who had previously been controller of the finances, and Master of the Queen's Household. And in the matter of boldness, Barbin was not a whit inferior to the Maréchal d'Ancre, as the world soon perceived.

The Prince de Condé, finding himself so popular, had ended

by thinking himself almost a king. His palace was called the new Louvre. There is a story that the English Ambassador—a very magnificent gentleman, Lord Savile—had proposed the health of the King of France in the Prince's house, looking at him in the most significant way when he drank it. When Condé came to the Council at the Louvre, he arrived with his hands full of petitions which had been confided to him. In this fashion, no doubt, he entered the palace on September 1, 1616, at about eight o'clock in the morning : " Here comes the present King of France, but his royalty will be like a Twelfth Night kingship, it will not last long ! " cried Marie de' Medici, who was watching him, as she leant on a window-sill : and seeing she had given orders for his arrest, she knew something about it. Within a few hours, in fact, Condé was shut up in the Bastille, and all in vain did the Princess his mother, robed in mourning garments, and attended by an escort of gentlemen on horseback, drive through the Paris streets in her coach, casting dramatic appeals from the windows : " To arms, gentlemen of Paris, to arms ! The Marshal has had M. le Prince killed ! " But the " gentlemen of Paris " never stirred, save to sack Concini's splendid house—a trifling misfortune for its owner, seeing that the suppression of his enemy made him master of France.

For little by little the Marshal's power had become irresistible. He had taken advantage of his military position to raise a veritable army, which would obey no orders but his. Safely entrenched in the fortresses of which he had caused himself to be appointed Governor, master of the courtiers, whom he had bound to his chariot-wheels either by favour or by fear, master of the ministers, who now held their sittings in his house, master of the Queen through his wife, and of his wife thanks to certain varied but excellent expedients, what had he to fear from any one ? His dream, in the old days, had been to make himself Constable of France : now, so men said, he was thinking of carving himself out an independent principality on the frontiers of the kingdom : in any case, his pride and insolence knew no bounds. Supple, cunning, excitable, capable alike of heroism and of cowardice, he was a true Southerner, and paraded his power more from sheer delight in it than from any deliberate calculation. Like all his countrymen, he would vary from one moment to the next; charming and kindly when he was pleased, he would fall into a sudden despair, and almost burst into tears, or break into the most terrible fury, if he found any obstacle in his path. Such as he was, this good-looking cavalier with his over-mobile countenance became absolutely intolerable to Frenchmen. He did indeed faithfully protect and support his own adherents, but he treated his followers like so many lackeys, and called the gentlemen who formed his guard, "coglioni di mila franchi." He himself demanded to be addressed as "Your Excellency": the most trifling failure in respect sent him into a fury: "Nobody could lay a finger on that mountain," says Matthieu, "without making it smoke with rage." He affected the airs of a dictator: he issued orders: he kept a body of police of his own: he had people cast into prison. At last, he fell perpetually out of one rage into another: he insulted and threatened every one he met—even the ambassadors. The ministers wanted to hand in their resignations: Leonora, alarmed by the hatred she felt seething in every quarter, would have fled into Italy. . . . But "the Sieur Conchine" only added to the number of his troops, and swore, pale with fury, that he would hold out to the bitter end: "If they do not love me, I'll make myself feared!" he vowed. . . . One man alone ventured to conspire against him: the King.

In 1617, Louis XIII was sixteen years of age. He was considered a simpleton, even a downright fool, and nobody who had watched the existence of the silly and passionate boy, that "most childish of children"—who never worked at all, and spent his days, not only in riding and a passionate pursuit of sport, but in games of baseball and soldiers, beating drums, gardening in the Tuileries gardens, doing kitchen work, larding joints and cooking them, helping the masons, harnessing dogs to little cannons and having them led past him—would have imagined he was ever to be capable of taking up the reins and governing his kingdom. His mother and her ministers let it be understood that he was feeble-minded. When his presence at a Council was allowed, it was on condition he should not open his lips: he ventured, one

Louis XIII as a youth.

17

day, to enter the Council-chamber without having been sent for ; his mother rose from her seat, took him by the arm, and turned him out of the room. At the Louvre, everybody avoided the King, for fear of displeasing the Marshal, and hardly two dozen courtiers would gather round Louis XIII of a morning, whereas the whole Court clustered bareheaded and eager about Concini, who heaped scorn on the royal boy, and may have even delighted to wound him for sport, as on the day he advised him to apply boldly to himself for the pocket-money the Queen refused to give him, and that other occasion on which he offered to lend him his army. So sorely did the sixteen-year-old King feel all this, that he fell ill. He may not have been over-intelligent, but he was brave, violent, and a dissembler : he passionately longed to see his tyrant's fall. But what could he do, all alone, against the masters of his kingdom ?

Only men of small account had been left about him—among them a needy Provençal gentleman who had been taken into **Assassination** the service of Henri IV, and then into the **of Concini.** Dauphin's household, on the recommendation of the Comte du Lude. His name was Charles d'Albert, Sieur de Luynes. Luynes was a handsome man of eight and thirty, with a high forehead, and an open countenance, easy, courteous, and attractive. He had charge of the King's falcons, and his functions brought him into frequent relations with his young master, who had taken a passionate liking for him, akin to that he was to feel, in later years, for Barradas and Cinq-Mars. The unassuming Luynes gave no umbrage to the mighty Marshal : Louis XIII was even allowed to provide his friend with a lodging within the Louvre, just over his own apartments. But from that time forward the King climbed the stairs to his Falconer's rooms every evening, and there, with a few other trusty persons, he considered means to rid himself of his tyrant. Luynes, who was cowardly by nature, would have had the King take to flight and seek refuge with the Princes, who had raised a fresh revolt and collected another army. But others, such as Déageant, and more especially the little King himself, were braver, and Louis ended by making up his mind to have Concini arrested. The man who should be bold enough to undertake this duty still remained to be found : neither Luynes nor his brothers cared to do so. The name of Nicolas de l'Hospital, Marquis de Vitry, Captain in the Guards, an exceedingly brave soldier and a noted duellist, was suggested. Summoned to the King's presence, he asked one question only : "But if he defends himself, Sire, what does Your Majesty desire me to do ? " The boy made no reply. "The King," quoth Déageant, "desires he shall be killed." Then Vitry answered : "Sire, I will carry out your commands." And on the morning of April 24, 1617, just as the Marshal walked through the wicket-gate of the Louvre, reading a letter as he went, and carrying a nosegay in his hand, Vitry issued from the guard-room. Concini was attended, as usual, by a bevy of gentlemen, so numerous that the Captain of the Guards, stopped here and there by the greetings of friends, had some difficulty in coming up with him. "I arrest you by the King's order ! " he was able to say to him at last. . . . "*A me?* To *me?*" cried Concini, aghast, laying his hand on his sword-hilt. Instantly he fell to the ground with three bullets in his body : the shots had been fired by Vitry's brother and brother-in-law and two or three of his friends.

IV

Thus perished the Maréchal d'Ancre, at the very moment when he seemed at the zenith of his power, condemned and Disgrace of the overthrown by a strong-willed boy whom he had Queen-Mother too bitterly offended. All France exulted. When and Leonora. the news of the murder spread, the courtiers all came crowding round the billiard-table on which the young King, flushed, talkative, and excited, had climbed to receive the congratulations of men who had just stepped across the corpse of him on whom they had been heaping flattery only the night before. Very soon the populace had torn the hated favourite's corpse out of its grave, and dragged it round the city streets. The great nobles submitted to the King. The Queen-Mother was sent to Blois. After a long and very unjust trial, Leonora was condemned to death, and her spoils were divided among the victors. Vitry was given 70,000 crowns and a Marshal's bâton : but after Leonora's execution Luynes got almost all the rest, and notably the Marquisate of Ancre, which was now to bear his name, Albert. Then he turned his attention to his family : he married his brother Cadenet, who owned an islet in the Rhone, to Mlle. de Péquigny, he made him a Marshal of France and Duc de Chaulnes, and a peer of France : his other brother, the mighty lord of a small vineyard, became the husband of Marguerite-Charlotte, Duchesse de Luxembourg et de Piney, and a duke and peer too : Luynes himself, likewise a duke and peer, married Marie de Rohan, daughter of the Duc de Montbazon (the future Duchesse de Chevreuse) : he was never weary of acquiring, at the King's expense, for his brothers and for the cousins (who came up out of their native province " by boat-loads ") money, titles, and governments : and at one and the same time a few years later, he was given the sword of a Constable of France, and the dignity of Keeper of the King's Seals. Did all this amount to the presence of a new Concini in France ? " It is the same old tavern," said the gossips, " nothing is changed but the sign ! " This was really unjust, for Luynes, who cared much more for titles than for money, was not a mere pirate, like Concini, and further, though his favour was immense, his political influence was in reality of the slightest. A cowardly though handsome fellow, vacillating, full of contradictions and inconsequence, who would take up a hundred different projects at a time, and not carry out a single one, a poltroon as little inclined to war as to duelling, he had none of the makings of a statesman in him. The part he played in politics has been grossly exaggerated : he was not appointed Constable of France till some eight or nine months before his death, and up to that moment he was no more than an ordinary member of the King's Council, and certainly not one of the most influential. That he had the King's ear is certain : but Louis, who was fond of authority, and full of strong good sense, often lost patience with his empty talk, as on the day when he exclaimed to him : " Hold your tongue, you do not know what you are talking about ! " Indeed the Council frequently arrived at decisions of importance without consulting M. de Luynes at all, and he did but little in the way

Marginal note: Monsieur de Luynes.

of keeping himself informed as to the progress of business. The almost amorous affection and remarkable favour shown him by the King certainly kept him in the foreground, and he was well pleased it should be so. Nevertheless, while the public believed Luynes to be directing everything and ruling France just as he chose, the favourite was really exercising no more influence over the general policy of the country than many another member of the Council, and very much less than the " greybeards " (who were ministers once more), or than the capable and violent Déageant.

While the Concini were in power, the Spaniards, emboldened by the two marriages, and encouraged by French indifference, Treaty of had made some progress in Italy. They had Pavia, 1619. attacked the Piedmontese and threatened the Venetians : they had lately taken Vercelli ; and were preparing to seize Asti. Louis XIII and his Council were in time to make it evident that France had no intention of relinquishing her interest in Piedmont : they forced Spain to sign the Peace of Pavia (October, 1619) which re-established things as they had been before the war, and further, to counterbalance the effect of the famous Spanish marriages, they bestowed the hand of Louis XIII's second sister, Christine, on the eldest son of Charles-Emmanuel of Savoy (February, 1619).

Marie de' Medici, who had been exiled to Blois, was not even invited to her daughter's wedding. She was keeping up intercourse with all the discontented persons in the kingdom, including M. de Luçon, Concini's former minister, who inspired her with an extraordinary sympathy, and who, it was asserted, directed her actions from afar, and had even gone in disguise to see her at Blois. The Council decided the most prudent course would be to exile the intriguing bishop to Avignon. But Escape of the Marie escaped by a window one night, and took Queen-Mother refuge at Angoulême, where d'Épernon, Governor from Blois. of Saintonge and the Angoumois, offered her an asylum. Henri III's former favourite had then attained his sixty-fifth year, and was one of the most powerful noblemen in the kingdom. His post as Colonel-General of the King's infantry, far more important, in reality, than that of any Marshal, enabled him to dispose of the greater part of the armed forces.

21

Thus a civil war, the result of which would have been most doubtful, might well have broken out. To escape it, the Council recalled the Queen-Mother's favourite from his banishment at Avignon, and Richelieu, having recovered all his influence over Marie, induced her, as he had undertaken to do, to sign the Treaty of Angoulême (April, 1619). This secured the government of Anjou to the Queen, and to her beloved bishop the promise of a Cardinal's hat—for which he was destined to wait a considerable time.

But Marie had hardly settled down at Angers before that town became a hotbed of conspiracy. In October, 1619, the Council had liberated the Prince de Condé from the prison into which it had thrown him, and on that occasion the King had caused Parliament to register a declaration, the tenor of which was, it must be confessed, anything but friendly to the Queen-Mother. As for M. de Luçon, he had done his best, in the first instance, to induce Marie to be reconciled to her son in a spirit of sincerity, but he was not the man to risk his own future for the sake of keeping a promise : the moment he was sure his advice was unwelcome to his protectress, he turned his coat, without the slightest hesitation, and worked as hard to make mischief as he had previously laboured in the interests of peace. He even proved his talent to be as remarkable in one direction as in the other, for before long, Soissons, Longueville, and Mayenne were all ready to league themselves with d'Épernon **Battle of Les Ponts-de-Cé, 1620.** and the Queen-Mother, and the Protestants, too, seemed inclined to side with them. . . . In Paris the Council would have entered into fresh negotiations, but Louis XIII decided to march straight on the rebels, with such troops as he had at his command. He acted wisely : the Norman towns (in the Duc de Longueville's Government) opened their gates to him, and the Queen-Mother's troops, which had been entrenched at Ponts-de-Cé, so as to defend the road to Angers, made but a " trembling defence," as Rohan called it, and dispersed with such celerity when the royal army came within sight of their lines, that this parody of a battle was christened the *Drôlerie des Ponts-de-Cé* (August 7, 1620). Three days later, peace was signed at Angers, and the ingenious M. de Lucon, who acted for the Queen-Mother, took good care to have himself included in its provisions. But France was now to find herself face to face with enemies of a more dangerous kind than this handful of factious nobles.

In the early years of the seventeenth century, thanks to a reaction against the doctrines of the Reformation, and also, it may be, against the " pagan " naturalism of the Renaissance, there was a strong revival of Catholicism : in every quarter the religious orders were reforming themselves, fresh orders were being established, convents and monasteries were being built. And though mysticism seemed to be blossoming anew in certain souls, the great majority of these new orders were active, not contemplative. Bérulle had imported the Carmelite Order from Spain in 1603, but he founded the Oratorian Order in 1611. In 1618, Saint François de Sales founded the Visitandines, and Saint Vincent de Paul the Sisters of Charity. The Jesuits, who had been recalled by Henri IV in 1603, were granted leave, in 1617, to open colleges for youths : and everywhere, even in the hostage-cities (*villes de sûreté*) their orators challenged the Calvinist pastors to theological controversies, frequently held in the presence of a sort of jury, and before a very large audience. The Protestants, on their side, were just as zealous as their opponents in the matter of preaching and discussing and converting, and as there was no conception in those days of religious tolerance, it followed, as a necessary consequence, that where the majority of the inhabitants were Catholics (in the greater part of France, in other words) they did all they could to persecute the Huguenots, and that the Huguenots exercised most skilful arts of oppression on the Papists, wherever they had the upper hand.

Royal sympathies, in France, naturally went to the Catholics. Marie de' Medici's government had been frankly clerical. Louis XIII, in a thoroughly honest spirit, did his best to treat his subjects of either religion with equal fairness : but he was exceedingly devout to begin with, and further, how could any King of France help feeling a prejudice against the Reformers ? Ever since the death of Henri IV, the Protestants, alarmed by

The Catholic Revival.

the reconciliation with Spain and the Ultramontane sympathies of the Government, had been multiplying their assemblies, legal or illegal, and their acts of sedition. They had supported every opponent of the Court, and recently they had even stood for the Queen-Mother against the King. . . . This was because the natural and almost inevitable tendency of the Protestants was to try to escape from the authority of a Government swayed by Catholics, and therefore by their enemies—a Government they regarded with distrust, seeing tolerance was a thing unknown in those days, and that they themselves would not have shown any had they been in that Government's place. This led them to organize with a view to resisting the King's authority, escaping from it more and more, and forming a sort of republic of their own within the kingdom. Greatly emboldened by their success and by the impunity they had enjoyed, and exasperated by the religious propaganda of the other side, they were ready to seize on any pretext for taking up arms. . . . This pretext was offered them in 1620.

Jeanne d'Albret had bestowed all the ecclesiastical properties in Béarn on the ministers of the Reformed Church. The Pope had called on Henri IV to restore this Church property to the rightful owners, but the monarch, shrinking from the inextricable difficulties of the situation, had put the question by. But Louis the Just (as Louis XIII has been very deservedly surnamed), in his simple loyalty, felt he must not refuse the Catholics a thing that was strictly in conformity with the provisions of the Edict of Nantes, and strongly pressed on him, not only by Luynes, who had no natural taste for fighting, but by all the other members of his Council. Wherefore, in the year 1617 he issued an order for the restitution of all property belonging to the clergy of Béarn. His decree remained a dead letter. Then in 1620 the King, exceedingly elated by the victories he had lately gained, vowed he was determined to be really King in France, proceeded to Béarn in person, and had the churches reopened by force.

Before he was back in Paris, a General Assembly of the Protestants had been convened at La Rochelle in spite of his orders to the contrary. And on May 10, 1621, this Assembly voted the division of France into eight " circles," commanded by chiefs who were to govern with the help of the provincial councils, raise armies in time of war, and collect taxes in the **Protestant** King's place. These decisions, which involved the **General** setting up, in the heart of the kingdom, of a **Assembly at** "republic drafted on the Dutch system," and **La Rochelle,** specially aimed against the King, and so against **1621.** France, would have been most serious if they could have been put into execution : as a matter of fact they did not alter the situation one whit. Still, Louis XIII could not do otherwise than proclaim the La Rochelle Assembly and all its supporters guilty of high treason (May 27). Then he put himself at the head of his troops, accompanied by his favourite, Luynes, whom he had just appointed Constable, occupied Saumur, took Saint-Jean-d'Angély, conquered Clairac, seized some fifty fortified towns in the course of a few months, and finally laid siege to Montauban : once that fortress had fallen, La Rochelle would be almost the only stronghold left in the Reformers' hands.

The majority of the Huguenot nobility had refused to have anything to do with the Assembly : they were Protestants, indeed, but they were noblemen too, and their interests by no means coincided with those of the majority of the party, who were clearly inclined towards a sort of theocratic and oligarchic republic. But La Force and Rohan hurried up to Montauban. While the first named was bravely defending the town with the help of Du Puy, the consul, the second fought skirmishes with the assailants, and passed supplies in to the besieged. The operations of the King's army, on the other hand, were conducted with considerable slackness by the newly appointed Constable—who, so Brienne tells us, had "never drawn his blade against anything but deer and wild boar "—so that after three months of ineffectual effort, Louis XIII was obliged, as winter was fast coming on, to raise the siege ingloriously.

This was a cruel humiliation, and one for which he kept a grudge against his favourite, for his vanity was especially sensitive to failure in his military undertakings. And further, for several months past, Luynes had not been showing sufficient consideration for his feelings. It would even seem as though his Constableship had completely turned the favourite's head : he would talk to the King with " his cap upon his ear," and contradict him too, with a " Gently, Sire!" and dilate behind his back on the power of the Mayors of the Palace, and humiliate him by giving away larger sums than he himself gave.

So that Louis XIII "was struck, at last, by the dimensions of this suddenly made colossus," as Saint-Simon puts it. In any case he began, very often, to draw his familiar friends into window recesses, and there confide to them that the Constable (who had also become Keeper of the Seals) wanted to " play the king," and these gentlemen do not appear to have made any great effort to persuade him to the contrary. In short, De Luynes' star was rapidly declining.

And at once everybody attacked him, and lampoons against him appeared in swarms. The pamphleteers said cruel things **Death of De** about his cowardice : at Montauban, they declared, **Luynes, 1621.** he had never dared to come within a cannon-shot of the ramparts, but had hidden behind a hill known as "the Constable's breastplate," and remembering he was Keeper of the Seals, " he amused himself by sealing papers while other men were fighting hand to hand." Even the Catholic party, whose policy he had always supported in the Council, now fell upon him. He succeeded in procuring the dismissal of the King's confessor, Father Arnoux, but he was on the eve of his own disgrace when he died of a " purple fever " (scarlatina or measles) on December 15, 1621, before the little fortified town of Monheurt, to which he had laid siege. His friend the King regretted him but little. His widow was remarried, within a few months, to the Duc de Chevreuse. " When his body was taken for burial—to his own duchy of Luynes, I think," writes Fontenay-Mareuil, " instead of seeing priests praying for his soul, I saw some of his lackeys playing piquet on his coffin, while their horses were baiting."

V

When Luynes died, Louis XIII made a vow that in future " he would act for himself in all State matters, as he was doing **Treaty of** at that time." The memory of his Montauban **Montpellier.** failure was still sore : like the brave soldier he was, and in defiance of all his advisers except Condé, he marched straight upon the enemy. Soubise, Rohan's brother, had won a few engagements in the west : the King overthrew him at the Isle of Riez. And then Louis seized Royan, received the submission of all Sully's fortresses in Quercy, took Nègrepelisse and Saint-Antonin, and ended by laying siege to Montpellier. This was one of the bulwarks of Protestantism. The besieged town—helped by Rohan, who kept skirmishing round and about as he had done at Montauban—made such a good defence that at the end of six weeks the King's troops were apparently worn out. And for this reason, when Lesdiguières, a new convert, offered his mediation, it was accepted perforce. A new treaty between the King and his Protestant subjects was signed at Montpellier in October, 1622.

Richelieu still continued to direct the policy of the Queen-Mother, who was more infatuated with him than ever. Louis XIII, unfortunately, could not endure M. de Luçon, and never lost an opportunity of jeering at his mother's devotion to her favourite, whose soaring ambition alarmed the monarch. But she, being miraculously obstinate, defended her Richelieu against all and sundry, and with a courage that never failed nor wearied, she went on begging favours for him. Hitherto she had not succeeded in getting him made a cardinal : Louis' attempts to carry out the promise snatched from him by the treaty of Angoulême had been of the most half-hearted description : and his ministers—more especially the aged Brûlart de Sillery and his son Puisieux—were secretly opposed to the idea of conferring the purple on the troublesome churchman : Richelieu had inspired them, too, with the antipathy most men felt for him all his life long. . . . But when the Treaty of Montpellier had been signed, and the Prince de Condé, who had advised against it, had taken himself off to sulk in Italy, they did not dare to fool the Queen-Mother any longer : in

September, 1622, M. de Luçon, sitting in a modest inn, learnt with a joy so intense that in spite of himself we detect it in his correspondence, that he was a Cardinal at last.

Thus, by slow degrees, we see him force himself on the King, but how difficult he found it! "I have had this mis-

The rise of Richelieu. fortune," he writes, without any mock modesty, at a later date, "that those who were powerful in the State have always had a spite against me, not for any harm I had done them, but because of the good they believed to be in me." The incapacity of Sillery and Puisieux was notorious : under their management, France was falling into discredit owing to the weakness of her foreign policy in Germany, in the Valtellina—everywhere, in fact. This the King well knew, so day after day his mother, primed by her gifted friend, repeated his lessons at the Council-board. But Louis XIII, a suspicious person, who lived in constant fear of being led by others, could not overcome his distrust of one whose imperious superiority was detested by every human being about the Court, as much as by the King himself. In vain did the haughty Cardinal make himself charming, compliant, modest, insinuating, reassuring : in vain did public opinion (which he bought) support his claims : in vain did the Queen-Mother return stubbornly to the charge : when the King decided at last on the dismissal of Brûlart (January–February, 1624), he did not even grant the new Cardinal a seat in the Council, and La Vieuville was made chief minister. But presently the condition of foreign affairs became still more complicated. What was to be done ? The advice of that much bepraised Richelieu really was badly needed. . . . Then La Vieuville fancied he had devised a means of making use of him without admitting him to the Council-board : he suggested his being given the presidency of a sort of secondary Council, less important than the King's, a "Council of Dispatches." But unluckily the Cardinal, quite aware that he was indispensable, did not care to accept a post which would have involved responsibility without liberty. . . . And at Compiègne, on April 29, 1624, towards two o'clock in the afternoon, Louis XIII was forced to summon to his Council, and introduce to all its members, his newly appointed minister, the Cardinal de Richelieu. . . . Within four months the new-comer was master, and showed Vieuville the door.

Works to Consult: *Memoirs* of Brienne, Fontenay-Mareuil, La Force, Pontchartrain, Richelieu, Rohan ; *Journal* of Héroard ; *Relazioni degli ambasciatori veneti nel secolo decimo settimo*, published by Barozzi and Berchet ; Vicomte d'Avenel, *Richelieu et la monarchie absolue* (1884–90) ; L. Battifol, *Au temps de Louis XIII* (1904) ; *La vie intime d'une Reine de France* (1906) ; *Le Roi Louis XIII à 20 ans* (1910) ; G. Fagniez, *Le Père Joseph et Richelieu* (1894) ; G. Hanotaux, *Histoire du Cardinal de Richelieu* (1896 *et seq.*) ; Mariéjol, *Histoire de France*, published under the direction of E. Lavisse, vol. vi, ii (1905) ; G. Picot, *Histoire des États-généraux* (1888) ; B. Zeller, *La minorité de Louis XIII* (1897) ; *Louis XIII* (1898) ; *Louis XIII* (1899).

CHAPTER II

RICHELIEU

I. Richelieu and Louis XIII.   II. The Valtellina business and the
Protestant revolts.   III. The Queen against the Cardinal :
Buckingham : Chalais.   IV. The ruin of the Protestant party.
V. The Mantua business ; the " Day of Dupes " ; Montmorency's
plot.

I

ARMAND-JEAN DU PLESSIS DE RICHELIEU was
born on September 9, 1585, the third son of a Poitevin
gentleman of fairly good position, and of his wife,
Suzanne de La Porte, the daughter of an advocate belonging
to the Paris Parliament.   The eldest of his brothers was
intended for the career of arms, the second,
Richelieu.   Alphonse, was to go into the Church, and he
himself—his parents had at first intended him, too, for the
army—received the education of a young courtier in the
academy of a certain Sieur de Pluvinel.   But one fine day,
Alphonse de Richelieu having resigned his bishopric of Luçon
to join the Carthusian order, Armand, to save the modest
bishopric from passing out of the family, had to make up his
mind to embrace the ecclesiastical career.   The decision cost
him an effort, no doubt ; but having taken it, he adhered to
it steadily, for he was not the man to wear his life out in hopeless
regrets, and he would appear, too, to have realized that as far as
worldly success went the Church might serve his purpose as well
as the army—or even better.   So he studied theology at the
University with industry and success, and was duly appointed
Bishop of Luçon in 1606 ; he was then twenty, five years below
the canonical age.   The country bishopric, " the ugliest
bishopric in France, the dirtiest and the most disagreeable," as
he calls it himself, was not the most tempting of benefices in the

eyes of a young prelate overflowing with ambition, such as Richelieu : but he had quite decided to employ every possible means of getting out of it.

The first he selected cannot be said to have been particularly good. On the morrow of the murder of Henri IV, he thought it judicious to send the Queen a protestation of his fidelity couched in terms so exaggerated that his brother, who was living at the Court, considered it ridiculous, and refused to transmit it. In vain did young M. de Luçon hasten to Paris ; in spite of the various intrigues he at once succeeded in setting on foot there, he failed to secure any place under the new government ; and being too poor to remain at Court was fain to get back to his province, tolerably crestfallen, and just the plain bishop he had been before.

He did not retire to his own diocese, which he found very dull, but to the Priory of Coussay, near Milhau, which was his property. And there he set to work to write to everybody, try to ingratiate himself, endeavour to make himself useful, and strive to gain new friends. In this fashion he spent four mortal years, and so contrived to get himself sent to the States-General by his province in 1614. We have already described the part he played in the quarrels between the three Orders. His sermons, his speeches, and his adroitness had

Richelieu Chaplain to Anne of Austria. brought him into prominence, and his friends succeeded in getting him appointed chaplain to the young Queen Anne of Austria, whose household was just then in course of formation. He soon contrived to insinuate himself into the good graces of the Concini couple : Barbin was his friend : through Barbin he obtained Leonora's friendship, and thanks to Leonora, he became a minister in 1616. . . . When one looks at the famous picture Philippe de Champagne painted of him when he was at the height of his glory, and notes the proud emaciated face, framed in black locks, the scornful eyes under the arched brows, the haughty mien, the imperious port, of the Cardinal-Duc de Richelieu, it is piquant to recall that young M. de Luçon, who put up so patiently with the stout Marie de' Medici, paid such attentive court to the fantastic Maréchale d'Ancre, worked so hard to make friends and acquaintances, was so unfailingly eager to please, so obsequious, persevering, tenacious, and calculating. During the five months he was in power (1616-1617), how unwearied was his endurance of Concini's rebuffs! His letters to him were almost humble (at first, in any case), and betrayed so compromising a devotion that those who seized the Marshal's private papers thought for a moment of including the Bishop in the approaching prosecution. But during the closing period of his ministry, Richelieu had contrived to secure a certain amount of support in the King's immediate circle, and those in power merely sent him into exile at his Priory of Coussay.

There, with a most reassuring zeal, he devoted himself forthwith to theological studies : "reduced to a tiny hermitage," he declared himself resolved henceforth "to spend his time peacefully between his neighbours and his books." Notwithstanding this assertion, the Council heard that he was keeping up communications with the Queen-Mother, and the King, much incensed, sent him to prosecute his beloved studies in his own diocese, first of all, and then at Avignon. I have shown how it soon became necessary to send him to Angers, to quiet Marie de' Medici, and how, when he had established his ascendency over that elderly lady's mind, he ruled her for the furtherance of his own interests, gradually forced himself on the Court and even on the King himself, by virtue of his genius, and above all by his gift of intrigue, and how, having laboriously attained a seat at the Council-board, he made himself master of the whole Council in the space of four months.

The finest portrait of Richelieu that we possess was neither painted, nor chiselled, nor engraved. It was penned by Cardinal de Retz, in the second chapter of the second part of his own Memoirs :

Cardinal de Retz on Richelieu.

"Richelieu," he says, "was a man who kept his word whenever no great interest forced him to do otherwise, and in that case he neglected nothing that was calculated to save his appearance of good faith. He was not liberal, but he gave more than he promised, and his way of adding zest to the benefits he conferred was admirable. He cared for glory far more than morality permits ; ·but it must be acknowledged that his abuse of the dispensation he had granted himself touching the excess of his ambition was no greater than his merit

warranted. . . . He was a good friend ; he would even have
desired the love of the people : but though he possessed the
civility, the appearance, and many other qualities necessary to
this result, he never had that indescribable something which is
more indispensable in this matter than in any other. . . . No
man could distinguish better than he between bad and worse,
between good and better, and that is a very great quality in a
minister. He was too apt to grow impatient over the small
things that lead up to the great ; but this fault, which is peculiar
to lofty minds, is always accompanied by a sagacity which
makes amends for it. He had sufficient religion for the purposes
of this world. He inclined towards that which is good, whether
by preference or by good sense, whenever his interests did not
lead him towards evil, which he recognized perfectly well, even
when he did it. . . . To conclude, it must be acknowledged
that all his vices were of a kind which a high fortune easily
renders illustrious, for they were of those which can only use
great virtues as their instruments."

This portrait, with the addition of a very few features, gives
us the whole nature of the man. In the first place, then, Richelieu, as my readers know, had by no means the soul of an ascetic :
all those things which the generality of men regard as the good
things of life, he passionately desired to possess. He was not
content with being powerful : to enjoy his power, he felt impelled to show it forth to all men. He was ostentatious : in
the days when he was Bishop of Luçon, and hardly able to pay
his way, he took a gentleman to be his steward ; "it looks well,"
he said ; " he manages the household and receives my company."
He delighted in luxury and splendour and expenditure, and in
money too, for he amassed a huge fortune (something like three
millions of *livres* a year, equal to about twelve millions in our
day) ; in honours, for he was always an ardent collector of titles,
and in women, who never cared for him at all. Like all the men
of his time, he was not content to be exalted in his own person
only, his " house " had also to be honoured : thanks to him, his
brother, the Carthusian monk, became Archbishop of Lyons,
received a cardinal's hat, was made Grand Almoner of France,
and accepted all these distinctions very readily ; he made one
of his nieces a duchess, and the other a Princess of the

Blood ;* he provided royally for his nephews and his cousins. His pride was enormous and insatiable : he claimed to be the first personage in the realm, after the King himself ; he took precedence of the Princes of the Blood, even in his own house : one day, shortly before his death, he ventured to receive the Queen without rising from his arm-chair, and when, far from excusing himself on the score of his illness, he informed the sovereign that she could not think his behaviour unusual, seeing that in Spain the cardinals had the right to remain in their arm-chairs in the Queen's presence, Anne of Austria appositely replied that she was now a Frenchwoman, and had forgotten all about the customs of Spain.

It must be added that Richelieu was not proud only, but conceited : he possessed all the vanities, in fact, even that of the literary man. The latter trait, indeed, seems pardonable enough ; this terrible actor in so many fine scenes, diplomatic and military, on the " European stage " was hardly a poet, nor even a dramatic author, but his talent and his power of writing prose are both evident in his dispatches and reports ; and, after all, is not an excessive love of literature a pleasing weakness in the case of a great minister ?

Now the Cardinal's ambition and his splendid greed were served by an energy that was sublime. Richelieu was a man who **Character of** knew no weakness, and pity least of all. He had, **Richelieu.** as people say," no heart." He would indeed, when the occasion served, display a sort of tearful sentimentality, but it was " all on the surface," and " never moved him from the line laid down by his calculations." It was not very often that he would relax, even among his most familiar associates, but when this did occur he would indulge in a sort of jovial merriment not uncommon among priests, and would laugh heartily at Boisrobert's sallies. Subject as he was to physical weaknesses and fits of nervous depression which he did not find

* Richelieu had two sisters older than himself : (1) Françoise, who died in 1615, married René de Vignerot, by whom she had a son who became General of the Galleys, and a daughter, Marie-Madeleine, married on November 26, 1620, to Antoine de Combalet (nephew to Luynes), who ultimately became Duchesse d'Aiguillon ; (2) Nicole, who married M. de Brézé, by whom she had a daughter who married the future " great Condé " in 1640, and a son who became Admiral of France.

RICHELIEU

it easy to conceal, he was never able to endure the smallest hurt to his vanity with indifference : this is what Retz calls his "weakness in not despising small things," and what Tallemant means when he writes that the Cardinal "had not the gift of imperturbability." But when we remember that till the very end of his life Richelieu suffered agonies from headache— he called his head "the worst head in the world"—that he was tortured by a disease of the bladder, that he was perpetually tormented by hæmorrhoids and boils, and that thus the man who spent his whole existence struggling, without an instant's respite, not only against the enemies of France, but against all the persons who surrounded Louis XIII, against Court intrigue, and plots, and attempts at assassination, was a sick man, we are forced into a boundless admiration for the inexorable Cardinal who ruled the whole epoch in which he lived, and moved across the page of history draped in his purple robe, like one of Corneille's heroes.

Richelieu was universally hated (and his unpopularity has survived him. Note the part he is generally made to play in our modern popular literature). The admiration inspired by men of despotic genius is usually accompanied by antipathy. He had tried, indeed, in the earlier days of his career, to gather friends around him, but his very silence was oppressive. Women— who were all-powerful in the romantic and gallant Court of Louis XIII—detested him ; he never knew what to say to them. Had he any real friends ? Faucan betrayed his confidence, and La Valette, Bullion, the Bouthiliers, Servien, Chavigny, even the Archbishop of Sourdis, whom he preferred, for a time, to all the other men about him, served him for their own ends and because he was known to stand faithfully by his creatures. . . . But did any one, save Father Joseph Le Clerc du Tremblay, the famous "Grey Eminence," ever love him ?

The son of a former parliamentary President, who had served as ambassador to the Venetian Republic, and great-grandson of **Father Joseph.** a Marshal of France, Father Joseph had been at Court, and had seen active service, before he joined the Capuchin Order in 1599. His fervent faith, his enthusiastic imagination, and the chimeras that filled his brain, never prevented him from being the most cunning of diplomatic agents. His dream, for many years of his life, was to organize a crusade against the Turks, and he believed that his activities would forward this.

His coarse gown, his great grave eyes under their bushy eyebrows, and the huge hairy beard that filled his cowl, and concerning which Richelieu declared that " he did not know any man in the world capable of shaving it, however dexterous he might be," were seen at every Court in Germany and Italy, whither the Cardinal sent him. From 1633 till 1638, when he died, he lived, for the most part, with the Cardinal, who entrusted to him the duty of communicating all his instructions to his secret agents and to the ambassadors. Father Joseph loved Richelieu because he had divined his greatness : in the days when his patron was still nothing but a poor shabby bishop, Joseph's " attentive soul," as M. Hanotaux puts it, " was already hanging watchfully over that young and brilliant destiny. . . ." But the nobles he had humiliated, the great ladies who were his enemies, the magistrates he despised, the people, bowed down by his taxation, every soul, in fact, except Father Joseph, detested the Cardinal.

The King, for his part, did not hate the Minister (whom he admired whole-heartedly), as he is said to have hated him—but he may not have looked on him with an over-sympathetic eye. He kept him in office because Richelieu served the country well, and because Louis XIII always put his kingly duty before his personal convenience, a truly noble characteristic. But indeed we all know, nowadays, that the son of Henri IV was not the melancholy and grotesque puppet of the old historians. True, he was unattractive at first sight : clad invariably in dull and sad-coloured stuffs, even when fashion imposed brilliant fabrics and ribbons and gold fringes on all his courtiers ; a poor dancer, still in need of dancing lessons at the age of twenty-two, he was miserably thin, his big head was covered with a bristling mane of hair, and the mouth, with slightly pendulous under-lip, that gaped perpetually under his great Bourbon nose, tended as little to endue his long countenance with intelligence as his habitual stammer tended to enliven his conversation. But all the stories about his moral weakness, his melancholy distrust of others, his lack of energy, are merely so many legends.

RICHELIEU

In 1624 the King was a young man of three and twenty, active, violent, healthy, and agile—a sportsman, as we should say nowadays, who spent his activity in an eager enjoyment of the delights of hawking herons and partridges, and hunting stags and wild boar. The elder Saint-Simon was appointed to the office of Master of the King's Horse because he contrived to bring up his fresh mounts quicker than anybody else. He also loved tennis, boating, shooting at a mark, riding, and so forth. He was already beginning to suffer, indeed, from the enteritis which was to kill him in the end, but his constitution cannot have been so very weakly, since it held out for over forty-two years against the treatment of his physicians ; and in one single year, we are told, Dr. Bouvard bled His Majesty forty-seven times, made him swallow two hundred and twelve purgatives, and gave him two hundred and fifteen injections.

Louis XIII at twenty-three.

Nor was Louis XIII a moral weakling. He was certainly not an " intellectual " : he never opened a book. When he was not hunting, he was carpentering, or building, or printing, or turning, or forging metal, and doing all this very skilfully : at an earlier period in his life he had spent hours over childish games, constructing imitations " of the artificial fountains at Saint-Germain with little canals made of quills," cultivating green peas which he sent to the market to be sold, larding meat, with his equerry Georges, making forcing-frames with the help of M. de Noyers, or cooking preserves, all alone ; one day he amused himself by shaving off the beards of several of his officers. But in spite of all this, Louis XIII was as brave as his father Henri IV, whom he had worshipped from his earliest childhood, striving, with a touching awkwardness, to imitate him, " trying to play the good comrade," but avoiding his father's loose morals, in the matter of which, as is generally known, the son's reserve was extreme, and, after his marriage, even excessive. He took a passionate interest in all military subjects : throughout his youth he had been in the habit of studying the movements of troops, and tactics in general, with the help of silver toy-soldiers which he set up on a table. He was not a first-rate general, indeed, for his only idea of a campaign was to march straight upon the enemy without subterfuge or *détour* ; but he was a good officer, who knew all his men by name, and would say a word to the brave fellows as they marched by him, who delighted in reviews and inspections of camps, and the sketching of maps and the drawing up of orders, quite able (as he did at the Isle of Riez) to spend seventeen hours in the saddle with his men, sleep on the hard ground, and eat whatever he could find in the nearest peasant's hut: "a big hunch of brown bread with nothing to drink," or some coarse omelet made with his own assistance. . . .

This being his character, careful of his own dignity and jealous of his kingly power, none of his contemporaries took Louis XIII to be a weak man, easily led. They considered him a great gentleman and a king. Sad he was, certainly, weakened by bleedings and merciless physicking, modest and reserved, his fastidious taste shocked by the loose behaviour of the people about him, "distrusting himself," but capable of a princely dissimulation, as also of energetic action and secrecy—did he not prove it as a boy of sixteen, when he plotted Concini's destruction?—just, soldier-like, conscientious, "passionately devoted to the glory of his State." Louis XIII was assuredly a king who was no slave to voluptuous weaknesses, one of the most virtuous monarchs that ever sat upon the throne of France, one who may not have possessed the intelligence, but who certainly had the heart, of a great sovereign.

Violent in temper and jealous of his own authority as Louis was, the Cardinal treated him with the greatest respect, and on **Louis' appreciation of Richelieu.** all questions, great and small, he drew up reports which he sent to the King when he was absent, or laid before him at his Councils. In these the solutions that might be adopted and the reasons in favour of adopting one or the other were clearly set forth. The King would read them, listen attentively, take great pains to understand them, and would then think over the matter : this done, he frequently decided in accordance with his Minister's wishes, but this did not always happen, especially when the question was one affecting military arrangements. The ambassadors always found the King thoroughly informed on current affairs, and with a perfect mastery of matters that had been debated in Council : they describe him as a prudent man, weighing the replies he gave them, careful to say just what was necessary, without compromising or entangling himself. . . . Those who represent Louis XIII as trembling in the presence of the Cardinal are quite in the wrong. Between 1617 and 1624, before the Minister was connected with the business of the State, the King had given proof, on several difficult occasions, of that very decision, vigour, and power of general direction which were to be the characteristics of French policy " under " Richelieu. The Cardinal certainly brought the depth and wisdom of his own views, the methodical consistency of his ideas—his political genius, in fact—into his conduct of public business, but Louis never needed his presence to make him energetic and resolute.

To sum up, it was never either feebleness or indolence that led Louis XIII to follow the counsels of his great Minister. He followed them because he was too sensible not to recognize the Cardinal's superior gifts, and that being so, too honest not to submit to them.

II

In March 1623, the Prince of Wales, attended by Buckingham, made a secret journey into Spain : romantic and utilitarian,

Marriage of the Prince of Wales and Henriette-Marie. like most Anglo-Saxons, his dream had been to make the Infanta fall in love with him, and thus carry off both her hand and her dowry—the Palatinate. Six months later (in September), he returned, sorely disappointed ; the Spaniards had tried to make him turn Catholic, and the Duke of Bavaria had become Palatine. Then he cast his eyes on the sister of Louis XIII, and his suit was accepted. The opinion of Richelieu, who had then just entered the Council, was that in return for Henriette's hand, France ought to exact the same conditions as those England had proposed when the Infanta's had been asked ; and he was deputed, with La Vieuville, to arrange the provisions of the marriage contract. The discussion did not prove an easy one: the fact was that Richelieu's colleague, desiring to play him a trick, sent secret messages to the English ambassadors, advising them not to give in. The Cardinal, becoming aware of this, complained to the King, who instantly gave orders for La Vieuville's arrest (August 13, 1624). Within three months of that date the contract was duly signed. Richelieu, now without a rival in the Council, was soon to be called on to prove the quality of his talents.

The Valtellina is the valley, some twenty leagues in length and one in breadth, lying along the upper Adda, and closed at its **The War in** two ends by the counties of Bormio and Chiavenna, **the Valtellina.** which command the Stelvio and Splügen Passes, and have always shared the valley's fate. To Spain it was an important matter to establish communications between her Italian colony in the Milanese State and the dominions of Austria, her natural ally, and with that object, to command the Stelvio and the Splügen. For this reason, when the Catholics of the Valtellina fell under the rule of the Protestants of the Grisons, the Spaniards at once felt that conscience imperiously dictated the duty of protecting the Catholic faith in the Valtellina. In 1620, therefore, they occupied the country, and then forced the Grisons to grant them the right of passage through it, in consideration of an annual subsidy of 25,000 crowns (January, 1622). While these events were taking place, France had been absorbed by her struggle against her own Protestants; but the moment the Peace of Montpellier had been signed (October, 1623), she leagued herself with Savoy and Venice, for the purpose of restoring their conquest to the Grisons (February, 1623). Then the Spaniards, in alarm, offered to make the forts over to some third Power—to the Holy See, for instance : a proposal the Brûlarts, who were directing the policy of France at that moment, very foolishly accepted. Yet it should have been clear enough that once the Pope had been appointed to hold the fortresses, it would be difficult to force him to return them, or agree to any measure in favour of the Grisons heretics, the oppressors of a Catholic population. It was on this that Spain had reckoned, and her wisdom was soon manifest. The Holy See, in fact, devised the following arrangement : the Spaniards were to have the right of passage, and the inhabitants of the Valtellina were to be free to practise their religion : the sovereignty over the country was still to remain with the Grisons, but they were to lose it if they were guilty of the slightest infraction of religious tolerance ; and as it was the Pope who undertook to verify these infractions, it will readily be imagined that they were likely to occur at once ! Yet the French ambassador at Rome, Brûlart de Sillery, gave his verbal adhesion to this agreement. And things had reached this point when Richelieu took the helm.

This is what he did. On November 25, 1624, the Marquis de Coeuvres suddenly marched a small French army into the Valtellina, to the general stupefaction, and by the end of three months the whole valley was in his hands : the Pope was left with nothing but Riva and Chiavenna. Richelieu at once proceeded to disavow his general's proceedings, and then opened negotiations. Unfortunately for him, the powerful party of devout Catholics, which he had alienated by forwarding the marriage of Henriette of France with the heretic English prince, and by signing a treaty with the Dutch Protestants, was raising an outcry about the " scandal "—the King's ordnance had actually fired on the standard of Saint Peter ! And at the same moment, the Protestants, thinking the occasion a favourable one, revolted once more. In January and February, 1625, Soubise, having seized seven great ships, took possession of Oléron, and when the news spread, all the Calvinists in the South, spurred on by Rohan, rose in revolt likewise.

The difficulty in which Richelieu found himself may be imagined : he was on bad terms with the Pope, he was threatened by Spain, and he had not only to cope with the foe within the borders of France—the Huguenots—but to hold out against the bigots and against his own personal enemies—in other words, practically the entire Court ; and all this at a time when he was not sufficiently powerful to reckon on imposing his will even on the Council. . . . He extricated himself from the difficulty with extraordinary dexterity.

Apparently only two courses were open to him : either to make peace with Spain and the Holy See, and so overwhelm the **Peace with** Reformers, or else to treat with the Protestants, **Spain and with** and so bring the Valtellina business to a satisfactory **the Huguenots.** conclusion. The Catholic clan tried to force the first of these expedients on him, but he did not feel himself strong enough, as yet, to crush the Huguenots completely, and desired to secure a little breathing-time. What, then, did he do ? In the most cunning fashion, he inspired each of his adversaries with a fear that he was going to ally himself with one so as to destroy the other, and in this manner he induced Spain to grant him the exclusive use of the passages into and out of the Valtellina (Treaties of Monçon, January 1 and March 5), and concluded the Peace of La Rochelle with the Protestants on February 5, 1626. " The Huguenots," he tells us himself in his Memoirs, " were led to consent to this peace by their dread of one with Spain, and the Spaniards to make peace out of their dread of peace with the Huguenots." The game had been skilfully won, but the Court did not thank him for his victory.

III

Now the Frenchmen of those days took but little interest in foreign politics. In the first place, because they knew very little about them—their means of information on the subject being of the scantiest description. The King, indeed, was perpetually publishing statements, *Declarations*, in which the affairs of the State, those of his own family, and the reasons which had guided his conduct, were all set forth at length—for the sovereign thought a great deal of public opinion, and took immense pains to conciliate it. But all this, as will be imagined, was exceedingly " official," and gave little satisfaction to curiosity.

There was a periodical publication, the *Mercure Français*, but it only appeared once a year, and was nothing but a summary of " the most remarkable " events. Besides this, a mass of lampoons and political pamphlets were retailed round about the Palace, on the Pont-Neuf, and in booths, but the authors of these confined themselves to dragging the great nobles, or the Cardinal, through the mud, according as their pensions happened to be paid by one or the other. So that almost the only source of information open to the public consisted of private correspondence (which accounts for the importance attached, in the seventeenth century, to the art of letter-writing).

The first Newspapers.

The first number of the first embryo of our present newspaper made its appearance on May 1, 1631. But this *Gazette*, edited by a physician, Théophraste Renaudot, was nothing but a four-paged weekly sheet, which printed news, but supplied no commentary. Renaudot's invention, we may add, was soon granted the Cardinal's encouragement, and the effect government encouragement produces on the Press, in most cases, is pretty generally known. . . . The public had no confidence whatever in the *Gazette*.

Thus it came about that after the appearance of Renaudot's paper, as before it, our forefathers lived, one might almost say, feeling their way. And for this reason we must not cry out too loudly against the lords and ladies of the Court, if, at the very moment when the Cardinal was simultaneously fighting the Huguenots and carrying on negotiations with Spain, they were doing their utmost to overthrow him altogether. The political services rendered to France by Richelieu, and at a later date by Mazarin, were very often misjudged by Frenchmen, or even utterly unrealized by them.

After the death of Luynes all that was young and gay at Court gathered round Anne of Austria, and opposed Marie de' **Anne of** Medici, whose creature the hated Cardinal was **Austria.** supposed to be. For, to all romantic hearts, the young Queen was a touching figure, persecuted and misunderstood !

After her marriage Anne of Austria was so utterly neglected by her timid lord that Spain, deeply offended, caused her ambassador to lodge a complaint. It was not till early in 1619, and then only by resorting to a certain violence, that Luynes succeeded in making the King play a husband's part : from that time, Louis XIII and Anne of Austria lived on good terms, until, after the Constable's death, Marie de' Medici came back to Court, and forthwith set herself to make mischief between her son and her daughter-in-law.

Poor Anne, now kept at a distance, amused herself as best she could. Just at that moment the *Astrée* was all the fashion : what harm could there be in listening to the doleful and flowery discourse of a lover respectful and fluent as one of the shepherd lads of the Lignon ? M. de Bellegarde, an old beau of the days of the Valois, still preserved " that politeness which Catherine de' Medici had brought with her from Italy," and his old-fashioned manners filled the young men brought up in the rough Court of Henri IV with admiration : Anne, then, permitted M. de Belle-garde " to behave to her after the fashion of the century in which he had lived, which had been the reign of gallantry and of fair ladies." But neither the speeches of the old Duke, nor those of the brave Henri de Montmorency, contributed to heal the breach between the King and Queen.

Nor did Anne's best friend help to improve matters. Marie de Rohan had married the Duc de Luynes when she was seventeen : **The Duchesse** by the time her first husband died, her reputation **de Chevreuse.** was already so extremely bad that the Nuncio thought it his duty to advise the young Queen not to keep so compromising a lady about her person. . . . But Anne did not dismiss her friend. One evening, on March 14, 1624, Mme. de Luynes and Mlle. de Verneuil amused themselves by running, with the Queen, along the apartment in the Louvre now known as the Salle La Caze. Anne, then in an interesting condition, " stumbled and fell, and hurt herself." Whereupon the King, in a fury, sent the young Duchess about her business. But she soon contrived to recover her position, thanks to her marriage with a younger member of the Guise family, the Duc de Chevreuse, to whom Louis XIII was very much attached.

But hardly had she married again when she fell in love with Henry Rich, Lord Kensington, Earl of Holland, " one of the **The Queen and** handsomest men in the world " it would appear, **Buckingham.** " but of an effeminate style of beauty." And this love affair would certainly have had no bearing on the history of France if Mme. de Chevreuse had not taken it into her head to provide the neglected Queen, her friend, with as charming a consoler as she herself had discovered. For such a purpose could anybody more attractive be imagined than the splendid Duke of Buckingham ? Charles I had just dispatched this nobleman as his Ambassador Extraordinary to the Court of France, to escort the new Queen of England, Henriette-Marie, to her future home (May, 1626). During the week he spent at the French Court, Buckingham took advantage of his mission to be a great deal with Anne of Austria, and his presence was certainly not disagreeable to her. . . . When Henriette departed to England, the Queen and the Queen-Mother accompanied her as far as Amiens. There, if we may believe La Rochefoucauld, Buckingham was very bold, and when he took leave of Anne, a few days later, those present noticed that he could not conceal his tears. He had only just reached Boulogne when he declared he had received a letter from his master which necessitated his return to Amiens; he went to pay his respects to the Queen; she was in her bed, he fell on his knees beside it. . . . All this extravagant behaviour made a stir. The King, who heard something of it, dismissed Anne's equerry and her footman, and his mother's favour with him was increased by all he withdrew from his wife. But Anne, thus persecuted, excited even more sympathy than before, and the Court ladies and coxcombs were hotter than ever against the Queen-Mother and her creature, the Cardinal.

These two had devised a perfectly reasonable plan for the marriage of Gaston d'Orléans (Monsieur, the King's brother) with **Projected mar-** Mlle. de Montpensier (who afterwards became the **riage of Gaston** mother of the " Grande Mademoiselle "). Many **d'Orléans.** people were hostile to this alliance: Anne of Austria, in the first place—for, being childless herself, she did not care to have a sister-in-law who might bear an heir presumptive to the crown; the Prince de Condé, too, the first Prince of the Blood after Monsieur, who was loath to lose all chance of seeing his own family on the throne; the Comte de Soissons, who wanted to marry Mlle. de Montpensier himself; the King's two natural brothers, the Duc and the Grand Prieur de Vendôme; Mme. de Chevreuse, carried away by her love of intrigue; Henri de Talleyrand, Comte de Chalais, carried away by his passion for Mme. de Chevreuse; and various other persons, who plotted for the same reasons as Chalais—for the sake of pleasing their lady-loves, or out of gallantry, or romance, or fashion, or because intrigue seems almost the only occupation open to courtiers. Thus love was mixed up with the whole cabal, and, one way with another, a most powerful party was labouring with all its might to prevent the marriage.

In those days Monsieur was a very good-looking man, " who always wears his hat like a halo, and whistles all the time, with **Character of** his hands in his pockets." Light of foot, lively **Gaston.** and wiry to the most extraordinary degree, he never ceased moving hither and thither and twisting about—to such an extent that his servants were obliged to put his clothes on him at random, and dress him, so to speak, by guess-work.

45

At night he would wander all over the town, frequenting low resorts like any wild young student, and often showing himself in places "where the police commissary of the quarter is sorely feared" : such habits scandalized the "severe and Christian" King, who would lecture him to the best of his ability. Hence, to the end of his life, Gaston's pleasantries always smacked of "page's wit" : but he was intelligent, he was fond of pictures and medals, and hair-splitting controversies ; he would note the best passages of a book, he was affable in his dealings with gentlemen, and more than affable with ladies : with all this, his "manners were incredibly easy," and, to conclude, he possessed, as Retz tells us, "everything that is necessary to the making of an honourable man, with the exception of courage" : he might have stood for a Prince Charming if he had not been such a coward. But what a coward he was ! All his life long he plotted "because he had not strength to resist the persons who dragged him into their intrigues for their own interest," and then betrayed his accomplices "because he had not the courage to support them." With his keen wit, his jeering tongue, and chicken heart, this prince appears quite out of place among the men of his period. His soft and feeble nature seems to set him far apart from his sturdy and independent contemporaries, even as the virtues of Corneille's heroes distinguish them from the neurotic heroes of our own times.

In 1625 he was blindly following the counsels of his Governor, the Maréchal d'Ornano. Ornano, "an old man, and the ugliest **Intrigues and** in France," who was much petted by Mme. de **punishment of** Chevreuse and also by the Princesse de Condé, to **Chalais.** whom he was deeply attached, and whose interests he desired to defend, joined the party of "those averse to the marriage," and easily persuaded his pupil to refuse to take Mlle. de Montpensier to wife. Whereupon Richelieu, having failed to win the old Marshal over to his side, induced the King to put him in prison. But this blow did not discourage the conspirators : the Vendôme brothers, indeed, went so far as to hatch a plot to have the Cardinal stabbed, and possibly to set the Duc d'Orléans on the throne. . . . Chalais was the confidant of all these black designs He was a gallant young fellow of eight and twenty, smiling and amiable and frivolous : "a handsome head, but with no brains ! " He was so imprudent as to repeat what he knew to one of his friends, who threatened to denounce him if he did not reveal the whole plot to the Cardinal instantly. Chalaïs obeyed. And forthwith the wily Cardinal wrote to the King, reported what he had heard, and offered to resign his office. " Whoever attacks you," replied the angry monarch, " you will have me for your second " ; and without a moment's hesitation he ordered the arrest of his two natural brothers, the Vendômes (June 11, 1626); while Richelieu, on his side, terrified Monsieur (no very difficult task), and made him sign a most humble declaration of submission to the King (May 31).

But Gaston, whose habit, as he says himself, was always to reserve "something when he took an oath," had only sworn to be faithful " with his lips." Every night, Chalais, who had plunged into the plot again for the love of Mme. de Chevreuse, would come to see him, in his dressing-gown, and exhort him to rebel openly, and then retire to some fortress. . . . Unfortunately for the imprudent Chalais, his own intimate friend, the Comte de Louvigny, with whom he had quarrelled, betrayed him to the King : he was arrested forthwith, and answered very awkwardly under cross-examination. He also rashly confided the letters he wrote to Mme. de Chevreuse to a lackey, who handed them over to his judges.

If my complaints [he wrote, in the fashionable jargon of his day] have touched the tenderest of hearts, when my sun failed to shine on the paths sacred to love, where are those who will not sympathize with my sobs, in a prison into which its rays can never penetrate ? And my fate is all the more harsh since it forbids me to reveal my cruel martyrdom. . . .

Meanwhile, Gaston, shaking with terror, confessed everything, gave up the names of all the associates who had put their faith in him, compromised everybody. When the Cardinal promised him a fine fortune on his marriage, he felt quite persuaded that " in this extremity the best thing was to make it up with the King," and on August 5, 1626, the triumphant Richelieu gave his blessing to the marriage with Mlle. de Montpensier.

A fortnight later Chalais mounted the scaffold. His friends, hoping till the last moment for a pardon that never came, had spent large sums in bribing the executioner to keep out of the way. But Richelieu granted their lives to two men who had been sentenced to the gallows, on condition that one acted as the executioner and the other as his man. The first blow struck by the amateur headsman, armed for the purpose with a sword belonging to one of the Swiss Guards, made only a trifling wound : he asked for an adze (he was a cooper by trade). Even at the twentieth stroke from this weapon, the sufferer was still crying out " Jesus Maria et Regina Coeli ! " . . . He received thirty-four blows in all, and before his head could be entirely severed from his body, the corpse had to be turned over. . . . Thus perished the frivolous Chalais, a conspirator for love's sake. Mme. de Chevreuse, compromised both by his letters and by his confessions while under trial, was exiled to Lorraine. Ornano died in prison, just when he was about to be tried (August, 1626). Two years later (February, 1629) the Grand Prieur de Vendôme died. The Duke his brother did not come out of prison till 1630. The Comte de Soissons departed on a little journey. As for Anne of Austria, she was summoned to the presence of the King, the Queen-Mother, and the Cardinal. Louis XIII reproached her with having desired his death so that she might marry his brother : " I should have gained too little by the change ! " she answered scornfully ; and it is probable, indeed, that the idea had never existed anywhere save in the over-fertile imagination of Mme. de Chevreuse : but to the end the King remained persuaded of his wife's guilt. " In the state in which I am," he was to say on his death-bed, " it is my duty to forgive her, but I am not bound to believe her." Gaston alone—as a reward for his treachery to everybody—gained a rich heiress and an apanage by " the conspiracy of Chalais."

IV

The Protestants were more dangerous enemies than the plotters of the Court. In 1625, according to their usual custom,

Protestant revolts. they had seized the moment when the Government, absorbed by external difficulties, was least able to make head against them, to raise the standard of revolt : and had thus once more acted in conjunction with the enemies of the realm. Yet their conduct should not be judged from our modern point of view.

RICHELIEU

No European, at that period, had the smallest conception of tolerance. Everywhere, in England, in Spain, in Germany, the church of the majority was forced by law on all the rest of the population. There was no question of liberty; the general opinion was that men were as much bound to live under a single religion as under a single ruler : *cujus regio, ejus religio*. So much so that the religious minority only contrived to impose itself on France by sheer force. The Huguenots snatched the Edict of Nantes from Henri IV by dint of threats, and threats uttered at a moment when he was engaged in a most difficult struggle with Spain. And this Edict was hailed with as much ill-will by the Catholics, whom its clauses infuriated, as by the Protestants, whom they disappointed. The first named did their utmost to oppose its application all over France, where they generally had the upper hand, and the others laboured with the same object in the parts of the country in which they had the mastery—as in Lower Languedoc and in Béarn, where the first outcome of the Edict would have been to re-establish that Roman faith which they had more or less suppressed. . . . Add to this the fact that, on both sides, under Louis XIII religious ardour had grown much keener, and tolerance, consequently, had not increased. In the Catholic parts of the kingdom the populace was constantly insulting the Huguenots, jeering at their funeral processions, disturbing their worship, destroying their dwellings or demolishing their churches, and sometimes even going so far as to take their lives—while the Protestants, in their own towns, applied similar treatment to all Papists. How could the Parisians possibly allow the " so-called Reformers " to refuse to uncover, like other men, and their women-folk to abstain from falling on their knees, on the line of passage of the Blessed Sacrament, which the King himself so respectfully attended on its way, whenever he chanced to meet it ? Yet that was the point on which the Protestants most frequently refused compliance ; and some fanatics would go to the length of cursing at the processions, or committing sacrilege during Mass ; while their pastors would call the Church of Rome the " wanton," and Catholics " idolators," or even, like Jérémie Ferrier, denounce the Pope as " Antichrist."

And on every side, among the people, reports were circulated of massacres planned by Papists, and of Huguenot plots. . . . In short, Frenchmen, thus divided between two religions, looked on each other as two hostile peoples.

And this all the more because the idea of nationality was not as yet very clearly defined in the national mind. Patriotism, as we understand the word—love of the true qualities of the Frenchman, and pride in them—probably did not develop **Patriotism a** into a general feeling till after the reign of the **modern virtue.** "Grand Roi." Amongst the nobility, at least, the feudal sentiment was still lively in the seventeenth century : the nobles were royalists rather than patriots ; civic virtue consisted in fidelity to the King : in a word (and the nobler *émigrés* of the Revolutionary period had exactly the same feeling), the King was the fatherland, he was France. And further, many men, in the days of Louis XIII, regarded religion as something even more important than royalism, because the theory of the League as to the temporal supremacy of the Pope over the King was still under discussion. And there certainly were numbers of Catholics who felt themselves much nearer to the Spaniards, for instance, who were Catholics like themselves, than to the French heretics : but, above all, the majority of the Protestants felt that their English and Genevan co-religionists were far more their fellow-countrymen than the French Papists. This explains the alliance of the Reformed party with the enemies of the kingdom. To all good Huguenots, and more especially to the men of La Rochelle, who kept representatives at the English Court and attacked all ships that flew the French flag on the high seas, Catholic France was a foreign nation.

But it is only fair to add that this was not the unanimous opinion of the Reformers : when Rohan strove to stir them up against the King he was frequently received with a very tepid enthusiasm. This was because the Protestant community was a sort of federation, each town in which was eager to preserve its own liberty, acting, above all things, in its own special interest. The cities of the South, which, with La Rochelle, constituted the chief strength of the party—each of them a small theocratic republic modelled on that of Geneva—desired war, as a rule, as little as they had desired the Edict of Nantes, which they did not want at all. Altogether, there was a great deal of division in the Reformed party. The nobles despised the political assemblies, which in their turn distrusted the nobles ; and the churches—as the Huguenots denominated what the Catholics called the parishes—distrusted both the nobles and the general assembly. And indeed the cohesion of the party was ensured, not by its political but by its ecclesiastical organization. Each church was ruled, in democratic fashion, by an elected assembly called a Consistory, and served by one pastor or more. The deputies sent from a certain number of Consistories composed a higher assembly, known as a Colloquy. Several of these Colloquies, again, made up a Provincial Synod, and these sent up their delegates to the National Synod, which thus represented the whole of Protestant France. These ecclesiastical assemblies, less regular in their sittings and less popular in their composition than the political assemblies, played a far more important part than these last in keeping the framework of the Reform party together.

The Consistory, which was charged with all matters of discipline, kept its eye on the conduct and the very thoughts of the " faithful." These might appeal from the decisions of the Consistory to the Colloquy, and from the Colloquy to the Provincial Synod, and to the National Synod in the last resort. This perfect subordination of the various classes of assemblies to each other endued the Reformed religion with a moral unity which rendered its adherents a most powerful minority.

Thus organized, and moved by such a spirit, the Protestants, though not always perfectly agreed on matters of general politics, possessed interests apart from those of the kingdom, a fact which, as they frequently proved, rendered them a very dangerous element within it. In 1611 Richelieu had begun to plan the suppression of the exceptional privileges they had obtained from Henri IV, and their conduct in 1625 was not calculated to lead him to alter his intention : as soon as he was rid of Spain, he set about preparing the destruction of La Rochelle—that " wasps' nest," as he called it. He constructed two forts on the Isle of Ré, and sent the brave Toiras to command the strong garrison he placed in them. Then, having been himself appointed Grand Master and Superintendent of the Navy, he caused a number of ships to be built. . . . England was to furnish him with the pretext for declaring war just when he wanted it.

Buckingham, who was Charles I's favourite, just as he had been his father's, had no reason to love Anne of Austria's "barbarous spouse," and Louis XIII, it may be fairly argued, had still less reason to love Buckingham. The Treaty of Monçon, which had reconciled France with Spain, had set enmity between her and England. Buckingham began by seizing French mer-

Buckingham's expedition against the Ile de Ré. chantmen, and next, on June 27, 1627, he set sail from Portsmouth, and bore down on La Rochelle, which he reached within a month. Protestant noblemen from all parts of the country had hurried to meet the English fleet : he formed them into a body of troops who were to lead every assault. But instead of entering La Rochelle, he amused himself by attacking the Isle of Ré ; and by September 10, when the heavy guns of La Rochelle opened fire, at last, on the royal forces, Louis XIII had had time to mass seventeen regiments of infantry and twenty-two companies of horse—carabineers, *chevau-légers*, and *gendarmes*—before the town.

Toiras, meanwhile, was still holding out at Saint-Martin-de-Ré. On the night of November 7 Schomberg broke the English blockade, and threw himself into the island, with the regiments of Navarre, Plessis-Praslin, La Meilleraye, and Piémont, the gentlemen of the Queen's household and the *chevau-légers*. Buckingham, in spite of his hasty retreat across the marshes, was caught and defeated ; he lost courage, and re-embarked his troops. We can imagine the despair of the men of La Rochelle, when, from the top of their ramparts, they watched the British squadron disappear over the horizon ! But hopelessly compromised as they were, there was nothing for it but to resist to the end.

The King's councillors would not run the risk of assaulting the town, and desired to starve its defenders out. On the land side they constructed a line of redoubts and batteries, connected by trenches, which extended over a distance of three leagues, and on the side towards the sea they built, after several ineffectual attempts, the celebrated dike, measuring 747 fathoms, bristling with cannon, pierced in the centre to give passage to the tides, defended from every attack by a floating barricade of beams and ships all bound together, and guarded by twenty-five large vessels, twelve galleys, and forty-five boats and barges : it took Métezeau, the architect, and Thiriot, the mason, six months to carry out the huge undertaking, in the teeth of the enemy's opposition.

The Cardinal had arrived with the King on October 12. Louis XIII liked to persuade himself that his commanding officers had no more respect for Richelieu than for some " cook-boy "; but as a matter of fact nobody felt inclined to laugh when the Cardinal rode by, attended by his pages and the Captain of his Guard, " very pensive and yellow-faced," with a pair of pistols in his saddle-holsters, his sword girt round his waist, and a plumed hat on his head, and clad in a light brown coat embroidered with gold, under a cuirass " the colour of water," or else in the garb of a " general in the army—a black beaver hat with a gold cord, a red satin coat, and over it a scarlet cloak covered with gold embroidery, silk stockings, and red slippers." Aided by Louis XIII, he had organized the troops in the most admirable way ; they were regularly paid, all supplies were bought, not taken, from the peasants, the soldiers were well clothed, comfortably lodged in huts, and made to confess and receive the communion at regular intervals. (It would be imprudent, however, to believe, as we have been assured, that they bore the most perfect resemblance to " monks under arms.")

Siege and capture of La Rochelle.

Early in the spring food was becoming very scarce within the town, which was bombarded with red-hot shot, night after night. But on April 30 the townsmen elected Jean Guiton, one of the aldermen, to be their Mayor, and this wiry little man, a bold sea-dog, who began by telling them all that it was no use to choose him unless they had made up their minds to die fighting, raised everybody's courage. And very soon (May 11) a splendid fleet, numbering fifty-two ships of war and attended by a bevy of transports, hove in sight of the port ; it was commanded by Buckingham's brother-in-law, Lord Denbigh. All the men of La Rochelle crowded gaily to the ramparts to admire the manœuvres of the squadron and watch the royal forces as they swarmed, in their haste, on to the dike and into the trenches. . . . Alas! after a few days' skirmishing the British admiral, convinced that the great dike was impregnable, weighed his anchors, and passed out of sight. Then the rations of the 2000 soldiers, 200 Englishmen, and 4000 burghers of the militia who formed the garrison had to be cut down by a third. Many women used to slip out of the town and beg food from the King's soldiers; in this quest the comeliest were more successful than their sisters. One day, at last, Guiton expelled all the owners of useless mouths, and as the royal army would not let them pass, a crowd of unhappy wretches perished between the town and the trenches.

At the earnest prayer of the envoys from La Rochelle, King Charles I dispatched a third fleet, which hove in sight of Ré on September 28. But it did no better than its two predecessors, and three days after its departure the men of Rochelle, " having no more grass that they could eat upon their counterscarps, no more of the ox- and horse-hides, the boots, shoes, leathern belts, sword-knots and pouches, out of which they had been making jellies with moist sugar and sweetened pap on which they had fed," made up their minds to sue for the King's mercy. On All Saints' Day, November 1, 1628, Louis made his entry into the town between two lines of skeletons, who raised feeble voices to cry, " Long live the King!" The Cardinal said Mass in the ancient church of Sainte-Marguerite, which, like all the others, was given back to the Catholics: a bishopric of La Rochelle was created; the liberties and privileges of the town were all abolished, and the walls razed to the ground; but the inhabitants (only 5000 remained out of 28,000, it was said), and even Guiton himself, were given their lives, and granted permission to follow the Reformed faith unmolested.

While the Cardinal had been successfully carrying on this memorable siege, Vincenzo Gonzaga II, Duke of Mantua and **Italian cam-** Marquis of Montferrat, had breathed his last **paign of 1628.** (December 21, 1627). His heir, strictly speaking, was his first cousin once removed, the head of the younger branch of the family, established in France, Charles, Duc de Nevers, a subject of Louis XIII. But Charles Emmanuel, Duke of Savoy, seeing the French troops all engaged in the struggle with the Protestants, claimed the Marquisate of Montferrat in the name of his own granddaughter Maria, who was niece to the late Duke. And immediately Maria Gonzaga, Duchess-Dowager of Lorraine and sister of Vincenzo II, put forward a similar claim.

Spain decided, meanwhile, to support the Duke of Guastalla's claim to Mantua, and entered into negotiations with Charles Emmanuel for a partition of Montferrat. On February 17 the son of the Duc de Nevers had taken possession of the inheritance in his father's name : on the 25th the Savoyards and the Spaniards opened their campaign against him ; very soon the town of Casale was invested. . . . At first Richelieu, whose hands were full at La Rochelle, was unable to do anything beyond negotiating. But the moment he was rid of that business he left the subjugation of the Huguenot towns in the South of France to a more convenient season, and started, with the King and the army, for Italy. Louis crossed the Alps in mid-winter, and carried the Pass of Susa at the head of his troops, in the most brilliant fashion. Before very long he had forced the Duke of Savoy to make peace, and relieved Casale (March, 1629). . . . He would fain have followed up his successes in Italy, but the Cardinal was able to persuade him to complete the destruction of the Huguenot party first of all. And while he himself remained at Susa to watch over the negotiations, the soldier-king marched to the help of Condé, whose savage devastation of the Cévennes and Languedoc had stirred the Reformers to fury.

They were led by a bold man, who may well have only lacked opportunity to become a great one : the Duc de Rohan. **Truce with the** His uprightness had won him popularity with his **Huguenots.** party, which had not, for many a day, seen any great gentleman in its ranks who had omitted to sell himself to the King in the long run. When the English failed him, Rohan had turned to Spain, and had signed a treaty with Philip IV whereby, in return for an annual subsidy of 300,000 ducats (May 3, 1629), he undertook to keep up an army and carry on the war in France. But on May 27 Louis took and burned the town of Privas, and captured Alais, while his generals were threatening Nîmes, Castres, and Montauban. Then Rohan realized that he must submit. On June 28, 1629, the King granted him the peace known as the *Paix de grâce*. By this the Reformers lost all their hostage towns, and ceased from that time forward to form " any separate body, independent of the will of their sovereign," but as regards all other points the provisions of the Edict of Nantes were confirmed : the King, in fact, made a declaration to the effect that his sole desire had been to " remove faction from the midst of his subjects, the rest " (the matter of faith) " being a work which must be waited for from Heaven, without the use of any 'violence save that of a good life and example." As a matter of fact, he subsequently encouraged the Catholic propaganda, and never grudged money for the purpose of buying apostasies. But the Protestants preserved their legal freedom of conscience. And Louis XIII deserves great honour for his tolerance, which was not the result of his personal indifference—for his piety was most fervent—but of his constitutional sense of justice, a quality in which he was greatly in advance of his times.

V

In Italy, unhappily, all the work had to be done over again. The Emperor Ferdinand, in fact, had interfered, on the plea that he had received no request from the Duc de Nevers to invest him with the States of Mantua and Montferrat. He had the Valtellina passes occupied by his troops, and meanwhile Spinola, the Spanish general, overran the Montferrat country. . . . Once the peace of Alais had been signed, and their hands were free, Louis XIII and Richelieu hurried to the scene, but they were unable to succour Casale, where Spinola was besieging the gallant Toiras, nor did they succeed in preventing the sack of Mantua by the Imperial troops (July 1). By great good fortune, and thanks to the efforts of the Legate and of an exceedingly clever young member of his suite, Giulio Mazarini, a truce, to last till October 15, was signed at Rivalto on September 4. Though this was not a final peace, the Cardinal had great hopes that before hostilities had to be renewed Father Joseph and Brûlart de Léon, whom he had dispatched to the Ratisbon Diet, would have arranged the treaty with the Emperor on which his hopes were set.

Campaign against the Emperor Ferdinand, 1629.

The King, who was suffering from dysentery, had been absent from the army since the end of July. At Lyons, whither he had proceeded, he grew rapidly worse : between the 27th and the 30th he thought he was dying. The Queen his mother and the Queen his wife both nursed him with great devotion ; his heart softened to them, and he begged them to forgive the pain he had caused them. Marie de' Medici now hated her former favourite, Richelieu, with all her strength ; had he not forsaken her interests, after she had made him what he was ? Had he not, only the year previously, objected to the bestowal on Gaston of the frontier governments of Champagne and Bourgogne, which she had asked for him ? . . . So while the King lay sick, Marie, backed by Anne, besought her son to dismiss the Cardinal as soon as the war was over, and the Mantuan business settled, and Louis, weakened by illness, very pious, and believing himself near his end, dared not refuse his mother the boon she so urgently prayed for. But the moment he recovered he repented him of his promise, and confessed to his Minister the fact that he had been weak enough to give it.

The Queen-Mother attacks Richelieu.

"There was no sort of complaisance and flattery," we are told, that Richelieu did not employ in his endeavour to mollify the Queen-Mother, "even to the point that one day, when the Queen had been angry with a jester of hers who had forgotten himself in her presence, he called him to his side and said to him, in the gravest and most serious way, before the assembled company : "What are you thinking of, Manuguet" (that was his name), "to displease the Queen? Do you not know she is so great a princess, and so powerful, that she is able to turn the Cardinal de Richelieu into a Manuguet, and a Manuguet into a Cardinal de Richelieu ? " What such a speech must have cost his pride we may readily imagine ! Yet it was labour lost, for the portly Marie, obstinate and shallow, doggedly pursued the idea she had taken into her head. . . . She dismissed Mme. de Combalet, the Cardinal's niece, who had been her lady-in-waiting, in the most public manner. Richelieu believed his downfall imminent.

The war was supposed to be over : the Queen-Mother determined to force the scrupulous King to carry out the promise she had snatched from him. On November 10, when he came to see her at the Luxembourg, where she was lodged, she shut herself up in her cabinet with her son, having given orders that nobody was to venture to disturb them. All at once, in the very middle of their discussion, a door opened : they looked up—it was Richelieu ! . . . The Minister, feeling it to be a case of " nothing venture nothing have," had contrived to get into the room by a door that opened into the chapel, and in later years the Queen was often heard to assert that " if she had not forgotten to shoot a bolt, the Cardinal would have been undone ! " . . . At the sight of Richelieu, Marie instantly flew into a passion, and lost all self-control. He did his best to defend himself, wept, humbled himself, tendered his resignation, and finally retired in despair. The King, very much " vexed," as Goulas tells us, departed to his small country-house at Versailles, and Marie made the mistake of allowing him to go there alone, staying on herself at the Luxembourg to receive the whole Court, which hastened to do homage to her victory. But while she was en-joying her triumph, the Marquis de Sourdis, Boutilier, and Father Joseph, seated in the King's coach, were using all their eloquence in Richelieu's favour, and Louis was thinking matters over. . . .

When the Cardinal, who had followed his master, reached Versailles, the King received him " perfectly," and had him lodged in a chamber just above his own : they ended by " talking together for four hours that night " (Arnauld d'Andilly). . . . The courtiers all turned round again, in the handsomest manner.

This was " the Day of Dupes." Knowing what Richelieu was, we cannot wonder that it was followed by a long series of " The Day reprisals. Michel de Marillac, Keeper of the Seals, of Dupes." whom the Queen-Mother's party would have brought into power after the Cardinal's fall, was exiled : the Connétable de Lesdiguières, the Duchesse d'Elbeuf, and the Princesse de Conti were banished to their country estates : Bassompierre, the last-named lady's close friend, was shut up in the Bastille, " not on account of any fault he had committed, but for fear he should be led into doing wrong " : the King's confessor, Father Suffren, was dismissed ; the Duc de Guise thought it prudent to travel abroad ; and the Maréchal de Marillac, brother of the

Keeper of the Seals, was arrested by Schomberg, one of his own colleagues. His trial was marked by scandalous injustice : the Cardinal, according to his usual habit, did not send him before the regular courts, but had him tried by a special commission ; and as this appeared to him too dilatory, he had a second appointed, which sat in his own house, at Rueil. One of the chief crimes with which the accused man was charged was that of having appropriated his soldiers' pay, and cheated in connection with the commissariat supplies ; but this was the constant practice of all generals, and the worthy Marshal, utterly astounded, declared that " the whole of this trial is a question of hay and cheese—trifles for which a page would hardly get a whipping ! " In spite of which he was condemned to death by a majority of one voice, and executed in May, 1632.

Marie de' Medici had obstinately refused to be reconciled to Richelieu, or even to sit at the Council-board with him. Then, **Exile and** when the King appointed her Governor of the **Death of the** Bourbonnais, and ordered her to retire to Moulins, **Queen-Mother.** she stayed on doggedly at Compiègne, pouring out endless lamentation concerning the " persecution " inflicted on her by her unnatural son : Louis XIII, sorely perplexed, could do nothing with her, whether by promises or threats. At last, in the month of July, she took to flight, and the King drew a long breath. She had calculated that one of her partisans would have put her in possession of the small fortified town of La Capelle, where she intended to establish herself, and make her own conditions ; but when she appeared before the town, she found the gates shut in her face, and was fain to move on into the Low Countries. There Louis XIII left her till she died. The soul passed out of her bulky body at Cologne in 1642, some six months before the death of Richelieu.

Gaston meanwhile, alarmed by the events that followed immediately on the Day of Dupes, began by lying low. But in January, 1631, urged on by his favourites, he proceeded into the Cardinal's presence, insulted him in the boldest way, and then, in a terror, galloped off to Orléans. An army was sent to attack the town, and Gaston got away into Burgundy ; but the Governor alone declared in his favour, not another person in the province stirred : then he took refuge in Lorraine, fell in love with the Duke's sister Marguerite, married her in secret (January, 1632), and in July, after publishing various manifestos against Richelieu, re-entered France at the head of an army.

Among his partisans he reckoned one very great and powerful personage, the Duc de Montmorency, brother-in-law to Condé, **Henri de** and godson of Henri IV. Though he squinted, **Montmorency.** and was not very intelligent, Henri de Montmorency was a fine-looking man, frank, brave, gallant, chivalrous, and greatly loved by women. Hitherto he had served the King, and even the Cardinal, with tolerable fidelity, against both Protestants and Spaniards, but he did not consider he had been rewarded as he would have desired. Now in Languedoc—of which province he was Governor, as his father and grandfather had been before him—his family had acquired a considerable following, and he himself had earned popularity by his pleasant manners and his generosity. As the master and patron of that powerful province, he might well have proved a precious ally for Gaston, and a redoubtable adversary for the Cardinal : but when the Duc d'Orléans made his unexpected entry into France, he was not quite ready. He proceeded to the States of Languedoc, at Pézenas, and obtained the adhesion of the deputies to the revolt, but the province in general did not follow them. Nevertheless, he effected a junction with Monsieur at Lunel, and together they marched on Castelnaudary. There they came upon a small army of the King's troops commanded by Schomberg : at the first onset their undisciplined bands fled, and Montmorency, who had courted death, was taken prisoner, with seventeen wounds, " making four and twenty holes in his body " (September 1, 1632). Though his dignity as a Peer of France gave him the right to be tried by the Parliament of Paris, even as Biron had been tried in the days of Henri IV, the King and Richelieu gave orders for his trial by the Parliament of Toulouse, presided over, for the occasion, by one of the Cardinal's creatures, Châteauneuf, Keeper of the Seals—a twofold abuse. In vain did the Paris Parliament raise a protest : it was forced to submit. Montmorency was condemned to death, and courageously met his fate on October 30, 1632. The whole Court had interceded for him, and all night long the populace had cried out " Mercy ! " under the monarch's windows—but in vain.

RICHELIEU

As for Gaston, he had undertaken at Béziers, on September 29, "to love his cousin the Cardinal de Richelieu most par-

Submission of Gaston. ticularly," and, further, "to take no interest in those who had been connected with him on

these occasions," and "not to make it a cause of complaint when the King should cause them to suffer that which they deserved"—in other words, to leave Montmorency, who had ruined himself for his sake, to his fate. However, when he saw that his late ally's head was really to be cut off, he thought it safer to join Marie de' Medici at Brussels (November). There he remained for two years, and then, urged on by Puylaurens, his favourite, who was tired of exile, he was reconciled to the King, who restored him " all his properties, apanages, pensions, and emoluments " (October, 1634). This, in his eyes, was the chief thing : he allowed Puylaurens to be arrested soon after- wards (February 14, 1635) without a protest, and his quondam favourite died in the donjon of Vincennes, after a few months' imprisonment (July 1, 1635), even as Ornano, the Grand Prieur de Vendôme, and Marillac had died before him.

WORKS TO CONSULT : Works quoted under Chapter I, and the *Memoirs* of N. Goulas, O. Talon, and Mme. de Motteville ; Tallemant des Réaux, *Historiettes*; A. Barine, *La Jeunesse de la Grande Mademoiselle* (1901); V. Cousin, *Madame de Chevreuse* (1862) ; Abbé Houssaye, *Le Cardinal de Bérulle et le Cardinal de Richelieu* (1910); La Roncière, *Histoire de la Marine*, vol. iv (1910); Dom Vaissète, *Histoire du Languedoc*, vols. xi-xii.

CHAPTER III

THE PREPONDERANCE OF FRANCE (1630–1643)

I. The House of Austria. II. Swedish successes. III. French successes. IV. The last intrigues of the Court. V. The Cinq-Mars affair. VI. Deaths of the Cardinal and the King.

I

WHEN the Day of Dupes was over, Richelieu felt that he was delivered from the Protestant peril and the Queen-Mother ; and fancied he had disheartened all conspirators and haters of discipline. Master, as he believed himself to be, of those " four square feet of the King's cabinet, **The House of** more difficult to win than all the battlefields in **Austria.** Europe," he was free to apply himself to the work of " raising the King's name to the place it ought to hold among foreign nations."

Since the days of Charles V the balance of power in Europe had inclined to the side of the House of Austria. The Hapsburgs of Madrid and the Hapsburgs of Vienna, allied by blood—which counted for much—were bound together likewise by common interests—and this was more. The King of Spain, indeed, stood in need of the Emperor's help to keep open his communications with his domains in the Low Countries and Franche-Comté, and without the King of Spain the Emperor's position in Italy would have been robbed of all its importance. And these two branches of the House of Austria, thus united by ties of blood, by interest, and by the struggle against Protestantism in which both were engaged, masters of Spain and of the Empire, with the huge territories dependent on them, wielded, to all appearances, a power beside which that of the King of France seemed a trivial thing. In reality this was not the case.

PREPONDERANCE OF FRANCE

On the one hand, Spain was beginning to decay : though she owned Portugal, the Kingdom of Naples, the province of **Decadence of** Milan, Franche-Comté, the Low Countries, and **Spain.** though all the treasures of the Americas were hers, her population was diminishing, she was ruled by a corrupt bureaucracy, ruined financially to such an extent that her successive bankruptcies brought her no remedy, and ruined hopelessly, too, since the expulsion of the Moors, the only hardworking subjects she possessed. For the Spaniards themselves were not a laborious race, and their industry and commerce were carried on, their colonies turned to account, and their very fields cultivated, by foreigners, who had even ended by monopolizing the small trades in their towns. Spain, it is true, did still possess a very powerful army, but two-thirds of the men serving in it were foreigners, and the French troops were soon to equal them.

As for the Emperor, he reigned over an inextricable confusion of races, and over several hundred States of varying size, kept apart, not only by the rivalries of their various heads, but by deep-seated religious disagreements ; and over these, as we have already said, his power was scarcely greater than that the first Capetian sovereigns had wielded over their vassals in France. His dominions were of two kinds: those under his direct rule and sovereign authority, and the " Empire," in regard to which his power was defined by an ancient constitution, contested by the Diets or Imperial assemblies, and frequently scorned by the reigning princes whose suzerain he was. Notwithstanding this fact, the seven Electors for two centuries past (four of these were Catholics in the days of Richelieu : the Archbishops of Cologne, Treves, and Mayence, and the King of Bohemia; and three Protestants : the Count Palatine, the Duke of Saxony, and the Margrave of Brandenburg) had always elected a member of the House of Hapsburg to the Imperial dignity. And little by little, alongside the Empire, the family had built up a huge patrimony of its own : Hungary, Bohemia, Austria, Styria, Carinthia, Carniola, Tyrol, Silesia, Moravia, Breisgau, and the greater part of Alsace. Naturally the Hapsburgs did their utmost to acquire a hereditary right in the Empire for their house, to add it to their other dominions, and, in short, to convert the great Germanic Federation into a monarchy resembling those of France and Spain.

Now in 1630 the chances in favour of the realization of this plan seemed tolerably good. For in the Catholic party in Germany, of which he was the leader, the Emperor had found a powerful support: from the day when the House of Hapsburg associated its cause with the cause of Catholicism, the progress of the Roman faith became identical with its own, and while it laboured to consolidate its own power it seemed to be fighting in the name of the Catholic religion. The advantages of this confusion are manifest: the Catholic princes of the Empire, against whose foes the Hapsburgs warred, helped them, or did not stand in their way at all events, and they owed their first successes to the Army of the Holy League, commanded by Tilly. . . . From 1629 onwards the Emperor's fortunes, served by the brilliant genius of Wallenstein, attained their zenith. Ferdinand II felt himself strong enough to decree, by the Edict of Restitution, that the Protestants must deliver up all Church properties taken from the Catholics for a century—notably the two archbishoprics of Bremen and Magdeburg, a dozen bishoprics, and a large number of abbeys. Wallenstein's army, which was firmly established all round Magdeburg, saw to the execution of the order, and the General did not hesitate to declare openly that the Electors ought to be reduced to the status of grandees of Spain, and the Princes of the Church to that of chaplains to the Emperor. . . . But the Catholics themselves, faithful allies of the Emperor though they were, began to feel alarmed at the ambitious projects that were gradually taking shape: when once the Protestants were utterly defeated, who, they began to wonder, would be strong enough to stand out against Wallenstein, if it should please him to overthrow the ancient constitution of the Empire, and set up his master as an absolute sovereign, to the detriment of the German princes ? For this reason, religious quarrels became a secondary consideration from that time forward, and even in Germany people began to realize that the real question was not the future of Catholicism, but the future of the House of Austria.

Ambitious designs of the Hapsburgs.

Richelieu was less disposed than any other person to allow the Emperor to carry out a plan for transforming Germany into one united and hereditary State, under colour of the promotion of a Catholic restoration. When he first began to deal with State affairs he had been forced into a conflict with the Hapsburgs : we have already noticed the fashion in which he opposed their projects in the Valtellina, and then at Mantua. In Germany his system was to reveal the designs of Ferdinand II to the Catholic Princes, unite them against him, and form with them what he had already formed with the Protestant States of Germany—a powerful league to resist the Emperor's encroachments. But at the outset his agents had but a chilly reception from the Electors. Then the King of Denmark, his secret ally, was defeated at Lutter, and driven back into Jutland by Tilly and Wallenstein (1627). Happily for France—or, as the French historians put it, for "the equilibrium of Europe"—his intrigues in the Ratisbon Diet were to meet with better success.

II

The Emperor had convoked the Electors of the Holy Empire to a meeting at Ratisbon on June 3, 1630. He reckoned on inducing them, in the first place, to elect his son **The Diet of** King of the Romans (in other words, his successor **Ratisbon, 1630.** in the Imperial dignity), and, in the second, to supply him with troops to fight his enemies : in short, to express their approval of his policy. But the Electors were anything but well disposed towards him : the Protestants reproached him with having published the Edict of Restitution, and the Catholics, as we have just said, felt by no means inclined to give any encouragement to the plans against their own independence attributed to Wallenstein and his master. Thus the very first condition they imposed on the Emperor was the dismissal of his general.

Ferdinand II, a little fat bigot, spent his life surrounded by priests and monks : it was no doubt piety rather than cunning that had led him to adopt his violently pro-Catholic policy, and he would quite possibly have been as earnest in his labour for the triumph of the Roman faith if it had threatened to cost him his throne. After due consultation with his confessor, he dismissed Wallenstein. But when he had thus laid down his arms, as it were, the Electors refused nearly everything he had asked of them, and notably the election of his son to be King of the Romans.

A crowd of foreign diplomatic agents had gathered round the Diet. Besides Brûlart de Léon, her ordinary ambassador, France had sent Father Joseph to Ratisbon : " The story goes," wrote an Italian, " that whenever Cardinal Richelieu desires to carry out some clever trick (not to call it some piece of deceit) he invariably makes use of pious and devout persons," and the French agents certainly did their work in the most artful manner: it is related (though the truth of the statement is anything but certain) that Ferdinand declared, when the Diet was over, " that a poor Capuchin monk had disarmed him with his rosary, and small as his monk's cowl was, had contrived to pack six electoral caps into it. . . ."

Officially Father Joseph and Brûlart had unlimited powers as to the arrangement of the Mantuan question with the Emperor : but the Cardinal had forbidden them to touch on other litigious matters : for Richelieu, though ready enough to wind up the Italian business, which did not promise to work out to our advantage, was determined to keep his hands free, and act as he chose with regard to all other points. Unluckily the Imperial ministers easily divined his plan, and plainly told the French agents that unless they signed a general peace they would sign no peace at all. The agents, thus driven into a corner, were in a state of great perplexity. It was most important, on the one hand, to conclude peace in Italy before Casale capitulated (immediately, in other words, for the truce of Rivalta bound the French garrison to march out of the town if it was not relieved before December 15) : but, on the other, neither Father Joseph nor Brûlart had been given powers to conclude any general peace. What was to be done ? Their dispatches to the Cardinal remained unanswered· (the reader will soon guess why). . . . After waiting on as long as they dared, they ended by making up their minds to sign the Peace of Ratisbon (October 13, 1630).

News of the signing of this treaty reached Richelieu at Roanne on October 22. He instantly feigned a furious rage, swore loudly that he had been betrayed, and then proceeded to disavow his ambassadors, on the plea that they had exceeded **The Treaties of** their powers (which, as a matter of fact, was true). **Cherasco, 1621.** He then hastened to enter into fresh negotiations with the Emperor, in Italy. The result of all this was the Treaties of Cherasco (April–June, 1631), the carrying out of which was another clever comedy, composed and put on the stage by Richelieu, by Vittorio-Amadeo of Savoy, who was friendly to France, and by the Pope's wily envoy, Giulio Mazarini. It had been agreed that the Imperial and the French troops were to evacuate all the strongholds either Power held in Italy on a certain date. The French troops, consequently, made a show of leaving Pignerol on September 21. But an envoy from the French King at once insisted that Vittorio-Amadeo should leave Pignerol to his government for another six months, on the plea that neither Spain nor the Emperor was carrying out the clauses of the treaty. The Duke of Savoy, with a great outcry for the benefit of the public, appeared to consent. In reality he had been under a secret engagement ever since the preceding April to make over the town to France. . . . This was the closing act and *dénouement* of the Mantuan business. Thanks to it, France had obtained possession of one of the gates of Italy. As for Spain and the Emperor, they could at all events feel they had been fooled in most masterly fashion—this was consolation of a kind.

And indeed Ferdinand had already lost the power of making any opposition. Greatly weakened by that Diet of Ratisbon from which he had expected so much advantage, and to which he had himself finally granted the dismissal of Wallenstein and the reduction of his army without receiving anything in exchange, he now found himself face to face with the new and redoubtable foe that had started up in his path supported by France— **Sweden under** Sweden. This was a small and poor nation which **Gustavus-** dwelt along the shores of the Gulf of Bothnia, **Adolphus.** though its borders did not reach the Sound, both shores of which belonged to Denmark. But the two millions of which this little nation was composed were brave folk, warlike, full of confidence, and led by Gustavus-Adolphus. In 1629 Gustavus, then only thirty-four years of age, had already vanquished Denmark, Poland, and Russia. This tall, burly Scandinavian, blue-eyed, fair-haired, broad-shouldered, jovial, strong, was filled with a most fervent piety, and proposed to descend upon Germany with the object of ensuring liberty of conscience to his coreligionists : but he reckoned at the same time on completing his conquest of the Baltic Provinces.

In his own kingdom, where military service was a tradition and wellnigh an obligation, he had raised an army of 40,000 men, national troops, and therefore immeasurably superior to the mercenary soldiery under the command of such men as Tilly and Wallenstein. At that period soldiers were recruited " to fight a battle, just as any private individual might hire labourers to build him a house." Captains bargained to supply a certain number of men, clothed, armed, and equipped at their expense. Naturally these mercenaries appeared on the scene in larger or smaller numbers according to the reputation of the men under whose command they were to serve, and the old soldiers, whose profession it was to fight just as an artisan's business was to work at his trade, charged more or less for their services according to the risks they expected to run and the profit they hoped to make out of the campaign : and even as a good captain found less difficulty than another in recruiting his men, a general of renown such as Tilly or Wallenstein would have a crowd of captains all desirous of enlisting under his command, and could thus raise an army at comparatively small expense. But in any case his troops could not compare with a homogeneous army such as this Swedish one, which did not fight solely for the sake of gain, but for its religion and its King, in whom it had a supernatural confidence : for this reason 40,000 Swedes, trained and led by so matchless a general as Gustavus-Adolphus, were equal to 100,000 Imperial troops.

Richelieu, warned by one of his agents, was aware of all this, and had already been negotiating for a considerable time with a view to securing little Sweden as his ally.

Alliance between France and Sweden. But Gustavus-Adolphus hesitated to embark on the adventure, and it was not till February 28, 1631, that he finally decided in favour of it. France was to make him an annual payment of 1,000,000 *livres*, and he, in consideration of this, was to keep up an army of 36,000 men to oppose Ferdinand. It was an understood thing that he was never to do anything to harm the Catholic faith in those places where he might find it already established. In this last clause of the agreement, Richelieu was endeavouring, no doubt, to reconcile his duty as a Minister with his scruples as a Cardinal: but his sense of the first was probably stronger than his realization of the last.

Tilly had laid siege to Magdeburg, and when the city capitulated (on May 20, 1631) it was sacked in the most merciless **Sack of Magde-** manner: soldiers were seen cutting off the heads **burg, 1631.** of fifty-three young girls who had sought refuge in a church, Croats impaled infants snatched from their mothers' breasts upon their swords, rough old troopers ripped up women with child, and outraged wives and daughters under the very eyes of their husbands and fathers. Tilly refused to put a stop to these atrocities—could he have done it even if he had so desired? " The soldiers must amuse themselves," he said. . . . When the news of this " Magdeburg merrymaking " spread over the country a shudder of horror ran through the whole of Lutheran and Calvinist Germany: there was a general uprising. The Saxons, who had been doubtful so far, threw in their lot with Gustavus-Adolphus, and helped him to crush Tilly's army at Breitenfeld, on the Elster, not far from Leipzig, on September 17, 1631; the peasants dispatched all the fugitives: " the Harz Mountains hurled themselves " upon the torturers of Magdeburg.

And then Gustavus-Adolphus began his triumphant progress through the rich Catholic countries of the Rhine, through Swabia and Franconia: he entered Frankfort, Mayence, Spires, Worms. . . . In the course of the winter of 1632, when only Alsace lay between him and France, he strove to spur on his ally—his sleeping partner—Louis XIII: he advised him to march on the provinces lying along the left bank of the Rhine. Most of the members of the Council were much tempted by the plan. But Father Joseph ardently opposed it: thus to fall on the Franche-Comté, on Alsace, Luxemburg, and Flanders would surely involve a final rupture with the Roman Faith and ensure the heretics' triumph in Germany. Richelieu was irresolute, and the Council dispersed without coming to any definite decision. At six o'clock the next morning the Cardinal, after a sleepless night, sent for the Capuchin and informed him he had resolved to follow his advice. How would the destiny of France have been affected if possession of her natural frontiers had been acquired at one blow in 1632 ?

When the spring came, Gustavus-Adolphus recommenced his victorious advance. Tilly was defeated and mortally wounded **Battle of** on the banks of the Lech, near Augsburg (April 15), **Lützen, 1632.** and the Swedes made their entry into Munich. Then Wallenstein emerged from his retirement, and raised an army. On November 19, 1632, Gustavus-Adolphus attacked him at Lützen : by nightfall the Swedes were in possession of the enemy's positions, but their King was dead, killed as he was leading a charge through the fog. He was only thirty-eight.

While the conqueror whom Richelieu had brought "from the Pole," as Voiture has it, was filling Europe with the fame of his victories, the Cardinal himself was slowly forwarding the interests of his country. During the earliest months of the year 1632 the Archbishop-Elector of Treves, thinking the Emperor too far away to afford him adequate protection, had given in his adhesion to Louis XIII, and shortly afterwards French garrisons made their appearance along the Rhine, at Philippsburg and Coblenz. At the same time, on the pretext of punishing Charles IV of Lorraine for having supported Gaston after the Day of Dupes, the Duke was forced to make over several of his towns (January–July, 1632). The death of Gustavus-Adolphus did not check the progress of France. On the very morrow of the Battle of Lützen, in fact, Wallenstein had opened negotiations in all directions. Was he contemplating some treason ? As to this point historians are not yet agreed. . . . Meanwhile Richelieu continued to strip the Duke of Lorraine : by the summer of 1634 the French had occupied all the fortified towns in his Duchy.

But in the midst of all this, fortune once more began to smile on the Hapsburgs. On February 24, 1634, Ferdinand **Assassination** had caused the disquieting Wallenstein to be **of Wallenstein.** murdered (he ordered two thousand Masses, however, to be said for the repose of his soul). In September,

PREPONDERANCE OF FRANCE

Gallas, his new general, crushed the Swedes at Nördlingen. Finally, in May, 1635, the Emperor rescinded his Edict of Restitution, and Saxony and the smaller Protestant States instantly made their peace with him. From that time forward Sweden stood almost alone against the House of Austria. . . . Richelieu perceived that the time when France must act had come. In the space of a few months, and with incomparable skill, he had gathered every one of the remaining foes of the House of Austria under the banner of Louis XIII, and on May 19, 1635, he sent a herald to declare war in solemn form, not on the Emperor, but on Spain.

III

What were the forces at his command ?

The army under Louis XIII consisted of various bodies of troops as unequal in quality and size as in the esteem in which
The Army under Louis XIII. they were held. The first of these bodies, the largest and the most highly honoured, was the regiment of the Guard: then came the old regiments of Picardy, Piedmont, Navarre, and Champagne, all the officers of which were personally known to the King : and then the " little old " regiments—Normandy, Ile-de-France or Rambures, Maugeron, Nerestang, Vaubecour, Bellenave, Saint-Luc, Saulx, Chamblay (these appellations were subject to change), which bore the names of their commanding officers ; and, finally, somewhere about one hundred new regiments, the strength and importance of which rose and fell perpetually according to the necessities of war and the wealth of the noblemen who commanded them. No effective strength was fixed, indeed ; the *mestre de camp* commanding the Guard might have some 6000 men under his orders, and the colonel of some other regiment might not have more than 300. Altogether, and reckoning the cavalry, the French army, about the year 1635, numbered some 130,000 men.

The rank and file consisted of an agglomeration of foreign ruffians and all the most good-for-nothing fellows in the kingdom. Even in France nothing could prevent " La Fleur," " La Jeunesse," " Champagne," " Belhumeur," or " Gargaillou " (every old soldier had some nickname of this sort) from leaving the ranks whenever the fancy took him, and going off *à la picorée*—in other words, to steal chickens, cattle and horses, furniture and forage, strip travellers, thrash tavern-keepers, and hang peasants, with the most deplorable ease. . . . This being so, my readers will conceive the horrors of war as these men made it. The Cardinal's memoirs relate, with a touch of indignation, that too often these soldiers " rubbed their boots with the holy oils, smashed images of the Virgin, trampled the Blessed Sacrament under their feet, and fired volleys of musketry at the Crucifix " : and no description can possibly be attempted of the horrors that took place when a town was sacked, for instance, or when a general thought it necessary to starve out the enemy by devastating the neighbouring country to some extent. . . . Further, robbers, incendiaries, murderers, torturers, as these soldiers were, they were far exceeded in all these respects by the vile crew who acted as their servants. One of these young wretches, a lad of sixteen or seventeen, makes a pleasing boast of having " strung up," with his own hand, some score of peasants of both sexes. Even in times of peace the passage of a French army through any province in the kingdom was a calamity.

"Musket on shoulder, his bandolier slung about his neck, his musket-rest in his right hand, a long walking-stick in his left—thus do we see the ' foot-soldier,' in the engravings of Abraham Bosse or Callot." When he fired his weapon he had to light his match, load his musket, take his match again, twist it round the cock, and then take aim : he can hardly have had time to discharge his piece more than once on the attacking force, for his fire did not carry much farther than sixty-nine yards. Thus, as a defence against the enemy's charge, each company contained a certain proportion of pikemen, who opposed the advance of the cavalry by crossing their heavy weapons, fourteen feet long. As for the cavalry, it consisted of musketeers, raised by Louis XIII (dragoons, they called themselves), mounted infantry, which dismounted before firing ; light horse ; gendarmes in armour ; and carabiniers, who acted as scouts and skirmishers.

Uniforms there were none, save for certain picked troops :

no special marks distinguished officers from their men. Colours (so huge, for the infantry, that the material of which they were made would have dragged along the ground if the man carrying each had not kept a corner under his arm), and the small standards used by the cavalry all differed from each other. So much so that the troops on one side frequently found their only method of mutual recognition was that every man of them should pull his shirt out of his hose, or else put it on over his doublet.

The military hierarchy was tolerably confused in its nature, and an officer's place in it depended less on his actual rank than on his regiment and his birth. A private in a crack regiment such as the Guards paid scant respect to a lieutenant belonging to one of the recently raised regiments : and what was a carabinier—some former lackey, perhaps—compared with a high-born gendarme who served the King attended by his varlets and his squire ? The Marshals of France were all equal, and as each directed the army's operations in turn, none cared to press the enemy so hard that some one or other of his colleagues would have nothing to do on the morrow—or the following week—but to cull the fruits of victory.

Besides all this, and in spite of the fact that a mere youth might attain officer's rank, what the leaders lacked was not so **Lack of disci-** much experience as discipline. Every nobleman **pline in the** intended for military life learned his business in **Army.** early youth at his " academy," and served some time in a regiment before he was given a command. He might be an officer at seventeen, perhaps, but he had been a soldier at the age of fifteen, or even, like Cinq-Mars, of thirteen years. The misfortune was that, once the battle began, each captain carried out the orders he had received after his own fashion and skirmished much as he chose. Every man strove to shine on his own account, and when Marshals of France could not deny themselves the pleasure of going under fire at the head of the leading battalions, it was of course difficult to prevent colonels from marching on the enemy, pike on shoulder, six paces ahead of their officers, and these, again, from advancing in a row in front of their men.

Further, since the French troops had won their brilliant successes, since the days of La Rochelle and the Pass of Susa, the art of war had undergone a total change. It no longer consisted, as in the old days, in moving a few thousand men this way and that, but in the handling of huge bodies of troops. Gustavus-Adolphus had completely changed military tactics, and the dealings of the German armies with him had taught them to manœuvre : their musketeers knew how to retire in good order behind their pikemen, after they had delivered their fire their infantry how to open its ranks in time to allow the ordnance it was covering to do its part, their cavalry to ride amongst the foot-soldiers without throwing them into disorder. Practice alone could accustom the troops of Louis XIII to these well-ordered evolutions, and their apprenticeship was to cost them several defeats.

IV

In the spring the Maréchal de Châtillon invaded Spanish Flanders, and on May 20, 1635, he defeated a small Spanish force **War with Spain.** near Liége. But his soldiers having committed the habitual atrocities of their kind, in a country which had quite forgotten what war was like, the population rose in every quarter, and the French army was obliged to retire across the frontier.

In the following year the Prince de Condé made an attempt on Franche-Comté, the only effect of which was to lead the **French reverses : " the Corbie Year."** Emperor to send Louis XIII a formal declaration of war. Then Don Fernando, Cardinal-Infante and Governor of the Low Countries, made an unexpected dash across the frontier, forced La Capelle, Le Catelet, and Corbie to capitulate without striking a blow, devastated the whole of the country between the Somme and the Oise, and actually sent his skirmishers up to Compiègne (August, 1636). At the news of this blow panic seized on Paris—the populace fancied it already saw the Spanish troops manning the towers of the Bastille. It ventured to hiss Richelieu's coach as it passed through the city streets. His guards, whom he had lately garbed in a gorgeous uniform, were hooted : one of them was actually assaulted at the Porte Saint-Denis. . . . Popular hatred has a peculiarly overpowering effect on certain nervous organizations, and Richelieu at first fell into a condition of profound despondency. But after a lecture from Father Joseph of a somewhat rough description (the Capuchin, we are told, called him a " milksop ") he soon pulled himself together. He was inspired with the idea of driving through all the roughest of the Paris streets with no attendants but a few lackeys, and with one of those sudden changes of front to which the idle elements of the population of that city is addicted, the populace gave him an ovation to begin with, and then rushed to enlist for the defence at the Hôtel de Ville. Here the aged Maréchal de La Force, whom the people loved because he was not haughty, shook hands with every vagabond who exclaimed, in his enthusiasm, " Yes, M. le Maréchal ! I will go out to fight with you ! " It was a splendid moment. Every corporation and guild—Parliament, Court of Aids, Aldermen, and so forth—undertook to raise and support a larger or smaller body of volunteer troops. Horses were requisitioned. Gentlemen hurried up from the provinces. Finally the King found himself at the head of an army of 45,000 men, with which he marched to meet the Spaniards. But the Cardinal-Infante would not wait for him, and proceeded to evacuate Picardy. Thus ended the " Corbie Year," which lived long in the memory of Paris. In all other quarters— Germany, Italy, and on the Spanish frontier—the warlike operations of France had been most unfortunate.

Happily the confederated forces which were opposing the Emperor's troops in Germany were commanded by the best of Gustavus-Adolphus' pupils, Duke Bernhard of Saxe-Weimar, whom Louis XIII had carefully won over to his interests by a secret treaty (October, 1635). Between January and December, 1638, Bernhard, liberally supplied with French money, conquered Alsace : soon after this (July 18, 1639), he died, at the very moment when, as he did not betray any particular inclina-

Alsace annexed tion to hand over his conquest, he threatened to
by France, give Richelieu a great deal of trouble. But the
1639. Cardinal enjoyed that special good fortune which no great politician has ever lacked. When Bernhard passed

away, the officers who had served under him, and their men—mercenaries all of them—were in a quandary as to which side they should take : Guébriant, a Breton nobleman in command of the small contingent of Frenchmen with the army, persuaded them to sell their services to the Most Christian King, and thus Alsace was finally absorbed by the French Crown. From that time forward Burgundy and Lorraine found a protector against the Emperor : and in the same way the communications between Milan and the Low Countries opened by the Spaniards' defeat of the French forces in the Valtellina under Rohan (1637) were finally cut.

Meanwhile the arms of the Comte d'Harcourt and the fine words of Mazarin, now one of Richelieu's agents, were carrying succour to Marie Christine, Duchess of Savoy and sister of Louis XIII, and strengthening the French King's hold on Casale and Pignerol. Thus, on every side, France, the last to join the fray, was overcoming her wearied adversaries.

Germany was now a mere ravaged desert, the inhabitants of which were returning to a state of savagery. In those parts **Horrors of war** of the country which had suffered most, such **in Germany,** peasants as had survived massacre, famine, and **1638.** pestilence could find no more carrion of beasts wherewith to stay their hunger, and had been devouring human flesh ; towards 1638, we are assured, the bodies of men who had been hanged were retailed as food in certain cook-shops in the Palatinate. . . . Starvation it was, far more than the troops of the newly elected Emperor, that checked the advance of the Swedish armies in that desolate land.

On the Spanish side there was less resistance still. From 1637 onwards the French generals had been capturing all the strong towns in Artois, one after the other : this slow war of sieges, which needed more patience than genius, suited them admirably. In 1639, at a huge sacrifice, Spain collected a squadron of ships which set sail with reinforcements for Dunkirk : but hearing that the fleet of the United Provinces, the allies of France, awaited them in the Channel, the Spanish ships sought refuge in British waters : and there, near Dover, in the neutral zone, they were destroyed by Van Tromp (October). In the following year (August, 1640) Arras capitulated. At the same time Catalonia and Portugal revolted against the Catholic King. No great effort was needed to overcome so feeble a foe: while Richelieu was promising help to the Portuguese, and actually sending it to Catalonia, the French troops were carrying out the conquest of Roussillon: this Louis XIII completed by laying siege to Perpignan, which surrendered in September, 1642.

Conquest of Roussillon, 1642.

Just after signing the "preliminaries" with the Emperor the Cardinal died, in the conviction that peace was to follow certainly and immediately. Nevertheless the end was by no means to be yet: but Louis XIII had acquired possession of Alsace, Artois, and Roussillon: holding Piedmont, he held the gate into Italy: his hand was on Spain, and "the great tree of the House of Austria, which overshadowed all the rest of the earth, was shaken to its very roots."

V

While he was so skilfully guiding the external business of France, Richelieu found it a hard task to stand out against his enemies on French soil. These, since the Day of Dupes, had indeed been weakened; and Louis XIII, who had a soul above all meanness, valued the Minister who did so much to increase his master's glory. But he was fond of authority, he was jealous, and his infatuations for his favourites were passionate beyond belief. Richelieu, whose sole support at Court, where he was generally disliked, was the distrustful King himself, must have dreaded the power of these favourites sorely: "People fall in his good graces, not by degrees, but by precipices!" he said of his sovereign one day—and the little sentence gives us food for reflection.

He had very dangerous enemies: women. In Anne of Austria's circle he was hated, and in her fight against him Mme. de Chevreuse combined the considerable resources of her intelligence with the no less potent charm of her beauty. Richelieu did all he could to conciliate his foes, and this occasionally by methods of the most simple description. It would appear certain, indeed, that he made an attempt to obtain the good

Feminine intrigues against Richelieu.

77

graces of Anne of Austria, who only laughed at him. " As for Mme. de Chevreuse," so Mme. de Motteville assures us, " her beauty never lost its charm " for the gallant Cardinal. And after the Day of Dupes, Richelieu acknowledged to the too fair Duchess that "in spite of the severity he had shown, he had never hated her." As will be readily imagined, the skilful coquette took good care not to discourage so illustrious an adorer : but the feelings she betrayed were no more to her than another means of lulling him to a false security and more successfully deceiving him.

He had just appointed a somewhat paltry fellow to the office of Keeper of the Seals. Charles de l'Aubespine, Marquis **The Marquis de** de Châteauneuf, had pronounced sentence of **Châteauneuf.** death on the upright Maréchal de Marillac, brother to his own predecessor in office, and on Montmorency : he owed everything to Richelieu, who had pushed his fortunes as he always pushed those of his own creatures, and he was fifty years of age. . . . But Mme. de Chevreuse had undertaken the task of turning his grizzled head, and her effort was crowned with the most complete success.

The lovely Duchess was then occupied, as was her wont, with intrigues of the most complicated nature. Just at that period Gaston had taken refuge in Lorraine, first of all, and then at Brussels, with his mother (1632) : certain persons were trying to persuade him to seek shelter in England, together with Marie de' Medici. But for that purpose it was necessary, in the first place, to overthrow the English Ministry, which was much inclined to keep the peace and had little desire to quarrel with Louis XIII, and then to bring the enterprising Lord Holland into power, and likewise substitute the Chevalier de Jars for Fontenay-Mareuil, then French Ambassador in London. Mme. de Chevreuse, like all Richelieu's enemies, was bent on Gaston's triumph, and, further, the fascinating Holland and the charming De Jars were still her friends, after having been, it may be, even more to her : this sufficed to make her apply that marvellous talent for intrigue which had made her almost a power in Europe to their service : but she drew Châteauneuf into the plot, and he, to please her, did not hesitate to fail utterly in his duty as a minister. He went mad about her : in

PREPONDERANCE OF FRANCE

November, 1632, while the Cardinal, sick unto death, remained at Bordeaux surrounded by his faithful friends, the Keeper of the Seals could not deny himself the delight of accompanying Anne of Austria and Mme. de Chevreuse to La Rochelle. The whole journey was one long series of merrymakings, but it had a disastrous end: on February 25, 1633, the amorous Keeper of the Seals was arrested and his papers were seized: among them, it is said, Richelieu discovered certain letters from Mme. de Chevreuse wherein his own sentimental hopes were treated with a most unflattering scorn. . . . Châteauneuf was cast into prison: De Jars was sentenced to be beheaded, and was only pardoned at the very last minute: as for Mme. de Chevreuse, she was banished to her estates in Touraine—where she plotted more busily than ever.

Louis XIII was in love, just then, with one of the Queen's maids of honour, Marie de Hautefort, and under the influence **Marie de Hautefort.** of this fair-haired merry young girl he was gradually becoming "of a gallant mood," and the Court was consequently "very pleasant." Several times in each week he would carry off a bevy of young ladies, in company with his dear Hautefort, to join his hunting-party. "In those days," says Mlle. de Montpensier, "he would allow people to speak to him of the Cardinal de Richelieu with considerable freedom, and a proof that this did not displease him is that he himself talked of him in the same fashion." Marie de Hautefort, who was the friend of Anne of Austria, did not fail to make a mock of the mighty Minister, and laud the Queen's good qualities to the King her husband. As for the Queen, her lord's love affairs troubled her but little, for Louis' affection for the young lady was purely platonic. The reader is no doubt acquainted with the famous story—of doubtful authenticity—about the letter Mlle. de Hautefort hid in the bosom of her dress, and the tongs the poor King would have used to pick it out.

Further, the courtiers noticed one day that the King was beginning to be fond of talking to Mlle. Marie-Louise de La **Marie-Louise de La Fayette.** Fayette. This young girl of seventeen, of pro-vincial origin and humble means, dark-haired, and of a somewhat ordinary type of beauty, was gentle, serious, and reserved, and her talk was far less startling than that of the fair-haired and lively Hautefort. The King soon fell in love with her. We may believe that she was touched by the chaste affection the King of France expressed for her, but she had always intended to become a nun : she felt herself called " by a strong vocation from God. . . ." Weeping, Louis XIII gave her leave to depart. On May 19, 1637, Mlle. de La Fayette retired to the Convent of the Visitation in the Faubourg Saint-Antoine.

While all these things were happening, Mme. de Chevreuse was busy with her intrigues at Tours. The beautiful Duchess was gifted with one of those imperious imaginations which make women, according to their circumstances, either heroines of the Fronde or most unhappy creatures. " She loved without selection, and purely because she had to love somebody. . . . Her devotion to her passion—which might be called eternal, though its object changed—did not prevent her from being led astray, now and then, by passing whims : but she always came back from these distractions with an ardour that made them appear delightful " (Retz). Plotting, in her opinion, stimulated the imagination, and the delightful dangers it entailed imparted an infinite zest to love. . . . From Tours, then, Mme. de Chevreuse was carrying on secret communications with Anne of Austria through the Queen's devoted servant La Porte, and a few faithful gentlemen such as Lord Craven and La Rochefoucauld : and as Spain and France were competing, at that moment, to obtain the Duke of Lorraine as an ally, Anne and her friend were doing their best to persuade the Duke to pronounce in favour of Spain. . . . More serious still, the Queen of France was sending her brother, the Cardinal-Infante, all the information she could collect : now warning him that Richelieu had just dispatched a monk to Spain, charged with a secret mission ; then that England was negotiating with France against the interests of Spain ; or again that the parleying between Louis XIII and the Duke of Lorraine seemed just about to reach a successful conclusion, and that it was high time to take measures. . . .

It is certain that Anne, when she did all these things, was acting the part of a Spanish Infanta rather than that of a

Queen of France, and that she was guilty indeed towards her adopted country. But we must recollect that patriotism, in
Intrigues of Anne of Austria.
those days, was not the clear and authoritative duty it is in our time; how many of the great nobles were guilty of appeals to the foreigner! In the eyes of a Condé, for instance, a revolt against the King was no more than a quarrel with his own cousin. And we may be sure Anne of Austria never understood that her sin lay, not only in the deception she practised on her husband, but in the fact that she had betrayed her people. Patriotism was an abstract idea rarely mentioned to little Infantas—who were hardly taught even to read—and we may very fairly believe that Anne had no precise notion of what it meant: whereas she saw M. le Cardinal—and hated him—every day of her life. Like the women of her own epoch and of every other, her political conduct was entirely governed by the sympathies and antipathies with which the various politicians inspired her. Her mental attitude was that of her romantic female contemporaries: all of them, from Mme. de Chevreuse and Mme. de Longueville to the Grande Mademoiselle, felt, and thought, and would have acted had the occasion arisen, even as she did.

It was in the Louvre, at night, or at the Val-de-Grâce, whither she habitually retired to perform her devotions, that the Queen wrote her secret letters. The faithful La Porte put them into cypher, and either he or the Superior of the convent had them conveyed to Mme. de Chevreuse, or handed them to a secretary of the English Embassy who sent them on to Brussels. One day the Cardinal intercepted one of these notes to Mme. de Chevreuse. Instantly La Porte was thrown into the Bastille and threatened with the rack: and Séguier, the Chancellor, proceeded to the Val-de-Grâce to make a search, and cross-question the Mother Superior, whom the Archbishop of Paris commanded to reveal everything on pain of ex-
The Queen's Confession, 1637.
communication. The Queen began by swearing on the Blessed Sacrament that she had never written any but the most trivial things. But seeing that the Cardinal knew more than she was telling him, she ended by a full confession, on Richelieu's assurance that the King would forgive her if she would make a clean

breast of everything. The scene was a pitiful one (if we are to believe what the Cardinal tells us of it). Anne humbled herself, and wept; she said, " What a kind heart you must have, M. le Cardinal ! " : she vowed she would be eternally grateful to the Minister : and ended by begging him to " give me your hand ! " which the Cardinal, as he carefully tells us, " refused to do, out of respect, drawing back for the same reason instead of coming nearer. . . ." The Queen was forced to sign a paper in which she confessed her ill-doing and swore she would never repeat it. This done, the King forbade her (still in writing) to hold any future communication either with Mme. de Chevreuse or her " go-betweens," or even to send any letter to any one that had not first been shown to her lady in waiting, who was to notify himself of its contents. Such were the humiliating conditions on which Anne obtained her pardon (August, 1637). And Louis never forgot.

Richelieu strove to preserve a certain amenity in his dealings with Mme. de Chevreuse, " that dangerous spirit " as he called her, fearing she might betake herself abroad, **Flight of** " and carry fresh disturbances, which cannot be **Mme. de** foreseen, into affairs." But she, mistrusting him, **Chevreuse.** thought it safer to slip away. And in September, 1637, having fooled the old Archbishop of Tours in the twinkling of an eye, she escaped, under circumstances of the most romantic kind, rode right across France, disguised as a man, and so reached Spain.

Meanwhile Louis XIII would go, from time to time, to see Mlle. de La Fayette in her convent : he loved her still. Father Caussin, the King's confessor, who directed the young girl's conscience, attempted, most imprudently, to use her as a weapon against the Cardinal. Primed by the priest, Mlle. de La Fayette endeavoured to make Louis see that his support of the German Protestants against the Catholic Emperor, and his severe treatment of his mother and his wife, were grievous sins. But at the very first word she uttered on the subject, the monarch " turned his back on her and departed without giving her any answer." Shortly afterwards (December 10, 1637) the King's archers conducted Father Caussin, a disgraced man, to one of the houses of his Order at Rennes.

And these visits of the King to Mlle. de La Fayette had a result of which nobody had dreamt. One December evening in **Birth of Louis XIV, 1638.** 1637, Louis, leaving his lady-love, was prevented by a fall of snow from returning to Versailles, where he was living at the time, and was fain to take refuge at the Louvre. Now in those days it was customary for the King of France to travel about with all his furniture : when he quitted one palace for another, the first was left completely stripped. The only chamber in the Louvre in which it was possible for the King to be lodged in this unexpected fashion was that of the Queen, who was residing there. And on September 5, 1638, Anne of Austria brought the future Louis XIV into the world.

VI

With Father Caussin the last vestige of the devout party, which had caused Richelieu so many difficulties during **Gaston again conspires against Richelieu, 1636.** the earlier years of his Ministry, disappeared. But the party of the " great " nobles was by no means extinct. In 1636, while the royal troops were besieging Corbie, a plot was concocted, and joined in by the Duc d'Orléans and the Comte de Soissons, to assassinate the Cardinal. At Amiens everything was ready : M. le Comte was to come out of the Council-room with Richelieu and keep him talking for a few minutes at the door : at that moment, Monsieur was to give the signal to the murderers. But once again Gaston's courage failed him : when the Cardinal appeared in the doorway, imposing and formidable, Monsieur lost his head and fled, despite all efforts to stop him. Richelieu lived and died in ignorance of the peril he had escaped.

But notwithstanding this, Soissons and Gaston thought it prudent to seek safety, one in the strong fortress of Sedan, and the other in his own town of Blois. M. le Comte was a good soldier, but apart from his ambition he had none of the qualities requisite for the leader of a party. Yet hatred stood him in the stead of skill. A huge conspiracy was formed, and was joined, in the train of the Duc de Bouillon, Prince de Sedan (brother to Turenne), by great nobles, lords, officers of the army, and even by prisoners in the Bastille, such as that Comte de Cramail, who swore that with the help of the Maréchal de Vitry he could raise the garrison of the fortress in revolt whenever it pleased him so to do. Spain was approached, and gladly promised to support a rebellion so favourable to her own cause : and Charles IV of Lorraine, in his turn, abjured the treaty he had lately signed with France. When all things were ready, Lamboy, the Spanish general, crossed the frontier with 6000 men, and defeated the Maréchal de Châtillon at La Marfée (July, 1641). But Soissons was killed in the battle, and his death disorganized the party formed in his name. Its collapse became complete some six months later, after Guébriant had utterly defeated Lamboy at Kempen (January, 1642).

But already a fresh plot was being hatched against the hated Minister. " The Cardinal, who had not found La Fayette **The Marquis** satisfactory, and clearly perceived the King must **de Cinq-Mars.** have some amusement," had chosen, to entertain his master, one Henri d'Effiat, Marquis de Cinq-Mars, son of one of his most faithful servants, on whose dutiful behaviour he relied. He was a handsome young fellow, lively and eager, extraordinarily winning and graceful in manners. The idea of shutting himself up in the palace of Saint-Germain with a cross-grained, overbearing old king had very little charm for him, and a year and a half went by before he resigned himself to it.

The passion the King did not fail to develop for him was both jealous and tyrannical : Cinq-Mars had to spend his days in the monarch's company, hunting stags and wolves, digging out foxes' earths, catching blackbirds in cast-nets, and all this in the company of a dozen other men of small account, and exceedingly foul-mouthed. By way of diversion he had to listen to hunting stories, and discuss the profession of arms. . . . Often, half dead with boredom, he would jump on his horse at night, and gallop straight away to Paris, where he would serenade Marion de l'Orme, who loved him—unless indeed he spent his evening with " Messieurs du Marais," a company consisting of " the most worthy people about the Court," it would appear—and the least dull as well—who held their meetings at the house of Mme. de Rohan. But he was late at the King's *lever* on the following morning : Louis, invariably informed by third persons of his favourite's pranks, was angry, complained, sulked : Cinq-Mars, weary and exasperated, stood out against him : there were scenes, in short, after which nobody but the Cardinal could contrive to make peace between the King and " Monsieur le Grand " (as Cinq-Mars was called, owing to his office as *Grand Ecuyer*, Master of the Horse) ; this he would do by drawing up an agreement for them in due form, as follows : " We, the undersigned, certify to whomsoever it may concern that we are well pleased and satisfied with each other, and have never been in such perfect mutual understanding as at this present time. In testimony whereof we have signed the present certificate. Given at Saint-Germain, this 26th day of November, 1639. . . ." Was not a favour so excessive enough to turn the head of any favourite of twenty ?

Now while Louis XIII was treating Cinq-Mars like a spoilt young brother, Richelieu, for his part, was snubbing him as though he were a little boy, and when he once guessed that Monsieur le Grand was dreaming of playing a part in State affairs, he scolded him " like a lackey." Cinq-Mars was actually venturing to aspire to the hand of the Princess Marie of Mantua. Further, he claimed the right to attend the Council, and to be appointed to some high military command. The Cardinal had a way of jeering at these pretensions that hurt the young man's vanity cruelly : and he reminded him, too, that he had put him about the King for a purpose, that of serving as his spy. . . . Thus Cinq-Mars ended by having but one object in life, that of destroying the bully who had so wounded him.

He had been informed of the Soissons plot : after the battle of La Marfée he entered into relations with the Duc de Bouillon. And at the same time he made active endeavours to prejudice the King's mind against the Cardinal. Louis did not at all object to hearing the most violent abuse of his Minister. In reality he did not take such talk very seriously : but the plotters were so encouraged by his listening to them that every one of them was convinced he secretly approved their plot. And thus, having come to an agreement, the eternal Gaston d'Orléans, the Duc de Bouillon, and Cinq-Mars boldly signed a treaty with Spain (March, 1642). Anne was aware of the existence of this document, and the fact was also confided to Cinq-Mars' best friend, François-Auguste de Thou, who, in spite of the alarm it caused him, did not feel himself bound to inform against his comrade.

Richelieu, then lying sick at Narbonne, felt, as it were, the existence of all these intrigues without being able to lay his hand on any decisive proofs. At last, however, one of his police-agents supplied him with a copy of the treaty: he was saved. For some time past Louis XIII had been telling Cinq-Mars that ill-natured remarks about the Cardinal were now displeasing to him. Once the treaty bearing the signatures of the various conspirators was in his hands, he did not hesitate to order the arrest of a favourite for whom he now felt little affection. He was ill, and had himself carried to the chamber in which the Cardinal lay in bed: the King was thoroughly ashamed of his own ingratitude, and the Minister had hardly recovered from the state of anxiety into which he had been thrown: they both shed tears of emotion—and agreed that young Cinq-Mars must be put to death.

Arrest and execution of Cinq-Mars and De Thou.

All this happened at Tarascon. Richelieu departed for Lyons by way of the Rhone, and the barge that bore the bed on which he lay dying towed the boat on board which De Thou was kept under watchful guard. Once at Lyons, the Cardinal himself appointed the commissaries charged with the duty of passing sentence on Cinq-Mars, and on De Thou, whose guilt consisted in his having failed to betray his friend. On September 12 the two young men were beheaded on the Place des Terraux: both strove to meet death stoically, after the manner of the heroes of antique times, then so much in fashion, and bore themselves admirably. As for Monsieur, he confessed, he informed, he wept, he humbled himself—in short, he was more utterly base than ever. He was pardoned, and so was the Duc de Bouillon.

Meanwhile Richelieu was making his way back to Paris. Dying, eaten up with ulcers, literally rotting away, he travelled in a litter—or a room, rather—hung with violet cloth, with one of his secretaries, who was accommodated with a table and a chair, seated beside him : when there was no possibility of placing this heavy machine on the deck of a barge, it was borne along by four and twenty guards, each with his hat in his hand. When the resting-place for the night was reached, a hole was broken in the wall of some house, an inclined plane was built from the ground to the upper story, and thus, still on the shoulders of the guards, the huge litter was carried into shelter.

The Cardinal reached Paris, and forthwith caused his enemy, the loyal Tréville, Commandant of the *Mousquetaires à cheval*, **Death of Richelieu, 1642.** to be deprived of his command. Then, on December 1, 1642, he secured a declaration whereby Gaston was stripped of almost all his power. The next day his death-agony began. When his confessor, the parish priest of Saint-Eustache, exhorted him to forgive his enemies, he replied that he had never had any, save those of the State. He died, courageously, on December 4, 1642.

"The King," says Tallemant, "only went to see the Cardinal just before he died, and having found him very ill, he came away cheerful." Louis did nothing, it is true, in the way of altering his great Minister's policy, and he even left Richelieu's creatures in power. But he was too ill himself to be able to stand out altogether against the reaction that ensued, and little by little the exiles returned : the Vendômes, the Duchesse de Guise, all the disgraced people began to reappear, **Death of Louis XIII, 1643.** Monsieur among them : the prisoners of the Bastille, Bassompierre and Vitry, issued forth. Yet when Louis XIII realized that death was close upon him, he roused himself. On April 2, 1643, in the presence of the whole Court and the Parliament, he read the final Declaration according to which the powers of the Regent, Anne, and the Lieutenant-General of the Kingdom, Gaston, were subordinated to those of a Council composed of Séguier, Bouthilier, Chavigny, and Mazarin. On the 8th of the following May, Louis XIII was dying, and on the 14th, towards three o'clock, he breathed his last.

A few days later Enghien won his victory at Rocroy.

(For bibliography, see end of chapter iv.)

CHAPTER IV

THE KINGDOM UNDER LOUIS XIII

I. Justice. II. Finance ; Commerce ; The Navy. III. The
Clergy. IV. The Nobility. V. Conclusion.

I

IN our day justice and administration are two separate
things. Our magistrates try cases, and our official
functionaries—our prefects, for instance — administer.
Under the *Ancien Régime* this distinction between the two
powers did not exist : there was no administrator who had not
judicial powers, nor was there any judge who was not also
charged with certain administrative functions—so much so
that the judges were almost as numerous as the royal
officials.

The jurisdictions were not only innumerable, but their
powers were ill-defined. In the first place there were the
Administration Parliaments, one of which, the Paris Parliament,
of Justice. had jurisdiction over almost half the kingdom,
while the nine others—Bordeaux, Dijon, Rouen, Toulouse, Aix,
Rennes, Grenoble, Pau, and Metz—covered very little more
than a province each. Below these ten parliaments there
were eighty presidial courts, distributed in yet more irregular
fashion. But at least all these presidial courts enjoyed similar
powers, whereas the bailiwicks and the seneschals' courts,
which were beneath them, possessed rights and performed
duties of the most varied kinds. And, finally, a number of
inferior tribunals did the work of Courts of First Instance in
the names of different towns, and noblemen, and abbeys, or in
the King's name—and the pretensions and powers of these last
were more various still. But this was not all. Side by side with
this judicial hierarchy there was another : that of the financial
administration : all cases connected with taxation were settled

by the Elections, the Finance Offices, the Court of Aids, the Chamber of Accounts, the Court of the Mint, and so forth. Then there was the King's Great Council, the powers of which were somewhat indefinite : its duty was to settle all disagreements between the higher courts, but it likewise acted as a Court of First Instance in all cases " evoked " by the sovereign. Add to all these a number of special jurisdictions : the Ecclesiastical Courts for the clergy ; the Provost-Marshals for military offenders ; the Admiralty Courts and the Salt Water Court for naval cases ; and the " Grand Provost of the Hôtel," who dealt with the persons employed in the royal residences, etc. . . . In a maze such as this a man might well lose his way from time to time.

Another vice of the judicial system was the slowness and complexity of procedure. Those were happy times for the **Slowness of** swarm of attorneys and lawyers, advocates and **Procedure.** bailiffs and process-servers, for the pettifoggers of every degree ! Prescription was a thing unknown, and the most insignificant lawsuit brought in a mass of memoranda and statements, and productions, and objections, scrolls and documents of every kind. These all helped to cram the bags that were perpetually being conveyed from the attorney's office to the court, and from the court to the magistrate. " I have seven and twenty lawsuits on my hands," quoth a financier in 1625, " and I have the wherewithal to keep them all going for seven and twenty years." Judicial procedure was a perfect jungle, attorneys and advocates had Roman law, Canon law, the Royal Decrees, the innumerable local " customs " which were accepted as law, all at their disposal : and thanks to these they were able to transform the simplest of cases into a hopeless tangle.

And meanwhile the bags of law papers, piled one upon the other, ended by costing a perfect fortune. A man who was called on to defend his property had to spend almost the whole of it in the process. Every item was charged in detail. For one single document, the attorney had first to be paid for his advice, and then for the memorandum, the assignation, the copy, the presentation to the court ; then there were the charges for time, and the travelling expenses—and what not besides ?

In the criminal courts, when the guilty man was not rich enough to pay for his own execution, it was the plaintiff who had to bear the expense of the sentence : and the cheapest of capital punishments did not cost less than three or four hundred *livres* : it is true, indeed, that the bill would contain such entries as the following : " to the executioner, for dressings and medicine for himself . . . to the surgeons who physicked the said executioner and dressed his hurts." And one crying abuse was that the judge's pay had to come out of the pockets of the persons under his jurisdiction. Till the sixteenth century the amount of the fees had been left to the option of the suitor, or very nearly so. Now they were fixed, and the magistrates took good care that they should be paid in advance. Without money payment, no justice was to be had. Poor folk could not go to law—and this made them desperate.

Money payments did not suffice : the judges had to be canvassed, waited on in their antechambers, and if the suitor **Civilities to** was not a man of quality this process would have **Judges.** to be repeated over and over again before he was allowed beyond them : in any case, the magistrate's goodwill had to be won by some offering—wine, or capons, or preserves. Were the magistrates thus courted and paid a corrupt body ? Not at all : on the contrary, their decisions were exceedingly equitable. These visits and presents, a custom, and an openly acknowledged one, involved no particular consequences, and the judicial functionary ran no risk when he delivered judgment according to his conscience, for his office was his own property, and his position consequently both permanent and independent. The magistrate of our day—a functionary serving under a minister on whom his advancement depends—who has no power, in a criminal court, beyond that of giving effect to the verdict of a jury, and whose decisions, in a civil court, are ordered and directed by the code and the laws of jurisprudence, has nothing **Hereditary** in common with the hereditary magistracy of **Magistrates.** those old days, with its huge authority—a separate caste within the nation, full of traditional pride and uprightness, pompous, perhaps, as to its habits, and imbued with an excessive sense of its own dignity, but profoundly conscious, also, of the importance of its social function. Every member of this body, rom the humble village bailiff to " Monsieur le Premier " who presided over the Parliament of his province, and made his way home, when he entered the town, to the impressive sound of cannon, delivered judgment in perfect freedom, and with much more care for equity than for mere jurisprudence. They did not invariably make the endless procession of laws and customs and decrees their first thought : they very often settled the question in hand according to the dictates of common sense rather than according to precedent. They were what are now known in France as *de bons juges*. And thus the confusion in the laws frequently ensured the triumph of equity.

What did Richelieu do in this domain ?

Very little in the way of perfecting the judicial machine and rendering justice easier of access to the King's subjects : his only endeavour was to make the magistrates more malleable and more submissive to the Government.

Richelieu's contribution to Justice.

We must remember, in fact, that these officers, financial and judicial, these magistrates who owned their posts and held them permanently, were anything but a docile body. When the King published an edict the first difficulty was to get it " received," and the next, when that was done, was to get it applied. The Parliaments had power to delay the " registration " of these edicts : in that case, the Government had either to constrain them to do so by force (and in the case of a strong Government this could be done), or else negotiate with them (and this succeeded if the Government was rich). Even when the edicts had been " received," they were rarely put into force. We see the kings perpetually renewing their own edicts and those of their predecessors : a proof that none of them had been applied so far. And it was this wall of passive opposition and inertia on the officials' part which was to break the force of Colbert's effort, to some extent.

Not only did the Parliaments, if it so pleased them, refuse to register the King's edicts, but they would address " remonstrances " to His Majesty. The Paris Parliament, more especially, claimed the right, when it registered royal wills, and treaties, and official documents, of examining their clauses—in other words, a certain political power. In these matters Richelieu called it to order.

When the Paris Parliament decided to "make its very humble remonstrances," the procedure was as follows. A "Remon- president and a councillor presented themselves strances." before the Chancellor, and inquired the date and hour at which the King would be pleased to hear the remonstrances. On the appointed day the members and nine or ten presidents and councillors met at the First President's house at seven or eight o'clock in the morning. He always accompanied them. If the Court was at Saint-Germain, which was Louis XIII's favourite place of residence, they reached the town at about eleven o'clock, dined with the First President who had a lodging there, and waited till the King could receive them : then they robed, and were solemnly introduced into the royal presence. Louis received them in his cabinet, surrounded by his whole Court : he invariably began by scolding them in his usual violent manner : then, somewhat intimidated already by the manner of their reception, they presented their case in the most respectful terms : the Keeper of the Seals, the Superintendent, the Cardinal, discussed the matter with them : fresh threats followed. When necessary, Louis would summon the most recalcitrant of the councillors to his presence, reproach them bitterly, and even send them into exile.

The provincial Parliaments were no better treated. During the siege of La Rochelle, for instance, the King ordered the First President of the Bordeaux Parliament, M. de Gourgues, another of the Presidents, the Attorney-General, one of the Councillors, and the Keeper of the Records, to his camp. When De Gourgues began his speech, Louis broke in exclaiming in a voice that shook with rage, "To your knees, little man, before your master ! " He even caught hold of his gown to force him to obey : it was a scandalous scene. Under Louis XIII the Parliaments, thus terrorized, invariably gave way.

Beyond their judicial functions, the Parliaments, presidial courts, bailiwicks, and so forth, had hardly any administrative powers, save that of the police, which they preserved, in Paris through the intermediary of the Attorney-General, more particularly, and also of the Lieutenant of Police : and in the provinces, through the Lieutenants of Police of the various bailiwicks and seneschals' courts (which offices were still purchasable and hereditary).

But the financial jurisdictions (Court of Aids, Elections, etc.) had power to exercise all sorts of administrative functions :
Financial Courts. they apportioned the taxes, administered the public properties, kept an eye on the public highways and all public works, controlled all matters connected with the pay, supply, and commissariat of troops, and so forth. Now these financial officials, who, like the parliamentary magistrates, owned their offices, and therefore held them permanently, were no more docile than the rest. Richelieu accordingly endeavoured to deprive them, as far as possible, of their administrative powers, which he made over to a set of functionaries whom he could dismiss at will, who were passive instruments in the hands of the Government, and absolutely dependent on it : the Intendants.

Since the close of the sixteenth century the sovereign had been in the habit of sending inspectors of a kind—Masters of Requests, or Councillors—into the provinces to
Intendants. supervise the magistrates and report any irregularities in judicial or administrative matters to him. Thus the Intendants were by no means Richelieu's own creation. Still, he both used and abused them : sometimes he made them into viceroys of some province or town, sometimes they were commissaries with the armies, sometimes they were judges, sometimes they acted as political emissaries or police officers. They were agents for carrying out the law, which, when the hereditary officials with whose interests it clashed were left to put it in motion, frequently remained a dead letter. But in spite of the Intendants, the chief difficulty of the so-called absolute French monarchy down to the days of Louis XIV and Colbert was to make itself obeyed.

To pronounce sentence on his enemies, the Cardinal needed judges more obedient, more exact in carrying out his intentions,
Special Commissions. than these haughty men of law. For this reason all his adversaries—Chalais, Ornano, Marillac, Châteauneuf, Cinq-Mars, and the rest—were withdrawn from the jurisdiction of the ordinary courts, and sent for trial before

commissions specially appointed to condemn them : a few magistrates, and occasionally several dukes and peers, were called to sit in the King's own cabinet, it might be, and obliged to express their opinions aloud, in the monarch's presence : such, for instance, was the commission that "tried" La Valette. Theoretically speaking, it must be admitted, the King did not exceed his powers when he took a criminal from his natural judges and arraigned him before others, chosen by himself for that purpose : the monarch was indeed the sovereign judge of all his subjects : the magistrates of the kingdom were no more than his delegates and representatives : all justice was dispensed in his name, and he had power, if he chose, to call any particular cause before himself : in virtue of this principle the murder of the Duc de Guise under Henri III, or that of Concini, was perfectly justifiable. But though Louis XIII in no way exceeded his rights when he confided the duty of trying one or other of his subjects to these special commissaries, the proceeding was tyrannical and odious in practice, and public opinion openly opposed it. Yet Richelieu constantly resorted to it, and parliamentary protests were all in vain. Masters of Requests travelled all over the kingdom, armed with discretionary powers, and acting with a complete disregard for formalities. Such a man was Laffemas, known as "the Cardinal's headsman," the "grand sportsman of France," or, *vir bonus strangulandi peritus*, who would frequently exclaim, "What a pleasure a hanging would be to-day ! "

"High treason is a crime of such importance," says Richelieu, "that he who is guilty of it, even by the merest thought, is worthy of punishment." Now it is evident that anything might become an act of high treason : to speak of the Government "with a little too much freedom," for instance, or to endeavour "to supplant the Cardinal," or even to be one of those "who would have exulted at his fall." This was the exact nature of the sin committed by young Barradas, a favourite "who sprang up in one night, like a gourd, thought the King loved him better than he loved the Cardinal, and—this was the last stage of folly—dared to say so to His Majesty." Wherefore the chastisement of banishment fell upon him. The Minister had been fully informed of his

Richelieu's arbitrary powers.

most trifling remarks !—one in particular, which he learnt from Du Plessis, who had it from Cardinal de La Valette, who had it from Bellegarde, who had heard Barradas make it to the Queen : Richelieu reports this with the utmost gravity.

" Gossip," and " reports," and " they say "—such grounds as these were almost sufficient to induce the Cardinal to banish a man, or hang him, or have him beheaded, or at least hand him over to his commissaries, which came to the same thing. His police service was well done : he had a swarm of spies, such as that cook of M. de Tréville's who was paid 400 *livres* out of the Cardinal's privy purse. And indeed, seeing, as he tells us himself, " that in matters of conspiracy it is almost impossible to obtain mathematical proofs," he was content with presumptions. Thus Châteauneuf was condemned, not on the evidence of facts, but on that of " certain designs " ascribed to him, which were " not altogether consonant with the service of the King " : for reasons of State, in fact. . . .

Such was the justice dealt out by Richelieu.

II

In his financial administration, likewise, Richelieu gave little thought to the remedy of abuses, and none at all to the improvement of the situation of the taxpayer : his only endeavour was to secure, by fair means or foul, the money necessary for the carrying out of his admirable foreign policy. He may, when he entered on his Ministry, have nursed some vague and lofty plan of administrative reform. But though he was a splendid diplomatist and a good War Minister, he was an indifferent legislator, and for figures, as he most readily confessed himself, he had no head at all. He left the squeezing of the taxpayers and fooling of the Government's creditors to the superintendents of the finances : from his point of view, D'Effiat and Bullion performed their duties marvellously well, because they always contrived to find him money. Whether this was done by perpetual borrowing at usurious rates of interest, by bankruptcies, or by reminting the coinage, deplorable expedients, all of them, which remained the usual practice of the French Monarchy, and aggravated the financial disorder destined to destroy the *Ancien Régime*, till it was beyond remedy, Richelieu cared not a jot. What he had to do was to overcome the House of Austria and his personal enemies.

One of these financial expedients was the sale of offices. Even in the earlier half of the seventeenth century the venality

Sale of offices. connected with these offices was universally held to be an abuse, and Richelieu himself had stigmatized it as such in a noble speech delivered in the States-General of 1614. But when he became Minister he added to the evil. After his time there were alnagers (cloth inspectors), for instance, and even *langueyeurs* whose business it was to examine pigs' tongues. It must be acknowledged that these newly created offices were no more, as a rule, than a veiled tax levied on officials who already existed. One fine day, for instance, the King would decide that such and such an office should be administered for six months in the year by its actual holder, and for the next six by some newly appointed person : or, again, he would increase the number of councillors of some presidial court. To save themselves from loss of income in the first case, or from loss of dignity in the second, the men in possession bought up the new offices. . . . And this explains how it was that when the State was pressed for money it cut down the pay of its officers or the incomes of the holders of State securities by a few quarters : the two categories occupied a precisely similar position in its estimation.

After 1636, more especially, the taxes grew very much heavier. The urban taxes, for instance, increased twofold

Increase in Taxation. between 1636 and 1646 : in most towns there were octroi charges, and these were doubled for the benefit of the Treasury. Yet we must not accept the figures of the official documents as absolutely correct : the accountants calculated according to the amount due on the lists they issued : and there was a considerable residue of unpaid taxes, which were remitted every year : but instead of reducing the nominal value shown on their returns, and thereby diminishing their own percentages, the assessors preferred a perpetual process of over-estimation, which made their fictitious total far exceed the amount really collected.

The distribution of taxation was very unequal. Brittany, Burgundy, Dauphiné, Provence, Languedoc, and the ancient possessions of the Kings of Navarre, such as Béarn and the County of Foix, had retained the right of summoning their own Estates—elected assemblies which voted the sum due to the King. But besides these districts with Estates of their own, there were others under the direct administration of the King, through his financial agents, in which the taxes, being fixed by the King alone, were far heavier. These were called the regions of Elections. . . . Richelieu undertook, or pretended to undertake, to convert the regions of Estates into Elections. In reality his sole object was to obtain a large sum of money, and thus he permitted the majority of the provinces to buy themselves out : the only one to lose its Estates was Dauphiné.

As the major part of the weight of this taxation fell on the lower classes, there was hardly a year after 1630 that did not **Revolts** witness a revolt of some kind : but the most **against taxa-** terrible was that of the *Va-nu-pieds* in Normandy. **tion : "Les** During the summer of 1639, the Avranches **Va-nu-pieds."** peasants murdered the *Lieutenant criminel* of Coutances, because they suspected he had come to the town to set up the salt tax, which had not existed there as yet. An ecclesiastic belonging to that neighbourhood, nicknamed Jean Va-nu-pieds, put himself at their head : before long he was backed by an army of 20,000 peasants. The revolt, which had been feebly or unsuccessfully repressed, spread to Caen, Falaise, Bayeux, and Rouen. The authorities had to send Gassion, then a Field-Marshal, with 4000 troops, to put the rebels down. It was a terrible process : the soldiers laid the province waste. "You cannot make too notable an example," wrote the Minister, "besides chastising individuals, you must raze the walls of the towns to the ground. . . ."

The reader will recognize that under Richelieu's guidance the monarchy was more qualified on the whole to cover France **Richelieu's** with glory than to rule her on the lines of a **Colonial** prosperous commercial undertaking. Yet the **Policy.** Cardinal did bestow a certain amount of care on commerce, and made some effort to encourage the great companies then being formed with a view to the profitable working of the French colonies, in which they all failed most lamentably. These colonies, which were wellnigh abandoned by the mother country, had hardly any population except missionaries, such as those Jesuits who by sheer heroism contrived to found a sort of primitive theocratic republic (something like that of Paraguay) among the Hurons of Canada, or pirates, like the " filibusters " of Tortoise Island, or the members of such short-lived commercial establishments as that of Pronis in Madagascar.

The fact was that merchants, emigrants, colonists, traders, sailors, and shipowners all found the risks, physical and pecuniary, more than they could face. The sea, in those days, was an area of evil repute, swarming with malefactors whose numbers far exceeded those of the inoffensive passengers, and wherein the strongest always had right on his side. It was a miraculous piece of good luck when any merchant ship made a **Corsairs and** voyage without coming across an enemy of some **Pirates.** kind, corsair or pirate, or even one of the coastguard ships belonging to the French King, which were very apt to strip his subjects on the pretext of protecting them. The Spaniards, the Dutch, the English above all, looted without the slightest regard for treaties, and plundered the French ships for choice; it must be admitted that these acts of brigandage were repaid with usury by the French sailors whenever opportunity served them. The Mediterranean was infested by Barbary Moors, Tunisians, Algerians, Moroccans, Turks, all of whom lived on the fruits of piracy. In vain did Richelieu's agents conclude truces with Bey, or Dey, or Sultan ; the Christians frequently made the first attack on the Moslem shallops and tartans. But the Infidels raided our very coasts. In 1633 there were 25,000 Christian slaves in Algeria, for whom a ransom of 3000 *livres* per head, on an average, was demanded, and the Dey would only consent to hand over 130 Christians in exchange for 1000 Turks : which proves that one Christian, in his eyes, was worth seven and a half Turks : a heavy price.

Richelieu made one splendid effort : besides all he did for the army, he succeeded in improvising a war fleet. In 1626 he **A Navy created,** bought the office of Admiral of France from **1626-28.** Montmorency, and transformed and enlarged its functions, under the title of Grand Master and Superintendent of Navigation. Two years later, by the end of 1628, a squadron of sixty-seven ships was already anchored before La Rochelle. Almost all of them were hired ships, indeed, and their crews were hired as well—for in those days a fleet was raised after the same fashion as an army, for temporary service. But by degrees the sailors learnt their business : the officers appointed to command them were no "nobles with curled locks," for whom the Cardinal had scant liking, but "bold stout mariners, bred to salt water and the bottle," and thus the foreign mercenaries, so often insubordinate— -such as those Dutchmen who refused, at the last moment, to fire on their co-religionists—were finally abolished. Soon, indeed, the King was able to have a few ships built in his own kingdom : in 1638 came a great day when the *Couronne*, a vessel over 200 feet long (the Dutch ships only measured 100), armed with 88 guns, was duly launched, the standard of France, a huge silken flag that had cost 1400 crowns, waving over her in the breeze ! Then, on the "Western seas" (the Channel and the Atlantic Ocean) floated galleons and advice-boats, three-deckers, heavy transports, light cutters for reconnoitring, and pinnaces of small tonnage. On the Eastern side (the Mediterranean) the Cardinal kept up a lively war on the Barbary Moors with his galleons, and carried on negotiations with the Dey. But he never succeeded in putting down the pirates, and did not even attempt to prevent the exactions of the Consuls of France and our Ambassador at Constantinople from their own fellow-countrymen. So that French trade in the Levant diminished, and in Louis XIV's time it had wellnigh disappeared.

III

Richelieu was the very opposite of a freethinker, a "Libertine," like Cardinal de Retz. Not only was he, like Louis XIII, **The** profoundly pious and regular in the performance **"Clericalism"** of his religious duties, he was even, if I may call **of the** it so, "clerical"—that is to say, he was fond of **Executive.** surrounding himself with ecclesiastics, and of confiding every sort of duty to them, even those for which we should now think a priest most unsuited, such as directing the navy

(Archbishop Sourdis), or military operations (Cardinal de La Valette), or leading the contingents of troops sent on active service from various dioceses (the Bishops of Montpellier, Nîmes, Mende, and Albi, in 1639). It is true that in those days priests, even those most fervent in their devotion, did not always profess to be patterns of angelic gentleness. Father Joseph is a case in point. " Kill them all ! " this pious Capuchin calmly replied one day to a captain who had asked him for orders, and then quietly went on saying his Mass. Indeed the habit of employing churchmen in the most secular occupations, and even in warfare, was widespread in every country. Richelieu himself set the example. He laboured with all his strength for what he believed to be the welfare of France, and far harder than he laboured for the good of the Church. Not, we may be sure, that he took no interest in the progress of Catholicism and of virtue, but these, in his mind, came after the interests of the State.

Now the Church of France was at this period a prey to undoubted abuses, such as *commendams*. A commendatory **Abuses in the** abbot lived in Paris, or elsewhere, and when the **Gallican** fancy took him to pay a visit to his monastery, he **Church.** set up his residence in a more or less pleasant habitation which he had built for himself, outside the monastery walls. He received the abbey revenues, on condition that he kept the abbey buildings in repair (which he did as little as might be), and ensured the support of the prior and monks (whom he starved when they had not forced him into an agreement as to the share each was to have, by a series of lawsuits). The same state of things obtained as to the parish cures. The men who drew the incomes were not, as a rule, the men who did the parish work. Many of the titular priests did not live in their parishes at all ; they had deputies, who heard the parishioners' confessions, administered the Holy Communion to them, and buried them. And the villages that were served to this extent were the lucky ones ! Many others were forced to go to law to escape total deprivation of religious services, and induce their parish priest to send down some other priest to perform his duties. Canonries were conferred on the same principle as the cures of souls : but the canons did not even send substitutes. As for the bishops, they were even less often in residence than the canons and priests and abbots.

At that period no priest had any right to an income in virtue of his priesthood : thus if he was to live at all it was essential **Status of the** that he should have a benefice. Now in the **Clergy.** kingdom of France the number of clerics far exceeded the number of benefices available ; and thus many ecclesiastics, and even priests, were forced to earn their livelihood by manual labour, like common workmen, and thought themselves most fortunate if they could contrive to get into the service of some wealthy nobleman who would employ them to do his errands, if he did not put them to even less exalted tasks, such as to stand on the footboard of his coach, dressed up in some lackey's jerkin : this at least was the fashion in which the Comte de Grammont utilized his chaplain, M. Poussatin.

Benefices of every kind, from the humblest parish livings to the richest abbeys, were bestowed without the slightest regard **Scandals of** for age or fitness. Richelieu gave the bishopric **Patronage.** of Grasse to young Godeau, in return for a copy of verses, and a monastery to Maugars, a violinist whose playing had pleased him : the son of the Duchesse de Guise held Saint-Denis when he was seventeen : Châtillon was given to the Comtesse de Guiche : Sully, a Huguenot, held four abbeys. These laymen, women, and Protestants were not the titular abbots : their benefices were held for them by a dummy, some ecclesiastic paid for the work, who collected the income in his own name : none the less was the abuse a crying one. As to the cures of souls, prebends, and bishoprics, they were given to clerics only, but with no greater consideration for individual merit. The nobles and magistrates looked on these benefices as so many gratuities which the King was bound to bestow on the junior members of their families. " An abbey would be stipulated for as a young girl's dowry, and a colonel would reorganize his regiment with the revenue of a priory " (Voltaire). And naturally these younger sons of great families, who had gone into the Church to ensure themselves the wherewithal to keep up their rank in the great world, these pious great ladies, and juvenile or schoolboy bishops, all these amateur ecclesiastics, if we may so describe them, made strange priests at times : some were atheists, like Bishop Lavardin, some debauchees, like the Bishop of Broc or the Abbé of Gondi, some men of scandalous life, like Canon Bois-Robert. And while many convents of nuns were not unlike those described by Boccaccio, the sisters in many others lived in utter indifference to the rules of their order, and received " all sorts of boarders, without distinction " : ladies who " desired to go to law with their husbands or to conceal the disorder of their own lives," girls who were " trying to escape the pursuit of one gallant, or await or catch another " (Francion). . . .

At the Court of Henri IV unbelief had been very much in fashion, and atheism the vogue. All through Louis XIII's **The** reign, but more especially during its opening **"Libertines."** period, the " Libertines " made a great uproar, and cast clumsy scorn on the mysteries of religion. We need not be astonished to learn that Father Mersenne reckoned Paris to contain at least 40,000 " Libertines," when we realize that Richelieu himself admitted avowed freethinkers to his intimate circle. M. de Matha and M. de Fontrailles charged at the crucifix, sword in hand, one day, shouting " The enemy ! " And trials such as that of Théophile de Viau had no terrors for these gentlemen. . . . But indeed more ardent missionaries than the tipstaffs of the French Parliaments would have been needed to stem the flood of irreligion.

Such missionaries there were : the period of the freethinkers was also the period of Bérulle, Bourdoise, Vincent-de-Paul, **Reaction** Olier, and Rancé. It saw the birth of the first **against** seminaries : Saint-Nicolas-du-Chardonnet (1620 **Unbelief.** and 1644), Saint-Sulpice (1641), and a whole efflorescence of religious orders, the Oratorians, the Nuns of Saint Magdalen, the Sisters of Charity, the Lazarists, the Eudists, who carried their good example into the provinces, warred against ignorance and reformed the clergy—aided by the *Compagnie du Saint-Sacrement*.

It was towards the year 1625 that a virtuous nobleman, the Duc de Ventadour, laid the foundations of this secret society, destined ultimately to obtain an enormous development. The " Brothers " who composed it belonged to every class : priests and laymen, small tradesmen, lawyers, great lords, and their names were known to the Superior only. Now this devout **The Company of the Holy Sacrament.** association was not content with exercising charity, improving the condition of the galley-slaves, for instance, visiting the sick and the prisons, and alleviating, with great success, the misery of the country-folk, during the Fronde : it also sought to fight against heresy and irreligion, and to " avenge the honour of God," by watching over the morals of the country. Thus it made a very successful struggle against Jansenism, which it took to be a kind of under-hand plot on the part of the Reformers, and against the Protestants themselves, whom it persecuted, individually, with an ingenuity which has never been equalled, putting Huguenot artisans on a sort of " index," making life impossible, by a variety of small annoyances, to a heretic physician here, a lawyer there, now to a pastor, and then again to an official. It was the duty of the " Brothers " to make private inquiries concerning the private life of every individual, to know who were well and who were ill conducted, to discover freethinkers, and inform against them in unobtrusive fashion. In the end the " Cabal of the Devout " exasperated the whole community, but though the identity of the pious spies was suspected, it was impossible to establish it. And, further, the Company had some very powerful protectors : after the death of Louis XIII, both the Regent and Gaston d'Orléans favoured it, and the Prince de Conti requested it to furnish him with " reliable reports as to everything that happened " on his country properties. But Mazarin had no liking for this clandestine and constantly increasing power, and Colbert liked it even less. So much so, that after 1661 the " Cabal of the Devout," betrayed and openly revealed, was laid under an interdict, its meetings proclaimed, its members hunted down. After the year 1666 it ceased to exist, save in a few provincial towns, and the Tartuffe whom Molière's contemporaries hissed would seem to have been a caricature of a " Brother."

Richelieu tolerated the activities of the devout party and the founders of new Orders, but gave them little encouragement, and his claim—in that political will and testament which sets forth what he would fain have done more than what he really accomplished, and is, in fact, a monument to his good intentions—to have originated the great improvement in Catholic **Richelieu and** morals that took place under Louis XIII is very **the taxation of** ill-founded. In reality he took far more pains to **the Clergy.** improve what we may call the yield of the Catholic clergy to the State than the morals of its individual members. The richest order in the kingdom contributed nothing to its treasury beyond the tithes and a " free gift " grudgingly voted, year by year, by the Assembly of the Clergy. In 1641 the King, without further ceremony, issued an order that all beneficed persons were to pay a considerable portion of their revenues into his coffers (abbeys, bishoprics, and ordinary benefices were to pay 33 per cent.; cures, 17 per cent.; and chapters, 10 per cent.). So great was the clamour that instantly rose from the Assembly of the Clergy that the Government compounded for a sum of 5,500,000 *livres*, to be paid in three yearly instalments. And two archbishops and three bishops refused to set their hands even to this engagement. Richelieu responded by a minor *coup d'état* quite in his usual manner. D'Émery was sent down to the Assembly, and ordered the protesting dignitaries, in the King's name, to retire instantly to their dioceses—a punishment keenly felt by a prelate in those days. The Archbishop of Sens replied that " he listened with honour and respect to everything that came from the King, even to abusive words," and when d'Émery answered that no words coming from the King were abusive, " You must give me time to finish," quoth Monseigneur de Sens, " and then you will hear that I call them abusive, coming from your lips ! " After which the Assembly was left to continue its deliberations in peace. . . .

Such was the religious work of the Cardinal de Richelieu.

IV

The first personage in the kingdom, after the King himself, the Dauphin, and the Queen, was Monsieur, the King's brother. He took precedence, of course, of the Princes of the Blood— Henri de Condé and the Comte de Soissons, second cousins of Louis XIII. Below these, and far below the members of the royal family, were the nobles. First in order came the "foreign princes" (younger sons of reigning houses) living in

The Royal Princes and Princes of the Blood.

France, or petty sovereign princes who were at the same time subjects of the French crown, such as Guise (a younger son of the House of Lorraine), Bouillon (Prince de Sedan), Valentinois (Prince de Monaco), Nemours, Nevers, Luxembourg, and so forth; and the "dukes and peers," greatly increased in number by Louis XIII, and more especially by Louis XIV. Dukes without a peerage were few and far between : Louis XIII did create a few by patent—that is to say, he gave a few of his courtiers leave to call themselves dukes for their own lives—but these were mere courtesy titles, semi-official, and not recognized by Parliament. As for the other titles, baron, viscount, count, or marquis, no one of them had any more value than the other. For in those days " nobility was attached to the individual, whereas titles went with the soil " (D'Avenel). If a nobleman sold his lands—a marquisate, for instance—he also sold to the purchaser (unless he was a commoner) the right to bear the title of marquis as well as the name of that particular marquisate. Fathers were in the habit of conferring the name of some one of their fiefs on each of their sons. But these sons could not take the name of the paternal property with titles of a lower rank, according to the custom obtaining in France since the thirteenth century : " a property raised to a marquisate conferred one title of marquis, and not the subsidiary titles of count, viscount, and baron as well." The antiquity and celebrity of the name was what was treasured, the title had no importance at all. At Court many noblemen put on the title of count or marquis just as they would have put on a fine coat, and nobody offered any protest : others, on the contrary, did not even adopt the *de* (wrongly believed to indicate noble birth), which was often used by plain artisans.

It was the moral right, and almost the duty, of the members of the royal family to take some share in the government of the country : " a Prince of the Blood must make civil war rather than forgo any part of his dignity," wrote Retz himself. Now Richelieu allowed Marie de' Medici to die in a foreign land : he forced Gaston into acts of the most dishonouring pusillanimity : Soissons perished at La Marfée : Condé—a rapacious, intelligent little old man, so filthy that Richelieu used to send him word that he was to clean himself on the days when he visited the King—only saved himself by his flattering tongue, and was too happy to marry his son, the future hero of Rocroy, to one of the Cardinal's nieces. . . . This was the treatment Richelieu applied to all these selfish and mischief-making princes.

In the provinces the old military nobility tended to die out, as a consequence of its pecuniary ruin. The whole of the **The Provincial** fortune of the nobles had been in lands, and very **Nobility.** often these lands only brought in the most miserable income, because their owners had alienated them, in the Middle Ages, in consideration of a yearly rent, the *cens*, fixed once for all, and permanently paid, by tenants who passed their holdings on from father to son : since that time the purchasing power of money had greatly diminished. A half-penny may have been a fair rent for an acre of ground in the Middle Ages, but when that acre brought in no more than a single copper coin in the days of Louis XIII, its owner found himself by no means a wealthy man !

To ensure themselves a livelihood, the ruined nobles married the daughters of rich magistrates and financial magnates—and thus the provincial aristocracy renewed itself. Or else they begged offices and benefices and sinecures of the King's bounty— and thus the Court nobility was formed. Richelieu—and in this he pointed out the way to Louis XIV—did all he could to develop this aristocracy of parasitical courtiers kept by the King, which was certainly injurious to the economic life and well-being of the nation, but which was to develop French wit to its most exquisite point.

Yet at the time of which I write the manners and customs of the nobility—even at the Hôtel de Rambouillet—were still **Education of** coarse, and very far removed from the refinement **the Nobility.** they were later to attain. A well-born youth was taught, in his boyhood, to fence, to dance, a little music, a still smaller amount of mathematics : when he was fourteen or fifteen he was attached for a certain period to some regiment, so as to be taught his military duties : then he spent fifteen

months at a Paris " academy " to learn to be " a good horseman " : and there his education ended. Wherefore noblemen,
as a rule, had no desire to gain a reputation for politeness or
wit ; their aim was to be known for their bravery and " magnificence." They were quite content if their houses swarmed
with servants and lackeys ; if they owned one or two of those
heavy coaches drawn by six horses and sumptuously lined with
velvet, but cruelly devoid of springs, the leathern curtains of
which afforded the traveller but little shelter from rain and
wind, but which bore at least three or four lackeys on their
footboards ; and if they could have this heavy machine attended,
as it bumped along the streets, by a bevy of servitors, who
made a hideous clatter and thus clearly demonstrated the
grandeur of their master's house.

Their chief quality was bravery—a mad, ridiculous, but
fascinating bravery. " Do you not know," said one Italian,
Duelling. " that Frenchmen go to their deaths as if they
were to rise again the next morning ? . . ."
About the year 1625 hardly a week went by without some duel
at the Court. Men drew their blades on account of the merest
trifles, and sometimes for no reason at all, simply for the
pleasure of so doing. " Sir," Boutteville would say to any
gentleman whose reputation as a duellist offended his own
claim to be the first in that particular, " I have been assured
that you are brave : we must fight ! " A certain Chevalier
d'Andrieux, we are told, killed seventy-two men with his own
hand. As a rule the " challenger " and the " challenged " did not
appear alone on the field : each party was supported by two or
three, or even four, friends, and these " seconds " fought with
each other. One day in 1638 Bussy-Rabutin received a visit from
a man of noble birth with whom he had no previous acquaintance :

Having heard that I had an affair with Busc, and was looking for him,
he came to offer to inform me of his whereabouts, on condition that I
would employ his services. . . . I thanked him a thousand times over. . . .
I begged him to consider that I already had four friends to support me,
and that if I accepted the honour he desired to do me, it would become
a battle. . . . He expressed his satisfaction with my reasons, and, said
he, " As I cannot be on your side, sir, you will not take it ill if I go and
offer my service to M. de Busc, and tell him you are here ! " I esteemed
this gentleman's behaviour highly.

Valençay, who was successively Knight, *Bailli*, and Commander of the Order of Malta, had been a famous duellist : this did not prevent him from dying a Cardinal. He it was who, as second to the Marquis des Portes, was fighting, one day, with Cavoye, who later became Captain of Richelieu's Guard. "Cavoye wounded the Chevalier de Valençay with two little thrusts, for he was very skilful, and said, 'Monsieur le Chevalier, have you had enough ? ' The Chevalier replied : 'A little patience, don't flutter about so much ! ' and dealt him so shrewd a blow that he very nearly died of it " (Tallemant). . . . And indeed duels very often bore a close resemblance to assassinations. Louvigny—the man who betrayed Chalais—was fighting one day with Hocquincourt, afterwards a Marshal of France, and said to him, " Let us take off our spurs." Then, " as the other bent down to do it, he gave him a sword-thrust that ran him through and through." The Chevalier de Guise ran his adversary through before he had time to draw his sword at all : every one agreed that this proceeding was somewhat " too princely " : yet many gentlemen of lesser degree behaved exactly like the Chevalier de Guise. One of Puymorin's servants gave Balagny, with whom his master was fighting in the middle of the Rue des Petits-Champs, a thrust with a pitchfork in his back. But it is only fair to add that such performances were more characteristic of the sixteenth century : as a general rule the duellists of the days of Louis XIII prided themselves on destroying each other with every courtesy.

Since the time of Henri IV the sovereign frequently endeavoured to check these fights, which were forbidden by the Church, and in which the flower of the French nobility sometimes fell. But law has never succeeded in overriding fashion, and the various edicts against duelling produced no more effect than the ordinances forbidding splendour of attire. And indeed Louis XIII was the first to scoff at men who would not fight. If Boutteville had not shown such insolence, the King would never have condemned him.

By the time François de Montmorency, Comte de Boutteville, Lord of Lusse and other places, had reached his twenty-third year, he had fought more than twenty duels. In 1624, after his meeting with Pontgibault, Parliament issued a writ for his apprehension : he left Paris in broad daylight, in a coach drawn by six horses, escorted by two hundred friends and ser-

The Boutteville Encounter. vants, and took service in Flanders : as soon as he came back, which he did in the most haughty fashion, without taking the smallest notice of the sentence of death by default which had been passed upon him, he slew Thorigny, and soon afterwards wounded the Marquis de La Frette.   Louis XIII had just signed a fresh edict : angered by this feat, he would have had Boutteville arrested, but the latter took refuge at Brussels in company with the Comte des Chapelles, the friend of his boyhood, and his usual " second." Young Beuvron went to Brussels, and challenged him to fight. Any avoidance of the challenge on Boutteville's part was impossible : as he had promised the Archduchess-Governor of the Low Countries that he would not draw his sword within her territories, it was settled that the meeting should take place in Paris.   And thus it came about that on May 12, 1627, six gentlemen got out of their coaches on the Place Royale, drew their swords, and fought so fiercely that in a few minutes Beuvron was disarmed by Boutteville, who granted him his life, Bussy d'Amboise had been killed by Des Chapelles, and La Berthe grievously wounded by Buquet.   While the dead man was carried back to his lodging in his coach, and the wounded duellist transported to the Hôtel de Mayenne, the survivors mounted their horses and fled.   Beuvron and his squire made for England, Boutteville and Des Chapelles hurried in the direction of Lorraine.   That night, by a mere chance, these two were recognized and detained in a tavern where they had halted for the night.   In vain did all Boutteville's relations plead for him.   His wife cast herself at the King's feet : Louis passed on without replying to her prayer, saying to those about him, " I am sorry for the wife, but I will and must preserve my authority."   He was convinced Boutteville had intended to defy him, and that he could not forgive.

In 1633 Corneille was able to put a duel on the stage (in the *Galerie du Palais*) without eliciting the smallest symptom of displeasure on the part of King or Cardinal.   Thus the executions of Boutteville and Des Chapelles caused no diminution in the number of duels fought in France : the Maréchal de

Grammont was to relate, at a subsequent period, that nine hundred gentlemen lost their lives in single combat in the course of the Regency of Anne of Austria.

The authorities were powerless against the abuse of duelling, only an alteration in the manners of the country was to bring about a change.

V

Before Richelieu's time the power of the sovereign was limited by the authority of certain constituted bodies, and **Checks on the Monarchy.** certain important personages, by the special rights of certain provinces, or certain towns, by very ancient institutions, or traditions that were centuries old, and by customs as imperious in their operation as any laws. Louis XIII and his Minister did their utmost to diminish these autonomous powers and customs and local rights, all the things, in fact, that hampered the sovereign's action. They were very far from attaining complete success : even in the days of Louis XIV the exercise of the royal will was held in check by local traditions and resistance. Nevertheless, after Richelieu's Ministry the ruling power was more successfully concentrated in the King's hands than it had ever been : and through the Intendants, who were absolutely subordinate to the Government, a really central administration was introduced in every quarter. What is known as the absolute monarchy, as it existed in France in the seventeenth and eighteenth centuries, dates from Richelieu rather than from Louis XIV.

Richelieu was neither a speculator nor a doctrinaire : he was a man of action, and not an administrator nor a legislator. **Richelieu's ideal of the State.** Thus he did not proceed methodically in his work of destruction and reform : he did not attempt to recast the administration of the French kingdom, on principles of his own, into one homogeneous system. He contented himself with adapting certain details. " In an ancient monarchy," he says in his Political Testament, with a wisdom that reminds us of Renan, certain " imperfections have passed into habits, and the disorder they cause becomes, not altogether uselessly, a part of the State." Yet it might not

110

have been a bad thing to arrange this disorder, as far as possible, and labour to render it easier of endurance for the King's subjects. This the Cardinal never attempted. He never tried, for instance, to make justice more just, or the financial agents of the sovereign less thievish; in short, to ameliorate the social condition of the inhabitants of the kingdom; his only aim was to make officials still more submissive, and existing institutions more flexible, to put more money into the coffers of the State, and render France, in fine, a better and stronger instrument of strength and power in the hands of the monarch who ruled her. This was the ideal of almost all the rulers of former days : the individual good of each Frenchman was not their first thought, as it is with those who now govern the country : the end and aim of all policy, in the eyes of such a man as Richelieu, was the glory of the collective body, of France—in other words, the glory of the King.

WORKS TO CONSULT FOR CHAPTERS III AND IV: Works already quoted, notably those of d'Avenel and Hanotaux, and the *Memoirs* of La Porte, Montglat, Campion, Du Plessis-Besançon, the Marquis de Chouppes, Puységur, etc. J. P. Basserie, *La Conjuration de Cinq-Mars* (1896); V. Cousin, *Mme. de Hautefort* (1856); Vicomte de Noailles, *Épisodes de la Guerre de Trente Ans* (1906–1908); Père de Rochemonteix, *Nicolas Caussin, Confesseur de Louis XIII et le Cardinal de Richelieu* (1911); A. Waddington, *La République des Provinces-Unies, la France et les Pays-Bas espagnols de 1630 à 1650* (1895); Raoul Allier, *La Cabale des Dévots* (1902), and Rebelliare in the *Revue des Deux Mondes* (1010); Abbé de Broglie, *Saint Vincent de aul* (1897); E. Glesson, *Le Parlement de Paris* (1901); Hanotaux, *Études sur le XVIᵉᵐᵉ et XVIIᵉᵐᵉ Siècles* (1886); *Origines de l'institution des Intendants* (1884); Perrens, *Les Libertins en France* (1899); P. de Vaissière, *Gentilshommes campagnards de l'ancienne France* (1904).

CHAPTER V

THE BEGINNINGS OF SOCIETY AND OF CLASSIC LITERATURE

I. Society : The *Astrée* and the *Précieuses*.   II. Literature, from Malherbe to Corneille.

I

AN important development marked the reign of Louis XIII : " the organization of the aristocratic class into a social world " (Lanson). The feudal aristocracy completed its transformation into a Court aristocracy, and the nobles, growing more and more into the habit of living either in the King's circle or in Paris, and having nothing to do save look at each other, and compare their ideas, their feelings, and their manner of life, became "men of the world." Already, under the later Valois kings, " society " had attained a certain brilliance, but this was at Court only, and during the first few years of the reign of Louis XIII the refined and gallant manners of the old courtiers of Henri III were as much admired as the superannuated graces of the *Ancien Régime* towards the year 1820. When the religious turmoil of the close of the sixteenth century subsided, and France began to rest and recover, under the restorative *régime* of Henri IV, a small society once more collected—not at the rough and unceremonious Court of the " Roi Vert-Galant," indeed, but in the city. This society was polite, fond of good talk and literature, almost pedantic, even at that period, and for its benefit a certain number of authors began to write novels the subject of which was love. By degrees the number of these " men of the world " increased : under Louis XIII they were so numerous as to be able to ensure the prodigious success of a fashionable and psychological novel entitled *L'Astrée*, and to create the vogue of the first French

Evolution of fashionable Society.

salon, that of Mme. de Rambouillet, while at the same time, by a due interaction, novel and *salon* both did a great deal to disseminate refinement and courtesy.

Honoré d'Urfé's *Astrée* was derived from the tales of love and chivalry of the sixteenth century and from the Greek, Italian, **D'Urfé's** and Spanish pastorals of Heliodorus, Tatius, **"Astrée."** Longus, Tasso, Guarini, Montemayor, and other writers—all very popular since the Renaissance. The story is somewhat insipid, the style most charming. It begins by showing us Céladon, a lover, after addressing most melancholy speeches to the ring and the ribbon his ungrateful mistress has left in his hands, throwing himself into the Lignon, in his despair at the unjust jealousy manifested by Astrée, a shepherdess. His life is saved by the nymphs of Isoure, and disguised as a shepherdess he soon becomes the unrecognized but intimate friend of his former lady-love. He does not gather courage to appear in the fair lady's sight clad in his own habiliments until she herself has expressed her desire to see him, and that is not until the scruples of Astrée, the unhappy passion of Galatée, the loves of Diane and Sylvandre, the adventures of the inconstant Hylas, the far too lengthy speeches of the over-sapient Druid Adamas, the war, the siege of Marcilly, and a hundred other episodes that perpetually cut the slight thread of the story, have filled up the five volumes of which the novel consists.

Now the success of this tale—the first three volumes appeared between 1607 and 1619, and the last two in 1627—was something incredible : for the space of thirty years the whole of France sighed for Astrée or dreamt of Céladon. In certain circles, so Tallemant tells us, " a favourite amusement, among others, was to exchange written questions about the *Astrée*, and those who gave faulty answers had to pay a pair of gloves for each mistake." In 1624 an "Academy of True Lovers" was founded in Germany, the members of which, all German gentlemen and Teutonic dames, adopted the names and habits of the shepherd of the Lignon, learned how to guide tender lambkins with their crooks, and strove to love each other gracefully. During the Fronde the *Astrée* was read as generally as the *Grand Cyrus*, and it is evident that the majority of Mazarin's terrible foes, masculine and feminine, plotted less from conviction or even self-interest than for the sake of romance and in the hope of resembling the heroes with whose doings their heads were filled. In Louis XIV's time, and even long after it, Honoré d'Urfé still nad many enthusiastic readers, some of whom, such as La Fontaine, Mme. de Sévigné, Racine, and Jean-Jacques Rousseau bore names far from obscure. . . . Yet how dull the flowing long-winded story with its endless succession of episodes and its graceful monotonous phrases seems to us now ! We do not possess the robust appetite our fathers boasted : *blasés* as to romances, and hard to amuse, we need livelier and more highly seasoned narratives, couched in language less noble, less majestic, but more dramatic and more spirited. . . . On the other hand, we must consider, when we try to understand the request in which this book remained, that for twenty years it was a kind of manual of good manners : the budding man of fashion found in its pages the pattern after which he must model his speech, his epistolary style, his manner of thought : it taught him how to treat ladies with the respect and admiration that was their due, to discourse to them in language at once respectful, flowery, and ingenious ; to write them pompous and literary letters ; in short, all his lessons in politeness and deportment were drawn from the *Astrée*. . . . Add to all this the fact that Honoré d'Urfé's book was entirely devoted to the glorification of the fair sex, at a time when the triumph of that sex in French society was greater than it has ever been, either before or since. From the day on which, under the influence of the Platonism of the Renaissance, the famous quarrel broke out between the partisans and the detractors of " the ladies "—a quarrel which absorbed part of the **The first** literary effort of the sixteenth century and was **" Feminists."** carried on into the seventeenth—the " feminists," if we may so call them, had gained the upper hand, at Court at least, both in the higher ranks of literature and in society, and had routed those who still persisted in simply regarding woman as the heroine of the ribald stories of the Middle Ages, the mere female, at once dangerous and despicable. And with them had triumphed the neo-platonic theory of love, the *credo* of the *Précieuses*—which one of their number, and certainly not the least important, Mme. de Sablé, has formulated in terms

114

that would have gained the approval, a century earlier, of the " Marguerite des Marguerites " or of Hérouet : declaring that

" Men, without committing any crime, might cherish the most tender feelings for women, that the desire to please them gave them wit, and inspired them with liberality and all sorts of virtues ; but that women, on the other hand, who were the ornament of the world and made to be served and worshipped, should never permit anything beyond respect on the part of men."

Did Mme. de Sablé, in her own practice, really never permit anything else ? " The love that lady bore herself," Mme. de Motteville tells us, " made her a little too sensitive to that she inspired in men. . . ."

Be this as it may, platonic love—*la belle galanterie,* as Anne of Austria called it—was all the fashion among the *Précieuses.* And the *Astrée,* entirely devoted to the glorification of intellectual passion, to the praise of respectful lovers and virtuous mistresses, and thus responding to the intimate feelings of the most refined section of contemporary society, well deserved to be, as it was, the gospel of the Hôtel de Rambouillet.

It was towards the year 1609 that Catherine de Vivonne, Marquise de Rambouillet, then about twenty years of age, **Madame de Rambouillet.** declared herself thoroughly disgusted with the habits and manners of the courtiers of Henri IV, and announced that she " would no longer attend the gatherings at the Louvre." She retired to her own house, and as she was amiable, extremely cultivated, knowing both Spanish and Italian, as she was rich, as she was so witty that, so Mlle. de Scudéry assures us, one afternoon spent in her *ruelle,* even without seeing her face, " and on one of those summer days when ladies darken their chambers artificially to exclude the great heat," was enough to make a visitor fall in love with her : as, besides all this, " all her passions " were " subservient to her reason " ; and as, to conclude, she possessed that gift of entertaining which is the vocation of certain members of her sex, her house soon became the rallying-point of a select society of lords, ladies, and men of letters.

This dwelling stood almost on the site of the block of houses on the Place du Palais-Royal just facing the present Magasins du

Louvre. In 1618 Mme. de Rambouillet set herself to arrange
it according to a plan of her own invention, most original, as it
would seem, and admirably suited to her future intentions. She
was the first person, so Tallemant tells us, who thought of
" having a room painted in any other colour than red or tawny
brown " : her own chamber, hung with blue velvet enlivened
with gold and silver, was soon to become famous. At that period
the various rooms in a Parisian house were not each reserved for
any particular purpose. Their denizens slept and ate, and
received company, in any cabinet, or chamber, or antechamber,
or large apartment, just as it suited their convenience at the
moment. Mme. de Rambouillet generally received her friends
in her blue chamber. Her bed, probably set with its head
against a wall, was separated from the rest of the room by a
balustrade, and it was a great favour to be admitted to the space
between the side walls of the apartment and the bed : the
ruelle. The furniture of this blue chamber probably consisted
of twelve or eighteen seats—arm-chairs, chairs, and folding-
stools—which the mistress of the house had to assign to her
visitors according to their quality ; not an easy art. Finally,
according to the number of guests present, Mme. de Rambouillet caused screens to be opened or closed, as a protection
against the cold.

Such were the surroundings in which, for the space of forty
years, but more particularly between 1630 and 1645 or thereabouts, the famous society of France was formed.
Duchesses and *bourgeoises* alike made their appearance there : Mlle. Paulet, the " beautiful lioness,"
whose proud beauty and golden hair did as much as her wit to
buy forgiveness for her stormy past ; marquises and men of
letters ; honest Scudéry and his ugly but charming niece ; the
keen-witted Abbé Cotin ; the discreet Vaugelas ; the learned
Ménage ; the influential Chapelain ; and young Godeau, who
suddenly, and to the astonishment of all men, transformed himself unto a most virtuous bishop : then, among the authors
every one who could be produced in the company of ladies, from
Malherbe to Corneille, not forgetting the young Abbé Bossuet,
and, above all, Voiture, a matchless talker and diverting com-
panion, the king of the whole society—*el rey chiquito,* they called

The Circle of the Hôtel de Rambouillet.

him, on account of his small stature—who, son of a wine merchant though he was, could hold his own, and proved himself as
touchy as if he had been born a prince.

Before all things, the Hôtel de Rambouillet was a literary
salon : poetry and letters were handed about like so many
dainties ; the guests listened to the works their authors read
aloud, and discussed them : within those walls Corneille de-
claimed almost all his masterpieces. This public, consisting of
well-bred men and women, who knew what good French was—
for in the Blue Room grammatical problems were courageously
discussed and immense stress was laid on refinement of style—
no doubt exercised a certain influence on the literature and
language of France. Its effect on the great writers must not be
exaggerated, of course ; *salons*, as a rule, have but little influence
on good authors (when the influence is strong, it is harmful) ;
but they spread a taste for intellectual things, they increase the
number of connoisseurs—and that was the work performed by
Mme. de Rambouillet's society. It supplied writers with an
excellent public, well-informed, passionately interested in art and
in psychology, and a public, too, which did not expect literature
to give it a picture of realities so much as models for its own
speech and thought ; with these desiderata literature forthwith
set out to provide it.

And the Hôtel de Rambouillet produced other excellent
results. In the Blue Room the habitual guest was only ex-
Its refining pected to be amusing, and to entertain others,
Influence on and there the originality came in. Before that
Manners. time a gentleman took little trouble to charm by
his conversation and his knowledge of letters : his desire was to
be thought brave, in the first place, and, in the next, to be considered powerful, magnificent, and able to spend large sums of
money : intellect was the last thing about which he cared. And,
further, before the days of the Hôtel de Rambouillet, the idea
that conversation might be a pleasure so great as to make it
worth one's while to meet simply for the sake of enjoying it had
never occurred to anybody : people met, as they met at the
Louvre, for a ballet, or to play cards, or for some sight or festivity,
but never for the sake of talking. Once the frequenters of the
' circle " had brought wit into fashion, men and women began

117

to be valued for the amount of that quality they displayed, and no longer for their birth or for their riches : the writers certainly did not become the aristocrats' equals, but they gained a certain professional consideration in general society ; and among the nobles themselves a man who did not prove himself a sufficiently " polite man " (or man of the world) lost the approval of his fellows.

But all this did not come about from the very day on which " the incomparable Arthénice established her empire." It was only by degrees, and exceedingly slowly, except in a very limited circle, that the nobility and upper ranks of the French *bourgeoisie* grew more refined. And to tell the truth, if the tone of the Hôtel de Rambouillet and of the *Astrée* seems refined, it is by comparison with the tone of the society immediately surrounding them rather than with that of the days that came after them. Mme. de Rambouillet's friends, and Mme. de Rambouillet herself, were amused by jokes which might seem somewhat coarse to the schoolboys of the present day.

There were a good many *Polexandres*, *Cassandres*, the *Grand Cyrus*, and *Clélies* before the *Princesse de Clèves*, and before the gradual evolution of the subtle, pompous, and superficial gallantry of the heroes of those novels into true delicacy of feeling. And, indeed, it is a fairly well-known fact, now, that the Great Age was by no means immovably fixed in that attitude of impeccable nobility formerly ascribed to it : long after Richelieu's day, and even under Louis XIV, French society continued to bubble with life, and youth, and vigour. Under their ribbons and feathers and ceremonious manners the Versailles courtiers concealed a passion and violence of the most extreme kind : there were hot heads under those flowing wigs of theirs. But if they were fierce, and even brutal, at bottom, they possessed an inimitable suppleness, elegance, and politeness of mind. And there can be no doubt that the Hôtel de Rambouillet, by setting women in the place they ought to hold in society, and asserting their claims to the influence they ought to exercise on the customs of a country, did much to promote the growth of this politeness. The incomparable Arthénice and the *Précieuses* rendered a priceless service to the intellect of France.

THE BEGINNINGS OF SOCIETY

The *salon* began to decline towards 1645, when Mlle. de Rambouillet, the celebrated Julie d'Angennes, made up her mind, at last, to "crown the flame" of the Marquis de Montausier, whom she had kept dancing attendance on her for twelve years, according to all the correct rules of "cruelty": it was time for the young lady to become less inhuman: she was just forty. She departed for Saintonge, where her husband was Governor, and with the heroine of the *Guirlande de Julie** the Blue Room lost the most inexorable of the *Précieuses* who had adorned it. Voiture died in 1648: then the Fronde broke out: Mme. de Rambouillet retired to the country, and though the doors of her *salon* were not closed, its glory gradually departed. But the fashion had been set, and in all directions other "nooks" and *ruelles*, formed on the same pattern, entered into competition with the original. There were Mlle. de Scudéry's "Saturdays," principally attended by middle-class folk and literary men; there were the Vicomtesse d'Auchy's pedantic "Tuesdays"; there were the receptions of the Marquise de Sablé, Mme. de Bouchavannes, and Mme. de Brégis; even in the provinces the *Précieuse* flourished. And as it is the peculiarity of every fashion to go on falling into greater and greater exaggerations, till at last it dies a sudden death by ridicule, these imitations of Mme. de Rambouillet's *salon* did not fail to transform the tendencies of the original model into abuses. Already the tendency of the "Blue Room" had been to talk about literature with an excessive gravity—gravity is a great pitfall in any *salon*—and even, if the truth must be told, to hold forth on the subject of grammar. And, further, the language of its frequenters, deliberately involved, did not lighten discussion, and the conversation was apt to be too laboriously playful to be really witty. Finally, it frequently happened that the most trifling matters of gallantry were discussed with an insistence that could hardly be called anything but pedantic, and the affectation of delicacy was carried to the verge of silliness. These defects, this "blue-stockingism," this pretentiousness of manner, language, and sentiment, this

Decline of the "Salon."

---

* This "Garland" was a vellum book, adorned with twenty-nine paintings of flowers by Robert, in which were written sixty-two madrigals composed by the habitués of the "circle."

seventeenth-century pose, in short, is what has been christened " preciosity."

This preciosity waxed stronger and stronger in proportion as the power of Mme. de Rambouillet's own *salon* declined. **Extravagances** Many of the " bureaux of wit " which opened their **of the Blue-** doors between 1650 and 1660 became ridiculous **stockings.** beyond all words. If the *chères* and the *alcovistes* were not to faint with disgust, their frequenters must " know the end of things, the great end, the uttermost end " ; they must exaggerate all that was " gentle, tender, passionate " ; they must not say " teeth," but " the furniture of the mouth " : nor speak of " cheeks," but of " the thrones of modesty " : nor of a police-sergeant, but of " the criminals' bad angel " : instead of " blow up that fire " the expression must be " excite that combustible element " : never " draw up that arm-chair," but " convey hither the comforts of conversation " ; and some of these ladies even want so far as to insist on the suppression of unseemly syllables, and claimed that in future their adorers must say *trois livres* instead of *un écu* !

This was too much. When, at the first performance of *Les Précieuses Ridicules*, on November 18, 1659, the audience saw M. de Mascarille appear before the delighted eyes of the two foolish ladies from the provinces, in those astounding habiliments of his, the garb of the fashionable " tuft " of the period— with his wig " so huge that it swept the floor every time he made a bow," and his hat so tiny " that it was easy to guess the Marquis carried it in his hand much oftener than he put it on his head," his neck-ruffle, which in all conscience " might be called a respectable dressing-cape," his breeches, with their lower trimmings " that looked as if they had been made on purpose for children to play hide-and-seek in them," the " bundle of tassels " hanging " out of his pocket as it is were a horn of plenty," his shoes " so covered with ribbons that it is quite impossible for me to tell you whether they were made of tanned English calf or morocco leather," and set up on heels so high that everybody was " sorely puzzled to know how heels so tall and slender could possibly carry the body of the Marquis, his ribbons, his trimmings, and his powder "—a shout of laughter rent the air. Very soon the name of *Précieuse*, hitherto a compliment, became a term of derision. . . . And, indeed, fashion, which had gone wild about delicacy, now took up learning, and Molière, after raising the laugh against the *Précieuses Ridicules* in 1659, was able to banter the *Femmes Savantes* in 1672.

II

Thus the Hôtel de Rambouillet gave literature a public consisting of the world of fashion. And before long these fashionable folk began to plume themselves on their own literary powers. In Richelieu's time no member of the aristocracy would have condescended to belong to the Académie Française : later, noblemen were to be seen canvassing to obtain entrance into that body. This interpenetration, if we may so describe it, of society by literature, and vice versa, produced excellent effects on both sides. . . . In the first place, before long, it did not suffice a cultivated man to be well-informed ; he had also to possess " style," he had to express himself clearly and gracefully, both in speech and with his pen—to sum up, in fact he had to be able to please, to fascinate, to amuse, to charm. And it was this art that the men of the world of that day carried to perfection, for they learned it in their childhood and practised it till they died— a very useful art indeed, and even indispensable, at a period when nothing was to be had as a right, but everything by favour or by the skill with which the applicant presented his request. . . . What classic French literature gained by the influence of the world of fashion was its admirable limpidity of expression. In fact " the public laid down the law. . . . It forced the authors to save it trouble without complaining of their own, to have a clear conception of what they wanted to say and to say it definitely " (Lanson). An absence of pedantry and of false profundity, no lyricism whatever, but a perfect limpidity and order in its ideas, and an extreme art and good taste in the matter of style ; the study of humanity in general, and certain of its social habits and passions, such as seventeen hundred years of Christianity had made them—these were the characteristics of the best literature of the seventeenth century.

Under Louis XIII, in addition to the Hôtel de Rambouillet

The marginal note beside the second paragraph reads: **Formation of the Classical Style.**

and fashionable society, three men specially contributed to the formation of the classic style: Malherbe, Balzac, and Vaugelas.

François de Malherbe (1555–1628) was a short-tempered old gentleman, very crusty, "boorish and uncivil," says Talle-
Malherbe. mant, licentious in his life and coarse in his talk, whom, however, his passion for his art endued with style. After a lifetime spent in the service of the fair sex, he found strength, on his death-bed, to reprove an incorrect expression used by his nurse, and when his confessor exhorted him to think thenceforth of nothing except his Saviour, he replied—and there was a touch of sublimity about the sally —that he intended "to uphold the purity of the French language till he died." . . . Now Malherbe has no natural sincerity, no spontaneity, no real feeling: he is a mere book-man, in fact: by this we mean that life and nature interested and touched him only as they appear in books; but the correctness of the composition and the harmony of the words employed invest certain of his poems with beauty. Many of his predecessors, in addition to the emotion and enthusiasm lacking in his case, had far more character, imagery, and colour than he, but none of them succeeded in writing a language so pure, so precise, and so intrinsically beautiful. Here then lies his great merit: he re-established the taste for technical perfection, he counselled all poets to labour at their work, to distrust obscure constructions in phraseology, to avoid cacophony and hiatus, to spend their pains, not only on their imagery, but on the sound and rhythm of the words employed—to write, so to speak, not only for the eyes of their readers' imaginations, but also for their ears; in fine, to make our language into music (see, for example, the stanzas on the *Dessin de quitter une dame qui ne le contentoit que de promesses* ("Design to quit a lady who gave him no satisfaction save in promises "). Unfortunately Malherbe not only clarified the language, he clarified poetic inspiration as well. So exalted, in fact, was his idea of art, that he would have had the poet abstain from subjects which he, Malherbe, thought unworthy, such as his own sorrows and his private life; and the noble themes he recom-mended were the taking of some city, for instance, or the King's

departure for the seat of war—official poetry, in a word: so much so that he certainly tended, by this process, to "purge poetry of every personal touch, and transform it into eloquence" (Brunetière): but lyric poetry died of the process, and two centuries passed before it rose again.

Taking him altogether "the old Court pedagogue," the "tyrant of words and syllables," as Balzac calls Malherbe, was as much a teacher of language and French versification as a poet, and it might almost be said that his poems were used by the generation following his own as a handbook of examples and *corrected exercises*.   Yet he had only two immediate disciples: Maynard (1582–1646) and the Marquis de Racan (1589–1670), and on contemporary poetry his influence was *nil*.   Everybody either attacked him or jeered at him, some in the name of the sixteenth century, which they declared he outraged (Malherbe professed to regard Ronsard and his disciples as mere bunglers, and told Desportes, one day, that his soup was better than his verses); others, in the name of liberty, inspiration, and fancy, against all of which, to their thinking, this man **The Minor Poets under Louis XIII.** whom they considered a mere manipulator of words had offended.   It is impossible, here, to quote the names of all those charming poets—*précieux*, burlesque, and libertine—who flourished under Louis XIII and in the earlier part of the reign of Louis XIV, and who seem to have been called the "minor poets" principally because, as a rule, their poems were short.   Almost every one of them wrote exquisite lines, and many succeeded, once in their lives, at all events, in achieving perfection and producing a masterpiece—so beautiful was the French language in those days!   And the best of them all was not Théophile, who wrote some fifty exquisite lines, and not many more; nor Saint-Amant, some of whose sonnets are like little Dutch pictures; nor Scarron, the wonderful, the dazzling, who committed the error of writing his *Virgile travesti*; nor M. de Sygognes, of whom we know nothing at all, who sang of dwarfs and weaklings, of milksops, and of elves—

> Petit rat de Brésil, qui vous a botiné ?
> Où allez-vous ainsi en robe de guenuche,
> Les bras sur les rognons comme ceux d'une cruche ?
> Vous froncez le sourcil ?   Êtes-vous mutiné ? . . .

> Le moindre petit vent, pour soulager sa peine,
> Comme un vent de lutin la porte à la fontaine,
> Car elle pèse moins, la nymphe du jardin,
> Que son vertugadin. . . .

—nor Jacques Vallée, Sieur des Barreaux, author of one of the most beautiful religious sonnets that has ever been written, entitled *Recours d'un pécheur à la bonté de Dieu*; nor the worthy Gombard, "a little infatuated with Parnassus"; nor Tristan l'Hermite, nor Cyrano de Bergerac, nor Sarasin—

> Achille beau comme le jour
> Et vaillant comme son épée,
> Pleura neuf mois sur son amour
> Comme un enfant pour sa poupée.

> À chanter ses fameux exploits
> J'emploierais volontiers ma vie :
> Mais je n'ai qu'un filet de voix,
> Et ne chante que pour Sylvie. . . .

—nor yet Voiture, nor Benserade, nor even the great Mathurin Régnier : but Jean de La Fontaine.

The work Malherbe did for poetic style was performed for French prose by Jean-Louis Guez de Balzac. No more dis-
Guez de Balzac. agreeable individual than this stiff and conceited personage would be conceivable were it not that he, like Malherbe, was ennobled by his lifelong and passionate devotion to the French language. He lived in the depths of his native province, but he kept up a voluminous correspondence. There were long intervals between his letters, truth to tell, for Balzac felt a well-deserved scorn for those who "wrote a book in less than a week," and spent weeks himself in polishing one of his own epistles, so that the missives he intended to answer lay piled upon his writing-table, and he occasionally found himself replying to the announcement of a marriage after the birth of the first child had taken place. But that mattered little : his letters were handed about, and every one desired to receive them. Yet their substance is ordinary, and the ideas they express are commonplace; but it may be that what now strikes us as the most obvious platitude seemed, in Balzac's time, a very impressive truth. And, besides, the qualities his contemporaries valued and discussed with the most eager interest were his style,

his language, and his long and well-constructed sentences. He taught his readers the proper development of a subject, how to build up a speech, how to compose a narrative, and how to order the various parts of a period clearly and harmoniously. . . . Altogether he was a good craftsman, and under his direction France, as it has been truly said, took her degree in rhetoric.

Towards 1629 " a certain number of private individuals " had formed the habit of gathering, on certain fixed days, in the house of M. Conrart, for the purpose of enjoying " all that is most delightful and charming in the society of wit and in a reasonable existence." Amongst these men of enlightened mind was Boisrobert, who mentioned his friends to the Cardinal, his master. Richelieu sent a message to the circle to inquire whether its members would be inclined to " constitute themselves into a body, and hold their assemblies under a public authority " : the proposal was accepted without any enthusiasm, but M. le **The origin of** Cardinal's wishes were imperious things. Thus **the Académie** began the Académie Française, which held its first **Française.** meeting on March 13, 1634, and sat, to begin with, in the house of one or another of its members, then, from 1643 till 1672, at the Hôtel Séguier, and finally at the Louvre, in the two rooms now called the Salle de Puget and the Salle des Coustou (Museum of Modern Sculpture).

The Academy had planned to prepare a Grammar, a book on Rhetoric, another on the Art of Poetry, and first and foremost a Dictionary, on which last it soon set to work. Now at this time there was a man living in France—timid, clumsy, ingenuous to the point of credulity, but who had also devoted himself to a passionately eager analysis of the French language, and had brought to it more good taste than Balzac, and even a greater **Vaugelas.** subtlety than Malherbe; he was called Claude Favre, Baron de Péroges and Sieur de Vaugelas (1585–1650). He had been attached to the service of Gaston d'Orléans, and had thereby lost the whole of his small fortune. In 1639, to enable him to work undisturbed on the Dictionary, which, people complained, was advancing far too slowly, Richelieu granted him a small pension ; nevertheless, when Vaugelas published his *Remarks on the French Language*, in 1647, the Dictionary was by no means ready for publication.

THE SEVENTEENTH CENTURY

These *Remarks*, which attained the greatest and most legitimate success, exercised a strong influence on the French language, and thus upon French literature. They were not embodied in a methodically arranged treatise, but were simply a collection of notes on various points. Vaugelas, like Malherbe and Balzac, laid it down as a rule that "the king and tyrant" of language is custom, and that writers must obey custom even if it should be absurd. But there are good customs and bad, and the good custom, which must be followed, is that of men and women of the world. . . .

For in those days the well-bred section of society had a language of its own : men and women of that society recognized each other as much by their speech as by their dress : we have already alluded to this special form of affectation. Grammar, indeed, formed one of the favourite entertainments of this society, and we come upon story after story concerning the eager discussions in the *ruelles* as to the use of the conjunction *car*, for instance, and as to whether it was correct to say *sarge* or *serge*, *muscadin* or *muscardin*. On the whole, even after the days of Balzac and Malherbe, society continued to purify the language, and this involved a certain drawback : that of impoverishing the vocabulary by the elimination of many old words, like those the loss of which La Bruyère regrets, and of all those special and technical terms for which the world of fashion had no use : but, on the other hand, this process had great advantages—that, in the first place, of fixing syntax, the sense of the various words, and rendering the language clearer, more precise, more adapted to the expression of thought ; and, in the second, that of enriching style with the mass of imagery and metaphor it put into circulation. For a very large number of those affected metaphors which made the subjects of Louis XIII laugh till they cried were rapidly absorbed into current use ; and as to the majority of the remainder, it may be safely wagered that if we were to find them now—and we do find many of them—in the works of Victor Hugo, they would not strike us as being in the least absurd, so far have we travelled beyond the frequenters of the Hôtel de Rambouillet in the matter of bold imagery.

The language of the *Précieuses*, then, was the language

Vaugelas made his study, and all that was best in it he selected with the most unerring taste : it was codified in the Dictionary of the Academy (1694), half a century after Vaugelas' **The Dictionary** death ; and employed by all the great authors, **of the** who prided themselves on their purism, and made **Academy.** it their boast that they " talked Vaugelas." The writers of the age of Louis XIV have proved that this language possessed brilliant qualities.

And now we come to the man who endowed classic literature with the philosophy that befitted it : René Descartes (1596–**René Descartes.** 1650). Son of a Councillor of the Parliament of Brittany, he was born in the village of La Haye, in Touraine. The early part of his life was spent in travelling about in stirring scenes : he served under Maurice of Nassau and the Duke of Bavaria ; journeyed through Holland, Germany, Austria, Switzerland, and Italy ; returned to France in 1625 ; then went back into Holland for the sake of quietness ; lived there for twenty years ; and, finally, yielding to the entreaties of Queen Christina of Sweden, he travelled to join her, and died five months later, in February 1650. He had been spending his days, early in the winter of 1619, "meditating alone in a stove " (that is to say, in a room provided with a stove), when, on November 10, in a dream he received a revelation which, according to his judgment, could only have been sent him from on high : this fact notwithstanding, he waited eighteen years before he published his *Discours de la Méthode*. In this he sets forth that, having remarked that the only method whereby some certainties can be attained is the use of mathematics, geometry, and algebra, he resolved to apply the same treatment to philosophy. He therefore begins by submitting every notion of his intelligence to this test : he rejects all that we learn from our senses because in certain cases our senses deceive us ; he rejects all mathematical propositions because we must commit paralogisms to demonstrate them ; he rejects all the thoughts he has hitherto had because a man may have the same ideas in a dream that he has when he is awake. The only truth that seems to him "certain and evident " is that M. Descartes must exist because he thinks : " I think, therefore I am." And this axiom is the principle of all his philosophy ; relying on it, he demonstrates the existence of the soul and of God, and recomposes, in imagination, the whole mechanism of the universe.

Thus Descartes' philosophy made reason the sole and only means for discovering truth, and proclaimed the fact that the use of reason alone would bring about the knowledge of every truth. This doctrine adapted itself perfectly well to the teachings of the Catholic Church : Descartes had been most careful to overlay his philosophy with religion, so to speak : piety and prudence alike had inspired him to draw a careful distinction between the things of reason and those matters connected with revealed religion which lay beyond the sphere of reason and critical inquiry. Hence the most religious minds of the seventeenth century, from Malebranche, an Oratorian, to Arnauld and Bossuet, could be, and were, Cartesians. On literature Cartesianism exercised a considerable influence. It would be too much to say, certainly, that the classical spirit proceeds from Descartes ; before his advent order, harmony, the taste for reason, were already in the ascendant. But Descartes endued the seventeenth century with the method and the doctrine best suited to its genius.

Cartesianism.

His influence had to contend with that of Gassendi, who had renewed the Epicurean theory of atomism. And it was also opposed by Pascal. But it should be noted that Pascal warred against philosophy in general rather than against that of Descartes in particular : if his thoughts turned to Descartes, it was because Descartes was the fashionable philosopher when he wrote ; and we must also remember that his contemporaries knew but one edition of his *Pensées*, that mangled and disfigured by the Jansenists : the first fairly exact version of his work did not appear till the nineteenth century.

When he was twelve years old, Blaise Pascal (1623–1662), alone and unaided, re-invented Euclid's geometry : at sixteen he wrote a Treatise on Conic Sections : at twenty he constructed an arithmetical machine : at twenty-four and twenty-five he was already celebrated, and formulated —though a recent attempt has been made to contest his claim to this honour—the earliest hypothesis as to atmospheric pressure : thus his learning alone would have sufficed to immortalize his name. In 1646 he became absorbed in religious matters, and

Pascal.

with all the passionate zeal he brought to everything he did, set himself, after his own conversion, to secure that of his father, of his elder sister, the prudent Mme. Périer, and his younger sister, the fervent Jacqueline. But he had not relinquished his scientific studies, and the flattering notoriety he enjoyed after the experiments in the Puy-de-Dôme exerted a cooling influence on his religious ardour. The truth was that his extraordinary sensibility forbade indifference on his part to anything of any kind. So he frequented the gay world, and if he did not fall in love (for we have no proof, unluckily, that the delightful *Discours sur les passions de l'Amour* is his work), he proved, at all events, that when occasion arose he could write pretty verses for fair ladies, and remarked, no doubt, that the " geometric mind " is less necessary to the man who desires to please than that " subtlety of mind " of which the Chevalier de Méré talked to him, and to which so many illustrious philosophers and learned men of every period, less great than he, have been total strangers. Under the sway of his lofty moral anxieties, towards the end of 1654 he once more plunged into theology, and thus, little by little, slowly, and in accordance with reason, his final conversion was achieved.

To realize the nature of Pascal's genius we must imagine the most limpid mathematical intelligence united to the tenderest and most exquisite feeling : it is this feeling which imparts life and movement to the *Provinciales* and pathetic force to the style of the *Pensées*. In 1655, when Pascal had become one of the *Messieurs de Port Royal,* he undertook to put together a few statements in defence of Arnauld, then threatened with condemnation by the Sorbonne : this undertaking resulted in those eighteen *Lettres provinciales,* all of which appeared between January 23, 1656, and March 24, 1657. In these, questions of theology were brought within the range of the public comprehension and popularly explained with the perspicuity of a consummate artist : the author succeeded in captivating his readers' interest as skilfully as the best journalist of our own time : his success was enormous. These letters, now eloquent and indignant, now dryly amusing, and then again full of an ironical compassion, written in a dramatic and picturesque style, which was a great novelty at that period,

The " **Lettres Provinciales.**

amused, charmed, and convinced their readers. In vain did the Jesuits strive to defend themselves in the literary lists : the rescripts they published in response to Pascal's "campaign" only served to demonstrate their adversary's talent more clearly.

But in the full tide of its success, the publication of the *Letters* was broken off. Had Pascal been stung by the reproach of one of his enemies to the effect that he was using against Catholics a talent which would have done better service to God if it had been employed against heretics ? That would have been a noble reason, and we would fain believe it true. Be that as it may, he instantly set himself to write a vindication of the Faith. He had been ill almost all his life. From 1568 onwards, amidst cruel sufferings, he began to jot down or dictate notes **The** for this work, instead of trusting, as had been his **"Pensées."** previous custom, to his prodigious memory ; and these notes, which illness and death prevented him from utilizing, are the *Pensées*. There is, unfortunately, no apparent order in their arrangement, and it is therefore very difficult to imagine the plan Pascal would have ultimately adopted, but Brunetière thus sets forth, in noble words, the general scheme as we may suppose it to have existed : " From everything within and around us the clamour of our distress arises : the weakness of our bodies, the vices of our social organization, and again the powerlessness of our reason, are only so many reasons for despair. Whence, then, comes the protest that rises from the depths of that despair ?—the exception, which, thanks to it, we constitute in the scheme of nature, and our invincible confidence in a happier destiny ? This we shall know if we accept the doctrine of an original fall, the obligation imposed on us to expiate it, and the doctrine of the redemption, which are, in fact, the essential teachings of Christianity. Do we shrink from accepting them ? Let us consider, in that case, that we need only believe them to become as good as we can be—living as we do amongst other men : that these doctrines, besides, have been typified in the ancient Law, foretold by the prophets, confirmed by miracles, and that if our reason cannot accept them, our will can always bow before them." Everything has been said in praise of the *Pensées*, and said with the utmost fervour and

enthusiasm. Certain expressions, certain broken sentences—
" pathetic like a ruin under the setting sun," . . . " man, a
reed endued with the power of thought," . . . " the infinite
spaces terrifying in their silence," . . . and even the famous
" foreshortening of the abyss," which may be a mere misreading
of the text, linger in the memories of us all. Mme. de Sévigné
asserted that Pascal's book gave one " a disgust for all others,"
and Sainte-Beuve has written as follows : " Pascal, an admirable writer when he works out his thought, is perhaps even
more admirable when he is interrupted."

The biography of Corneille has no bearing of importance on the
history of his works. He was born at Rouen in 1606, was a very

Corneille.
ordinary kind of man, devout," provincial," a functionary of some sort, and died poor in 1684. " The
first time I saw him," says Vigneul-Marville, " I took him for a
Rouen merchant : he never talked French very correctly."
" My father," writes Voltaire, " had drunk in Corneille's company : he used to tell me this great man was the most tiresome
mortal he had ever seen in his life, and that his conversation was
of the commonest kind." And La Bruyère writes, " Another
is simple-minded, timid, wearisome in his conversation : he
takes one word for another, and only judges the quality of his
play by the amount of money it brings him : he cannot recite it,
nor even read his own writing. . . ." But this simple fellow
was fired by a sublime inspiration.

Until his day, tragedy had been hardly more than a sort of
exercise of the lyric and declamatory powers, or else a romantic
imbroglio, or a spectacle to delight the eye, like our fairy entertainments and operatic libretti : but Corneille showed that the
real subject of the drama ought not to be the events themselves,
but the feelings they evoke in the minds of the characters :
thus in his first masterpiece, the *Cid* (acted at the close of 1636
or the beginning of 1637), he took good care not to present the
duel between Rodrigue and the Count on the stage, for instance,
but applied himself to revealing the mental attitude of his
heroes as they were modified under the influence of external
accidents.

The considerable success attained by the *Cid* displeased

Richelieu—perhaps because he himself had pretensions to talent as a playwright, and his feeling for Corneille was tinged with the jealousy of an unsuccessful writer, but much more probably because it was disagreeable to him, as a Minister, to know the public was nightly applauding a play that glorified Spain, just at the very moment when the war between that country and France was at its fiercest. So the Cardinal submitted the piece to the consideration of the French Academy, and the too severe, but very remarkable *Sentimens de l'Académie française sur le Cid* (which are more especially the sentiments of that judicious critic and pitiful author of *La Pucelle*, Jean Chapelain) resulted in the correction by the worthy Corneille of some fine lines, alas! and of a great many poor ones.

" Le Cid."

To moderns, one of the objections to the play expressed by the Academy is most curious. If the *dramatis personæ* of the *Cid* were transported into one of our modern plays, with their characters, at all events, even if without their habits of life, they would certainly strike the public of the present day as being of a quite improbable virtue and moral perfection : for the only one of them all who ever betrays a symptom—and that a passing one—of any evil feeling is the Count, when he gives way to the jealousy with which Don Diegue's favour inspires him. Now the thing with which the Academy reproaches Corneille is the moral weakness of his characters. To the critics of the year 1638, Chimène was " an unnatural daughter," because, though she does all she can to ensure the punishment of Rodrigue, she still loves him, and even grants him interviews which in their eyes exceed all the bounds of propriety. And the remarkable thing is that the Academicians' feeling on this subject was also that of the connoisseurs amongst the public of the day, and probably that of the author himself. For from that time forward we see Corneille make it his special care to paint his stage heroes as men without a touch of weakness, showing more and more perfect as time goes on, and when he criticizes any of his own plays, he invariably reproaches himself with not having caused his characters to take the most sublime resolution—if any resolution more sublime than that they have taken can be conceived. Such then were the model beings whereof the subjects of Louis XIII dreamt : these superhuman heroes embodied their ideals.

In Corneille's heroes the will is everything, even in love. But their love bears no resemblance to love as Musset knew it. **Corneille's conception of tragedy.** It is the pure outcome of reason : lovers hold each other dear because of the virtues and good qualities each discovers in the other : their affection is founded on their reciprocal admiration, and in this way their love comes back to the one starting-point—the longing for perfection. Thus, they frequently change the partner of their flame ; should one of them discover some fresh object whose merits seem still greater, the first is straightway forgotten. It is easy to see that this " intellectual love " (Jules Lemaître) is the same platonic love as that conceived by the readers of the *Astrée* and by the *Précieuses*. And, indeed, the self-analysis of Corneille's heroes is not much less subtle than that practised by those of Mlle. de Scudéry, nor is their manner of expressing themselves essentially different.

It has been frequently demonstrated (as by M. Jules Lemaître) that Corneille's plays did not embody the " triumph of duty over passion," as the old-fashioned formula has it, at all, but the victory of the human will over all the obstacles which the poet skilfully raises in its path. Corneille exalts energy, not holiness : it is not always virtue that spurs on his characters to heroism : sometimes it is one motive, sometimes another—and for the most part it is pride. When Chimène, for instance, seeks the death of the man she loves, it is not so much out of filial love that she crushes her own heart, but as a point of honour, out of regard for her " renown," and that of her " house," because, as she says :

> . . . Je veux que la voix de la plus noire envie
> Élève au ciel *ma gloire* et plaigne mes ennuis.

The incomparable audience which applauded the *Cid* shared the young girl's view. It approved and admired the Infanta in the *Cid*, the Queen in *Don Sanche*. All those spirited princesses evoked by the great Corneille considered their love for heroes whose merits and exploits far exceed our wildest imaginations, but who, not being the sons of kings, were unworthy of these ladies by their " birth," a shameful weakness which must

be overcome. And so in real life their admirers, unlike ourselves, regarded those unions which we call "love marriages"
as something quite inadmissible. In their eyes, the strict and
elementary duty of every man and woman of noble birth was
to contract an alliance founded exclusively on rank, name,
and fortune, with as many advantages as could possibly be
secured for him, for her, and for their descendants : to their
thinking, the man who married a "beloved" (but poor) object
was not doing a noble, but rather a shameful thing, he was
sacrificing his "glory" to his passion ; and to give way to his
passion was no sublime action, it was a not very creditable
weakness. (This, whatever some people may say, was also, to
some extent, the point of view of Racine, but it is the exact
opposite of that of the Romantic School, which is our own.)

On the whole, the nobles and ladies of the times of Louis XIII
and of the Fronde tried to behave like the heroes of their
The literature. Cinna and Chimène were the models
precursors of whereon such beings as Richelieu, and Retz, and
Romanticism. the Grande Mademoiselle probably strove to form
themselves. Those vigorous men and women of the year 1650,
so much admired by Nietzsche, were full of greatness, pomp,
generosity, candour, and brutality ; they had a passionate taste
for the heroic and the theatrical. Those who desire to understand Chevreuse and Longueville, De Thou, Chalais, and Retz,
their pretentious and somewhat heavy gallantry, their useless
and Machiavellian conspiracies, their heroism and their swagger,
must remember that they had been brought up on the *Conciones*
and on Plutarch, on *Cassandre* and on the *Grand Cyrus*, on
Polyeucte and on the *Astrée*. Now Sainte-Beuve noted certain
similarities of accent and inspiration forming a link between
the tragedies of Corneille and the great romances of the Hôtel de
Rambouillet, on the one hand, and the romantic literature of his
own time, on the other, and further he observed that after having
been ridiculed, killed, and cast aside by Boileau and the realist
school of 1660, this "elevated, romantic, sentimental style"
had been taken up again "in the days of Jean-Jacques
Rousseau."

This is perfectly true : is not Céladon languid, gloomy ,and
melancholy, like Saint-Preux ? Certain of Corneille's tragedies,

such as *Rodogune, Héraclius,* and *Don Sanche,* are nothing but melodramas. "*Clitandre,*" says M. Faguet, "is simply a novel of adventure put upon the stage, with masked assassins, and archers, and single combats, and earthquakes. . . ." And the romance of the heroes of the Fronde bears a prodigious resemblance, in many respects, to the romanticism of the conspirators of Young Italy—or even to that of the "Jeunes-France" of the days of *Hernani.*

WORKS TO CONSULT: Brunetière, *Manuel de l'histoire de la littérature française* (1898); E. Faguet, *XVIIᵉᵐᵉ Siècle* (1889). The bibliography will be found in G. Lanson, *Manuel bibliographique de la littérature moderne,* vol. ii (1910); G. Lanson, *Histoire de la littérature française,* (10th ed. revised, 1908); J. Lemaître, *Corneille*; Petit de Julleville, *Histoire de la langue et de la littérature française,* vol. iv; Sainte-Beuve, *passim* (see the two alphabetical tables); the collection of *Grands Écrivains français,* published by Messrs. Hachette.

CHAPTER VI

THE FRONDE AND MAZARIN

I. Anne of Austria and Mazarin. II. The great victories. The Westphalian Treaty. III. The Fronde. IV. The end of the war. The Treaty of the Pyrenees. Apotheosis of Mazarin.

I

ONLY a few hours after Louis XIII had breathed his last, disturbance began to threaten among the Princes assembled at Saint-Germain. The Queen, leaving a few of the Crown officials to watch the late King's body, had gone to join her sons. But the crowd of courtiers in their **Accession of** apartment was so great that Anne grew faint, and **Louis XIV.** begged the Duc de Beaufort to clear the room. This Beaufort, second son of the Duc de Vendôme, and grandson of Henri IV and Gabrielle d'Estrées, was a good-looking fellow, rude, presumptuous, boastful, but brave, whose sense " was below the average " (Retz), his wit " heavy and rough " (La Rochefoucauld), and his language that of a street-porter, in spite of which he was popular with women, and even Anne herself looked upon him with a favourable eye. He proceeded, after his usual insolent fashion, to carry out the Queen's command, whereupon the Prince de Condé asked him what authority he had to issue any orders at all : the quarrel was patched up with some difficulty.

A few days later (May 18, 1643) Anne of Austria proceeded to the Parliament, to secure its assistance in setting aside the will by the provisions of which the late King had endeavoured to limit her powers. It was a fine sight. The great hall hung with violet velvet, all the Councillors and Presidents, and Masters of Requests, and the King's servants, in their red or black gowns, the Princes and Dukes, the guards, the heralds, the mace-bearers : the Queen draped in a great crape veil that almost totally concealed her face : the King, just four and a half years old, who made his entry borne in the arms of M. de Chevreuse. Silence was proclaimed, and the child was made to stand in front of his " bed "—five cushions laid under a violet velvet canopy dotted with golden fleurs-de-lis—between his mother and his governess, to recite his speech, " but he sat down again, comically, and would not say a word." Forthwith the Chancellor and the Advocate-General made him long harangues. Each member voted, and then the Chancellor mounted the steps to where their Majesties were seated, came back to his own place, and said, " The King, seated on his Bed of Justice, has declared, and now declares," etc. etc. Anne was given the right to govern as she chose, and admit any one she pleased to the Council. The precautions poor Louis XIII had taken so carefully had only been in force for four days.

Anne was a handsome woman of two and forty, superbly healthy, fresh and buxom, with fine eyes and quantities of fair **Anne of** hair, which her women delighted to watch her **Austria.** curling skilfully round her beautiful white fingers, when her head was dressed. She generally woke at ten or eleven o'clock, gave a few audiences, and breakfasted before she heard Mass. " She was served, after her broth, with cutlets, sausages, and bread-porridge. She generally ate a little of everything, and did not dine the less heartily "—nor sup less well either. Her style of dress was modest, " but like that of persons who wish to look well, without luxury, without gold or silver, or rouge or any extraordinary ornament," and it was easy to see that " she might be capable of a little vanity." Unlike Marie de' Medici, who had never been able to pronounce French correctly, Anne spoke that language with as little accent as if she had been born in the Ile-de-France. She was fond of unceremonious amusements, and during the great heats of the year 1646 she actually held a Court for her ladies in the River Seine, not far from Thomery : the little King bathed too, with his Governor, the Maréchal de Villeroy, and everybody, from the Marshal to the ladies, was decently clothed in a long garment that trailed upon the ground, so that " modesty was not offended."

Anne was very devout, spent much time at her prayers, made retreats in convents, and offered gifts, after the Spanish custom, to the Virgin and the saints. Ignorant as any Infanta, she knew some little about politicians, but nothing at all about politics. Even-tempered as a rule, she was, however, subject to furious fits of anger, and then her voice would grow strident and harsh, as on the day when she called out shrilly to the members of the Parliament, " Hold your tongues ! Hold your tongues ! " On the whole, she was likeable, noble, and simple, both in character and demeanour, a perfectly well-bred woman —she " knew better than anybody how to do what is called ' holding a Court.' "

She was coquettish : she loved admiration. Her late husband had not spoilt her by over-attention, and under Louis XIII to declare oneself in love with the Queen was not thought such a very extraordinary action as it would have been held thirty years later. It was quite well known at Court that the gentlemen who were not prevented by the majesty of the sovereign from realizing the beauty of the woman in her were not unpleasing in her sight. Their adoration was platonic, indeed, for Anne was virtuous and scrupulous. Gondi, the Coadjutor, had hoped to gain great advantage by following the counsels given him by Mme. de Chevreuse : " Only look dreamy when you are with the Queen," said she, " keep gazing at her hands ; inveigh against Cardinal Mazarin—and leave the rest to me ! " And Retz goes on : " I played the game well : in the talks I had with the Queen I passed from reverie to frenzy. . . ." But he got no more for his pains than the conceited little Marquis de Jarzé. Anne was a fond lover, as is clearly shown by the fashion in which she defended her Mazarin. " Till my last breath," she wrote him one day. " Farewell, I am tired out ! " When he died, she relinquished power as though she had never desired to have it : all reason for ambition had disappeared when she could no longer be ambitious for another. At her son's Court, her one care, from that time forward, was to play the part of an old lady tastefully, and right well did she succeed.

Giulio Mazarini, born on July 14, 1602, the son of a Sicilian attached to the Colonna household in the quality of business man, was a good-looking and very intelligent gentleman, tall, chestnut-haired, bright-eyed, of pleasant and open countenance, always gay and smiling, who told a story better than anybody else, excelled in every game, and, in short, had " charms which unfailingly endeared him to those he desired to please." Being himself subject neither to hatred nor to friendship, he knew how to manifest just so much of one feeling or the other " as his interest obliged him to do," and this practice had served him well. He had been a model student at the Jesuit College at Rome, and had then studied at the University of Alcala in Spain, where, being ruined by his gambling debts, he contemplated marrying a notary's daughter. He afterwards became a doctor *in utroque jure*, an infantry captain, a diplomat, and tried many trades in fact. At the siege of Casale in 1630, when all the negotiations failed, and the French and Spanish armies were preparing to renew hostilities, suddenly the young Papal agent made his appearance, hurrying towards the front of the troops, and brandishing the treaty the signature of which he had just obtained, with cries of " Peace ! Peace ! " This triumph, and the theatrical manner of its announcement, made Giulio Mazarini's fortune. He entered into relations with Richelieu, put on the ecclesiastical habit (though without taking orders, it is thought), was appointed Nunico in France, and ended by entering the King's service. Richelieu obtained the Cardinal's hat for him in 1641, and after that he contrived to become the King's favourite and continue at one and the same time to be his Minister. And when, in 1643, Louis XIII appointed him one of the four Councillors on whose will Anne of Austria was to be dependent, does the reader imagine this made him that proud lady's enemy ? No, indeed ! Three days only after that on which the late King's will was set aside, and the Regent's powers fully restored to her, she chose Cardinal Mazarin to be her chief Minister.

He was so accommodating ! Business never was complicated when he had it in charge : politics became quite easy. And, besides, he had been at the French Court for so short a time that he had had no opportunity of compromising himself with any party—let alone the fact that he had taken good care

to avoid such an error. The Regent, on the whole, had no
complaint to make of this clever man, who did not seem to
have set his heart on anything in particular, and was always
talking of going back to Rome. And then he was perpetually
telling Her Majesty of the deep, the tender, the respectful
affection with which she had inspired him ! Her Majesty ended
Mazarin and by being profoundly touched. Day by day, in
Anne of Mazarin's private notebooks, we follow the pro-
Austria. gress of the suave and handsome Cardinal in his
sovereign's affections. The earlier books are full of protestations in Spanish and Italian : " I would it had cost me dear,
and that I had been Her Majesty's servant for long years
already ! " " If I believed what is said—that Her Majesty
employs my services out of necessity, without any inclination
whatever—I would not stay here three days ! " At the same
time one feels Mazarin was far, as yet, from being certain of
his favour with the Regent, for he grows uneasy sometimes as
to the sympathy she betrays for one person or another, the
assertions of the Commandeur de Jars, who " boasts of his
intercourse, his credit, and his familiarity with the Queen, in
days gone by," or the remarks of the Mother-Superior of the
Carmelites, who has plainly warned Her Majesty that her
Minister is compromising her reputation. And then suddenly,
in the later books, the tone changes ; " a jaundice, caused by
excess of passion," is the first thing we read : and after this
Mazarin trembles no more, but writes in the firmest, though the
most respectful tone : " Let Her Majesty find out privately from
His Highness what is to be done with M. le Duc de Vendôme " :
" Her Majesty should do her best to gain me the support of all
those who serve her, and that by causing all the favours they
receive to pass through my hands." " If Her Majesty does not
make herself obeyed, all is lost, because every man will dare
everything," etc. These counsels, no doubt, Mazarin imparted
to the Queen in her cabinet, where she shut herself up with him
every night. Before long, in November, 1644, the Regent was
to inform the Council that she was granting her Minister rooms
in the Palais-Royal, where she herself lived, " so as to be able
to confer with him on her business more conveniently. As
Anne was then forty-three years old, no very great perspicacity

was needed to see that Mazarin had every chance of holding permanent office.

At the outset the Queen still retained the sympathy evoked by the manner in which Cardinal Richelieu had persecuted her. And, then, it was a time of general gladness : pensions, honours, offices, were poured out as in the days of Marie de' Medici : " There are only five little words, now, in the French language," said La Feuillade, " La Reine est si bonne ! " (The Queen is so kind !) Even Mazarin was not disliked : " On the steps of the throne, whence the terrible Richelieu had crushed rather than ruled the human race, we saw a successor who was gentle, benign, who desired nothing for himself, who was in despair because his dignity as a Cardinal did not permit him to humiliate himself before all the world as he would fain have done, who drove through the streets with two diminutive lackeys behind his coach " (Retz). And further, everybody believed Anne would dismiss him " in five or six months," when all business **The " Cabale** matters had been cleared up. Yet month after **des Im-** month went by, and still the Cardinal remained. **portants."** . . . At last, all those to whose interest it was to bring about his fall joined forces—this was the " Cabal of the Mighty Ones " (*Cabale des Importants*).

" The great strength of M. le Cardinal de Mazarin lay in soft words, hinting, giving reason to hope : he would let in a glimmer of light, and then take it back, he would give an idea, and then confuse it." And good Father Tixier ingenuously confesses : " I have never approached the Cardinal without being persuaded I was going to talk to the greatest impostor in the world, and I never left his presence without being charmed by him." It was wonderful, indeed, how " Pantaloon " as he was coarsely nicknamed by Retz, his bitter enemy, contrived, while he was completing the conquest of Anne of Austria's affections, to use the Condés against the Vendômes, foil the plans of Mme. de Chevreuse, and attack her, so to speak, at her weakest point. She tried the power of her charms—the charms of a woman of forty-three—upon him, and he, on his side, endeavoured to make her believe she had inspired him with a genuine passion ; but he was just as gallant, meanwhile, in his dealings with the fascinating Mme. de Guéménée, and in the end these two fair ladies, sorely nettled, began to wonder which of them was to prevail. . . . Finally the " Importants," perceiving how little they were gaining from this warfare masked by flowers, coolly made up their minds to have the obnoxious Minister assassinated. But day by day Mazarin's influence over the Queen had increased in strength, until one fine morning the Duc de Beaufort, grandson of Henri IV though he was, was conducted to the Castle of Vincennes, Mme. de Chevreuse was banished to Touraine, and the rest of the conspirators were either exiled or imprisoned (September, 1643). . . . This done, the mild-mannered Cardinal did his utmost to persuade everybody that it was not he, but the Duc d'Orléans and the Prince de Condé who had counselled such severe repressive measures. " The morning after the event he seemed more moderate and civil than ever. Access to his person was quite free, audiences were easily granted, people dined with him just as with any private individual : he even put away a great deal of the stately manner affected by cardinals of the most ordinary sort. In fact, he played his cards so well that he had his foot on everybody's head, while everybody thought he was still standing beside them " (Retz).

II

Louis XIII had spent the winter of 1643 in planning the campaign which was to open in the following spring. He had intended to march in person against Don Francisco de Melo, Governor of the Low Countries, who was threatening to invade Champagne : but when his illness destroyed all his hopes of being able to start, he appointed the elder son of his cousin Condé to take his place.

The Spanish Campaign of 1643.

The Duc d'Enghien was then a young man of two and twenty, more than careless about his toilet, whose thin, lank, active body bore a head like that of some strange bird of prey : a narrow receding forehead, hollow cheeks, a nose as sharp and hooked as a beak, and eyes with so fierce a flame in them that men shrank from their gaze. Like all the well-born men of his time he had gained his first experience of war as a volunteer (at the siege of Arras), and had then fought through the cam-

THE FRONDE AND MAZARIN

paigns of 1641 and 1642 : thus he was not a mere novice : nevertheless, it was thought wise to supply him with a Mentor in the person of the Maréchal de l'Hôpital, then a man of sixty.

Since May 10 Don Francisco de Melo had been laying siege to the fortress of Rocroy, intending, when that place had fallen, **The Battle of** to make his way to Paris through Champagne : **Rocroy.** the Spaniards had not forgotten the Corbie Year. The Duc d'Enghien went to meet them, and on May 17 the French army arrived at the entrance of the passes it had to cross, amidst woods and marshes (now dried up), to reach the enemy before Rocroy. But just at this juncture the news of the death of Louis XIII arrived. Forthwith a council of war was called : was it best to take the risk of a pitched battle, or merely try to throw some reinforcements into the besieged town ? Against the advice of the aged De l'Hôpital, and of the majority of the military chiefs, who all leaned towards the more prudent course, the young Duke insisted on fighting. And it was because he had imposed his will on all the rest that, on May 18, the French troops deployed without let or hindrance (wherefore, nobody seems to know) in face of the enemy on the plain of Rocroy. Though it was already six o'clock in the evening, Enghien was making his arrangements for an immediate attack, when the whole Spanish line moved forward and marched upon the Frenchmen, with trumpets sounding and drums beating the charge. A false step at that moment would have thrown the whole of the French army into confusion : if the Spaniards had driven home their attack, their adversaries would have been defeated, it would have spelt utter disaster. . . . Happily, after marching some 400 paces, Don Francisco halted : his only object had been to ensure room for his rear lines. And the struggle was deferred till the following day.

Before daybreak on the 19th, his attendants roused the stripling who was to command the French troops from his youthful slumbers. He put on his armour, but refused to wear a helmet, and donned a white-plumed hat instead : then he mounted his horse and showed himself to his men : wiry, eager, and authoritative, with that " noble ardour " of his (*Grand Cyrus*), he was truly " a young Prince of the Blood who carried victory in his eyes " (Bossuet).

He gave the command of the left wing to the Maréchal de l'Hôpital : the Baron de Sirot, a veteran who had fought in the Thirty Years' War, was put in charge of the reserve : he himself, assisted by Gassion, an excellent cavalry officer, led the right wing. And now the French advance began. At the very first contact Enghien completely drove in the Spanish left : then, leaving Gassion to pursue the fugitives, he turned suddenly upon the Walloon and Italian infantry which formed the second line of his opponents' centre, and having broken it, finally threw himself on the rear of the Spaniards' right wing. It was high time : the Spanish troops, commanded on that side by Don Francisco himself, had already very nearly routed the force the Maréchal de l'Hôpital had led against them : but when they felt Enghien's sudden attack upon their rear, they broke. The only resistance now was that offered by the leading ranks of the Spanish centre, " that redoubtable infantry of the army of Spain, whose great serried battalions, like towers capable of repairing their own breaches, stood unshaken in the midst of all the rest of the rout, and darted forth fire on every side " (Bossuet). These were the proud *tercios viejos*, commanded by the Comte de Fontaines, who was forced by his infirmities to have himself carried into the fray on a litter— war-worn old regiments, famous throughout Europe : Avila, Vilandio, Villalva, Albuquerque, Garcies, Castelvi, entirely composed of those "native Spaniards" whose bravery, as Condé himself tells us, was of an essence more exquisite than that of any other nationality. These regiments, swelled by a large number of men belonging to those which had just been broken, and provided with eighteen cannon, formed themselves into squares. Three times did the whole French army, led by Condé, throw itself upon them : at the fourth attack, which assailed them on three sides at once, they gave way. The battle, begun at three o'clock in the morning, was over at ten. The Spaniards left seven or eight thousand dead on the field, besides four and twenty guns, 170 infantry colours, fourteen cavalry standards, and a considerable amount of treasure, and though their Captain-General, Don Francisco de Melo, succeeded in making his escape, the French took his bâton, covered with inscriptions commemorating former victories.

THE FRONDE AND MAZARIN

The victor of Rocroy moved on towards the Moselle, took
Thionville on August 10, and Sierk on September 3, and then
returned to Court to clamour greedily for his reward and
indulge in immoderate triumph, like the very young man he
was. . . . About the same time the old Maréchal de Guébriant
met his death gloriously at the siege of Rothweil (September 25),
and Mazarin sent the Duc de Bouillon's second son, Henri de la
Tour d'Auvergne, Vicomte de Turenne, whom he had just
created Marshal of France, to replace him in command of the
troops on the Rhine.

Turenne was then a man of thirty-two, ten years older than
Condé, to whom he bore no resemblance of any kind. With his
Turenne. brick-red complexion, his hairy face, thick-set,
heavy figure, and broad shoulders, and his big
head that always hung down, he looked anything but dashing,
whether on horseback or on foot. " I send you a courser that
will suit you," writes Mazarin to him on July 9, 1644, " for he
served my purpose perfectly, though I am not a good rider, and
to tell the truth you are not a much better horseman than I."
Morally Turenne was perhaps devoid of any vice save that of
pride in his noble birth : he was awkward in his mode of
expression, but he was a diligent thinker, he turned his ideas
over slowly " under those great eyebrows of his that met," and
even his most daring actions were the result of a methodical
process of decision. His first performances, after he had been
created a Marshal, proved him a past-master in the art of taking
advantage of the ground he held : later he acquired the art of
sudden action in which he had been lacking at first. Indeed he
improved all his life long, and the most splendid, probably, of
all his campaigns was the last he fought.

Guébriant's army welcomed him gladly : the " Weimarians,"
Protestants like himself, remembered that their famous general,
Bernhard, had valued him highly. . . . Meanwhile, Mercy had
taken possession of Freiburg : it was necessary to drive him
out, and Turenne had not sufficient troops to attempt this
successfully. On August 2 the Duc d'Enghien joined him,
and took over the command. No pitched battle ensued, but
there was a series of somewhat disconnected engagements.
Mercy was firmly established in a mountainous region, with a

145

force inferior to the French. On August 3 his entrenchments were stormed : Enghien got off his horse and crossed the first *abatis* with his infantry. But in the course of the night the Bavarians formed up again on a somewhat steep and thickly wooded hill, the Josephberg, and in spite of three attacks delivered in oppressively hot weather, and a hand-to-hand fight which lasted all through the day of August 5, their dislodgment proved impossible. Then, for a few days, the two armies lay watching each other, till, early on the 9th, Enghien made up his mind to move : he marched away. Mercy, who could get no supplies, and whose horses were reduced to eating the leaves off the trees, did the same thing, and executed a skilful disappearance. But the Weimar cavalry caught him and delayed his march : Enghien was close on their heels : Mercy only contrived to save the 6000 men who remained to him by abandoning his artillery and baggage. The Bavarian army was not utterly wiped out, but for a lengthy period it was practically destroyed.

The Duc d'Enghien wisely gave up all thought of laying siege to Freiburg, which threatened to hold out for a very long time. He marched down the Rhine, took possession of Philippsburg without any difficulty, entered Spires, Worms, and Mayence, conquered Landau, and then returned to France. Turenne, who replaced him in the command, reopened the campaign early in March, 1645 : this was earlier than usual, and the old Weimarian leaders grumbled about the change of routine. When Mercy attacked Turenne at Marienthal, in May, 1645, he had no difficulty in driving the discontented army of King Louis back across the Main.

Then Enghien hurried up to Turenne's aid. Mercy had entrenched himself in a very strong position at the village of **Battle of Nordlingen, 1645.** Allerheim, near Nordlingen : on August 3, 1645, the Duke attacked him with 38,000 men. A first infantry assault on the village was repulsed with loss, and the enemy was vigorously pursuing this advantage when it was checked by the death of Mercy. During this time, the French right had been completely driven in by Werth, who, instead of imitating Enghien's wise behaviour at Rocroy, allowed himself to be carried away by the eagerness of the pursuit. By the time he returned, Turenne, who commanded the French left, had routed the troops opposing him, and, acting on his chief's orders, had taken the village in the rear while the infantry of the French centre delivered another frontal attack : Allerheim was carried. Werth was forced to order a retreat. This was the battle of Nordlingen. So heavily had the victors lost that they were obliged to take their way back to Philippsburg.

But all this while the laurels won by the House of Condé were filling the soul of Gaston d'Orléans with bitterness, and he resolved he too would become a mighty warrior. He was appointed to command the army in Flanders (several good generals were to give him their aid), and this army took Gravelines from the Spaniards in 1644, Mardick and Cassel in 1645, and Courtrai in 1646 : this time the victor of Rocroy served under Gaston's orders. But after these exploits, Monsieur went back to Court satiated with glory. And his departure did not by any means prevent Enghien from carrying the very strong fortified town of Dunkirk (1646).

On the Spanish frontiers the French operations were less successful. Even Enghien, now Prince de Condé, owing to his **Siege of** father's death, won but little success there. On **Lerida.** May 14, 1647, he laid siege to Lerida. "The fortress was nothing : but Don Gregorio Brice (or rather de Brito), its Governor, was somebody," and this was soon to become evident. Condé had "ordered the trenches to be mounted at noonday by his own regiment, at the head of which marched four-and-twenty fiddlers, as if it had been to a wedding," so Hamilton tells us.

"Night approaching, we were all in high spirits ; our violins were playing soft airs, and we were comfortably regaling ourselves. . . . All this was going on in the trenches, when we heard an ominous cry from the ramparts, repeated two or three times of, 'Alerte on the walls !' This cry was followed by a discharge of cannon and musketry, and this discharge by a vigorous sally, which, after having filled up the trenches, pursued us as far as our grand guard.

"The next day Gregorio Brice sent by a trumpet a present of ice and fruit to the Prince de Condé, humbly beseeching his

Highness to excuse his not returning the serenade which he was pleased to favour him with, as unfortunately he had no violins ; but that if the music of last night was not disagreeable to him, he would endeavour to continue it as long as he did him the honour to remain before the place. The Spaniard was as good as his word ; and as soon as we heard ' Alerte on the walls ' we were sure of a sally that cleared our trenches, destroyed our works, and killed the best of our officers and soldiers."

So loud was this brave Don Gregorio's music that Condé was fain to raise the siege of Lerida. The struggle was to be fought out to the end on the north-western frontier of France.

In 1646 and 1647 Turenne and the Swedish General Wrangel, who had succeeded that glorious cripple Torstenson, reduced Bavaria to submission. The following year saw Condé at the head of the army in Flanders : he seized Ypres, but when he reached Lens, he found that town occupied by the Archduke Leopold (the patron of Teniers). He deployed his troops opposite his adversary's, and then suddenly, on the morning of August 20, he feigned a retreat. The Archduke instantly quitted his strong position and fell on the French rearguard—so vigorously, indeed, that Condé, who was with it, narrowly escaped being taken prisoner. But all at once the King's army made a half-turn, as if it had been on pàrade, and marched straight on the enemy. Surprised by this counter-attack, the Spanish lines were driven in, and the Archduke, in his flight, left 3000 dead, 5000 prisoners, 118 pieces of ordnance, and more than 100 colours behind him. . . . About the same time, Turenne and Wrangel, who had beaten the Imperialists at Zusmarshausen, were preparing to besiege Prague and march on Vienna, when they heard that peace had been signed (October 24, 1648).

The Great Condè in Flanders.

The negotiations had been going on for four years. The plenipotentiaries of Sweden and the Empire (whose differences were to be arranged apart from the rest) held their meetings at Osnabrück : the others—those of France, Spain, Holland, and the Empire—sat at Münster. But diplomatic etiquette and jealousies had delayed progress. At last, in January, 1648, a private treaty was signed between Spain and the United

Provinces, and these two retired from the conferences : Holland, on the whole, thought it better to have the Spaniards than the French as her neighbours in the Low Countries : as for Spain, she preferred to carry on the war, hoping that the troubles of the Fronde, of which she perceived the beginnings in France, would provide her with allies like those she had found in that country in the days of the League.

But on October 24, 1648, the Emperor affixed his signature to the Treaty of Westphalia, which reduced him to a position **Treaty of** little higher than that of the first among the **Westphalia,** German princes. The allies of France—Sweden, **1648.** Brandenburg, the Elector Palatine, the petty Protestant princes—gained considerable advantages. France received Pignerol and the three Bishoprics of Metz, Toul, and Verdun (which she had been occupying, *de facto*, for a long period of time, but her ownership of which the Emperor now formally recognized), and also Alsace—that is to say, the two landgraviates and the inextricable chaos of lordships and imperial towns which made up the territory known under that geographical name : unfortunately this cession of Alsace was couched in terms the ambiguity of which was to be the pretext for much future contestation and war.

III

Mazarin's successes in the departments of foreign politics and war were almost unnoticed, like those of Richelieu in earlier **Unpopularity** days : the whole of France had grown to hate **of Mazarin.** the foreigner, the intruder, the Italian. The populace ascribed the increased weight of taxation to him, and reproached him with having amassed a fortune for himself. Even in 1645 women had cast themselves at Anne of Austria's feet in the church of Notre-Dame, crying out that she " had a man about her who took everything " (d'Ormesson). At Court there had been a hope that this Regent's rule would be as weak as that of others, and that the usual profits would consequently be made out of it : and behold, Anne had chosen a Minister who took good care nobody should play on her ignorance or her indolence to extort favours, pensions, honours, and benefactions. The princes, too, loathed this tiresome fellow who kept them out of power with a gentle hand, indeed, but one that never failed. And like them, the former " Importants," the ambitious men, and all those who had reckoned on fishing in troubled waters, from Retz to Mlle. de Montpensier—the "Grande Mademoiselle" as Gaston's daughter was called, on account of her height—were bent on the Cardinal's ruin. Even those who had nothing to gain by such an event longed for it too, for the sake of being in the fashion—for the Fronde was a fashion.

What more fascinating adventure could there be, in fact, in the eyes of those fair and romantic ladies and the fops of their period, passionate admirers, every one of them, of the *Grand Cyrus* if not of Oroondate the Scythian (just as their grandchildren, at a later date, were to go crazy over Saint-Preux or René), whose dreams were all of heroic loves and splendid intrigues, and doughty sword-thrusts, than such a civil war as this one—not " savage " and " barbarous," but chivalrous and well-ordered, with its battles fought under the eyes of the fair sex, and that famous siege of the Bastille in 1649, graced by the presence of the most fascinating ladies of the Fronde, who brought their chairs " as if they had come to hear a sermon," and sat behind the battery which fired five or six shots—a mere formality—on the ancient fortress before it surrendered. And was it not a prodigiously fine thing to come back, like M. de Noirmoutiers, from firing off pistols in the faubourgs, and find your way, all covered with heroism and dight in armour, into Mme. de Longueville's own chamber, where the very air rustled with talk of warfare and of love ? " The medley of ladies and blue scarves and cuirasses, of violins in the room, and trumpets in the square, made up a sight more commonly seen in novels than elsewhere," says Retz : " Noirmoutiers, who was a great admirer of the *Astrée*, said to me, ' I imagine to myself that we are besieged in Marcilly.' ' You are quite right,' I replied." What more unforgettable indeed, to romantic imaginations, than scenes such as the following :

The Fronde.

The smallpox had left Mme. de Longueville all the radiance of her beauty, and that of Mme. de Bouillon, though somewhat impaired, was still most brilliant. Imagine, I beg of you, these two ladies on the steps of the Hôtel de Ville, their appearance all the more lovely because it seemed unstudied, *although it was not*. Each held one of her children in her arms, as beautiful as their mothers. The Place de Grève was crammed to the roofs with people : all the men shouting with delight, all the women shedding tears of tender emotion ! (Retz).

The Parliament—like the Court, like the town, like every one in fact—was at enmity with the Cardinal. It had considerable **The Paris** pretensions, which it constantly put forward, and **Parliament.** more particularly, for the best of reasons, during the minority of any sovereign. It claimed to be the sole representative of the ancient Court of the Peers, the Assembly of the Champ-de-Mai, and the States-General of the Three Orders, and to have a right, in consequence, to control the King's Government : unfortunately, in the King's opinion, his Council sufficed for all his needs. But the Parliament was powerful. It had a huge following of attorneys, sheriffs' officers, serjeants, lawyers, and pettifoggers of every kind, who exercised a great influence on public opinion. When, in conjunction with the three sovereign courts—the Court of Aids, the Chamber of Accounts, and the Great Council—it discussed the King's edicts, its deliberations attracted the greatest attention. All the Parliamentary magistrates in their scarlet mantles trimmed with ermine, and those of the other courts in their black gowns—of velvet, satin, damask, or silk—gathered themselves together in the Chamber of Saint-Louis, and there solemnly exchanged speeches, frequently violent in tone, and interrupted by the hooting and the plaudits of the young Councillors of the Court of Inquiry—more than four hundred of them, between the ages of twenty-five and thirty, far outnumbering the greybeards of the " Grand' Chambre." The public acclaimed the " fathers of the country " as it called them, and this popularity was by no means displeasing to them. Nurtured as they had been on the Latin authors, they were delighted to hear their speeches described as " magnificent harangues with something of ancient Rome about them," and themselves likened to Roman senators defending the rights of freedom. That was their special form of romance.

THE SEVENTEENTH CENTURY

On ordinary occasions the Palace of Justice was full of all sorts of people who had nothing to do with judicial matters, **The Palais de** and besides the throng of attorneys, advocates, **Justice.** lawyers, and litigants of every kind, innumerable idlers spent their whole days there. For in all the public halls, and every corner of the old building—but above all in that " Galerie Mercière " in which Corneille laid the scene of his comedy *La Galerie du Palais*—every variety of fashionable ware and elegant trifle was sold : fans, gloves, slippers, fine linen, trinkets : even engravings and books were to be had : every pillar in the Great Hall had its bookstall. On the days of great political sessions the news was carried from shop to shop, spread to the street, reached the Place Dauphine, and thence was passed on to the Pont-Neuf. . . . Once there, all Paris caught it up.

The Pont-Neuf was the real heart of the city. There were no houses along its parapets, as on all the other bridges, and **The Pont-Neuf.** the view over the river was open on both sides. Looking up-stream, this was bounded, at no great distance, by the buildings of the Pont-au-Change and the Pont-Saint-Michel, but down-stream the yellowish ripples of the Seine could be seen shining in the far distance. The river was more useful in those days than in ours, and quite as busy. Its banks were crowded with stores and open-air markets, and boats, barges, roofed passenger-boats, and pleasure-galleys, carved and gilded, shot in all directions over the face of the stream, which was narrowed, wherever there was a landing-stage, by the rows of boats moored close to it. On the left bank, behind the Hôtel de Nevers and the ruined Tour de Nesles, which stood on the edge of the quay, was the shadowy outline of a great mass of houses, intersected by streets, and dominated by the steeple of Saint-Germain-des-Prés. But on the right the Louvre extended in noble beauty. In the foreground, in the angle formed by the Little Gallery and the southern front of the old palace (that which runs parallel with the river), there was a sort of garden of orange-trees bounded by a terrace and a wall, against which stood several houses in what has now become the Rue du Louvre. Then, from the southern end of the Little Gallery, the Great Gallery ran right down to the

THE FRONDE AND MAZARIN

Tuileries, flanked, just before it reached that palace, by an ancient fortified gate, the great wooden tower of which corresponded with the Tour de Nesles. At the end of the garden of the Tuileries was the town wall and the Porte de la Conférence, through which the King had easy access to the Cours-la-Reine and the open country. . . . It was a delight to pass out of the close network of the Paris streets, full of stinking mud and encumbered with filth of every description, which the townsfolk threw indiscriminately out of window, and find oneself on the fine road over the Pont-Neuf, spacious and airy, swept by the river breeze, and offering the most amusing sight conceivable.

For all day long a huge crowd swarmed there. People going about their business, in the first place : horsemen with ladies behind them, gentlemen who galloped along without the smallest regard for the passers-by, burghers bestriding their mules, women of the humbler sort sitting on their donkeys, market-gardeners and washerwomen leading their pack-horses or their asses, laden with linen, lackeys with led horses, carters driving long strings of tumbrils ; often a coach would appear, leather-curtained, more or less sumptuous, covered with gilding and armorial bearings, lined with velvet and fringes—a weighty machine filled with lords and ladies, and drawn by great coach-horses under whose hoofs the pavement shook. But the special colour of the Pont-Neuf was due to the fair that was held there all the year round. All along the parapets, in front of the fine new and regularly built houses—brick with stone facings —of the Place Dauphine, facing the open space on which the colossal statue of good King Henri IV stood, and even along the neighbouring banks of the river, swarmed jugglers, and singers, and conjurers, and tooth-drawers, and dog-sellers, and vendors of silk stockings, and parasols, and flowers, and fruit, the shabby poets, and the second-hand book-dealers. Close to the pumping machine that rose out of the river and was set against the parapet not far from the right bank—the "Samaritaine," as it was called, because its handsome clock was adorned with figures of Jesus and the Samaritan Woman—the small book-sellers laid out their wares, and did an underhand trade in lampoons and "mazarinades" : there the gazetteers had their newspapers cried—sometimes these were in manuscript, sometimes they were printed—and the song-writers produced couplets about the victories of M. le Prince or the misdeeds of M. le Cardinal : " Beware of the *ponts-neufs*," said Condé at Lerida. . . . Farther on, protected by their canvas tents or sheltered by red umbrellas, the wineshop-keepers and orange-sellers offered their wares, the jugglers blew their horns, perched on their trestle-boards, the quacks, successors of the illustrious Mondor and his servant Tabarin, vaunted their remedies. Here the " Orvietan," round whom four fiddlers scraped their instruments, dispensed his miraculous ointment. Elsewhere, Carméline, Cormier, and Rondin pulled out teeth and sold their opiates, warranted not only to restore youth to the old, but to beautify the human countenance and heal the most incurable ills. Philipot, a blind man, otherwise called the Savoyard, and the famous Baptiste (two of Boileau's " victims ") sang couplets of their own composition. Brioché made his monkey, Fagotin, dance (the monkey which Cyrano ran his sword through one day), and there were plenty of rogues ready to imitate him.

> Vestus comme des harlequins
> Avec trois guenilles de linge,
> Qui font sauter un pauvre singe
> Et grimper dessus un baston,
> Afin de gagner un teston. . . . (F. Colletet).

Till the sun went down the bridge rang with talk and shouts. Then, when darkness approached, each man prudently closed his shop, for at that hour thieves, and bravoes, and highwaymen reigned supreme : once, towards the year 1700, they ventured to hold up the mail-coach to Tours, when it halted at the " Samaritaine."

Though the Fronde came into existence in the Palais de Justice, it was on the Pont-Neuf, and amongst the populace, that it gathered strength, and flamed into action. Yet the Fronde did not respond to any deep national feeling. Apart from the touch of romance, and the hatred of the Minister, the parties that made up the opposition had not a single idea or passion in common : the Fronde possessed no programme. From the very outset, jealousy between the chief leaders, Orléans and Condé, was as bitter as between their subordinates, and these rivalries resulted in some ridiculous incidents. On

THE FRONDE AND MAZARIN

one occasion, in 1644, " Madame la Princesse " had herself bled, so as to avoid taking part in some ceremony in which she would have had to yield precedence to Gaston's daughter, the " Grande Mademoiselle " : forthwith Mademoiselle took physic, so as to escape appearing without Madame la Princesse in her wake—nothing but the threat of having her carried bodily to Notre-Dame settled the matter. In 1648 her attendants hardly dared to inform her of the victory won at Lens by the Great Condé, her father's adversary, and when she did hear of it she was in despair. The Cardinal, as may easily be conceived, made no effort to reconcile the princes, and he was quite right : when they did join forces, it was against him. . . . These divisions were a source of weakness to his enemies (who were, after all, the enemies of France as well), but a greater one was their lack of conviction. The name bestowed on the Fronde was that of a childish game, and this was appropriate enough, for the rebellion really was a game, a silly comedy, played by France for her own entertainment : in it the members of the Parliament were to be seen figuring as " magistrates of Ancient Rome," fine gentlemen and fair ladies played at war and politics, and even the worthy Paris burghers played at soldiers on the Place Dauphine and the Place Royale : the " common folk " were the only people who did not play ; they paid instead, as usual.

It was the Parliament that opened the battle, so to speak. For several years past it had been opposing all edicts for taxation, and had gained immense popularity as the result. Mazarin, out of prudence, had nearly always persuaded the Queen to give way, but Anne, thoroughly embittered, was impatiently awaiting the moment when she should be strong enough to take her revenge. That moment seemed to her to have arrived on the day when the *Te Deum* for the victory of Lens was sung in Notre-Dame. So on August 26, 1648, she ordered the arrest of two Councillors well known for their violent language regarding the Court—Blancmesnil and Broussel. The latter of the two, " who had grown old amongst the bags and dust of the Grand' Chambre, with more reputation for integrity than capacity," was an exceedingly obstinate old fellow, whose imperturbable opposi-

Arrest of Blancmesnil and Broussel.

155

tion and blind obstruction in connection with the financial edicts had made him the popular idol. While Comminges, a lieutenant of the Guard, was preparing to remove him in a closed coach, his servant-maid, leaning out of the window, roused the neighbourhood. Instantly a crowd collected, and the coach startéd on its way amidst a storm of hostile cries : then the news spread like wildfire all over Paris : soon the shops were shut noisily : chains were stretched across the streets as though darkness had already fallen : the rusty old weapons of the League began to reappear : within a few hours the city was barricaded right up to the Palais-Royal. . . . In those days, and even under Louis-Philippe, a few paving-stones and two or three hogsheads filled with earth and horse-dung sufficed to block up many of the old Paris streets very thoroughly : when Baron Haussmann widened the city highways he did the rioters a very bad turn. At the Palais-Royal, in spite of it all, the Court had not as yet taken alarm. M. le Cardinal kept a cheerful countenance. The Duc d'Orléans went on whistling with his hands in his pockets, as was his wont. To amuse the Queen, the courtiers took off old Broussel's " nurse " at her window. Anne herself seemed as calm and placid as usual : but when Gondi, the Archbishop's Coadjutor, whose hatred of the Court had won him huge popularity, waited upon her, and hypocritically advised her to give in, she suddenly lost all patience. " ' I know what you mean, M. le Coadjuteur ! ' she cried, and her voice grew shrill with anger, ' you would have me set Broussel at liberty : I would rather strangle him with these two hands ! ' And as she spoke the last syllable she almost struck me in the face with them, and added : ' and those who . . .' The Cardinal, convinced that she was on the point of saying everything to me that fury could inspire, came forward and whispered something in her ear. She composed herself, and that to such an extent that if I had not known her so well I should have thought her very much appeased. . . ."

But the next day the populace began firing on the Guard. Very early in the morning the Parliament met in solemn **Popular** assembly, and while a great crowd in the Grand' **risings.** Salle sent up shouts of " Broussel ! Broussel ! " the Councillors decided to go in a body to the Palais-Royal and demand the prisoners' release.   They were very badly received : the Queen, in a furious rage, slammed the door of her chamber in their faces : but the Cardinal, to console them, assured them in the most civil fashion that Broussel and Blancmesnil would be set free at once if Parliament would undertake to discontinue its seditious meetings.   Whereupon the Councillors resolved to go back to the Palais de Justice and there discuss the matter.

But seeing them issue forth without the prisoners, the crowd assembled in the square hooted them.   When the red-robed procession reached the barricade of the Croix-du-Trahoir, at the corner of the Rue Saint-Honoré and the Rue de l'Arbre-Sec, it was obliged to halt :   a cookshop-keeper's apprentice marched straight down upon Molé, the First President, caught him resolutely by his flowing white beard, and ordered him to go back and fetch Broussel.   In face of this pressing danger the President was as bold as the antique senators whose courage he no doubt panted to emulate :   but all the same, the Councillors, sorely frightened, were fain to retrace their steps.   Back they went to the Palais-Royal, where, after some pretence of a discussion, they agreed to the Cardinal's conditions, and the Queen granted the prisoners their freedom.   But it was not till the morrow, and after the populace had seen Broussel return to his own house, that the barricades disappeared.

Now while the good man was being borne in triumph to Notre-Dame, Mazarin was writing as follows in his notebook : " Parliament has performed the functions of the King, and the populace has completely complied with its will :   it has given Broussel to the King as his partner :   it has used imprudent language touching the Queen and myself " :   all of which things the Prime Minister regarded, very justly, as intolerable.   And for this reason, on September 13, 1648, the little King made his surreptitious exit from Paris and was joined by the Queen at Rueil the same day.   Mazarin's intention had been to collect troops at that place, and then administer exemplary chastisement to " those knaves."   But Gaston, as usual, was horribly frightened.   And as for that incoherent being Condé, so clear-sighted and resolute in war, but half-crazed with pride in civil life, he certainly thought the boldness of " those devils of square caps " an insult to the crown, but at the same time he kept telling everybody that he loathed that "rogue of a Sicilian." And so the two parties came to a compromise. The Queen, with rage in her heart, signed a sort of "charter" in twenty-four articles, which gave satisfaction to the Parliament. And the Court returned to Paris.

Mazarin had not abandoned his original idea. He was firmly resolved to violate the Rueil understanding the moment he could find means to do so. For this purpose he issued secret orders for the advance of the Army of Flanders nearer Paris : and that done, set himself to win over Condé, whom he took to be the only good general in the country. Wily fellow ! His notebooks show that he desired Anne to make public complaints of himself, to blame his mildness and weakness, and say to M. le Prince, with a sham air of resignation, "that if men, even M. le Cardinal, should fail her, God would help her ! " Anne followed these instructions, as other documents prove, to the letter : and the proud Condé's vanity was exquisitely tickled. . . . Two months after the Court had returned to Paris (at the end of December), the troops began to collect round the city, Monsieur had been won over, M. le Prince was conquered, and Mazarin felt it was time for him to act.

On the evening of January 5, the eve of Twelfth-Night, Anne seemed, to all her circle, as calm and placid as was her **Removal of** wont. To amuse the little King she shared a **the Court to** Twelfth-Night cake with him and two or three of **Versailles.** her ladies, found the bean herself, and shortly afterwards retired to rest. But at three o'clock in the morning she left her bed, had the child-King and his little brother dressed, took them with her down a secret staircase, passed out of the gardens by a side door, entered a coach that stood waiting for her, and departed to the Cours-la-Reine, there to await the Cardinal and the Princes-: her only attendants were her principal waiting-woman and three officers of the Guard. Gaston, Condé, and Mazarin had supped and spent the evening with the Maréchal de Grammont : when they left his house they proceeded to the Cours-la-Reine to join the Queen. Meanwhile lackeys were running hither and thither all over the town, to warn the most important persons of the Court ; these, in their turn, informed their own friends ; and thus a whole caravan of coaches, laden with sleepy gentlemen and ladies, set forth and jolted along in the thick darkness, behind that in which the Queen was seated. She halted at Saint-Germain-en-Laye. The only furniture the palace boasted consisted of a few camp beds. On these the King, the Queen, and the Princes lay down : the courtiers slept where and how they could, on mattresses, on straw, or on the hard floors.

When Paris woke up on January 6, the population learnt with astonishment that the Court had fled. But the first moment of consternation once past, it put a good face on the matter. Parliament decreed the impeachment of Mazarin, ordered " all burghers and heads of families " to take up arms, and published an exceedingly insolent edict forbidding soldiers or people connected with the business of war to come within twenty leagues of the capital. All this, of course, was done in the King's name, for the constant anxiety of the supporters of the Fronde—so strong was the worship of monarchy in the hearts of that period—was clearly to establish the fact that they only rebelled against Mazarin the better to serve the King : *Querimus regem nostrum* was one of the legends on the flags carried by the Paris burghers, and the Parliament wrote : " Your preservation, Sire, and that of the Kingdom, are the sole cause of our prohibition, and the motive of our decree ordering Paris to take up arms."

Thus began this burlesque warfare, in which the amount of gunpowder used by the warriors was far exceeded by the quantities of ink and paper consumed by the lampooners. Condé was quite unable to blockade Paris with his 5000 or 6000 men : he held the chief strategic points, and did his best to starve out the city by occupying the Gonesse bakeries, for instance, and the cattle markets at Poissy. The Parisians began by taking a huge delight in playing at soldiers. But, if the truth must be told, they had little taste for downright fighting. For the burgher, we are told,

> . . . est prudent et craint la touche,
> Outre qu'il n'aime la cartouche. . . .

Yet leaders there were in plenty. Mme. de Longueville, sister to M. le Prince, had refused to flee with the Court, having sworn an oath to play a noble part in the Paris revolt. This indolent beauty, who looked "like an angel," with her pink and white skin, pale golden hair and eyes of turquoise blue, dreamt of a life of perils, like Mme. de Chevreuse, like Mademoiselle, like the Princess Palatine, and many another lady of her generation. She would pass from fits of languor to "awakenings that were luminous and surprising." She, too, was romantic, and of the stuff whereof Corneille's heroines were made : she cared for her "glory." She longed to be like the heroines of whom she had read : and, as she said, "I do not care for innocent pleasures. . . ."

And Mme. de Longueville was not the Parisians' only refuge : they had Condé's own brother, Conti : they had Mme. de Bouillon : they had the Coadjutor, they had all the men of noble birth who came hurrying up from Saint-Germain, day after day, to put themselves at their head, after the example of La Rochefoucauld, Elbeuf, and Beaufort. . . . But all these gentlemen, whose profession was bravery, tried to lead the city troops into undertakings against the enemy which the said troops took to be imprudences of the most culpable kind, so much so that the officers of the city militia were obliged to point out, at last, "that the Colonels and Captains of Paris had not been appointed for the purpose of exposing themselves and the burghers of the said town to sorties in which they might very well risk their lives." And further, all these high-born gentlemen expected to be worthily entertained, together with their attendants and their soldiers—a most ruinous proceeding. In addition to all this, the behaviour of the populace was beginning to cause alarm : it fancied it saw "Mazarins" in every corner, and had begun a series of domiciliary visits, after which the persons visited very seldom found their silver intact. . . . All these things put the burghers so out of conceit with heroism that when the Archduke Leopold sent an agent to offer the Parliament an alliance with Spain, a great many people perceived that to support the foreigner against the French Government would really be a preposterous manner of serving the King. One man of courage, Molé, the First President, braved the rage of the demagogues, and took upon himself

The "Fron-deuses."

The Peace of Rueil, 1649.

to open negotiations with the Court : this brought about the Peace of Rueil (March 30, 1649). Neither Parliament nor city lost anything by this agreement, and the rebellious nobles gained various favours : the lesson was not lost on the rest.

The Court returned to Paris amidst the most extraordinary enthusiasm (August 18, 1649). A great ball was given at the Hôtel de Ville. Mazarin himself was much applauded. . . . And after that the Fronde grew stronger than ever in Paris. Condé, especially, literally drunk with vanity and surrounded by a band of young coxcombs as insolent as himself, became unendurable, now that he had saved the Court. And indeed he gave offence to everybody—to the Parliament by his incredibly rude speeches, to the Cardinal by the extraordinary scorn with which he treated him, to the Queen by his clumsy attempt to foist on her as an admirer one of his friends, a good-looking fop of the name of Jarzé, : so that the cunning Mazarin soon succeeded in forming a coalition against him : on January 18, 1650, Condé, his brother Conti, and his brother-in-law Longueville were all arrested, without a word of protest from anybody. The ladies still remained : the Dowager Princess of Condé, the Princess her daughter-in-law, and the Duchesse de Longueville : they managed to raise a revolt in Bordeaux. But a royal army soon appeared on the scene : October had come, and the Bordelais were beginning to think about their vintage : the Cardinal offered them very easy terms, and they capitulated.

Meanwhile, a small Spanish army commanded by Turenne, who had not accepted the Peace of Rueil, was advancing by the north, and its scouts were already threatening Vincennes. But it was completely defeated at Rethel (December 15, 1650). . . . Thus Mazarin's triumph seemed assured : but he had been guilty of an unpardonable fault : that of not keeping the promises with which he had bought the Coadjutor's support.

Yet this Paul de Gondi, future Cardinal de Retz, was a man he should have humoured. Though his appearance was against
Paul de Gondi, him—he was small, swarthy, badly built, short-
Cardinal de sighted, and extraordinarily clumsy in his move-
Retz. ments—his real character did not answer to his face. We shall never know whether he possessed true genius or not—for it is not prudent to credit statesmen with this

till they have turned it to account—but at all events he gave many signs of it. Brave, adventurous, violent, caring for nothing but women and sword-play, the last man in the world, in fact, to be a priest, the necessity of keeping the Archbishopric of Paris in his family had forced him, like Richelieu, into the Church : the step had cost him much pain, but once he had made up his mind to it, his whole ambition was fixed on the great prospect it had opened to him, that of becoming chief minister in Mazarin's place. To this end he struggled, all through the Fronde, with astonishing skill, vigour, and unscrupulousness, displaying every quality needful in a party leader— eloquence, courage, tact, knowledge of men, quickness in seizing opportunities. . . . But great politicians, like great generals, cannot win the day unless fortune is on their side ; events turned out badly for Retz, and the accession of Louis XIV to power was to deal a terrible blow to his hopes. Then, like the gamester who knows how to lose, we see him show a smiling countenance ; he becomes a cultured man, much addicted to belles-lettres, and never giving a thought to politics. Only now and then, in the Conclave, he will use all his talent in the service of France—the King might perhaps remark him, employ him ? . . . But once thoroughly convinced that Louis XIV will never, on any pretext whatsoever, call the Frondeur of other days to his councils, he forthwith humbly resigns his honours as a Prince of the Church, and sets himself to be, at all events, a holy man—that being the only noble part left him to play. . . . Thus Retz, in every circumstance of his existence, remembered his future biographers and lived with a view to the verdict of posterity. He was a true specimen of the kind of character dear to Corneille. " His whole life, from one end of it to the other, was ruled by his will. His immorality was sublime, and his greatness of soul never failed him " (Lanson).

To drive so cunning a personage to extremes was a grave piece of imprudence. Within a very short time Gondi had contrived to set everybody against the Cardinal. Monsieur himself, under his skilful guidance, broke with the Court, and made up his differences with Condé ; he had been promised that once Mazarin was dismissed he himself should be placed at the head of the Council. One of his daughters was to marry

Condé's son, the Duc d'Enghien : Conti was to marry Mlle. de Chevreuse : the Coadjutor was to have a Cardinal's hat, and so forth. The ladies had thrown themselves joyously into the plot : the Princess Palatine, Anne de Gonzague, Mme. de Chevreuse, Mme. de Montbazon, the whole bevy of voluptuous dames were rapturously engaged in making mischief. . . . Already Gondi was stirring up his parish priests, and Beaufort was talking to the market-women of the Halles in the language they best understood. . . . Mazarin finally believed his life to be in danger, and slipped away secretly (February 6, 1651). Anne and her son, closely watched by the populace, which suspected their intentions, were unable to join him. He hoped for help from the imprisoned princes, and went himself to Le Havre to release them : but we are told that when he bowed low—very low indeed—before M. le Prince's coach, a disagreeable burst of laughter was heard to issue from the vehicle. Nothing was left him save to get across the frontier : and this he did.

Condé hurried up to Paris, where he succeeded in completely ruining things for the Fronde. The Queen, to whom Mazarin, from his retreat at Bruhl, constantly sent the wisest counsels mingled with passionate protestations of his own feelings for her, flattered him most skilfully, and this made him lose his head completely. In less than no time M. le Prince had contrived to give mortal offence to Monsieur, the Coadjutor, Beaufort, the Parliament, and Mme. de Chevreuse, and make them all band themselves together against him. Then he left **Majority of** Paris and departed to his own government of **Louis XIV.** Guyenne, where he raised a rebellion. Meanwhile (September 7, 1651) the majority of Louis XIV was declared : resistance no longer meant opposing the Regent " for the good of the King," it meant flat rebellion. This excellent pretext permitted Condé's last remaining allies to forsake him.

Thereupon Mazarin re-entered France at the head of a small army which wore his colours—a green scarf (December, 1651). He had feared, no doubt, that mischief might be made about him with the Queen, or even worse things yet—and this the most charming gentlemen about the Court were doing their best to achieve. But his inopportune return stirred up the Fronde, which had been dying of sheer inanition. The moment his reappearance was known, in fact, the Parliament set a price on his head (and sold his splendid library of books). But —a most miraculous happening—Monsieur did a decisive thing ; he opened negotiations with Condé (January, 1652), who had already come to an arrangement with Spain. In the end, two or three armies took the field at once : that of the Princes, that of Mazarin, and that of the King and Queen, which was under the command of Turenne, who had joined the Court party in consideration of a liberal reward.

The Grande Mademoiselle threw herself into Orleans, an apanage of her father's : there she took, or fancied she took, **Adventures of** command of the troops : the officers praised her **the Grande** sagacity in military matters. . . . These were the **Mademoiselle.** happiest days she ever knew. But indeed the King's troops made no attempt to enter Orleans. Condé surprised D'Hocquincourt's headquarters at Bleneau, but Turenne saved the situation (April, 1652): then he placed the army of the princes (which Condé had left, hurrying off to Paris) in a most critical position. He was unfortunately obliged, just at this moment, to move against the Duc de Lorraine, who had hired himself and his troops to Spain, and the princes' forces slipped away. He did not find them again till he met them under the walls of Paris, commanded, once more, by the victor of Rocroy.

The Parisians energetically refused to allow any troops, whether friendly or otherwise, to enter their walls. And when, on July 1, Condé's forces, which had been driven out of Saint-Cloud, arrived by the Cours-la-Reine on what is now called the Place de la Concorde, they found the " Gate of the Conference " closed in their faces. The little army was fain to make a *détour* round the town and so reach Charenton : all night long it marched along what we now call the Grands Boulevards. But at six o'clock on the morning of July 2 it was met and attacked, in the Faubourg Saint-Antoine, by the King's troops, which came down from Belleville. Condé was driven back against the wall and the Porte Saint-Antoine, which was still shut against him, and guarded by the militia of his friends the Parisians, who stood to their guns with matches ready lighted. The ramparts were crowded with spectators : Mazarin himself watched the fray from the heights of Charonne. After a fight that lasted six hours, and prodigious deeds of valour accomplished by the Prince, the troops of the Fronde seemed on the point of being finally crushed against the wall, and Turenne was just about to call on his men for a final effort, when, all of a sudden, the drawbridge was lowered, the gates opened wide, and the fugitives were seen disappearing into the town, while a puff of white smoke rose over the Bastille. The Grande Mademoiselle had persuaded the Parisians to open the gate, and had then caused the King's soldiers to be fired on. Turenne stopped short: Condé was saved.

At that moment Paris was in a state of utter anarchy. Authority over the city was in the hands of Monsieur, who had **Anarchy in Paris.** assumed the title of Lieutenant-General of the Kingdom: but whenever he was asked for an order, Gaston took to his bed and swore he was dying. Each of the leaders, consequently, had rioters of his own, in his own pay. The populace, at a loss to know in whom it was to believe, stopped any passing burgher, and made him shout "Death to the Mazarins"—which was far from pleasant. . . . When Condé and Gaston entered the assembly specially elected to govern the town (July 4, 1652), they found the chief subject of discussion was the possibility of coming to some arrangement with the Court. They left the meeting. The Place de Grève was black with people. All at once shots were fired in the midst of the crowd: this was the work of hired agents placed there by Condé, who had fired on the city archers. The archers returned the fire, and forthwith the populace rushed upon the Hôtel de Ville, burned down one of the doors, made its way in, sacked the whole building, and murdered five deputies who had not been able to get away. This riot was **The "Straw Sedition."** called the "Straw Sedition," because everybody, from the Princes to the meanest counter-jumper, had adopted, for the day, the badge worn by Condé's men at the fight before the Porte Saint-Antoine—a wisp of straw stuck into their hats.

> Si sans paille on voyait un homme,
> Chacun crioit : Que l'on l'assomme,
> Car c'est un chien de Mazarin !

However, within a month half the hats in Paris were adorned with paper, which was the royalist emblem.

The Princes, and Retz, who had calmed down considerably having at last attained the purple, were all making terms for **End of the** themselves. So ill-guarded were the gates of Paris **Fronde.** that Turenne was thinking of taking the city by surprise and sending in troops to support " the gentlemen who wear paper." There was no necessity for this : Mazarin having been so obliging as to take himself into exile in August, 1652, the King returned to his good town of Paris two months later (October 11). Four months after this, again, Mazarin himself returned, and was loudly acclaimed (February 6, 1653). Save at Bordeaux, where it was kept up by the Dowager Princesse de Condé, by Conti, and by Mme. de Longueville, the Fronde was dead. At Bordeaux, too, it was killed, as it had been killed in Paris, by popular excesses : and in August, 1653, the advent of the King's troops was enthusiastically welcomed by the Bordelais.

A certain amount of chastisement was meted out to the great nobles. Monsieur, who had fled to Blois, easily secured his pardon on condition that he should betray his friends (which he did very willingly) : Mademoiselle, the artless virago who had dreamt of winning the hand of Louis XIV at the point of the sword, was sent in disgrace to a splendid country-house : Retz was imprisoned at Vincennes, first of all, and then at Nantes, whence he escaped : Beaufort, La Rochefoucauld, and their fellows were exiled to a certain distance from Paris for a time. As for the Parliament, it was discussing some later edicts of the King's, one day (April 13, 1655), when the monarch, in his red jerkin and grey hat, suddenly appeared in its midst ; he did not say, " I am the State," but with his own lips, and without the intervention of his Chancellor, he forbade the continuance of the discussion. This prohibition produced no effect, indeed, till the members had been bought over one after the other—all, at least, who were worth buying. When this was accomplished, everybody was pacified—save Condé.

THE FRONDE AND MAZARIN

IV

Condé had left Paris a few days before the King's return, and joined the Spanish army : but there his pride clashed with the arrogance of Archduke Leopold and the haughtiness of Fuensaldaña. Repulsed in Champagne in 1652, and held in check by Turenne on the Somme in 1653, he was solemnly declared guilty of high treason and treachery to his country, and condemned to death by default on January 19, 1654. Then **Alliance with** the war was carried on in somewhat desultory **England, 1657.** fashion till Mazarin succeeded in persuading Cromwell, the ruler of England, to become his ally. The Protector exacted a considerable price for the support he gave ; Turenne, after effecting a junction with the English troops, 6000 in number, took Mardick, and then proceeded to lay siege to Dunkirk, while the British fleet blockaded the town from the sea. In vain did the Spanish army, commanded by Don John of Austria (son of Philip IV by an actress), and led, under that prince's orders, by Condé, endeavour to succour the besieged town : it suffered a complete defeat at the Dunes, in June, 1657. This glorious victory was announced to his wife by Turenne, who was not given to eloquence, in the following letter :

" The enemy came upon us. They have been beaten. God be praised ! I have worked rather hard all day : I bid you good night, and am going to bed." *

Spain, worn out, was forced to sue for peace. The chief condition Mazarin imposed was the marriage of Louis XIV **Peace with** with Philip IV's eldest daughter, the Infanta Maria-**Spain.** Theresa. To this Philip objected, for so far he only had two sons, puny and sickly boys, and nobody expected them to live. As the succession of females in default of male heirs to the throne was a fundamental law of Spain, the poor King was disinclined to give his brother of France, who was his traditional rival, any hope of ultimately wearing his crown. To overcome his hesitation Mazarin arranged a very entertaining comedy.

* This is the text as Ramsay gives it ; Grimoard has another version.

Louis XIV was at that moment a healthy young fellow of twenty. He had already been in love, and each time "for his **First loves of** whole life," with Olympia Mancini, one of the **Louis XIV.** Minister's own nieces, in the first place, with Mlle. de La Motte-Argencourt, and, at the time of which we are now writing, with yet another of Mazarin's nieces, the skinny Maria Mancini, his adoration for whom was likewise to last for ever : all this made it evident that it was high time for him to be married. So the Cardinal arranged an interview, with a view to matrimony, between the young King and the daughter of Christina of Savoy. The King had "always said he must have a wife who was beautiful," and Princess Maria of Savoy was far from lovely ; but Louis was of the age of Cherubin : he at once discovered that his future wife was "very pleasant-looking," "well made," and only "a little swarthy." And Christina, on the faith of his declarations, already saw her daughter Queen of France, when she heard of the hurried arrival of an envoy from Spain; he had been sent to promise Louis XIV the Infanta's hand in his sovereign's name. The Cardinal's cunning little comedy had ended as he had foreseen.

Nothing now remained except to conclude peace. The two plenipotentiaries, Mazarin and Don Luis de Haro, met at the frontier, on a little island in the Bidassoa. A whole month was spent over the settlement of the problems in etiquette and precedence arising out of the meeting : four more elapsed before the treaty was finally arranged. "The Cardinal's policy depended on his subtlety, that of Don Luis was founded on delay. The last named would never say a word, those spoken by the first were always ambiguous. The genius of the Italian Minister lay in his attempt to take others unawares, that of the Spaniard in the way in which he defended himself against surprises. We are told that he said of the Cardinal : "He has one great political fault, he is always trying to deceive" (Voltaire). On the whole, the treaty reflected great credit on Don Luis de Haro : according to its provisions, France forsook her ally, the King of Portugal, restored the greater number of the fortified towns she had taken in the Franche-Comté and the Low Countries—Ypres, Oudenarde, and so forth—and pardoned Condé : in return she acquired definite possession of Roussillon and the Cerdagne, the whole of Artois except the towns of Aire and Saint-Omer, and a series of northern towns which provided her with a solid girdle of defence in that quarter : further, the Duke of Lorraine, who had been the paid soldier of Spain, only recovered his Duchy on condition that he ceded a great slice of it to France : and finally Louis XIV was to marry the Infanta, who renounced all her rights to the Spanish throne in consideration of the dowry of 500,000 gold crowns which her father was to give her. Philip IV was utterly unable to find such a sum. Did Mazarin, who could not have been ignorant of this fact, say to himself that the day would surely come when either the Queen of France or her children would have a right to the throne of Spain ? Perhaps so, and if so, **Treaty of the** events were to prove he was right. . . . In any **Pyrenees, 1658.** case, when this Treaty of the Pyrenees was signed, and the Cardinal had succeeded in placing the Rhenish League under the protection of France (1658), Louis XIV found himself master everywhere. Mazarin had completed what Richelieu had begun, and proved himself a great diplomatist.

Within the kingdom he was a greater figure at that time than his predecessor had been, and even greater, in a way, than **Magnificence** the King himself. He lived splendidly in Paris, **of Mazarin.** in his magnificent palace (standing almost on the site of the present Bibliothèque Nationale), which was filled with works of art and rare books, and protected by guards and musketeers who wore his livery. " The Councils were held in his chamber while he was being shaved or dressed, and often he would play with his bird or his pet monkey while people were talking business to him. He never asked any one to be seated in his chamber—not even the Chancellor or the Maréchal de Villeroy." His fortune was enormous, much larger than Richelieu's : it amounted to at least 200 millions of modern French money, and he never ceased adding to it, not out of avarice—for he was fond of showing off his splendour, as on the day when he spent a million on a lottery for his friends—but, like many another man, less because he loved money than because he delighted in the art of making it. Assisted by a most crafty man of business, named Colbert, " poor M. le Cardinal " lent the King money for short periods and at heavy

169

interest, sold the Crown offices for his own benefit, received, on various pretexts, sums of money intended for the use of the army and navy, and exacted from all and sundry payments too considerable to be called gratuities, to which the more high-sounding title of " commissions " must be applied.

He was on excellent terms with the King. La Porte has asserted that he allowed the monarch, as a child, to sleep in sheets that were full of holes, and grow quite out of clothes that were too short for him, and it would appear that at a later period he did not fail to economize on the expenses of the young man's establishment as far as he could contrive to do so without causing a scandal. Nevertheless, he seems to have had a sincere affection for the handsome, manly, thoughtful youth. As we have already related, Louis XIV fell **Maria Mancini.** in love, in 1658, with the Cardinal's niece Maria Mancini, a tall girl of seventeen, thin, dark-haired, violent, witty—" a contradictory and passionate spirit " the Cardinal himself said of her—who had set her mind on making him marry her, and very nearly succeeded in doing so. The Cardinal made a most heroic resistance to the plan : he packed off his unmanageable niece to Brouage. When the moment of parting came, Louis wept hot tears, and his lady-love said to him fiercely : " Sire, you are the King, you love me, and yet you let me go ! "—a celebrated sentence, which Racine was to reproduce later, in a less trenchant form, in his *Bérénice* :

Vous êtes empereur, Seigneur, et vous pleurez !

Why did the Cardinal refuse to permit his niece to mount the throne ? Like all the men of his time, he had the strongest feeling for his own family : in proof of this it may be pointed out that his nephew, Filippo Mancini, was made Duc de Nevers, one of his nieces, who died in 1637, was Duchesse de Mercœur, and therefore granddaughter by marriage to Henri IV ; another was married to Conti, and consequently a Princess of the blood-royal ; a third was Duchesse de Bouillon ; a fourth the wife of Eugène of Savoy, Comte de Soissons ; a fifth Duchess regnant of Modena ; Hortense, indeed, married a mere Marshal of France (De la Meilleraie), but even he was promoted to be Duc de Mazarin. Might not Maria Mancini, sister and cousin of

so many princesses, have aspired to be Queen of France ? . . .
But Anne of Austria was already drawing up formal protests
against the marriage : and then Mazarin did not like Maria : and
he did, besides, feel a most passionate interest in his own political
work : no doubt he would not permit the failure of the Spanish
marriage, his crowning achievement.

However this may have been, when he had made the final
sacrifice to virtue involved in his renunciation of any attempt
to place his own kinswoman on the throne, he felt he had done
enough, and from that time forth all his attention was devoted
to preventing any possibility of the fortune he had amassed
being confiscated after his death.   On March 3, 1661, he craftily
made over everything he possessed to Louis XIV.   Alas !
for three whole days the young King hesitated as to whether
he should accept so magnificent a gift, and Mazarin lived in an
anguish of apprehension.   At last, on March 6, Louis returned
Death of   the document embodying the donation, and gave
Mazarin, 1661. his Minister authority to dispose as he thought
fit of the riches enumerated in it.   After this fashion " M. le
Cardinal " quieted his own conscience, and ensured the inheritance of his wealth to his family.   To console Hortense for being
no more than a duchess, he gave her thirty millions.   The others
contented themselves with what was left.   As for the King, he
received a great deal of wise counsel—especially he was advised
never to take another Prime Minister.   And all this being completed, the Cardinal made a good end : on March 9, 1661, he died
in the odour of piety, fortified by the rites of the Church, and with
the name of Jesus on his lips.

WORKS TO CONSULT : See henceforth *passim*, M. E. Lavisse's fine
history ; vols. vii, 1, 2, and viii, 1, deal with the reign of Louis XIV. See
also, in addition to works already quoted : A. Barine, *Louis XIV et la
Grande Mademoiselle* (1905) ; *Princesses et grandes Dames* (1909) ; Chéruel,
Histoire de France pendant la minorité de Louis XIV (1879–80) ; *Histoire
de France pendant le Ministère de Mazarin* (1883) ; Funck-Brentano and P.
d'Estrée, *Les Nouvellistes* (1905) ; G. Lacour-Gayet, *L'éducation politique
de Louis XIV* (1898) ; J. Lair, *Nicolas Fouquet* (1890) ; Normand, *La
bourgeoisie française au XVIIème Siècle* (1908) ; L. Pérey, *Le Roman du
Grand Roi* (1894) ; J. Roy, *Turenne* (1884) ; A. Renée, *Les nièces de
Mazarin* (1858) ; Rod. Reuss, *L'Alsace au XVIIème Siècle* (1897) ; Val-
frey, *Hugues de Lionne* (1881) ; Voltaire, *Le Siècle de Louis XIV* (1893).

CHAPTER VII

THE " ROI-SOLEIL "

I. The King.   II. The Court before the advent of Mme. de Maintenon.   III. Court life.

I

FOR several days Anne of Austria, Louis XIV, and his nurse had been spending their nights at the Castle of Vincennes, in a room next to that in which Mazarin lay dying. On the morning of March 9, 1661, the King called his nurse, and asked her in a whisper, so as not to wake the **Louis XIV** Queen, if the Cardinal were dead. When he knew **asserts his** this to be the case, he dressed himself, summoned **power.** the ministers, and forbade them to do any business whatsoever—even to grant a passport—without having taken his orders. When Monseigneur de Rouen said to him, on the following day : " Sire, I have the honour of presiding over the Assembly of the Clergy of your kingdom : Your Majesty ordered me to address myself in all business matters to M. le Cardinal : to whom does Your Majesty now desire me to apply ? " " To myself, Monsieur l'Archevêque," replied the King.

There was universal stupefaction at Court. When her son's words were reported to the Queen, she could not help laughing. But Louis had begun to work six and seven hours a day at his kingly duties ; fifty-four years later he was working harder still.

His Memoirs tell us that he had long been making himself ready against the day when the Cardinal's death should leave him sole master. That day he at " once desired and feared " : this was apparently because " though he had been brought up in ignorance, his innate good sense had made him timid " (Voltaire). He has himself set forth, in very noble words, the
172

emotions he experienced after he had publicly declared his intention of governing alone :

> I felt my heart and my courage rise up within me, as it were ; I found I was quite different, I discovered that within me of which I had been unaware, and I reproached myself, with joy, for having been so long unconscious of it. This first timidity, which judgment always brings with it, and which distressed me—more especially when I had to speak at some length and in public—vanished in a very short time. Then I really seemed to myself to be a king, and born to be one. I experienced a delight, in fact, which it is difficult to express. . . .

His education had been very much neglected. As a little child, his governesses had generally left him to the care of **Youthful** their waiting-women. In those days the great **training of** King was a fair-haired little boy, much addicted **Louis XIV.** to the pleasures of his age. " He ate everything he could lay hands on," Mme. de Maintenon indignantly reports, " and no one cared what might disagree with his health : it was this which gave him the habit of being so severe with himself. If anybody cooked an omelet, he always contrived to get hold of some scraps, which Monsieur, his brother, and he went and ate in a corner. He would sometimes relate that most of his time was spent with a little girl, the daughter of a woman who waited on the Queen's waiting-women : he called her Queen Marie, because they used to play together at being grown-up people " . . . Later on, the child did not learn very much : nobody in those days imagined that knowledge was indispensable to a prince. The only item as to which Queen Anne was strict with him was that of his religious duties. The chief object of M. de Villeroy, his Governor, was to secure the affections of a pupil who was soon to become his master, and he thought it useless, for this purpose, to force the youthful Louis to apply himself to studies for which he had no taste. As for Mazarin, who had caused himself to be invested with the title of Superintendent of the King's education, he derided La Porte, the King's valet, who displayed his zeal by reading Mézeray's history to his young master at night " to put him to sleep " (for which purpose the means may not have been ill-chosen). For Mazarin, a practical man, held the teaching of things to be far more precious than the teaching of books : he preferred talking to the boy, and instilling, in familiar converse, mistrust of men : it may well be that Louis XIV owed his prudence, and that famous saying of his, " I will see," to the counsels of his earliest instructor. In spite of which his real knowledge, in 1661, was of the scantiest description, and he was himself so well aware of this that he resolved to put himself to school once more. This is one of the noblest passages in his life : the young King, just three and twenty, intoxicated with the delights of reigning, went back to his studies like any child. . . . As a matter of fact, he never knew any foreign language really well, except Italian ; Maria Mancini may have taught him that.

The King was exceedingly handsome. Tall and strong, masculine in stature, and in face elegant, " the figure of a hero," **Appearance of** with firm well-rounded cheeks about which **Louis XIV.** his magnificent chestnut hair fell in soft waves— it was not till 1673 that he could make up his mind to hide it under a wig, and this was made with holes in it, to give passage to the locks he refused to have cut off—a large nobly shaped nose, and a scornful mouth : dark eyes that shot intimidating glances : " his whole person so impregnated with the most imposing majesty that it revealed itself alike in his slightest gestures and his most ordinary actions, without any appearance of pride, but with an air of grave simplicity " : " a voice the sound of which agreed with all the rest : a great deal of reserve : a politeness that was always grave, always majestic, always distinguished, and suitable to age, station, and sex, and, towards women, an air of natural gallantry " : " his figure, his bearing, the charm, the beauty, and the noble aspect which succeeded that beauty," the air of splendour and authority, in short, diffused over his whole person, marked him out, in the midst of his Court, " as the king-bee " (Saint-Simon and Primi), and made him, in his subjects' eyes, the most perfect King of France they could have imagined.

In his youth Louis was an accomplished dancer, and a still better shot ; even at seventy he was a perfect horseman, and **His physique.** drove his own chaise and four, at full speed, on every hunting day. He had an iron constitution. More than once, in the course of the year 1661, he travelled forty leagues in a day, to see Mlle. de La Vallière. In 1662 the Grande Mademoiselle fell ill from sheer fatigue after dancing the ballet entitled *Hercule amoureux* in his company. And the incessant festivities of the period, the jousts, and hunting parties, and love-making, never prevented him from working all the rest of the day. His appetite was gigantic : " So hugely and so solidly did he eat, at night and in the morning, and so regularly, too, that nobody could grow accustomed to the sight " (Saint-Simon). " I have often seen the King eat four full plates of soup of various kinds, a whole pheasant, a partridge, a great plate of salad, two large slices of ham, mutton dressed with gravy and garlic, a dish of pastry, and after all that, fruit and hard-boiled eggs," says his sister-in-law. And when the doctors made a post-mortem examination of the old King's body, " what especially astonished them was his stomach and bowels, on account of their size and length—twice as long as the ordinary—which explained his being so large and regular an eater " (Saint-Simon). It is not astonishing, after such a regimen, that the King should have suffered at an early age from gout, from gravel soon after, and all his life long from sensations of heaviness, and vapours, and fits of giddiness, for which his physicians, —those depicted by Molière—treated him in the manner familiar to us. He had smallpox in 1647, and scarlet fever in 1658 : in 1663 he had measles, and for the space of four and twenty hours was in some danger ; in 1686 he suffered from that " troublesome fistula " the operation for which he endured with a courage that transported his whole Court with admiration. And, indeed, his splendid endurance never failed. " No fatigue, no ill-treatment by the weather, was too much for him, nor made any impression on that heroic countenance : under rain, snow, cold, sweat, or covered with dust, he was always the same." And, as his own "robust and splendidly formed body " easily endured all things, he insisted that those of others should do likewise. Great ladies—kinswomen, daughters, or favourites— had always, whether well or ill, " to appear in full dress (with bare shoulders and uncovered heads), fully adorned and laced into their stays, and go to Flanders or even farther, dance, sit up late, join in every merrymaking, eat, be gay and pleasant company, go hither and thither, never look afraid or uncomfortable because of the cold or the wind or the dust, and all this exactly on the very days and at the very hours set forth, without failing by the space of one minute." For so the King would have it.

Too much stress can hardly be laid on the physical qualities of Louis XIV, because " the infinite graces and the imposing **His good** majesty of his incomparable countenance " did **manners.** more than can be told for the greatness of his reign. His politeness was at once a masterpiece in itself and a method of government. It was charming, it was also useful. Everybody knows that " he never passed the humblest woman without raising his hat, even to waiting-women, I say, and whom he knew to be such. . . . To ladies he lifted his hat right off his head, but from a greater or lesser distance : to men of title, he half lifted it, and held it up, or over his ear, for a few moments, more or less markedly : to gentlemen—who were really such— he contented himself with raising his hand to his hat. He took it off to the Princes of the Blood just as he did to ladies." His words, like his salutations, were measured, graduated according to the quality of the persons to whom they were addressed. He **His character.** spoke little, and gravely, saying what it was neces- sary to say, and to the person to whom it was proper to say it ; and, indeed, a word from him was an honour about which people talked. In short, " no man ever sold his words, his smiles, and his glances to better advantage." There is something admirable in it all : does any one realize the effort imposed on himself by this man whose whole existence was spent in public : who never, for a single moment, forgot he was the Great King, and played the part for which he had cast himself on the earthly stage without once weakening in the course of fifty-four years ? " Being in his chamber with some other courtiers," says Primi Visconti, " I remarked several times that if the door happened to open, or if he left the room, he at once composed himself in an attitude, and his face took on a different expression, just as if he were about to appear on the stage of a theatre : altogether, he knows how to play the king right well in every particular." Saint-Simon reckoned that in all his life he was only in a rage four or five times. " He had a bearing which was appropriate to himself and his rank only, and would have been ridiculous in any other man," says Voltaire. But in any case, and whatever might have happened, Louis XIV could never have been ridiculous : he certainly is the only man to whom the epithet of majestic may be applied with impunity. Majestic everything about him was, decent, noble, great, and at the same time very natural. His strength of will and force of character overawed every one : the merciless Saint-Simon, who hated him, himself acknowledges that "you had to accustom yourself to the sight of him if you did not wish to expose yourself to the danger of breaking down when you had to address a speech to him." More fully than any other man, Louis XIV possessed the art of being a king.

He was not highly intelligent, but he was judicious, thoughtful, hard-working, practical, master of himself; he possessed powers of discernment, dignity, gravity, strong common sense, and, in short, what he himself described as " a solid and active mind " : just the qualities useful to a monarch or a business man. So much good sense roused Boileau to a sort of enthusiasm : " this prince never speaks without having thought ; everything he says is admirably constructed "—and everything he writes, Boileau might have added, for Louis XIV's Memoirs and his letters are models of correctness and good taste, of lucid eloquence, and clear and straightforward expression. Added to all this, Louis was passionately devoted to his " calling as a king " ; to him it was " a great, noble, delightful " thing : he had a lively sense of the pleasure to be derived from informing oneself carefully as to a particular question, discovering all that was true and just and useful in it, and bringing it to a practical solution. Further, he was by nature kindly, gentle, and indulgent : when he granted an audience, " however prejudiced he might have been beforehand, he would listen with patience, kindness, with a desire for enlightenment and information, and would never interrupt, save to procure this ; he proved himself imbued with a spirit of equity and a desire to know the truth, and this though he was sometimes angry, and up to the very end of his life." To conclude, he knew how to appeal to men's hearts, and the way in which he granted his favours doubled their value : the tone in which his praises were delivered inspired those on whom he bestowed them with the blindest devotion, and when he blamed, he did not discourage the wrongdoer, but filled him with a longing to succeed better another time. Being, then, what he was, with his clear reason, his knowledge of men, his inherent dignity, his prudent tact, Louis XIV remains the perfect type of the finished gentleman, the *honnête homme* of the seventeenth century. He was not at all brilliant : Racine, who collected his *bons mots*, only found a bare half-dozen, and these by no means of the wittiest (but to console us, he quotes some delightful traits of his personal charm). "At every moment," says Sainte-Beuve, "he makes us feel the attraction there is in the exercise of good sense."

His somewhat moderate intellectual gifts were heightened by his nobility of character. Louis XIV had a very pure and **His intellect.** very beautiful ideal, embraced with passionate ardour and followed up with the most splendid energy : that of figuring in history as a "great king." Often, in his Memoirs, in which he puts forward his passion for "glory" as the moving principle of his conduct, he speaks of it in really touching terms : "I realized that the love of glory has the same sensitiveness, and I may even say timidity, as the most tender of all passions" : and elsewhere :

It is after this fashion, my son, that glory will have us love her. The ardour we feel for her is not one of those feeble passions that cool with possession. Her favours, which can never be obtained except with effort, never cause disgust, and he who can refrain from longing for fresh ones is unworthy of all those he has received.

But the idea of a great monarch, as it appeared to Louis XIV and to his contemporaries, bore but little resemblance to our **Louis XIV and** present conception of royalty. The King of **Divine Right.** France did not consider himself at all in the light of a sort of permanent functionary or hereditary steward, whose duty it is to administer the affairs of the nation to the best of his ability. He looked on himself as an owner, free to manage his patrimony—in other words, his kingdom—as he chose, an owner, in fine, whose own good sense, uncontrolled save by God Himself, led him to manage it wisely.

"Rome est à vous, Seigneur, l'empire est votre bien," says Maxime to Auguste, in *Cinna*. The bishops were, in a sense, the sovereign's chaplains, the officers of justice or finance were his police and his cashiers, the intendants were his business agents, the ministers and courtiers were "servants" of his "house," secretaries, or members of his Guard of Honour. . . . And a "great king," a "glorious" king, was simply, in his eyes, a king who enlarged the borders of his kingdom and made his rivals tremble—a warrior, a conqueror : wherefore he made war. No doubt he likewise strove, as far as he was able, to ensure his subjects equal justice and freedom from taxation, but that was not his first care, for in his eyes to sacrifice his "glory" to his subjects' happiness would have been "base." We may not share his opinions nowadays, but it would be a sovereign injustice to judge Louis XIV solely from our modern point of view.

Unfortunately this splendid and well-balanced nature had one weak point—vanity : and from the very beginning of his active reign Louis gave proof of this in various ways. The young man, so serious and resolute in 1661, began by degrees to lose his head : flattered by his courtiers like any sultan of *The Arabian Nights*, worshipped like a god by his subjects, favoured by fortune herself, intoxicated with adulation, the vainglorious Louis went a little mad with pride. It will be seen that the errors of his reign had no other cause than this mental malady.

II

Mme. Scarron was one of the spectators of Louis XIV's entry into Paris with his young newly married Queen : " I do **Louis XIV's** not believe anything so handsome can be seen **Marriage.** anywhere," she wrote to one of her friends, " and the Queen must have gone to bed well pleased with the husband she had chosen." Now Marie-Thérèse had not chosen her handsome husband, by any means, but she loved him with all her strength, nevertheless. She was a very small fair woman, with chubby cheeks, a fleshy nose, and loose-lipped mouth, whose round blue eyes looked out upon the world with an astonished air. Brought up, like all the Spanish Infantas, like an idol, she was a pattern, all her life long, of the most solid virtue and the greatest stupidity. When she had lived in France for twenty years, she was still saying *una servilietta* for *une serviette, Sancta Biergen* for *Sainte Vierge*, and *eschevois* for *chevaux*. But her love for the handsome man political arrangements had given her for a husband was really touching : if Louis only " looked kindly at her," says Madame, " she was merry the whole day long," and people about the Court laughed a little on the sly when she appeared, one day, to please her lord, " all covered with coloured ribbons," an adornment under which her plump little person looked odd indeed ; or when a proof of the King's tenderness filled her with open delight. " She was so exhilarated when this happened to her that everybody found it out at once. She liked to be joked about it, then she would laugh, and her eyes would twinkle, and she would rub her little hands together." She bore five other children after the birth of the Grand Dauphin, all of whom died in their infancy. When she died, in her turn (July 30, 1683), Louis might well exclaim, " This is the first sorrow she has caused me ! "

Less than a year after the King's marriage, his brother, Monsieur, took a wife. Though the younger brother was very "Monsieur" unlike his elder, there was a great affection be-(Philippe tween the two. Philippe d'Orléans had hair and d'Orléans). eyebrows as black as jet, a thick nose, dark eyes, a small mouth, and his face looked long and narrow under his immense wig. Whereas Louis was tall and masculine and fine-looking, Philippe was small and plump and effeminate. " He cared neither for horses nor for hunting : his only pleasures were gaming, receptions, good eating, dancing, and wearing fine clothes." Foppish, frivolous, coquettish, as loquacious " as two or three women," he delighted in gossip—Saint-Simon calls him " a king of mischief-makers "—he took care of his complexion, laughed prettily, minced, simpered in the most marvellous way, and painted his face, " which endued him with a beauty more fitted to a princess than to a prince," as Mme. de La Fayette judiciously puts it. Further, he loved his friends with a passionate affection, and more especially the Chevalier de Lorraine, a younger son of a great family, " like a painted angel," who soon became " a more absolute favourite with Monsieur than a man can permit himself to be if he does not choose to be taken to be the master, or the mistress, of the house " (Choisy). . . . At the age of fifty, " short and full-bellied, looking as if he were walking on stilts, so high-heeled were his shoes, always adorned like any woman, covered with rings and bracelets and gems, with a long, black, powdered wig brought very much forward, and ribbons wherever he could put them, exhaling perfumes of every kind, and cleanliness itself in all details," the Duke of Orleans was still simpering. A fairly good-natured man, apart from all this, and not at all devoid of intelligence ; he was not afraid, when his elder brother's jealousy permitted him to go to the seat of war, " to expose his beauty to a merciless sun " and ride under fire and into the most dangerous positions, " painted and indolent " indeed, but as unconcernedly as if he had been going to pay a visit to the Queen.

His young wife, Henrietta of England, sister of Charles II, had one shoulder a little higher than the other, and yet the beauty of her figure was the subject of universal praise. The fact is that her grace and charm blinded all men to her faults. She lived for nothing but to fascinate. She openly acknowledged her belief that she had really been born the day on which she had been loved for the first time. " One would think she was asking for one's heart, however indifferent the words she spoke," writes the author of the *Princesse de Clèves*. " When anybody looked at her, and she noticed it, it was impossible to believe that she had any other desire than to be pleasing in the sight of him who was gazing upon her " (Choisy). The King, in the first instance, had appeared by no means attracted by Henrietta's charms : he thought them lacking in opulence, and was fond of telling his intimate friends that they reminded him of " the bones in the Cemetery of the Innocents." . . . But here we will hand the pen to Mme. de La Fayette : she wrote Madame's Memoirs, and though, as she herself acknowledges, it was " a work of some difficulty to interpret the truth, in certain instances, in such a way as to make it known without rendering it either offensive or disagreeable to the princess," she succeeded fairly well in her attempt, as we shall see :

Henrietta Stuart, Duchesse d'Orléans.

Madame [she says] had no thought beyond that of pleasing the King as his sister-in-law : I think she did attract him after another fashion, and I believe, too, that she thought he only pleased her as a brother-in-law, although he perhaps attracted her more strongly : but in any case, as they were both infinitely charming, and both born with an instinctive inclination to gallantry, and as they met every day or two, in the midst of pleasures and entertainments, it seemed to every one else that each possessed for the other that charm which is the usual precursor of great passions. . . .

And indeed, within a fortnight of her arrival at Court Madame was the queen of every festivity : moonlight drives round the Fontainebleau canal, torchlight dances, Benserade ballets, alfresco collations, theatrical performances, reviews, which the ladies attended on horseback, mingling their scarves with the cuirasses : so much so that Monsieur thought his wife's triumph excessive, and Louis, to reassure him, was obliged to make love to one of Henrietta's maids of honour. He chose the simplest and most modest of them all, Louise de La Vallière.

This charming girl of sixteen, fair-haired and black-eyed, gentle, frail, delicate, had a slight limp, " but it did not suit her

Louise de La Vallière. badly " : it was on horseback that she looked her best, for not only had she a perfect seat, but " the riding-jacket hid her bosom, and the cravat made it look fuller." The King's contemporaries could not understand his admiration for so thin a lady : at that period slight beauties were not at all the rage. D'Ormesson, when he saw her, thought her " emaciated, with hollow cheeks, an ugly mouth and teeth, a thick end to her nose, and a long face " : an anonymous critic indignantly informs us that she had no bosom to speak of, flat arms, and that everybody agreed in declaring her " intelligence rather limited." But it was not her mind, nor yet her beauty, that enchanted Louis, it was her gentleness, her maidenly reserve, her glance, " at once so tender and so modest," and, above all, her absorbing love for him. And the feelings of this young King, who could talk to ladies in those days like the most fascinating of Benserade's shepherds, were still so fresh that he could not be insensible to her deep and timid passion.

It was at this period that the modest country-house—as it still was in those days—of Versailles became the scene of the

Fêtes at Versailles. *Plaisirs de l'Ile enchantée*, a famous festival, the subject of which was " the Palace of Alcina." The first day saw Roger and his knights—represented by the King and some of his courtiers, blazing with jewels—riding in

front of a glistening car on which Apollo sat enthroned, supported
by the Four Ages, the Golden, the Silver, the Bronze, and the
Iron. After much reciting of verses and singing of madrigals
and cantatas, the joust began, and when night had fallen, the
Seasons, attended by fauns, and wood-nymphs, and dryads, and
harvesters, and vintagers, all escorting a hill that moved on
rollers whence Pan and Diana duly descended, served a supper
in the light of four thousand torches. The next day there was a
performance of Molière's *Princesse d'Elide,* and the cavalcades
and ballets went on for five days more. All this was secretly
dedicated to Mlle. de La Vallière, " and she enjoyed it, hidden
in the crowd." But the poor girl's happy days were of short
duration. The King loved her, indeed, but this did not prevent
him from climbing about on the palace roofs to visit the other
maids of honour. And indeed her position as the royal favourite
made Louise blush with shame : when Louis, who had made his
relations with her more and more public, established her in
Paris, and created her a duchess, in 1666, she almost died of
it. . . . And even then the King had no eyes save for one of
her own friends, Mme. de Montespan.

In the person of Françoise-Athénaïs de Tonnay-Charente,
Marquise de Montespan—fair-skinned, golden-haired, " beauti-
Mme. de   ful as the day," says Saint-Simon, " *tonnante et*
Montespan.   *triomphante,*" writes Mme. de Sévigné—a perfect
form was united to a most enchanting wit. " She was always
a person of the highest breeding, with charms that made one
overlook her haughty ways and suited them. It was not
possible to possess more wit, a more delicate politeness, with a
quaintness of expression, an eloquence, a natural correctness
which formed a language peculiar to herself, but which was
delightful, and which others caught up to such an extent that
her nieces, and the persons who assiduously frequented her
company, all adopted it, and even now we feel and recognize it
in the few of them who still remain." . . . Mme. de Montespan could entertain a circle of guests like a really great lady ; she
would take risks, fasten on what was ridiculous, " and make
others feel it by a manner peculiar to the Mortemart family " ;
she was a woman of taste ; she patronized Quinault, helped
Lulli, encouraged Racine, took an interest in Boileau : what

was poor little La Vallière beside this radiant lady ? So it came about that in 1667 " the wondrous," " the incomparable," "the beautiful lady," " Quanto," as Mme. de Sévigné calls her, having given herself some trouble to attain this end, took her rival's place in the King's affections. For the space of ten years her fine manners, sparkling wit, and dazzling beauty were to increase the glories of Versailles.

But in spite of this new passion, the King did not dismiss Mlle. de La Vallière. For Mme. de Montespan was a married woman. And, indeed, her husband was a most inconvenient spouse, an " extravagant fellow " who ventured to " inveigh very loudly against the King's friendship for her," and who " had a great deal of wit " into the bargain. " When he betook himself to Saint-Germain and poured out his admonitions, Mme. de Montespan used to be in despair : ' Here he is putting stories about the Court,' said she to Mademoiselle, in her rage. ' I am so ashamed to see that he and my parrot provide amusement for the mob ! ' " One fine day Montespan donned mourning for his wife, put his whole household into mourning too, proceeded, in a coach hung with black, to bid a solemn farewell to all his friends and relations, and then departed into his own province, where Louvois cynically did his utmost to implicate him in some shady business. For a long time afterwards, the King and the Marquise felt by no means easy as to what his next prank might be. . . . But it may be mentioned that many of Montespan's contemporaries ascribed his uncompromising attitude to his not having obtained all the advantages for which he had hoped from his position.

In that very year when the haughty Marquise's favour became known to all men, on Sunday, June 29, 1670, Madame **Death of** fainted after drinking a glass of chicory water : **Henrietta** at half-past two the next morning she was dead : **of Orleans.** hardly a week previously she had returned from the most triumphal journey to England whence she had brought Louis XIV the Treaty of Dover and the alliance of her brother, Charles II. Two months later, on August 21, 1670, at Saint-Denis, Bossuet, Bishop of Condom, pronounced, with an emotion that deepened as he proceeded, his funeral oration on Henrietta-Anne of England. When he spoke those celebrated words," Oh, night of disaster! night of horror! whereon, as with a clap of thunder, the astonishing news rang out, 'Madame is dying! Madame is dead!'" the whole Court broke into sobs. . . . Many of the courtiers who could not restrain their tears were persuaded Henrietta had been poisoned by the Chevalier de Lorraine, whose banishment she had brought about, perhaps even with the assent of Monsieur himself. This was a falsehood: the physicians of the present day, at all events, have expressed their unhesitating opinion that Madame was carried off by a violent attack of peritonitis. But the calumny brooded over Philippe d'Orléans all his life.

Hardly a fortnight after Henrietta had breathed her last the King sent for his brother, and invited him to espouse their cousin the "Grande Mademoiselle," daughter of Gaston d'Orléans, and the richest heiress in the kingdom, But Monsieur asked for time, and betrayed considerable repugnance to the idea. It was written, no doubt, that Mademoiselle's likeness to the heron of the fable was to be complete: after she had scorned a Prince of Wales, an Infante of Portugal, a Duke of Lorraine, and fancied she was to be Queen of France, of England, of Spain, and of Hungary, if not an Empress indeed, this proud princess was to end by setting her whole heart on the younger son of a Gascon gentleman.

"Nobody would dream what his life has been," La Bruyère writes of Lauzun. . . . He was a little man, insipidly fair, **Lauzun and** "the most insolent little man that has been seen **the "Grande** for a century" (La Fare), half bald, with red eyes **Mademoiselle."** and a sharp nose, and a "face like a skinned cat," dirty and slovenly to boot, but in him the ladies delighted, just as he was. Witty and illiterate, full of scoffing jests, brave, at times, even to heroism, or servile as the lowest menial, he had won the King's regard by affecting an almost religious admiration for the sovereign, which indeed he did not scruple to intersperse with the most amazing scenes, as on that day when he broke his sword in Louis' presence, crying out in a rage "that he would no longer serve a prince who broke his word to him so scurvily." The King, beside himself with fury, retorted by one of the finest gestures of his life: he turned about at once, opened the window, threw out his cane, said he would have been "sorry to have struck a man of quality," and left the room. It was by such traits as these that Louis XIV was continually proving himself the most perfect gentleman in his own kingdom. . . . Mademoiselle was a tall, stout woman of three and forty, with a great majestic nose, above which the two most innocent eyes in the world looked out. Having made Lauzun's acquaintance, so she tells us, she clearly felt " that for once in her life she must taste the delight of feeling herself loved by some one it was worth while to love " : and hence, on October 15, 1670, Mme. de Sévigné wrote her friend Coulanges the news, " the most astonishing, the most surprising, the most miraculous," and so forth—the marriage of the little Lauzun to Mademoiselle, own cousin to Louis XIV, and the most richly dowered old maid in France. . . . Alas ! the King, who had begun by consenting to this union, retracted within three days; the whole of the royal family, and Mme. de Montespan above all, had pointed out the impropriety of such an alliance ; and it had perhaps occurred to him, without any outside interference, that if Mademoiselle died unmarried, her immense wealth must all fall back into the hands of the reigning family of France. . . . The " Grande Mademoiselle " wept and sobbed and raged Lauzun bowed to his fate with heroic fortitude. This did not prevent him from marrying his lady-love in secret, and he consequently spent ten years in the fortress of Pignerol : that done, he was restored to favour and was made a duke. " We have seen him a favourite, we have seen him drown, and here he is back on the crest of the wave," wrote Bussy to Mme. de Sévigné. " Don't you know a game in which one says, ' I've seen him alive, I've seen him dead, I've seen him alive after his death ! ' ? That just describes him."

Mademoiselle being no longer in question, Monsieur married Elisabeth-Charlotte, daughter of the Elector Palatine, familiarly **Second** known as " Liselotte " (1671). Liselotte was not **Marriage of** beautiful : Saint-Simon has told us she had " the **Monsieur.** face and the manners of a Swiss Guard," and she herself, at the age of forty-six, described herself as follows :

You cannot remember me very well if you do not class me among the ugly ones. . . . My figure is monstrously fat, I am as square as a cube ; my skin is red, with yellow patches on it ; my hair is getting quite grey ;

my nose, and my two cheeks as well, have been horribly scarred by small-pox ; I have a large mouth and bad teeth : and there you have a portrait of my pretty face.

When this daughter of the Palatinate arrived at Versailles (1671), the courtiers thought Monsieur had been made to marry a servant-girl, and Philippe himself could not suppress a frown. The new Madame could neither talk, nor curtsy, nor play cards, nor dance, nor even, at first, ride a horse, and her rustic and rubicund figure was as much out of place in the midst of that brilliant Court as her " honest German stomach " was offended by French cookery. " For the first three days she ate nothing but one olive, and said not a word, so uncivilized was she " (Primi). Later, she talked and ate more, even " more then she should," but this Liselotte, whose whole delight was to " fill her jaws " as she calls it herself, never grew accustomed to the French *cuisine* ; nor did she become used to French habits, so that her letters present a melancholy alternation of regret-ful longings for German food and the most violent abuse of her French surroundings. Mme. de Maintenon was her pet aversion, " the wizened old thing, the old slut, the old wretch, the old horror, the filthy old creature," or simply, and more eloquently, " the old woman " : but what displeased her always was France and everything French—mind, manners, cooking, and inhabitants. So, to console herself, she would dream of her beloved Palatinate, that virtuous country—and her corre-spondents filled her with deep astonishment when they replied that the morals of that part of the world were hardly so pure as she took them to be : her melancholy fancy dwelt on its land-scapes and its dainties : some " good beer-soup," " a good dish of sauerkraut with smoked sausages," or " a good salad made of German cabbage with bacon." Ah ! that German cabbage ! With what emotion does she laud it, with what poetic feeling does she sing it, in every page of her correspondence ! We can easily understand how nowadays, on the other side of the Rhine, her patriotic tastes are esteemed extremely meritorious. And indeed this princess, so chaste in morals, so ribald in speech, who contrived to live at the Court of Versailles for half a century without any tincture of corruption or of politeness, is a fair specimen of the qualities of the German race.

Poor La Vallière was present at Monsieur's marriage; she, like Mme. de Montespan, was to be seen everywhere. The two ladies were lodged in the same apartment: so that when the King went to see the fair Marquise, it was said "the King is with the ladies." In February, 1671, Louise fled for the first time, and sought refuge in the convent at Chaillot: Colbert undertook to fetch her back, and the two ladies became more inseparable than ever. At Saint-Germain, at Fontainebleau, at Versailles, the courtiers saw "La Vallière get into the King's chaise, first of all, then the King, and then Mme. de Montespan, all three on the same seat, the King in the middle. Louis very well dressed in brown stuff, but heavily laced with gold, gold round his hat, too, and a high colour in his face: Mme. **Louise de La** de Montespan very handsome, with a most **Vallière a Nun.** beautiful complexion": Louise thinner than ever. This went on for a long time. . . . Then one fine day the news spread abroad that the Duchesse de La Vallière was going to enter the Carmelite Order. On April 20, 1674, she who was no longer to be known save as Sœur Louise de la Miséricorde cast herself at the feet of the Queen, who lifted her up and embraced her. A fortnight later she took her vows (June 3). The King, it would appear, condescended to preserve for her "an esteem and cold respect which he expressed, indeed, rarely and curtly."

A month later Louis XIV was triumphantly celebrating his conquest of Franche-Comté at Versailles. The festivities opened on July 4, 1674, with a collation in one of the groves: marble tables arranged amidst the green boughs bore dishes of fruit, decanters filled with liqueurs, and baskets of marzipans or dried preserves; the tinkle of the falling waters mingled with the sound of violins and hautboys: at eight o'clock, an opera was performed in the Cour de Marbre: the eight columns supporting the gilded balcony formed the background of the stage, the sides of which were marked out by the great orange-trees in their boxes, while dwarf trees of the same kind spread their greenery in porcelain vases set between the larger ones. All this was lighted up by quantities of wax tapers placed on the balconies and on the entablatures, and in crystal and silver chandeliers on stands painted blue and gold. After listening to a performance by the artistes of the Academy of Music of Quinault's *Alceste*, to Lulli's music, their Majesties proceeded to the Palace to eat a *médianoche* (midnight supper). . . . On July 11 there was another collation in a verdant glade at the Trianon, where the *Éclogue de Versailles* was afterwards played. On the 19th yet another collation at the Ménagerie, at the end of the Great Canal : an excursion on the water in gondolas, attended by a boat-load of musicians : and a performance of the *Malade Imaginaire* at the Grotto of Thetis. On the 28th a collation at the Théâtre d'Eau, a performance of the *Fêtes de l'Amour et de Bacchus* close to the ornamental water called the *Pièce d'eau du Dragon* : fireworks on the Canal : *médianoche* in the Cour de Marbre. On August 18 the Court proceeded in eighteen coaches to partake of a collation in the Allée Royale, and then attended a performance of *Iphigénie* which took place in the avenue leading to the Orangery : this over, their Majesties entertained themselves with an illumination of the sheet of water which ultimately became the *Bassin d'Apollon*, and a display of fireworks over the Canal. And at last, on August 31, the rejoicings were closed by a general illumination of the whole park, and an excursion in gondolas on the Canal, to the sound of musical instruments. . . .

Mme. de Montespan was the sultana of all these festivities. Louis was then having built for her, at Clagny, by Mansard, a Eclipse of "little Versailles," a "palace of Armida." In her Mme. de own apartment she never condescended to rise Montespan. from her chair to receive any one, not even the King's brother, a most unheard-of thing. . . . Yet, when Bossuet persuaded Louis to break with her in 1675, surely this was done, to some extent, because the King was growing tired of her ! . . . Be that as it may, no sooner had the beautiful Marquise taken her departure, than Louis felt the lack of her presence so severely that the good Bishop was soon to be seen acting, quite unconsciously, as his royal penitent's postman. . . . Mme. de Montespan came back, and then it was that Lenglée made her that celebrated gown " of gold on gold, and gold-embroidered on that, and above that again a gold in relief figured with gold, mixed with a certain gold which makes the most divine material that ever was imagined." . . . That year she was still in great beauty.

I thought her back very flat, but seriously her beauty is a marvellous thing. Her figure is not half so thick as it was, and yet neither her skin, her eyes, nor her lips are the worse for it. She was dressed from head to foot in *point de France*, her hair dressed in thousands of curls, the two on her temples falling down very low on her cheeks : black ribbons on her hair, the Maréchale de l'Hôpital's pearls, embellished with diamond buckles and drops of the most extreme beauty : three or four bodkins, no cap : in a word, a triumphant beauty for the ambassadors to see. (Sévigné.)

But from the very beginning she had treated the Great King to angry scenes (" she has often scolded him, he has not been proud of it," as Mademoiselle tells us) : did she not even venture to tell him one day that at all events she did not smell as nasty as he did ? And the fits of temper, which had charmed him once, were thoroughly disagreeable to him now. . . .

Mlle. de Fontanges. In short, in 1679 the King allowed it to be officially known that he was in love with a lovely auburn-haired girl—" as beautiful as an angel, from head to foot," says Bussy ; " as fair as an angel, as stupid as an owl," adds Choisy ; " beautiful from her feet to her head, but with no more intelligence than a kitten," so Madame sums up—called Mlle. de Fontanges. And all men turned their faces towards the rising star.

In August, 1679, the whole Court crowded into the chapel at Fontainebleau to see the wedding of Mlle. d'Orléans and the King of Spain. Mme. de Montespan, so the Duchess of Osnabrück relates, appeared in " a very careless dress, with embroidered lappets, and in dismal grief at beholding the triumph of a younger woman than herself." Not far from where she sat, Mlle. de Fontanges was reading her breviary, which " gave her on excuse for keeping her eyes cast down on the King, whom she loved better, no doubt, than the King of kings, which is not astonishing, for he is most lovable." Louis XIV, on his side, kept gazing at Mlle. de Fontanges " with more devotion than at the altar," and yawned with all his might, closing his eyes whenever he was not looking at her. Marie-Thérèse was stifling, meanwhile, under the weight of a gown " heavier than the trappings of a horse." After the ceremony the Duchess of Osnabrück paid a visit to the Queen. Monsieur, who had accompanied her, took a taper to show her the jewels with which his sister-in-law was laden : and good-natured Marie-Thérèse obligingly submitted to the scrutiny : "You must look at these," she said, pointing to her diamonds, "and not at this," she added, pointing to her face.

The poisoning scandals had just come to light. For ten years past sorcery and magic had been tremendously in fashion. **The poisoning scandals.** Those charming creatures who, according to Mme. de Longueville's unforgettable sentence, did not care for innocent pleasures, no longer desired, as in the days of the Fronde, to resemble Chimène or Clélie : their new dream was simply to transform "everything into gold, carry on life for ever, cure by spoken words, make themselves loved by any one they chose, know all the secrets of the future, command evil spirits," etc. (Molière, *Amants magnifiques*).

> Perdait-on un chiffon, avait-on un amant,
> Un mari vivant trop au gré de son épouse,
> Une mère facheuse, une femme jalouse,
> Chez la devineuse on courait. . . . (La Fontaine).

And from the fortune-teller these clients obtained whatever they desired, for the sorceresses of every kind who swarmed about the city were not content with selling magic philtres as disgusting as they were inoffensive, they likewise dealt in "powders" for tiresome husbands or rich relatives, who shortly suffered from the consequences, for poisonings could be carried out without much risk in those days, when the legal science of medicine was unknown.

There had been a first scandal in 1668. Two quacks who had been arrested revealed the fact that Mme. de Montespan had ordered the use of spells to assist her in obtaining and preserving the King's affections. But Louis, at that moment, was still in love, and had not as yet turned devout : all he did was to laugh at his credulous mistress and her peccadilloes. . . . But in 1673 the priests of Notre-Dame warned the judicial authorities that numbers of penitents were confessing abominable crimes, and one of the most famous of these sorceresses, Voisin by name, was arrested with her confederates. All these wretches set themselves to compromise a whole bevy of persons, and in the highest places (this was to their interest) : towards the end of 1679 they began to relate the most horrible stories about Mme. de Montespan herself, accusing her of having had "Black Masses" said on her own body, slaughtered little children, given powders to the King, and even conceived a plan to poison both him and Mlle. de Fontanges. Was all this true ? It is very doubtful : the cross-examinations were all directed by Louvois, Mme. de Montespan's mortal enemy. Yet it seems clear that though the Marquise may not have committed all the abominations of which she was accused by this hideous crew, she had at least kept up relations with the sorceresses, more especially about the time of her temporary dismissal in 1675. The full details of the business are not known : the King had the whole inquiry stopped, in the most sudden manner, in July, 1682. To what conclusion does this fact point ? For several years longer the Marquise continued to enjoy a prominent position at Court : apparently, therefore, she was able to clear herself of the gravest of the misdeeds imputed to her.

In January, 1680, she was present, with Mlle. de Fontanges and the whole Court, at the marriage of the daughter of Mlle. **Marriage of** de La Vallière, Mlle. de Blois, with the Prince de **Mlle. de Blois.** Conti, nephew of the Great Condé. On this occasion an astonishing sight was seen : " M. le Prince, the hero," freshly shaved and decently dressed. "Mme. de Langeron, seizing her opportunity when his paws were crossed like a lion's, had a coat with diamond buttons slipped upon him, a valet, who likewise imposed upon his patience, curled his hair, powdered it, and reduced him at last to the appearance of the best-looking of Court gentlemen, with a head that made all the wigs look shabby : this was the great wonder of the wedding " (Sévigné). Ever since 1675, in fact, Condé had been living in retirement on his splendid property at Chantilly, bravely enduring torture from the gout, as odd as ever, and as full of genius, violent, dirty, careless, charming—" he has been heard to say ' *I fled* ' with the same grace as that with which he said ' *We beat them !* ' " (La Bruyère) ; and besides, since the signing of the Treaty of the Pyrenees he had been a good courtier, as submissive and humble, indeed, in his behaviour to the King as he had once been intractable. This man, so deservedly surnamed the "great"—"genuine, simple, magnanimous, lacking nothing but the lesser virtues"—was to die in 1686.

In 1680 it was Mme. de Montespan again, "being the woman of fashion who knows most about all things," who was **The Grand Dauphin.** deputed to choose the wedding gifts intended for the Dauphiness, Anne-Marie-Victoire, daughter of the Elector of Bavaria. The bride was an insignificant and not very healthy German, who never played any part at Court beyond that of bringing the King's grandchildren into the world—the Duc de Bourgogne in 1682, the Duc d'Anjou in 1683, and the Duc de Berry in 1686. As for the Grand Dauphin—Monseigneur, as he was called—he had been brought up with the most ridiculous severity by his Governor the Duc de Montausier, husband of Mlle. de Rambouillet, and instructed by the famous Bossuet, whose far too intensive method of teaching had dulled rather than awakened his slow mind. Cruelly beaten with a ruler by his Governor—so severely indeed that his hands were constantly swelled and his "arm all stiff," as on the day when he "had omitted one word" in reciting his Sunday prayers in French—with three lessons from Bossuet every day of his life, even on Sundays, and his austere tutor seated beside his bed at night, "to put him to sleep with some pleasant story," the child had grown, by 1680, into a heavy young fellow of nineteen, dull and apathetic, sickened for ever of "everything that smacked of study," never happy except when he was out hunting, terrified at Court, and always quaking with the fear of doing anything to displease his awe-inspiring father, whose jealousy would never have permitted him the smallest share in the management of State affairs.

Mlle. de Fontanges, who had been created a duchess in 1680, was obliged to leave Versailles almost immediately afterwards in consequence of an accident which compromised her health. She died on June 28, 1681, at the age of twenty-two, and her place was not refilled: religion, Mme. de Maintenon, and Louis XIV's own innate good taste saved him from an undignified old age: at the age of forty-four he settled down.

This Mme. de Maintenon had led an adventurous life. The granddaughter of the rough Huguenot poet, Agrippa d'Aubigné, born under the walls of the Château-Trompette, the Bastille of Bordeaux, in which Richelieu had caused her **Mme. de** father to be shut up, taken away, as a child, to **Maintenon.** Martinique, whence her mother returned widowed and penniless, brought up on the charity of one of her relatives, who employed her to keep her turkeys, with no hope before her, in short, save that of entering a convent or domestic service, Françoise was only too glad, in 1652, when she was just sixteen and a half, to marry the crippled poet Paul Scarron. Now Scarron belonged to a good legal family, but " the burlesque style he professed discredited him, while it made him popular " (Voltaire). His contemporaries looked upon him as a sort of merry-andrew : his marriage was considered one of his best buffooneries. Naturally the young girl was nothing to him save a sick-nurse. . . . Françoise endured her position with a singular dignity, decent and simple, which impressed all who came in contact with her. After her husband's death she obtained a pension of 2000 *livres.* Her reputation, of which she was very careful, was as good as could be expected in the case of a young widow in most needy circumstances. Tall, with " an air of nobility, gentle, merry, and modest," regular features, " soft brilliant black eyes, full of passion and intelligence, she did not set up to be a beauty, though she had a thousand obvious charms " (Scudéry). " Her mind suited her beauty— it was large, tranquil, agreeable, elegant." She dressed simply, but " like a woman who spends her life among persons of quality " (Sévigné). In the best society, which she frequented, her conversation was considered " delicious."

Mme. de Montespan, who met this wonderful creature in the house of the Maréchale d'Albret, chose her, in 1670, to educate her children, and then presented her to the King. Little by little the quiet beauty of his children's governess, her distinction, her reason, so calm and subtle—Louis XIV, who was a connoisseur in the matter of good sense, was later to call her " Your Solidity "—the correctness of her language, " gentle, well chosen, naturally eloquent, and concise," all charmed the King. Mme. Scarron's conversation was an agreeable change from Mme. de Montespan's stormy scenes : for the first time in his life, perhaps, a young woman talked to him simply and seriously, " without seeking to attract a declaration on his part, nor attempting to amuse him with trifling discourse " (Arvède Barine). And on December 27, 1674, " Dame Françoise d'Aubigny, widow of Messire Paul Scarron, lord of Fougerets and Councillor of the King," purchased, for the sum of 240,000 *livres*, the Marquisate of Maintenon : shortly afterwards Louis XIV addressed her publicly as Mme. de Maintenon : from that moment the " Widow Scarron " was no more.

Mme. de Maintenon was a pious person : she took a great interest in the King's salvation, and to exhort him to virtue she told him fables which Louis, it appears, thought amusing, but at which Mme. de Montespan did not laugh at all. . . . When the lovely Fontanges supplanted the haughty " Quanto," the favour of the lady whom the courtiers already called *Madame de Maintenant* (Madame Now) showed no sign of diminution, quite the contrary. The King went to see her every day, and she would seem to have exhorted him to very good purpose, seeing that after the departure of Mlle. de Fontanges she induced him to return to the Queen (August, 1680). But presently the kind-hearted Marie-Thérèse herself died (July, 1683) ; and Mme. de Maintenon no doubt continued to preach the doctrine of conjugal virtue, for in the course of the following winter Louis XIV married her.

The King marries Mme. de Maintenon.

And indeed Françoise d'Aubigné was anything but an ambitious and wily woman, nor was she even, it would seem, a designing coquette ; she was a prudent, thrifty being, who loathed adventures like the plague ; further, she was a person of delicate taste ; and, again, we have every reason to believe her to have been perfectly virtuous, while her deep piety is manifest to all. In November, 1702, she wrote to her dear Mme. de Glapion in that fine style of hers, pure and noble like herself :

Do you not see that I am dying of melancholy amidst a fortune that can hardly be imagined, and that nothing but the help of God prevents me from perishing ? I have been young and pretty, I have tasted pleasure, I have been loved wherever I went : at a rather more advanced age, I spent years in the society of intelligent minds : I have risen to favour, and I protest to you, my dear daughter, that all these conditions leave a hideous void, an anxiety, a lassitude, a longing to know some other thing, because in all this there is nothing that really satisfies. . . .

Foundation of Saint-Cyr. It is in fact probable that events rather than any exertion of her own raised Mme. de Maintenon to the throne. Indeed, her vocation was not to be Queen of France, she was manifestly born to be a teacher. The work of her life was the House of Saint-Cyr which the King founded, at her request, close to Versailles, for the education of two hundred poor young girls of noble birth (1686). Weary of the Court, which she disliked exceedingly, she sought refuge at Saint-Cyr whenever she found it possible, and threw herself with passionate interest into all its arrangements, even the most trifling ; teaching the children herself, or advising the mistresses. She had a gift for reading character, and pointing out each person's special duty ; she cared much more about training " good girls " who might, when occasion offered, be " turned into good wives and good nuns," than about forming " talkers, inquisitive, bold," etc. . . . Gentle, but firm, unerring in taste, loved and respected by all who approached her, Mme. de Maintenon was an incomparable schoolmistress.

III

On the spot where the Palace of Versailles now stands, there stretched, in 1624, a plain, owned by a number of small holders and two large ones : the Maréchal de Retz and a certain Jean Martin. Louis XIII was fond of the village of Versailles, whither he often came when he was hunting, and where he habitually halted for breakfast on his way to Saint-Germain or Fontainebleau by way of Palaiseau. He decided to build himself a hunting-lodge there, and in 1624, after the occupants of the ground had been expropriated, a small country-house was erected on a hillock covering a modest space of some few square yards, built of brick with stone facings, with a wing on each side, adorned with the high-pitched roof then in fashion— a manor-house, in fact, of a quite unpretentious kind, which he carefully paid for out of the funds set apart for his " small enjoyments," so as to put no expense on the public purse, and

the cost of which did not at all exceed that in which any gentleman in comfortable circumstances might have permitted himself
to indulge.

Louis XIV had all his forefathers' love of building : early in
1661 his architects, Le Vau for the buildings, Le Nôtre for the
Enlargement of gardens—these two had been the makers of Vaux,
the Château the property he had so greatly admired, too much
de Versailles. indeed for the safety of its owner, Fouquet—
began to rearrange this " gentleman's small country-house,"
this " little house of cards " ; but they did not greatly alter its
general aspect : in 1668 the hillock at Versailles was still
crowned by a palace in the Louis XIII style, but richly decorated,
with red façades, and white chimney-stacks, and sharp-pointed,
gilded roofs : away in the distance the future " Great Canal "
was still a flat plain, and though the general outlines of the
gardens were there, few statues and fountains adorned them as
yet. This was the setting in which the entertainments offered
to Mlle. de La Vallière took place : the *Impromptu de Versailles*
in 1663, the *Delights of the Enchanted Island* in 1664—and even
the first of those given in honour of Mme. de Montespan in
1668, the *Fêtes de l'Amour et de Bacchus,* by Quinault.

Louis XIV disliked his capital, to the despair of Colbert. . . .
For Colbert, a practical man, loved his Paris ; it was a delight
to him to see the people hurrying along the streets, and the
customers dawdling about the shops, and the crowd swarming
upon the bridges ; the noise that rose up from the city and
filled his study with its busy hum was a joy to him ; it was a
sound of commerce and of health, the throbbing of the life of
France ; and he would write, insidiously, " Oh, what a sad pity
it would be if the greatest of all kings, and the most virtuous—
with that true virtue which makes the greatest of princes—
should be judged by the standard of Versailles ! " . . . But
Louis XIV was never able to forget the battle of the Porte
Saint-Antoine : and the city, with its stinking, winding streets,
and the confused mass of people moving hither and thither in
them, was not, to his mind, so worthy a setting for the King's
Majesty as a park laid out by Le Nôtre. What delighted him
was the regular avenue along which his great white horses
could trot, with the heavy red and gold coach rolling smoothly

THE SEVENTEENTH CENTURY

behind them; the walks cut through the grove and round about the flower-beds; the prospect " disposed for the perfect delight of the eye "; the surprise of a statue set at the corner of a clump of trees; water, enclosed or running freely, murmuring low or spouting forth; clipped trees, rare blossoms. He disregarded his Minister, and forsook Paris more and more: after 1671 he ceased to live there: after 1678 he did all he could to avoid entering the city, and when he dined at the Hôtel de **The Court** Ville in 1689 it was considered an extraordinary **installed at** thing. The Court took up its quarters at Ver- **Versailles.** sailles, and there soon formed a society apart, quite different from that of the " town," and even using a language of its own: [thus the King of France, to whom his faithful people had formerly obtained access very easily, ended by living in isolation, as far as the nation was concerned; a misfortune, probably, for the monarchy.

As a permanent residence for the King and his Court the Versailles of 1668, which contemporaries were already extolling as a marvel, was too small: after 1669 it was rebuilt. But Louis XIV would never consent to the pulling down of the remains of his father's hunting-box, and Le Vau was fain to content himself with masking the little country-house, on three of its sides, with a series of new buildings: thus there were three new fronts, looking on the gardens, but the original façade, looking over the *Cour de Marbre*, was left standing, though greatly altered by the various adornments added to it. Then the State apartments of the King and Queen were decorated, very much as we see them now, and finally, in 1671, the town of Versailles was founded by an edict which gave any one who chose to do so, leave to build on the ground lying between " the pump of the said Versailles and the farm of Clagny." This was the Versailles of Mme. de Montespan.

But the Court grew larger, and the King's taste for building stronger. From 1678 onward, and in 1682 particularly, a third **Versailles** rearrangement of the palace was commenced, **rebuilt by** on plans supplied by Mansart: by the last week **Mansart.** in August, 1684, 22,000 men and 6000 horses were toiling on the works at Versailles; in the following year the labourers numbered 36,000. The *Galerie des Glaces* was

198

finished first ; then the south wing, and the north wing, in which the courtiers were lodged, the stables, the *Grand Commun*, the Orangery ; the gardens were all laid out over again, the Grand Trianon was erected in the place occupied by the old " porcelain " Trianon, with its charming blue and white façade. The chapel was not completely finished till 1710 . . . but by that time all Louis XIV's interest had been centred for several years in Marly.

It was towards the end of 1678 that the King began the work of making himself a " hermitage " at Marly. In one of **Marly.** his most lively pages Saint-Simon has criticized the choice of this " deep narrow valley with its steep sides, inaccessible on account of the marshes around it, without view of any kind, shut in by hills in every direction," where even by cutting through the hill-sides, so he declares, nothing but a " most imperfect outlook " was obtainable, " a filthy hole," which had to be dried by filling it up with earth, " a den of snakes and offal, of frogs and toads," where, to get any shade at all, it was necessary to transplant " whole forests of full-grown bushy trees," " great trees from Compiègne and from much farther off than that, more than three-quarters of which died, and were replaced forthwith." . . . Marly really was a pretty little valley lying between pleasant hills, so thickly wooded that in 1679, when the palace was built, it was necessary to clear some of the land, and from the palace, when finished, there was a charming view over Saint-Germain and its neighbourhood. As for the " thousands of millions " spent, so the censorious duke assures us, on gratifying what he ventures to describe as " the King's invariably bad taste and the vain-glorious delight of doing violence to Nature," they amounted to just 13,200,000 *livres*, laid out in the course of thirty-seven years. This was the expenditure necessitated by the erection, on the brow of a hill, and on a white marble terrace, of the *Pavillon du Soleil*, a little fairy dwelling, the walls of which were covered, on their outer sides, with frescoes after drawings by Le Brun, adorned with wreaths and bas-reliefs, and pilasters with gilded capitals, and crowned by a balustrade consisting of gold-coloured pillars with groups of figures representing children at each corner : twelve other pavilions for the courtiers, painted like the larger one : and the gardens, the unequalled beauty of which has been described by the admirable Saint-Simon in indignant terms : " huge stretches of thick wood and shady paths, suddenly transformed into great sheets of water on which the company floated in gondolas, and then turned back into forests so close that they shut out the daylight the moment they were planted—I speak of what I saw myself in the course of six weeks : the fountain basins altered a hundred times over : the cascades as well, in a succession of shapes, and always different ones : habitations for fishes adorned with painting and gilding of the most exquisite kind, and hardly finished before the owners changed and rearranged them in some different style, and this an endless number of times." . . . Thirteen millions of *livres* for this marvel of " sure and polished taste," this " lesson in proportion, precision, and grace," for the expression of an idea so eminently French, was not too high a price.

In that " sumptuous and delightful abode " the King imagined himself to be enjoying a country life. The exiguous proportions of the dwelling forbade his bringing more than a few courtiers with him : thus it was a favour to be invited to " the Marlys," and the remark of the Cardinal de Polignac, when the King and those attending on His Majesty were overtaken by the rain while out walking, is historic : " 'Tis nothing, Sire ! The rain of Marly does not wet ! " Nevertheless, even in that " hermitage " etiquette was scarcely relaxed.

In the old days the courtiers, though they respected the King as their master, still treated him like a man. The simple friendliness with which Henri IV would talk to his comrades, and invite himself to dine with any one who took his fancy, is legendary. The exceedingly coarse compliments with which the fascinating Bassompierre habitually entertained Marie de' Medici cannot well be quoted here. In 1621 the English Ambassador was astounded to see Bellegarde slip up on the tips of his toes behind the Queen and drop some " small comfits " into Her Majesty's hair, to startle her. As to the freedom of the language in use among the courtiers of Louis XIII, the following lines will give my readers some idea of it :

THE "ROI-SOLEIL"

Being at my gallery window [writes Louis XIII himself to Richelieu] I saw Saint-Preuil coming towards me, all swelling with rage, and when he reached me, he said, "What have I done to you that you should wish me so ill ? I thought there was something to be gained by serving you, but I see there is nothing that I can hope for. . . ." [He had been a Captain in the Guard for many years, and a young lieutenant had been given a regiment over his head. The King replied :] "At Chantilly, the last time you were there, you asked me leave to get rid of your company, and I granted it. . . ." "I do not choose to get rid of it now ! " "But I insist on your getting rid of it ! . . . You are a cross-grained fellow, nobody can get on with you : I'll have you given 20,000 crowns for your company. . . ." "No, you can take it from me ! . . ." "You would be well caught if I took you at your word, but I do not choose to do so ! " "Here are 20,000 francs that I have wasted in your service, without your having ever done the smallest thing for me. . . ." "Say 100,000 crowns that you have lost at the gambling-table. . . ." And thereupon everybody came up and stood between us. . . . (D'Avenel, *Richelieu*, iii, p. 49.)

The kindly King adds, "His aim was to make me say something to him at which he might take offence, but I was very wise."

Louis XIV himself did not at first claim to be more than the foremost of the elegant young gentlemen covered, like **The Court in** himself, with gems and laces, gay with ribbons **the King's** and feathers, who fluttered round the fair ladies **young days.** of his Court. And indeed the Court of the year 1662 or thereabouts bore but little resemblance to that of later days : the courtiers only made their appearance from time to time, and the comparative smallness of their numbers rendered the continual removals from Paris to Fontainebleau, from Saint-Cloud to Saint-Germain, an easy matter : the youthful courtiers of that time, lively, merry, and unaffected, seemed to owe their freedom from constraint to the graceful ease of the master of them all. These were the days when the Duc de Guiche posed as the King's rival in the good graces of Mlle. de La Vallière, and then boldly sought to replace him in the favour of Henrietta of England : when His Majesty was not unfrequently seen climbing about the roofs at night : and when Mlle. de La Motte-Houdancourt pinched her royal admirer so sharply in the Queen's room, one morning, that in spite of himself he exclaimed " Ha ! the bitch ! " at the top of his voice. We are far, indeed, from the future husband of Mme. de Maintenon !

Thus it was by slow degrees that the King became an idol : but by the year 1685 a look from him singled a man out, a **The etiquette** word with him was an honour, a favour bestowed **of later years.** covered the recipient with glory. To hold his bedroom candlestick for a single evening made the fortunate holder the envy of his brethren. When he was operated on for a fistula, all the courtiers came crowding to Fagon, beseeching him to treat them likewise. When he turned pious, the whole Court hurried after him to church. And indeed divine honours were paid him : on March 28, 1686, M. de La Feuillade set up on the Place des Victoires, at his own expense, an equestrian statue, in gilded bronze, of Louis the Great, and by his will he **The Monarch** charged his son with the duty of having lanterns **an idol.** lighted, every night, all round the sacred image ! This no doubt was pure flattery, " the most enormous, the vilest, the most pagan," as Saint-Simon phrases it. In 1699 another statue was set up on the Place Vendôme : " but for the fear of the devil, the King would have had himself worshipped, and he would have found men to worship him." And indeed he does seem to have actually found them : in the Chapel at Versailles the courtiers " turned their backs on the priest and the sacred mysteries, and lifted their faces to the King, who was to be seen kneeling in a gallery, and on whom their whole hearts and spirits seemed bestowed : this custom certainly indicates a sort of subservience, for the gathering appears to worship the prince while the prince worships God " (La Bruyère). And Mademoiselle piously exclaims : " He is like unto God, we must wait on his will, and hope all things from his justice and his goodness, without impatience even, so as to gain more merit by so doing."

The worship of the Ruler of Versailles began with the morning. Even before his eyes were open the approaches to his chamber were filled with a spruce and gilded crowd. There, by right of office, we see the Great Chamberlain, the first gentlemen of his chamber, the pages, and chief *valets de chambre*, the other *valets de chambre*, the ushers of the antechamber, the Grand Master, the Master, and the Valets of the Wardrobe, both valets proper and valets in ordinary, the gentlemen of the household, the private secretaries, and so forth ; and in the year 1687 these retainers bore the names of the Ducs de Bouillon, de Saint-Aignan, de Beauvilliers, d'Aumont, de Gesvres, de La Trémoille, de Montausier, de La Rochefoucauld, etc. etc.—198 persons in all, for nothing beyond the monarch's own personal service, and without reckoning the servants properly so called. One man had the right to look after the royal lap-dogs, another was in command of the mules that carried the King's bed from place to place, another had the sole responsibility for a less picturesque item of His Majesty's personal belongings.

At the hour given out on the previous evening (generally at eight o'clock, Saint-Simon tells us ; at 8.30 according to the **The King's** *État de la France* of 1687), the First *Valet de chambre* **"Lever."** woke the King. At that moment the *Grande Entrée* was admitted to the room—the Duc de Bouillon, Great Chamberlain, and the Chief Gentlemen of the Bedchamber ; the Duc de La Rochefoucauld, Grand Master of the Wardrobe, the Masters of the Wardrobe, the Chief *Valets de chambre* ; the King's Physician in chief, Daquin, the Chief Physician to the late Queen, Fagon ; the King's nurse, and a few favourites who had succeeded in attaining this treasured honour, such as the Duc de La Feuillade. " This was the moment to speak to the King, if they had anything to say to him or ask of him," and in this case the others discreetly retired to a distance from the person who was conversing with His Majesty. Meanwhile Louis crossed himself, recited the Office of the Order of the Holy Ghost, put on his slippers, presented by his First *Valet de chambre* (a duke), and his dressing-gown, held for him by the Great Chamberlain (a prince), and while the barber was dressing the King's hair, the usher opened the door to the *First Entrée*— that is to say, the four private secretaries, the three First *Valets de chambre*, who were not doing their quarterly term of service, the two Readers, the two Comptrollers of the King's Plate, the Physician in Ordinary, the King's Apothecary, and a few courtiers to whom this special favour had been granted, among them Dangeau and Villeroy. Shortly after this the " *Chambre* " made its appearance : then came all the most distinguished of the company waiting in the antechamber, such as the dukes and peers and the Marshals of France : after these the chief officials of the King's household, and finally the general Court.

"It is part of the usher's duty to inquire the names and qualities of the persons who are unknown to him," remarks the *État de la France*. "Nobody is permitted to open the door for himself, it must be opened by the usher," and to this end the person desiring to enter must scratch very gently on one side of the folding door : to knock on it with the knuckles would be an act of rudeness.

While all this was going on, the King was dressing himself : he put on his wig : then his breeches, to which his stockings were fastened, were slipped on his legs : every second day, the barber shaved him : his early breakfast was carried in with endless ceremony : his night jacket was taken off, his shirt duly presented to him—a serious business, this, the honour of accomplishing which belonged to Monsieur if he were present, or in his absence, to his son : if neither were on the spot, the privilege fell to a Prince of the Blood or else to one of the legitimized princes, and failing these, to the Great Chamberlain or to the officer holding the highest rank after his : the First *Valet de chambre* held up the right sleeve of the shirt, the First Valet of the Wardrobe held up the other, and the Master of the Wardrobe would not have surrendered the honour of helping His Majesty to pull up his breeches to any other being upon earth : after all this, Louis was garbed in his vest of red, or blue, or green cloth or satin, richly embroidered : his blue ribbon was slipped over his head, his sword buckled on for him ; over all this he put on his coat—" brown, more or less dark, lightly embroidered, but never on the seams, sometimes with plain gold buttons "— knotted his own cravat, chose one of the four handkerchiefs presented to him on a salver, took his hat, with its white feather, his gloves, and his tall cane from the hands of the Master of the Wardrobe, and retired to the space beside his bed to say his prayers. By the time the King reappeared the whole Court was present, and the *lever* was over.

The whole existence of Louis XIV was a ceremony, governed by fixed rites of this description. When his *lever* was over he **Programme of** announced his plans for the day : "thus every-**the King's day.** body knew, to a quarter of an hour, what the King was to do." Then he heard Mass. Then he went to his Council. When he left the Council Chamber, at about one o'clock, he proceeded to his own room, where his meal was laid on a small square table opposite the centre window, and there, surrounded by his gazing courtiers, and in a silence only occasionally broken by the few words he would sometimes say to persons to whom he desired to show favour, he ate, with the mighty appetite of which we have so often heard—and without any fork.

As a matter of politeness, the Duc de Bourgogne and his two brothers had been taught to eat with a fork. But when they were admitted to sup with the King, he would not hear of it, and forbade them to do it. He never forbade me to do anything of the kind, for all my life I have never used anything to eat my food save my knife and my fingers. (Madame, January 22, 1713.)

One day, Father Tixier tells us, he saw King Charles of England supping with Louis XIV and the two Queens at Compiègne : every time Marie-Thérèse spoke to the English King, he lifted his hat to her, and " by the end of the meal his hat was most terribly greasy. . . ."

After his dinner the King would take a walk in the gardens, or go to look at the new works, always followed by a troop of courtiers, hat in hand, his head alone being covered : but oftenest of all he went a-hunting. Towards three o'clock, or later, he again met his ministers in council. At seven o'clock the evening entertainments began. Three times a week there was a theatrical performance ; on Mondays, Wednesdays, and Thursdays, the *appartement* ; on Sundays there was nothing at all.

What was known as the *appartement* was the assemblage of the whole Court—from seven in the evening till ten, when the **Evening** King sat down to supper—in the *grand apparte-*
amusements of *ment* ; that is to say, in the series of saloons that **the Court.** lie between the Galerie des Glaces and the Chapel Gallery. These huge rooms were decorated with luxurious comfort and splendour, with a profusion of tapestries, paintings, marbles, and heavy plate, set everywhere on massive silver stands. At night, under the blaze of the lustres, candelabra, candlesticks, and girandoles, the gilded furniture gleamed, the damask of the arm-chairs blushed red, the colours of the velvet doublets and brocaded gowns played in the light, the diamonds

sparkled, the golden and silver vases and salvers, flagons and
ewers, shone brightly. . . . There were tables for every kind of
game : a lansquenet table at which Monseigneur (the Dauphin)
and Monsieur (the King's brother) almost always played, a
billiard-table, too, and every one had leave to ask anything he
desired to have of the lackeys, all in blue coats braided with
silver. Meanwhile the musicians were making themselves
heard, and a collation of fruit, oranges, citrons, and dried fruits
was laid out in the *Salon de Vénus*. . . . All these things, " the
numerous and august company, the magnificence and richness
of the furniture, the rare pictures and busts," the huge size of
the billiard-table, the grace of the ladies as they danced, " and
the charming scraping of the fiddle-bows," greatly dazzled the
learned M. Bourdelot, who was permitted to view them in 1682,
but not so much, perhaps, as the sight of the King himself
moving majestically to and fro in the rooms.

When there was dancing, a special festivity, or a State reception, the *Galerie des Glaces* reflected the light of hundreds of
tapers arranged in a sort of pyramid form, on stands and on gilt
tables. The chairs were placed in a double line, and sometimes
small graduated stages, covered with Savonnerie carpets, were
placed in the window recesses. And even so there were not
seats enough, for the crowd at the French Court was something
tremendous, and by no means so respectful as might have been
imagined. When the King received the Doge of Venice, there
was no keeping the way clear between the *Salon de la Guerre*
and the *Salon de la Paix*, in which the sovereign was awaiting
his visitor : the Doge had the greatest difficulty in getting
through the press. Constantly Madame complains of the heat,
the smell, of having been half smothered. Another German,
Mme. d'Osnabrück, who was present at a theatrical performance at Court in 1679, likewise declares that the " crowd "
and " the terrible heat " cause " the pleasures of the Court of
France to be mingled with many discomforts," and that, in
fact, the number of curtsies that have to be made to every
new-comer, the infernal noise that goes on all day long, and the
trouble people take to amuse themselves, make the Court a
most tiring place to live in.

At ten o'clock, when the *appartement* was over, the King

supped in great state, with the " sons, daughters, grandsons, and granddaughters of France." Towards midnight there was the **The King's** *coucher,* for which the rules were as minutely **"Coucher."** prescribed as those for the *lever.* Then at last " the Court was over."

Like the King—although, so Madame vows, "there is nothing more tiresome than to eat alone, with a score of big fellows standing round, watching you chew, and counting every mouthful "—the members of the royal family all lived in public from morning till night. In 1665, an Italian traveller had no difficulty in obtaining admission to the Queen's *lever* :

While her hair was being dressed she wore a pair of light white linen stays, well boned and tightened round her figure, and a petticoat so narrow **The Queen's** that she looked as if she were wrapped up in a silken **"Lever."** bag. When the Queen's hair was dressed, her upper garments were brought in by pages. They were of a pretty fabric, of extremely rich material, with alternate flowers of blue and gold, on a silver ground, and, with her ornaments, were all put on her person by male attendants. They even laced her into her gown and finished dressing her ; but her women fastened the jewels she wore on her head and in the front of her gown. When she was completely dressed, she turned towards the foreigners, a certain number of whom had been admitted, made them a very fine curtsy, and flew, so to speak, to the apartments of the Queen-Mother, her aunt. . . . (Locatelli.)

It will thus be perceived that access to the royal residences was not difficult to obtain. At Versailles there were beggars and hucksters selling trifles even on the landings of the stair-cases. Thieves plied their trade, and one rogue went so far, one day, as to steal the diamonds on the hat the King had just laid on a table. The number of persons in attendance was immense, for the Queen, as well as the King, the Dauphin, Monsieur, Madame, every member of the royal family, had his or her Household : when we add to these the soldiers on duty and the swarm of lackeys, tradesmen, loafers, and parasites of every kind that helped to swell the numbers of the Court, it becomes evident that its total population must have been well over 10,000 souls.

Richelieu had done his utmost to attract the French nobility to Paris : Louis XIV made it the duty of that nobility to live at Versailles. He had a great prince's eye and memory for

THE SEVENTEENTH CENTURY

faces. "He saw and noticed everybody, not a soul escaped him—not even those who had no hope of being seen." If any

Concentration of the Nobility at Versailles.
favour was asked for an absentee : "That is a man I never see," he would answer dryly, or "I do not know him." So the nobles forsook their beautiful dwellings in the provinces, or their convenient houses in Paris, in the hope of obtaining, after years of intrigue, "two small, dark, garret rooms, into which neither light nor air could penetrate," but which were in the King's palace, close to him : and the greatest punishment he could inflict upon them was to order them back to their own homes.

"I would rather die than spend two months without seeing him," was the Duc de Richelieu's confession to Mme. de Maintenon : and Vardes, on his return from exile, said, "Sire, far from your presence a man is not only unhappy, he is ridiculous !" "The creation of that horror of exile," says Stendhal, "was the masterpiece of Louis XIV."

WORKS TO CONSULT : In addition to those already quoted, the *Letters* of Mme. de Sévigné, Mme. de Maintenon, Bussy-Rabutin, and Madame, Duchess of Orleans ; La Bruyère's *Caractères* ; the *Works* and *Memoirs* of Louis XIV ; Locatelli's, *Voyage en France* ; Dangeau's *Journal* ; the *Memoirs* of Choisy, de La Fare, Mme. de La Fayette, Saint-Simon, Primi Visconti, etc.

A. Barine, *Madame, Mère du Régent* (1909) ; Boislisle, *P. Scarron et Françoise d'Aubigné* (1894) ; Bourgeois, *Le grand Siècle* (1894) ; P. Clément, *Louis XIV et Mme. de Montespan* (1868) ; A. Dayot, *Louis XIV* (1909) ; E. Forichon, *Marly*, in the *Revue de Paris*, 1909 ; Fr. Funck-Brentano, *Le Drame des Poisons* (1900) ; Funck-Brentano and P. d'Estrée, *Les Nouvellistes* (1905) ; *Figaro et ses devanciers* (1910) ; H. Gauthier-Villars, *La Princesse Palatine*, in the *Grande Revue* (1907) ; D'Haussonville and G. Hanotaux, *Souvenirs sur Mme. de Maintenon* (1903–4) ; J. Lair, *Louise de La Vallière* (1907) ; J. Lacour-Gayet, *L'éducation politique de Louis XIV* (1898) ; J. Lemoine, *Mme. de Montespan et la légende des poisons* (1908) ; Lemoine and Lichtenberger, *Trois familiers du grand Condé* (1909) ; *De La Vallière à Montespan* (1905) ; P. de Nolhac, *Histoire du Château de Versailles* (1900 et seq.) ; A. Pérate, *Versailles* ; G. Piton, *Marly-le-Roi* ; A. Taphanel, *La Beaumette et Saint-Cyr* (1898).

CHAPTER VIII

THE GLORIOUS YEARS, 1661–1678

I. The forces of France : The Ministers : The Army. **II.** First
successes : The Devolution War. **III.** The Dutch War.

I

SPAIN, already decadent in the time of Richelieu,
seemed moribund in 1661. True, her King, Philip IV,
a kind of fetish whose every thought and action were
governed by etiquette, still reigned over territories so vast that,
as men said, the sun never set upon them, and the memory of
past grandeur, not less than the national pride in
which the most poverty-stricken hidalgo can drape
himself as in a cloak, still lent a certain prestige to
the Spanish monarchy ; but it was undermined by the bureaucracy, overwhelmed by the weight of a huge clergy, and hopelessly ruined, for its population, which diminished steadily, lived
" nobly " without working; a skeleton proudly tricked out in
glittering ornaments, it subsisted solely by the support of its
allies. The Hapsburg at Vienna was hardly more powerful
than he of Madrid : the Emperor Leopold I reigned by various
titles over ill-assorted races ; moreover, he had to make a stand
against the Turks who were attacking him, and the League of
the Rhine, which was threatening him in the name of the King
of France. For the Princes of Germany were doffing their hats
and holding out their hands to Louis XIV ; the majority of
them were ignorant, brutal, drunken, venal, selfish, and particu-
larist, utterly devoid of any national sentiment. The Free
States of Italy seemed falling into decline, and the rest of the
peninsula was a kind of European colony. Puritan England
felt a loyalist respect for the King she had restored in 1660, but
did not in the least understand him : Charles II (Stuart), a

209

charming and polished gentleman after the French fashion, brought up in France, which he loved, aimed at restoring the **England under** Papacy and absolute power in his kingdom ; when **Charles II.** she came to realize this, old England made up her mind to get rid of him, but while working to this end she was not particularly dangerous to her neighbours. Sweden in 1661 held sway over a considerable domain, but she was always short of money, and could do nothing without subsidies from Louis XIV : indeed, she had been the client of France for thirty years. Beside her, the vast Russian Empire was still in process of formation. Denmark scarcely counted any longer. Poland was failing, and her neighbours were casting covetous eyes on her territory : in 1663 Colbert was to work ardently, but in vain, to make her elect one of the Condés as her king.

Meanwhile there had grown up on the lower shores of the North Sea a new State, small as regards population, but great **The United** by reason of its wealth and valour ; this was the **Provinces.** Republic of the United Provinces. Since the decline of Spain, it had become the first of maritime Powers ; it had seized nearly all the Portuguese provinces, and its merchant ships, protected by a formidable navy, had almost a monopoly of the trade of Europe, whether making long voyages from China to Brazil, or coasting, transporting from port to port the salt fish of Amsterdam, the spices of Batavia, the sheep and oxen of the polders, the wools of Dutch manufacturers, the boats built at Saardam. The Bank of Amsterdam ranked as the first in the world. The University of Leyden reckoned 2000 students. Dutch printing-presses published the works of Grotius, Vossius, and Huygens, and the famous political gazettes which appeared freely. It was in Holland that Descartes composed his *Discours de la Méthode*, that Spinoza speculated, that Frans Hals, Ruysdael, Rembrandt, Potter, Cuyp, and Jan Vermeer painted. This vigorous and flourishing little country, inspired by an indomitable man, was to be the most terrible adversary of the great King.

But in 1661, flourishing as the United Provinces were, and great as was the consideration shown by Louis XIV himself to the Grand Pensionary of Holland, no comparison seemed possible between them and France, which indeed no other country in

Europe could claim to rival. In the first place the French population amounted to some 20,000,000 inhabitants, as many as those of Germany and Austria together, and almost four times as many as those of England, which at this period had but five or six millions. Great France, as fashioned by the administration of Richelieu and the Treaties of Westphalia, dominated all the other States by her strength and discipline, just as her sovereign himself surpassed the conscientious but discouraged Emperor Leopold I, Philip IV, King of Spain, the laconic idol of an exhausted country, and the needy and venal Charles II of England.

Louis XIV was served by the most adroit ministers, as by the most brilliant generals. His Secretary of State for Foreign **Hugues de** Affairs was Hugues de Lionne. The nephew of **Lionne.** Abel Servien, he had learned his profession of minister from childhood; he had worked under Mazarin, and practised the methods of that incomparable diplomatist. He took part in the negotiations of Westphalia, invented for the Treaty of the Pyrenees that famous little *moyennant* (in consideration of) which made the renunciation of the Infanta conditional on the payment of the dowry, worked at the League of the Rhine, travelled as political agent throughout Europe, with the secrets and intrigues of which he was marvellously familiar. He was a man of pleasure, enjoying idleness, yet indefatigable and ready to spend whole nights at work when necessary, eager, subtle, energetic, an experienced diplomatist, and supple as the " late lamented Cardinal " himself, witty, cultivated, with a lively imagination tempered by a classical good sense, a great gambler, a great lover of women, and for the rest so charming that Mazarin during his exile in 1651 did not fear any of those who attempted to take his place with the Queen so much as he dreaded his dear pupil, Hugues de Lionne.

Lionne died in 1671, worn out by work and pleasure, and was replaced by Arnauld de Pomponne, who had nothing in common **Arnauld de** with him but his efficiency. Pomponne, who in **Pomponne.** former days had been a *habitué* of the Hôtel de Rambouillet, had remained the worthy man of a bygone generation, and as a diplomatist he had " an art, a singular skill in getting the best of an argument in negotiation, a subtlety and a flexibility devoid of cunning which enabled him to gain his ends without irritating his opponents." But he was no fanatic for work like Colbert ; he enjoyed conversation in town and correspondence with Mme. de Sévigné; in short, he cultivated friendship, as if the worship of the God of Versailles had been compatible with private affections. He even quitted the Court occasionally, without any show of despair, to go and rest on his estate. . . . Colbert and Louvois did their utmost to discredit so impertinent a rival, and Pomponne, who, in addition to his other offences, was suspected of Jansenism and was a nephew of the great Arnauld, was disgraced in 1679, on the occasion of the Matthioli affair. However, his merit was so indisputable that he was restored to office in 1691. He died four years later.

If Colbert and Louvois had combined for the overthrow of Pomponne, it was because each of them proposed to fill his **The younger** place with a henchman of his own. Colbert **Colberts.** triumphed; the King appointed his brother, Colbert de Croissy. The latter had the harsh and rapacious disposition of his elder brother, the same deference towards the great ones of the earth, and, according to d'Ormesson, a " very heavy " but well-stored mind. Professionally he was a clever business man, cunning as a Norman, ready for anything, and full of resource. His son, Colbert de Torcy, married Pomponne's daughter, and succeeded him : he proved himself a good diplomatist, adroit and trustworthy ; like Lionne, Louvois, and Seignelay, he had begun his apprenticeship to ministerial functions at his adolescence.

Such were Louis XIV's principal diplomatists. To these must be added Turenne and Condé, whose disgrace, contrary to tradition, was really a very short one. But the actual director of foreign policy was the King himself; he was well versed in the calling, having learnt it from Mazarin, and he worked at it daily with that solar regularity which excited the admiration of his courtiers as it still excites ours. Prudent and judicious at the outset, his policy became preposterously arrogant as he himself became so.

The Secretaries of State for War were at first Le Tellier and his son Louvois. Michel Le Tellier was a lawyer, intelligent, handsome, gentle, insinuating—and so modest ! Spanheim tells us of his " natural repugnance to any manifestation of pride " ; he scarcely increased his scale of living when he

Michel Le Tellier. became Chancellor. " In social intercourse," says Choisy, " he scattered only flowers " (indeed, these were the sole tokens of friendship to be expected from him). " He was an accomplished humbug," says the honest Saint-Hilaire bluntly. " He was inclined to bear malice," adds Gourville. And Saint-Simon sums him up exhaustively as " supple, adroit, artful, modest, always between the two extremes, keeping his end well in view, full of intelligence, vigour, and, at the same time, of amenity, gentleness, foresight," etc. etc. For the rest, the gentle Le Tellier was an excellent administrator. In 1661, when he was fifty-eight and had been Secretary of State since 1643, he had already indicated the main lines of the reforms which were subsequently carried out. From 1662 onwards he obtained for his son Louvois the right of " signing " together with himself ; but he continued to direct administration until about 1677, and it is doing him less than justice to attribute all the credit for reforms to Louvois : Le Tellier's part in these was at least as considerable as his son's, and Louis XIV was as well versed in military organization as in diplomacy.

In 1661 Louvois was twenty-two, just a year younger than the King, and from the age of fifteen his claim to succeed his

Louvois. father had been assured. From that father he had inherited a handsome face, the effect of which on the fair sex he enhanced by the care he bestowed on his dress, though it may be doubted whether this was as powerful a factor in his successes among ladies as his prestige as a minister. In other respects the Marquis de Louvois bore little resemblance to the modest Le Tellier ; as brusque, overbearing, violent, and arrogant as his father was the reverse—tall, strong, and full-blooded, " his body heavy and fleshy " (Spanheim), he " treated all the world in a domineering fashion, and the natural ferocity painted on his countenance terrified all those who came in contact with him " (Saint-Hilaire) ; in short, he was " the most perfect clerk and the greatest bully imaginable " (Siri). His favour was based primarily on his merit, which was unparalleled in all things pertaining to war, but also to some extent on the fact that he had posed as the pupil of the King : Louis was greatly attracted by this clever

213

personage who came to him for advice and instruction, and whom he undertook to train for the business of the State ; finally, it was derived from his skill in encouraging the King's inclination for war and flattering his conquering instincts : Louis XIV considered Louvois the Minister *par excellence* of his "glory." Thus Louvois was a disastrous force ; all the memoirs of the seventeenth century accuse him of having fomented wars and incited religious persecution solely that he might remain "the necessary man" and counterbalance the influence of Colbert ; and we cannot but agree with the memoirs.

Often, in the seventeenth century, some florid, well-dressed fellow, sometimes accompanied by several robust veterans, and **System of** even by a few pretty girls, might be seen perorat-**recruiting.** ing in public places, jingling a purse of crowns which sounded harmoniously in the ears of loafers, while his followers brandished white bread and fowls on a spit under their noses. This was a non-commissioned officer recruiting men for his captain. Enlistment was concluded between two drinks at a neighbouring dram-shop, and it was useless for the new recruit to protest as soon as he became sober ; the recruiting officer never had any trouble in finding witnesses to swear that they had seen him drinking the King's health.

When once the recruits were enrolled, they had to be equipped. At the beginning of the reign only the troops of His Majesty's Household wore uniform, but the custom of dressing the men all alike gradually spread throughout the army ; towards 1673 it was almost universally adopted.

In April, 1665, the Italian Locatelli was present at one of those grand military parades which Louis XIV loved to show **Household** to ladies on the plain of Saint-Denis. The gigantic **Troops.** Swiss Guards, crowned by black velvet caps with red, white, and blue plumes, marched past first to the sound of fifes and drums, their halberds on their shoulders ; they were uniformly dressed in blue and red ratteen, relieved by facings ornamented with tufts of silk and silver. After them, on tall white or dappled horses, with crimson trappings, came the Grands Mousquetaires, whose blue cloth tunics were embroidered on the chest and back with a silver cross surrounded by golden rays,

214

and the King's cipher. Then the Petits Mousquetaires, without any silver braid on their tunics, riding black horses with blue trappings, adorned with an L and a golden crown; and finally the soldiers, in grey, blue, or red cloth and black silk cravats embroidered with silver. The young King bestrode a large dapple-grey charger, whose saddle and trappings, covered with gold and precious stones, were of a " warm dry rose " tint, and his stirrups of silver-gilt; the King changed his mount several times, " and all these horses, proud and joyous at bearing the King, did nothing but prance and gallop." Two wide flame-coloured ribbons, matching the immense plume which adorned his hat, fastened back Louis' long hair; his collar of Venetian point floated over his gilded gorget; his doublet of light-coloured *moiré*, so thickly braided with gold and silver that the tint was barely distinguishable, was unbuttoned, showing a vest of brocade *à la Polonaise* trimmed with wide gold lace adorned with brilliants; two large diamonds sparkled like stars at the points of the two golden lilies which formed the clasp of a belt of an antique pattern; his wide Walloon trunk hose surrounded him like a little petticoat; garters of flame-colour and gold held up his stockings, which were of the same shade of brown as his shoes of English calf, and spurs of violet enamel were fastened to his feet by gold and diamond buckles. In his hand he held a switch " twisted like two serpents entwined," made of a black flexible wood said to have come from China: a present from Mazarin, like the little sword which hung at His Majesty's side. Thus equipped, and beautiful as Mars, the young warrior bore little resemblance to the King nobly but soberly attired in brown slightly relieved with gold known to Saint-Simon and a later generation.

Under Louis XIV, a foot soldier received 5 *sols* a day, a cavalryman 15 *sols*, and a dragoon 11 *sols*. The captain's pay **Pay of** was only 75 *livres* a month. But no great skill **soldiers.** was required to add considerably to his income. In the time of Louis XIII it was almost a rule that the French infantry companies, composed on paper of some sixty men and paid on this basis, consisted really of from fifteen to twenty; on the days when the war-commissaries came to inspect their troops, captains made up their effectives by supers (*passe-*

volants) : lackeys, loafers, beggars of every sort, hired for a few hours, dressed and equipped, marched past in the ranks of the true soldiers. Le Tellier and Louvois did their best to suppress this practice, but they were never altogether successful.

Above the private soldiers there were the *anspessade* or soldier of the first class, the *corporal* or *caporal*, and the *sergeant*, **The Military** called in the cavalry the *maréchal des logis* ; these **Hierarchy.** inferior officers could never hope, save in very exceptional cases, to become officers. The superior officers were the *ensign* or sub-lieutenant (called a *cornet* in the cavalry), the *lieutenant*, the *captain*, the *major*, the *lieutenant-colonel*, the *colonel*. Above these were the general officers : *brigadier, field-marshal,* and *lieutenant-general.* Finally, the *Marshals of France.* Under Louis XIII the generals took over the command in turns, and we have pointed out the disadvantages of this custom. They ceased to alternate one with another after the decree of 1675, which established "the order of the list," or in other words, decided that the officer of highest seniority in his rank should always command his equals.

Not all officers, and not even all generals, were of noble birth. Catinat and Gassion were the sons of lawyers, many others were plebeians, like Saint-Hilaire, or Gangnières, whose father was a butcher at Jargeau. Louvois deserves credit for having established that henceforth military rank should be everything and nobility nothing : duke or marquis, a man had to obey his superior officer ; and Mme. de Sévigné tells us how the son of Le Tellier used to remind the officers of the Court of their duty.

M. de Louvois said loudly the other day to M. de Nogaret : " Sir, your company is in a very bad state." " Sir," he replied, " I did not know it." "It is your business to know it," said M. de Louvois ; " have you seen it ? " " No," answered Nogaret. " It is your business to have seen it, sir." " Sir, I will put it in order." " You ought to have done so already. You must be one thing or the other, sir ; either declare yourself a courtier, or do your duty as an officer." (February 4, 1689.)

Sébastien Le Prestre de Vauban, a simple country squire of Morvan, passed in one stride from the rank of captain to that of brigadier, and became a Marshal of France. **Vauban.** This was because nature had endowed him with such marvellous talent as a military engineer that he never failed in any siege. " The town defended by Vauban," said his compatriots, " is impregnable ; the town invested by Vauban is taken " ; and it was true. The siege of a fortress became in his hands an operation the successive stages of which followed logically and inevitably one after the other, " like the five acts of a tragedy." For defence, he invented forts on a level with the ground, and replaced the high walls of former ages, useless against cannon-balls, by trenches ; he introduced *covered ways*, and bastions so designed that their cross-fire could always enfilade the trenches. By his efforts France was surrounded by a girdle of fortifications so solid that they resisted the enemy until the time of the Revolution, and so imposing that their ruins are still the pride of our towns. " He was a man of medium height and sturdy build, very warlike in appearance, but at the same time superficially coarse and rustic, not to say brutal and ferocious." This was by no means his disposition ; he was, on the contrary, very respectful of human life, and opposed to unjustifiable bombardments. In 1707, at the age of seventy-four, moved by popular suffering, the worthy Vauban published a book, *La Dîme royale*, in which he expresses his indignation against the collectors of customs, and sensibly demands that taxation should be in proportion to income. The financiers could not forgive him for this, and he was disgraced.

The great point in the reforms of Le Tellier and Louvois, seconded by Vauban, was the organization of the artillery and **Army Reforms.** the administrative services. Down to 1669 the artillery was a sort of commercial enterprise : the artillery officers, who were hardly more military than the officers of the *Cour des Aides* (Court of Subsidies), for instance, contracted with the King, under penalties, to establish batteries, and their men were mere workmen or soldiers borrowed from other corps. Louvois created special artillery troops. Then he organized *magazines* of victuals and forage close to the frontiers ; thanks to him, the cavalry was enabled to take the field even before the grass had grown again, and the troops could live in the ravaged districts, advantages which His Majesty's marshals did not fail to turn to the best account.

For at this period war really resembled a game of chess. On the field of operations, duly marked out and delimited, the generals began the contest every year in the spring. When, after complicated manœuvres, one of the adversaries had lost or gained several pieces—towns or fortresses—the decisive battle took place ; from the top of some slope, whence the whole chess-board—the battlefield—lay before him, the Marshal moved his fine regiments backwards and forwards . . . Check and mate, the loser cleared his board : " the pawns were put back into their boxes, or the regiments into their winter quarters, and each one went off to attend to his private affairs while awaiting the next game or campaign."

II

Louis XIV, who proposed to acquire the fame of a great sovereign, could conceive no other method of achieving this end than war and conquest : now the traditional enemy of the King of France was the King of Spain. On the other hand, Hugues de Lionne could not but feel impelled to follow the policy of Mazarin, which was also his own, and to realize the advantages which the Spanish marriage and the Treaty of the Pyrenees had apparently been concluded to ensure some day. Thus it is by no means absurd to conclude with Mignet that " the Spanish succession was the pivot of all Louis XIV's policy." Nor is it any more so to believe the exact opposite, for Mignet's famous phrase is indeed but a hypothesis. As a fact we only see from the correspondence of ambassadors, ministers, and the King himself that the projects and diplomatic enterprises of the reign were very varied, that they changed, arose from conjunctures, were interrupted or developed according to events. That Louis XIV's ruling thought was the Spanish succession, that he wished to unite in his house the two most illustrious crowns of the world and to reconstitute for his own advantage a power superior to that of the Emperor Charles V is possible, but we have no proof of this. Be this as it may, such a dream would have been no chimera in the seventeenth century : nations were then looked upon as the property and inheritance of kings, and their fate was decided between diplomatists just as that of private fortunes is weighed between men of business : why

Rivalry of France and Spain.

should Louis XIV have hesitated to add to his own possessions, which were France, those destined to revert to his wife, which were Spain ? Whatever his plans may have been, we see him from the moment of his accession slowly elaborating them, because he was prudent and patient, by strengthening and perfecting his army. Meanwhile he made trial of his power in certain small adventures.

At this period it was an accepted axiom that an ambassador represented the actual person of his master ; it followed that the **Precedence of** order of precedence of the various ambassadors **Ambassadors.** in official ceremonies was very important, and that, on the other hand, their ages and individual qualities had nothing to do with the question. By common consent the envoy of the Emperor came first, but the envoy of France claimed the second place, to which the envoy of Spain also aspired. In 1661 this competition had disastrous results in London ; at the solemn entry of the Swedish ambassador, the coach of the Baron de Watteville, the representative of Philip IV, tried to take precedence of that of the Comte d'Estrades, who represented Louis XIV ; there was a regular battle, with dead and wounded ; but the followers of the French ambassador were outnumbered, and had to yield. Louis XIV at once demanded an apology from his father-in-law; he obtained it, together with the recall of Watteville and a promise that the Spanish ambassadors throughout Europe should henceforth forbear to " compete " with his.

Shortly afterwards (1662), when the King of England demanded that foreign vessels should give the salute first to his flag " on the English seas," Louis XIV wrote a very proud letter (rather too proud, indeed, for good taste) ; and Charles II was obliged to give way in this " matter of the flag."

Finally, this same year, 1662, was the date of the affair of the Corsican Guard. The King had sent to the Holy See the least **Affair of the** patient of men, the Duc de Créqui, with secret **Corsican Guard.** instructions to make himself intolerable, which Créqui at once succeeded in doing, for if his first interview with His Holiness was chilly, the second was unpleasant, and the third absolutely stormy. Neither the imperious Alexander VII not his Cardinals could brook such treatment. On August 20,

1662, a dispute arose between some of M. de Créqui's men and several Corsican soldiers of the Pope's Guard ; supported by their comrades, the latter fired upon the Farnese Palace and the coach of the ambassador's wife. Créqui immediately withdrew from the Papal States, and the King confiscated Avignon, and then assembled an army with great clamour. The Holy Father had to disband his Corsican Guard, raise an expiatory pyramid, and also give satisfaction to the Dukes of Parma and Modena, the *protégés* of Louis XIV, in certain territories ; finally, in July, 1664, Cardinal Chigi came to Fontainebleau to read an apologetic declaration ; " he was the first Legate of the Roman Court who had ever been sent to ask pardon," said M. de Voltaire gleefully.

Meanwhile Louis XIV was eager to prove his fine army. In 1663, 120,000 Turks having invaded Hungary, he offered the Emperor 60,000 soldiers, 30,000 as King of France, and 30,000 as a member of the League of the Rhine. The unhappy Leopold, uneasy and distrustful, did not dare to accept more than 6000, commanded by Coligny. On August 1, 1664, the Turks were defeated at Saint-Gothard by Montecuculli. The French troops had played a gallant part in the victory ; it was said that when the Grand Vizier Koeprilü saw our gentlemen with their fair periwigs, their feathers, ribbons, and laces fluttering in the wind, he asked who these young girls were ; and that for his part La Feuillade, who had taken over the command on the death of Coligny, made this curt but eloquent speech to them : " Comrades, there are three hundred leagues between us and Vaugirard, and there is no way to get there but over the bellies of these ——. Forward ! " They advanced, and at their first charge Koeprilü learned by the flight of his Turks what was the worth, if not what was the sex, of M. de La Feuillade's young ladies.

In 1662 Louis XIV pointed out to his father-in-law that as Marie-Thérèse's dowry had not been paid over within the stipulated time, the Infanta's renunciation of her claim to the throne must be annulled. Moreover, Hugues de Lionne was already at work forming a series of alliances against Spain. The needy King of England, who had become the brother-in-law of Louis XIV by the marriage of his sister Henrietta with Philippe d'Orléans, in 1662 obtained, through the French King's intervention, the Infanta of Portugal and her rich dowry (Tangiers and Bombay), and sold back to us Dunkirk and Mardick for five millions (a profitable transaction). In Germany the Emperor, harassed by the Turkish peril, and opposed even in the Diet itself by the clients of Louis XIV, was powerless to help Spain. In 1663 France was treating with Denmark ; Sweden seemed still fettered by French gold. Finally, in 1662 Lionne signed a treaty of alliance with the United Provinces. But such a treaty was necessarily illusory ; for, on the one hand, Holland did not want powerful France as her immediate neighbour, and, on the other, the French King had no idea of renouncing Marie-Thérèse's claim to the Spanish Netherlands. This claim he based very ingeniously upon a custom observed in certain Flemish provinces, known as the law of *devolution*, according to which the children, after the death of father or mother, became sole owners of the fortune of the deceased, while the surviving parent retained only the usufruct. According to Louis XIV's argument, Marie-Thérèse, by the death of her mother, had become the owner of the territories of the Spanish monarchy in which the law of devolution was recognized—that is to say, in the Netherlands—and these territories would revert to her on the death of Philip IV, who had only a life-interest in them. The Dutch did not accept these conclusions for a moment ; they were soon to give rise to a conflict.

The Law of Devolution.

In 1665 an unforeseen event upset the diplomatic manœuvres of Louis XIV : England, the friend of France, attacked Holland, the ally of France, and Holland called upon the King to carry out the treaty of 1662. The King was greatly embarrassed, but he had no thought of evading his engagements with the Republic, on the neutrality of which he counted as necessary to the success of his projects concerning the Low Countries. As the treaty allowed him an interval of four months before intervention, he tried first to induce the two Powers to accept his mediation. But he failed, and as Philip IV had just died, leaving no heir but a child of his second marriage (September 17, 1665), his one thought was to finish off this war as quickly as possible in order to have his hands free to deal with Spain. On land his troops accordingly marched against the robber-bishop of Münster, Bernhard von Galen, who was attacking the Dutch

221

from behind. On the sea his fleet sped towards that of De Ruyter, which, however, it was unable to join, owing to the inadequacy of the French warships of that period. And as soon as he saw that his allies the Dutch were beginning to get the better of their adversaries, Louis invaded the Spanish Netherlands with 50,000 men and Turenne, to occupy the territory he claimed for Marie-Thérèse by virtue of the famous right of Devolution (May, 1667).

The Governor, Castel Rodrigo, had very few soldiers ; for the war against Portugal kept the best troops of His Catholic

Louis XIV occupies Flanders. Majesty in Spain. Louis XIV accordingly gathered a veritable harvest of fortresses ; in a campaign of two and a half months, he took possession of Flanders by a simple military march ; after which he returned to celebrate his triumph in France, while the army went into winter quarters.

Europe was greatly stirred by the news of this sudden conquest. Holland was distracted by it, but her struggle against England was not yet at an end. At last she succeeded in signing the Peace of Breda under the auspices of Louis XIV (July, 1667) ; six months later the United Provinces entered into a league with their recent enemy, England, and with Sweden, against France.

But Louis XIV had had time to prepare a new stroke. At the end of January, 1668, 15,000 men, gathered from various directions, punctually assembled in Burgundy, the province governed by the Great Condé. On February 3, the Prince invaded Franche-Comté at their head. On the 7th, Louis XIV arrived in great haste to join the army ; he had ridden 250 kilometres. Twelve days later, when he set out to return to Saint-Germain, the Comté was conquered ; it had taken less than three weeks, just a quarter of the time it had taken for the conquest of Flanders. The Spaniards wrote that " the King of France might have been content to send his lackeys to take possession of the Comté."

Louis XIV would gladly have continued the war and followed up his successes. But the Swiss, very uneasy with regard to their new neighbours, were stirring ; Portugal made peace with Spain ; and finally the King heard of the Anglo-Swedo-Dutch

Triple Alliance. It cut him to the quick; his conduct to the United Provinces had been very correct, and he had supposed that they in return would have allowed him to carry out his plans undisturbed. Urged on by Colbert, he thereupon determined to punish them. But always prudent, and judging that he had not as yet enough troops and allies to embark on this enterprise, he signed at Aix-la-Chapelle a treaty the moderation of which caused great astonishment (May 2, 1668): Franche-Comté was thereby restored to Spain, and Louis retained only the Spanish fortresses.

III

Colbert was the person mainly responsible for the Dutch war. True, the King had every reason to feel resentment against the United Provinces. Foremost among these was the one just mentioned: the Dutch had checked his progress by means of the Triple Alliance. Then their gazettes never ceased ridiculing the *Roi-Soleil*; on the occasion of the negotiations of 1668 they had struck medals such as that on which five horsemen were seen beneath a sun, with this inscription: *Stetit sol in medio coeli*, and the other on which Holland boasted of having " strengthened the laws, purified religion, aided, defended, and reconciled kings," etc.—which was too much. Colbert, for his part, could not meekly accept the action of the United Provinces in replying to his protectionist tariff of 1667 by tariffs still higher and a sort of " boycott " of French products. And wealthy, desirable, insolent little Holland tempted him. He accordingly incited the King to make war on her.

The War with Holland.

The Government of the Seven United Provinces was as republican and decentralized as that of France was monarchical and centralized. As a fact, the Provinces, which differed one from the other by language, manners, and race, being partly German and partly French, lacked unity; it was the persecution by Philip II and the war against Spain which had made them a nation. Each of them, and within them each of their towns, formed an almost autonomous little State, governed by an assembly, and before any decision of a general order affecting the federation as a whole could be adopted, it had to be *unanimously* voted by the States-General, composed of the delegates of the seven Provinces. Nevertheless, one of the provinces, Holland, was greatly superior to the rest in wealth and influence ; if it was Zealand which nominated the ambassadors to be sent to England, Holland alone chose the ambassadors to France, Sweden, and Germany (and this is why in France the Seven United Provinces are usually called by the generic name of Holland) ; in like manner the States-General, which met in one of her villages, The Hague, generally followed her counsels, and consequently her Grand Pensionary, a sort of political administrator or minister whom she nominated every five years, became the Prime Minister of the United Provinces. In 1668 this Pensionary, who had held office since 1653, was called Jan de Witt. His brown hair, big prominent eyes, and thick moustache did not make him handsome. But he was an upright man and a skilful politician ; industrious, intelligent, supple, adroit, and an orator of great parts, he excelled not only in giving general satisfaction in the United Provinces, but in steering a safe course between France, Spain, and England. And this middle-class republican who went on foot through the streets followed by a single servant, who despised the mob, but prayed God every day to save his country from the fury of kings, was to die a death worthy of the pages of Plutarch.

The rich, cultivated, and tolerant citizens who administered the Seven Provinces inclined, like their chief, Jan de Witt, to **The** peace, favourable to commerce and the arts. " Stathouder." But there were many malcontents in the Republic ; insignificant persons who aspired to be admitted into the municipalities like the more important citizens, soldier-squireens who wished for war, proletarians naturally hostile to the commercial aristocracy, fanatical Calvinists opposed to religious toleration. The head of this opposition was the *Stathouder*. In the beginning each of the provinces had had its special *Stathouder*, a sort of president of its government, but from 1620 onwards six out of the seven provinces had made it a custom to nominate the same man to this office : the Prince of Orange, the head of the House of Nassau, who was, in addition, the Captain-General of the forces of the Union. Now the

Prince of Orange—necessarily a partisan of war, during which his military functions gave him greater influence in the State, and at the same time inimical to the middle-class Republic by reason of his birth—thus became the natural leader of the opponents of the Government and of the Grand Pensionary. In 1651 the latter had scored a great success against his traditional adversary the *Stathouder* : William II of Orange had died without children save an unborn infant, and the States-General seized this opportunity to declare it useless to appoint a successor to the office. In 1668, therefore, there was no *Stathouder*. But William III of Orange, the posthumous son of William II, was now seventeen years old. His birth made him the leader of the opposition to the States-General, and the enemy of the Grand Pensionary. The reverses of Holland brought about the death of Jan de Witt and the Prince's triumph.

For four years, from 1668 to 1672, Louis XIV prepared methodically for war upon the United Provinces. In England, **The Treaty of** Charles II volunteered his aid. He cherished **Dover, 1670.** various secret designs, such as the re-establishment of the Roman Catholic faith and of absolute power in his kingdom. But it was certainly difficult for him to ask his Parliament for subsidies for such purposes. He therefore applied to the French ambassador, Colbert de Croissy. His sister, the fascinating Mme. Henriette, was sent over to induce him finally to sell himself. She came back bearing the Treaty of Dover (1670) and the alliance of Charles II. Sweden, for her part, put herself up to auction. Louis XIV offered 200,000 crowns ; Holland bid higher ; finally France carried the day with 400,000 crowns (1672). The King secretly incited the Hungarians, always ready to revolt, against the Emperor. In Poland he negotiated for the elevation to the throne of a French prince—Condé, for instance. Finally, in Germany French gold succeeded as usual. And while Lionne and Pomponne were weaving this web of alliances, Vauban fortified the strongholds of Flanders, where the Court made a sumptuous " progress " in 1670, and Le Tellier and Louvois collected vast stores of provisions, and an army of 120,000 soldiers, more numerous perhaps than any ever yet seen in Europe.

To meet all this, the United Provinces had about 80,000 men, obtained with great difficulty from the States-General, for the pacific middle classes are not fond of opening their purse-strings for men of war. And these 80,000 men, distributed in half-dismantled fortresses, were ill-trained and ill-provided with victuals and powder. (Louvois had, indeed, by unknown machinations procured part of the munitions of the French army in Holland itself.) But the inefficient Dutch troops were commanded by the youthful William of Orange, whom it had been necessary to nominate Captain-General. This prince, a thin stripling, with bowed shoulders, a hooked nose between hollow cheeks, and a face seamed by small-pox, asthmatic, always ailing, carried in his frail body one of the most energetic souls that have ever existed. A wretched general, his tenacity was his substitute for talent ; on the morrow of the most flagrant disaster, he would set to work again with his phlegmatic persistence, and soon he would reappear, a threatening presence. This terrible man, insensible to luxury, vanity, love, pity, pleasure, to everything save political passion, came very near to vanquishing powerful France and that Louis XIV whose antithesis he was in every respect. But in 1672 he was only twenty-one, and the States-General felt so weak that they wrote humbly to the King asking him how they could have offended His Majesty, and offering him any satisfaction he might desire. They received only a mocking answer. In the spring of 1672 Louis XIV and his ally Charles II took the field.

The King with Turenne and 80,000 men was joined near Maestricht by Condé and 40,000 soldiers, and, as in 1667, his first successes were overwhelming ; at the beginning of June his army was already on the right bank of the Rhine, and he had only to cross the Yssel to reach Amsterdam. As the Prince of Orange had entrenched himself behind this deep river with 20,000 men, it was decided to turn him on the right and cross the Rhine, which was scarcely defended at all ; and while Luxembourg distracted the attention of the Dutch by a curtain of troops, scouts went in search of a place where the great river seemed fordable. " Some of the natives then informed the Prince de Condé that the recent drought had formed a ford on an arm of the Rhine near an old tower which was used as a tolls-

The Prince of Orange Captain-General.

226

office, and called the Tolhuys, the toll-house [beyond Schenk].
. . . The King ordered the Comte de Guiche to sound this ford;
there were only some twenty paces to swim in the middle of the

The Passage of stream. . . . This space was nothing, for twenty
the Rhine. horses abreast broke the current which was not at
all rapid " (Voltaire). On the opposite bank a single infantry
regiment and a few horsemen were drawn up to oppose the
landing. But while the French artillery rained projectiles
upon them, " the King's Household troops and the pick of the
cavalry to the number of 15,000 men passed safely across; the
Prince de Condé crossed beside them in a copper boat. The
Dutch cavalry began to retreat and the infantry to surrender
very peaceably, when the Duc de Longueville, Condé's nephew,
" his head full of the fumes of wine, fired a pistol at his adversaries, who were begging for their lives on their knees, crying:
' No quarter for this rabble ! ' The Dutch infantry in despera-
tion snatched up their weapons and fired a volley which killed
the Duc de Longueville. A cavalry captain, who had not fled
with the rest, ran to the Prince de Condé, who had just landed,
and was mounting his horse, and held a pistol to his head. The
Prince made a movement to avoid the shot, which only broke his
wrist. This was the only wound Condé ever received in all his
campaigns. The French, exasperated, threw themselves upon
the Dutch infantry, which began to flee in all directions.
Louis XIV passed over on a pontoon with the infantry, having
himself directed the entire march." . . . " Such " adds Voltaire,
" was this passage of the Rhine, a brilliant and unique action,
celebrated at the time as one of those great events destined to
live in the memory of man." Boileau extolled it in his well-
known Epistle. But Napoleon considered it " an operation of
the fourth rank." Be this as it may, each of the provinces, on
hearing of the arrival of the royal army in the heart of the
Republic, recalled its individual contingents in terror for its
own defence, and the Prince of Orange, reduced to a few thousand
men, was obliged to retreat hastily from the line of the Yssel.
Hereupon Nimeguen, Arnheim, Zwolle, Utrecht, all the towns
surrendered when called upon to submit. An officer named
Mazel sent this message to M. de Turenne : " If you will send
me sixty horses, I could take two or three fortresses ; " and this

was hardly an idle boast. A few French horsemen advanced to Muiden, where are the principal locks of the Zuider Zee. Now Muiden is at the gates of Amsterdam; the great town was already in panic; the richest inhabitants thought of embarking for Batavia; the municipal council were discussing the handing over of the keys even before they had been demanded; there is no doubt that had a few French troops presented themselves at this moment, Amsterdam would have opened her gates. . . . But the King, Turenne, and Louvois were over-prudently employed in taking towns instead of marching straight upon the capital. The delay was irreparable : on June 20, the very day of the capitulation of Utrecht, the States ordered the lock-gates at Muiden to be opened.

"Holland is a conquest of man from the sea ; it is an artificial country, a country that has been made." If the system of dikes and locks by which she holds back the sea upon her shores, and keeps her rivers within their beds, be cut, the waters at once resume their sway, spread over the country, submerge fields and meadows, and leave only the narrow threads of embanked roadways uncovered. Holland had already defended herself in 1629 by the inundation of her soil ; in 1672 she not only broke open the dikes of the canals, but those of the Zuider Zee, and allowed the sea to mingle its waters with those of the rivers. A truly heroic resolution : all the beautiful country-houses of the rich merchants, with their exotic gardens, their rare plants, and their famous collections, perished ; flocks and crops disappeared ; and the salt water made the land barren for years. But then "Amsterdam was like a huge fortress in the midst of the waters," surrounded by gunboats, for after June 23 it could only be approached in boats. The capital was saved by this suicide of the country.

The Dutch open the sluices.

Meanwhile deputies of the States-General had come to sue for peace from the King. They offered him the towns on the Rhine, Dutch Brabant, and an indemnity of ten millions. When he refused this offer Louis did not commit a great " error " as has been asserted ; he was merely prudent ; for there is every reason to believe that the proposals of the Dutch were not sincere.

228

THE GLORIOUS YEARS, 1661-1678

The whole Republic had turned to the descendant of William the Silent. On July 4 the young Prince of Orange was elected **The Murder of** *Stathouder*. In August, Cornelis, the brother of **the De Witts.** Jan de Witt, was accused of having plotted the death of the Prince of Orange by poison, and was tortured for an hour and a half. On August 20, when Jan came to visit him, the excited mob invaded the prison, dragged the two brothers into the street, murdered them, tore them limb from limb, and gibbeted their remains. . . . Meanwhile more dikes had been thrown down, and the French were closely invested by the waters. The King had returned to France, leaving the command to Luxembourg. When the first frosts set in, Luxembourg, wishing to make a brilliant stroke, left his headquarters at Utrecht in the hope of reaching The Hague on the ice. But a thaw suddenly took place ; his army was forced to fall back on Utrecht by a narrow highway, wading waist-deep in mud and water. Shortly afterwards Luxembourg's communications were very nearly cut ; the Prince of Orange advanced towards the Meuse, but was unable to take Charleroi (December).

Thus the luck seemed to be changing. Before his death, Jan de Witt had successfully concluded an alliance with the Elector of Brandenburg and the Emperor Leopold, who were both uneasy at the progress of French power. As a result of this it became necessary, by the end of 1672, to detach an army to hold the Imperial and Electoral troops on the Rhine. Turenne was entrusted with the task. But in 1673 the King, who hitherto had commanded only with the help of his famous generals, wished to show the world that he could make war on his own initiative, and while Condé in Holland and Turenne on the Rhine were quietly keeping the enemy in check on his right and on his left, Louis ostentatiously laid siege to Maestricht, which he took in a week (June, 1673). To tell the truth, he had the " Sieur Vauban " with him.

This new success determined the coalition against France : the Emperor, the King of Spain, and the Duke of Lorraine **Coalition** (August 30, 1673) joined the Prince of Orange. **against France.** " It became necessary to abandon the three Dutch provinces no less promptly than they had been conquered. The triumphal arch of Saint-Denis and other monuments of the

conquest were scarcely completed when the conquered territories had to be abandoned " (Voltaire). Moreover, Luxembourg, who was in command of the little French army in Holland,
feared that he would be crushed by the more numerous troops of
the *Stathouder* ; but he was able to deceive his adversary by a
feint, and bring back his soldiers without hindrance. Thus it
was France who now had to retire. And in 1674 England,
weary of a war which injured her trade, and in which her fleet
had been constantly beaten by that of Admiral de Ruyter,
abandoned her ally and made peace with Holland. When the
minor German princes in their turn broke with Louis XIV,
France was alone against Europe.

In 1674 she had to maintain three large armies in the field,
without counting the troops who were operating in the Pyrenees
against Spain. The task of the first, commanded by Condé,
was to contain the Dutch and the Spaniards in Flanders ; that
of the second, under Turenne, to check the advance of the
Imperialists in Alsace and in Lorraine ; the third, commanded
by the King in person—he had again, as in the previous year,
reserved the showy part for himself—took the offensive in
Franche-Comté, entered Dôle and Besançon, and for the second
time Louis found himself master of the province in less than
six weeks (May–June, 1674).

In Flanders Condé had to face the sixty or seventy thousand
Dutch, Spanish, and Imperial troops of the Prince of Orange
with forty or fifty thousand men. He had entrenched himself near
Charleroi, in a position so well chosen that the coalition judged
it to be impregnable, and preferred to turn it. The Prince
allowed the main body of their forces to defile quietly, but he
fell upon their rear-guard, composed of Spaniards, and routed it
at Seneffe. William at once halted, and deployed from his
centre. Condé launched a second furious attack. The Dutch
fell back, but, reinforced by the Imperialists, the stubborn
Prince of Orange formed his troops again upon the heights of the
village of Fayt. Condé attacked for the third time, throwing
himself upon the left and then on the right of the enemy, but
failing to break either. "At the end it was evident that only
M. le Prince wished to go on fighting " (La Fare). In the night the
two exhausted armies both retreated. The losses were consider-

able : eight thousand men of the finest French regiments, ten or twelve thousand men on the side of the allies. On the whole it was an indecisive action (August 11, 1674).

On the Rhine Turenne's tactical skill enabled him to resist forces infinitely superior to his own : this campaign of 1674–5, **Turenne ravages the Palatinate.** which was to be his last, was also his most admirable achievement. In June and July, 1674, with 15,000 men, he twice surprised his adversaries and twice defeated them, at Sinzheim and at Ladenburg. But the forces of the allies grew incessantly. Then, by Louvois' orders, Turenne ravaged the rich lands of the Palatinate abominably— that so it might become a desert which would prevent the enemy from marching on Alsace ! The cattle were driven off, the crops destroyed, the small towns and villages methodically set on fire. Useless cruelties, moreover, for the coalition troops quietly invaded Alsace by the bridge of Kehl, which was placed at their disposal by the free town of Strasburg. Turenne flew to meet them with the 30,000 men at his command, and succeeded in checking them temporarily near Strasburg (October). Meanwhile the allies, reinforced by the soldiers of Brandenburg, had mustered 60,000 men. Then Turenne, as if recognizing the impossibility of further resistance, retired into Lorraine by the Col de Saverne, and installed himself in his winter quarters. The enemy, thinking hostilities were suspended till the spring, dispersed throughout Alsace to winter at their ease. But all at once, on the last day of November, Turenne left his quarters without sound of drum or trumpet, marched his army swiftly forward under shelter of the Vosges, from north to south, and after twenty-seven days of a march which the cold made intensely painful, arrived at Belfort, and fell suddenly on the scattered allies. In a fortnight, he had hustled them at Altkirchen, Mulhouse, and Colmar, and thrown them back to the other side of the Rhine. Better still, he had done all this in spite of Louvois, who had desired him to retire upon Champagne in order to oppose a possible advance of the allies towards Paris ; this resistance " to the all-powerful Louvois was not one of the least tokens of Turenne's courage, nor one of the most insignificant exploits of the campaign " (Voltaire). When the great Marshal arrived at Saint-Germain after a journey which had been one long triumph, the King advanced to meet him, embraced him in the presence of the whole Court, and said to him : " You have raised up afresh one of the lilies of my crown."

The campaign of 1675 was a continuation of that of 1674. While Condé was manœuvring against Orange and the King was **Campaign of 1675.** taking a few Flemish towns as was his custom, Turenne, on the right bank of the Rhine, had the illustrious Montecuculli as his adversary. After several months of scientific marching and counter-marching, a great battle at Salzbach seemed imminent between the two famous generals on July 26. M. de Turenne seemed pleased with the order in which he had arranged his troops : " Positively, I think it is not at all bad, and I believe M. de Montecuculli will think what we have just done pretty good," he declared in the morning. At two o'clock he mounted his horse, and advanced along the line of battle to observe the enemy positions once more. As he was passing near some guns, M. de Saint-Hilaire approached him, hat in hand, saying : " Monsieur, just take a look at the battery I have placed here." As he spoke, a cannon-ball tore off the arm and the hand with which Saint-Hilaire was holding his hat and struck the great Marshal on **Death of Turenne.** the left side. Thus died Turenne in the height of his glory, at the age of sixty-three. The whole army, which worshipped him, was filled with grief. De Lorges and De Vaubrun wrangled over the leadership : " Let the Magpie loose," cried the soldiers, " she will lead us." (The Magpie was the Marshal's mare.) The troops were obliged to fall back upon the Rhine. Happily Condé came to take Turenne's place, and succeeded in driving Montecuculli out of Alsace. But for him, too, this was a last campaign. Tortured by gout, and almost helpless, he retired to his estate at Chantilly, where he spent the ten years he had still to live cultivating art and letters with great enthusiasm.

Three days after the death of his glorious Marshal-General, on July 30, Louis XIV had nominated eight new Marshals of France, among them the Duc de Luxembourg. But, as Mme. Cornuel remarked, they were merely " the small change of M. de Turenne," and the war languished. In Flanders, Louis XIV entered Condé and Bouchain, but he missed the opportunity of a pitched battle with the Prince of Orange, having taken counsel with his generals, who dared not accept the responsibility of "endangering the glory of the King" (1676). The following year, while he himself took Valenciennes and Cambrai, Monsieur, with the help of Luxembourg and d'Humières, gained the battle of Cassel, receiving a bullet in his cuirass with an indifference which the courtiers magnified into heroism, and causing the King, who could not brook a rival, to determine thereupon that he would never again entrust his brother with an army. Simultaneously, on the Rhine, Créqui, Turenne's best pupil, as Luxembourg was Condé's, following his master's tactics, got the better of the skilful Duke Charles of Lorraine ; finally, in the Mediterranean, an old sea-dog of sixty-six twice routed the fleet commanded by the great De Ruyter near the coast of Spanish Sicily. This gentleman—a crabbed Protestant squire, an old beau, and a great lover of Hungary water and lace cravats—was called Abraham Duquesne.

In spite of these successes, and although Holland and France were both very weary, the negotiations which had been going **Peace of** on at Nimeguen for a year came to no conclusion **Nimeguen.** —first, because the *Stathouder* set himself strenuously against peace; and, secondly, because neither of the two nations could decently abandon her allies, which tended greatly to complicate matters. And at this juncture Charles II, impelled by English public opinion, which was very hostile to "Papist" France, was obliged to give his niece, the Princess Mary, daughter of the Duke of York, in marriage to William of Orange, and then to conclude a treaty with this redoubtable nephew (January, 1678). Louis XIV bore this double blow in a manner worthy of a great king and an intelligent man ; by way of showing that France was by no means beaten, he at once mustered a new army, seized Ypres and Ghent (March, 1678), and hurled an ultimatum at the United Provinces. . . . Greatly alarmed, they at last signed a treaty of peace (Nimeguen, August and September, 1678).

Spain had to pay for every one ; for though she recovered certain towns such as Charleroi, Oudenarde, Courtrai, and Ghent, which would have been mere isolated outposts for the French, she ceded Franche-Comté and the strongholds of the ancient frontier : Cambrai, Bouchain, Valenciennes, Condé, Saint-Omer, Ypres, Cassel, Maubeuge, etc. As for Holland, she came out of the war immune, recovered even Maestricht, and obtained a promise that Colbert's famous tariff on foreign merchandise should be suppressed. On the whole she triumphed, for it was the establishment of this tariff in 1667 which had caused hostilities. Nevertheless, the Peace of Nimeguen was abhorrent to the *Stathouder*, for it put an end to the war. Four days after it had been concluded, William of Orange attacked Luxembourg near Mons, in defiance of treaties ; but once more repulsed, he saw his last chance of renewing hostilities brought to naught.

When Louis XIV had signed agreements with the Emperor and the Duc de Lorraine—the first losing Freiburg, and the second the last remnants of his duchy, which he would not accept·in the mutilated state in which it was offered to him—and subsequently with Denmark and Brandenburg, which were obliged to restore what they had taken from France's sole ally, Sweden, the French nation was left greater and more glorious perhaps than she had ever been. At Nimeguen, indeed, her King may be said to have imposed his ultimatum on, and dictated his conditions to, all Europe. " Victorious from the outset of his reign, never having besieged any fortress without taking it, superior in every way to his united enemies, the terror of Europe for six consecutive years, and finally her arbitrator and peace-maker, adding Franche-Comté, Dunkirk, and half Flanders to his States " (Voltaire), Louis XIV was unquestionably a great sovereign. Yet he had not succeeded in crushing insolent little Holland, and he must have recognized this.

WORKS TO CONSULT : See those already quoted ; *Mémoires* of Saint-Hilaire ; *Mémoriaux du Conseil de 1661*, published by Jean de Boislisle ; Vast, *Grands traités du règne de Louis XIV* ; André, *Michel Le Tellier* (1906) ; L. Delavaud, *Le Marquis de Pomponne* (1911) ; Gérin, *Louis XIV et le Saint Siège* (1894) ; Lefèvre-Pontalis, *Jean de Witt* (1884) ; Legrelle, *La Diplomatie française et la Succession d'Espagne* ; Michel, *Histoire de Vauban* (1896) ; Mignet, *Négociations relatives à la Succession d'Espagne* ; Pagès, *Le Grand Electeur et Louis XIV* (1903) ; Pagès and Japiske, in the *Revue Hist.* (1905) ; C. Rousset, *Histoire de Louvois* (1886) ; P. de Ségur, *La Jeunesse du Maréchal de Luxembourg* (n.d.) ; Tuetey, *Les Officiers sous l'ancien Régime* (1908).

CHAPTER IX

DECLINE

I. The Reunions. The League of Augsburg. II. The Court in
the days of Mme. de Maintenon. III. The War of the League
of Augsburg.

I

LOUVOIS regretted the peace, for he was the Minister for
War. But Louvois was a man of great ingenuity ; he
managed to make this peace fertile in conquests, and
thus to remain " the necessary man " in the King's eyes. After
the disappearance of Colbert and Pomponne he had no rival in
the Council ; he constituted himself the champion of " Reunion." What may not be evolved from ancient documents
with a little intelligence ? France's neighbours were about to
have a lesson in the art.

The question was to determine which were the territories
pertaining to the towns which the treaties of Nimeguen and
The Reunions. even those of Westphalia had made over to
France. The archives were searched, and yielded
all that the searchers wished to find. Relying, when this was
necessary, on documents dating from the early days of the Middle
Ages, the King claimed and occupied eighty small towns or
villages of Franche-Comté, everything that was still at liberty
in Alsace (with the exception of Strasburg), and a number of
fiefs in Lorraine. Finally, in September, 1681, the French troops
entered Strasburg with the approval of the municipality—on
the same day that in Italy they occupied Casale, which they
had disputed with the Spaniards for two centuries, and finally
wrested from the Duke of Mantua. (It was on this occasion
The Man with that the King ordered the imprisonment of
the Iron Mask. Matthioli, the Man with the Iron Mask, an agent
who had sold to Spain the secret of the negotiations.)

THE SEVENTEENTH CENTURY

As may be imagined, "this gnawing and encroaching peace," as it has been called, and the arrogant policy of France raised difficulties. In 1681 a pretty diplomatic contest took place. On the last day of September our ancient ally, Sweden, specially offended by the "reunion" of the duchy of Zweibrücken, which belonged to her, made an alliance with Holland. Louis XIV, whose diplomacy was once again admirable, answered by signing a treaty with Brandenburg and Denmark, the irreconcilable enemies of Sweden (January–March, 1682). But the Emperor and Spain joined Holland and Sweden (February–May, 1682). Then French agents let loose Turkey upon the Empire, and very soon the troops of the Crescent arrived under the walls of Vienna : the King hastened to offer his services ; if the Emperor had accepted them he would thereby have recognized the "reunions." But the King of Poland, the chivalrous John Sobieski, came to the rescue of the Emperor, bringing him an army to fight the Infidels ; Vienna was saved : Louis XIV accordingly hastened to complete his acquisitions before the Emperor's hands were free. Meanwhile Spain, despoiled and exasperated, declared war. The French troops at once took the field, and occupied Courtrai, Dixmude, Luxemburg, and Oudenarde ; after which the King imposed a truce of twenty years on his feeble enemy, forcing her not only to recognize the "reunions" as legitimate, but further to cede Luxemburg and Oudenarde to him (Truce of Ratisbon, August, 1684). The game was played out.

This year, 1684, was to all appearances the culminating-point of the reign of Louis XIV. The kingdom of France was larger **Apogee of** than it had ever been. The King's person, his **Louis' glory.** Court, the culture, graces, and wit of the French were famous among all the people of Christendom. But the impossibility of living secure of the morrow and without fear of some new enterprise on the part of France began to make itself plainly felt among other nations. Europe was alarmed to see "this power, which was extending in every direction, and acquiring in peace more than ten kings, the predecessors of Louis XIV, had acquired by their wars." The King's navy even seemed to be developing into the strongest in Europe. In 1681 Duquesne and d'Estrées harried the Mussulman pirates in the Mediterranean ; then they bombarded Tripoli twice, and Algiers three times, with the new " galleons with bombs " invented by Petit-Renaud, and imposed peace upon the people of Barbary (1687). Finally, as the Republic of Genoa continued to build galleys for Spain in spite of Louis' prohibition, Duquesne's fleet appeared one day off the coast, and in less than ten days threw over 10,000 bombs into the town ; after this the suburbs and their magnificent palaces were set on fire. To avoid a fresh bombardment the Doge was obliged, in spite of the laws which forbade him to quit the Republic, to come to Versailles and read an apologetic speech prepared for him by Seignelay (1685).

This policy, at once brutal, arrogant, and cunning, roused resentment even stronger than the terror inspired by the King **Revocation of** of France. Moreover, William of Orange had **the Edict of** not ceased to work against him. In 1685 the **Nantes.** Revocation of the Edict of Nantes caused great indignation among the Protestant Powers. In 1685 the famous monument of the Place des Victoires deeply offended the rulers of Sweden and Brandenburg : it represented Louis the Great trampling underfoot Cerberus, the symbol of the Triple Alliance, while two allegorical figures, personifying the Elbe and the Oder, paid homage to him, and the King of Sweden was represented as a slave in chains. Finally, at about the same time, Spain was again threatened, and the allies of France were disgusted by encroachments without compensation. At last all the malcontents—the Emperor, Spain, Sweden, Bavaria, Saxony, the Elector-Palatine, and (in secret) the Elector of Brandenburg—formed the League of Augsburg (July, 1686). When Holland, Savoy, and England joined this coalition, France had all Europe against her.

A fresh act of violence on the part of Louis XIV provoked war.

For nearly ten years the King had been struggling against Rome on the subject of the *Régale* right, and after the Declara- **Disputes with** tion of the four articles in 1682, France was almost **the Pope.** in a state of schism. In 1687 the situation was aggravated by a fresh conflict. It had become a tradition that all ambassadors in Rome should exercise a right of sanctuary throughout the quarter they inhabited, and that, further, goods entering the city in their name should be duty-free; the results were that a great many criminals of all sorts were able to elude justice and that smuggling was freely practised. Innocent XI undertook to reform these abuses. After discussions more or less prolonged, all the Powers of Christendom agreed to renounce the " immunities " and privileges of their ambassadors. Louis XIV alone declared that God had established him "to give an example to others and not to take one from them," and he caused his new envoy to Rome, the Marquis de Lavardin, to be accompanied by a formidable escort of naval guards and armed followers. The Pope excommunicated Lavardin, but such was the prestige of the King of France that his ambassador nevertheless found a church even in Rome itself in which to receive the Sacrament : Saint-Louis-des-Français. The Pope laid the church of Saint-Louis under an interdict. But the King thereupon threatened to seize Avignon (January, 1688).

Such was the state of affairs when the Archbishop-Elector of Cologne died (June, 1688). Louis XIV at once supported the candidature of the Cardinal von Fürstenberg ; but the Emperor put forward that of Prince Clement of Bavaria. The votes of the Chapter were equally divided between the two candidates, and the Pope chose Clement of Bavaria, in spite of the threats of Louis XIV, who retorted by forcibly installing the Cardinal von Fürstenberg.

At the same time he perpetrated further acts of violence. The Elector-Palatine, brother of the Duchess of Orleans, had died in 1685, and the King had then claimed part of his estate on behalf of his sister-in-law. In 1688, under pretext of taking possession of Madame's inheritance for her, French troops suddenly entered Germany, and conquered the Palatinate in less than seven weeks. It was war ! But alas ! Louis XIV could not foresee that William of Orange, having ousted James II of England from his throne with incredible facility, would, within three months, reinforce the coalition with his new and powerful kingdom.

DECLINE

II

At the moment when the war of the League of Augsburg began, nearly all Louis XIV's great servants had disappeared :
War of the League of Augsburg. Turenne had died in 1675, Condé in 1686, Colbert in 1683, and Le Tellier in 1686 ; Seignelay was to die in 1690 and Louvois in 1691, more or less in disgrace. True, the King was still to have some good ministers, such as the Torcys and the Pontchartrains, and good generals, such as Luxembourg, Vendôme, Berwick, Villars, and Boufflers ; but these could not attend to everything, and during the closing years of the reign such men as Chamillart were to direct policy, and too often a Villeroy or even a La Feuillade was to command the army.

The King, by no means piously inclined at the beginning of his reign, was now converted (1686). But his religion was to some extent more material than sentimental. " The King never misses a station or a penance, but he cannot understand the necessity of humbling himself and acquiring the true spirit of repentance," wrote Mme. de Maintenon. Indeed, Louis XIV was cruelly lacking in Christian humility, and his piety was inspired less by love than by the fear of hell and the hope of Paradise, which he thought that Heaven would certainly grant him, provided he attended divine service assiduously, observed Lent, and, in short, gave God His due, or paid respectful court to the Almighty.

The courtiers had all been converted with the King, for irreligion had become an obstacle to promotion. " To the devil
The Court becomes devout. with all this whining and psalm-singing, aaa, iii ! " cried Madame ; but no one followed her on this dangerous ground. Under the gilded ceilings where the haughty " Quanto " once flaunted her beauty there were now only pious gentlemen and devout and modest-spoken ladies to be seen. " The courtier of the past had flowing hair, was dressed in doublet and hose, wore wide boots, and was a libertine. This is no longer the mode : he now wears a wig, a closely fitting coat, plain stockings, and is devout " (La Bruyère). Light colours, trunk-hose, fluttering ribbons, plumes, shoulder-knots are no more ; now the mode is a long severe jerkin, closely

buttoned, dark purple or brown in colour, close-fitting breeches, and dark stockings; no ribbons save one at the neck; no lace save in the cravat and cuffs; no plumes save in the three-cornered hat, and then a very small one. Gallantry and intrigues were also at an end: love was hunted down and lovers were reprimanded. "The King," said Madame, "imagines he is pious when everybody is bored to death." In 1685 Louis ordered his Grand Provost to denounce all members of the Court who should eat meat in Lent; in 1694 he would have suppressed the acting of plays, if Père de La Chaise had not warned him of the danger of banishing harmless amusements; in 1696 he laid the Fair of Saint-Germain under an interdict for a fortnight. Scarcely any entertainments were permitted save the official "circle" (*appartement*), where, to put it briefly, the same persons met all their lives three days a week, and where Louis XIV, who now spent his evenings working with one of his ministers in the Marquise's apartments, no longer appeared. The principal attraction was gaming: bagatelle, barette, reversi, trente-et-quarante, hoca, dice, backgammon, and, above all, lansquenet—"a game without any limits and without any rules, which to you is no longer a mere diversion, but a profession, a trade, an occupation, an attachment, a passion, and, if I may venture to say so, a rage and a fury!" (Bourdaloue)—and a game in which everybody had not, like Dangeau, the good fortune never to be suspected of helping his luck adroitly. Add to all this a system of espionage, letters opened in the *cabinet noir*, the King's spies keeping him informed of everything, and the most comfortless life in the great icy-cold rooms, where in winter at the King's table, "both wine and water froze in the glasses," and in the small, inconvenient bedrooms, approached by filthy passages. Such was the Court. Nevertheless, every noble desired to live there, so great to most of them was the prestige of him who reigned there, and so persuaded were the ambitious that the only road to success was to please him, but also, as the Duc d'Antin once said, because there were to be found "a small number of men and women with whom it was possible to spend one's life agreeably, and more easily here than elsewhere, on account of the difficulty of getting them together"; finally, above all, because

Discomforts of the Court.

curious observers (so numerous in the seventeenth century) were never weary of the absorbing spectacle of characters in conflict and of courtiers expending all their resources of energy and cunning to obtain advantages often purely conventional, it must be admitted—such as that of the patent conferring the right to amuse the King when on his close-stool—but which then seemed, and so indeed became, the greatest in the world.

After the death of Louvois (1691), Louis tried more than ever to do everything himself. He carried out very heavy **The King's** labours with admirable perseverance and con-**industry as** scientiousness. He mastered the contents of **a ruler.** every diplomatic report, and prescribed the reply; he it was, henceforth, who corresponded directly with the generals, sending them almost daily letters of from fifteen to twenty pages carefully studied and elaborated, and often admirable; on the whole, " there were few days on which the King did not work eight or nine hours " (Dangeau). It was thus that Louis XIV conceived his " grand, noble, delicious craft of kingship."

Every day he held a Council (sometimes two) and worked with one of his ministers from about seven to ten o'clock in Mme. de Maintenon's apartment. Louis XIV and the Marquise were seated in arm-chairs on either side of the fireplace; before each of them was a table; in front of the King's table stood two stools, for the minister and his bag. Mme. de Maintenon read a book, or worked at her embroidery-frame, careful not to seem too much interested in the conversation. When the King asked her opinion, she gave it, without insisting too strongly upon it, for any such insistence would have been enough to make Louis, who was more anxious than ever not to be dominated, decide the exact opposite. About nine o'clock in the evening two ladies' maids came to undress the Marquise; immediately afterwards her steward and a man-servant brought her some soup and something light to eat; as soon as she had finished her supper, her women put her to bed; all this in the presence of the King and the Minister of State, who did not interrupt their work. At last ten o'clock would strike, and His Majesty would take leave, and go off to sup.

What, under these circumstances, was Mme. de Maintenon's political influence ? According to Saint-Simon, she had a secret understanding with the ministers, not one of whom would have dared to resist her. On the day when the business in which she was interested came up (it would seem to have been always some appointment to make or some favour to grant), the minister showed a list of candidates ; if the King stopped of his own accord at the name pointed out by the Marquise, the minister "managed to go no further ; if the King paused at some other name, the minister proposed to see those who were eligible ; he rarely proposed the one he meant to come to directly, but always mentioned several whose claims he affected to weigh impartially in order to perplex the King " ; hereupon the King generally consulted Mme. de Maintenon ; she would smile, affect helplessness, sometimes say a word in favour of another candidate, and then, if she had not already pronounced in his favour, would come back to the one the minister had supported." . . . All this seems to show that Louis XIV, suspicious and distrustful, greatly feared to be influenced. If Mme. de Maintenon was obliged to display so much skill and cunning merely to secure a place for one of her *protégés*, can we suppose with Saint-Simon that she ruled "without an interval, without an obstacle, without the slightest cloud, for over thirty, and indeed for thirty-two years " ?

Influence of Mme. de Maintenon.

Perhaps she had no great desire to rule ; the character of Françoise d'Aubigné was not that of a woman of vast ambitions. She was honestly fond of quiet, embroidery, the education of young girls, and meditation. Court life was irksome to her, and she had no pleasure in ostentation. At Versailles she led by choice the most modest and retiring life possible ; a queen in her own apartments, remaining seated in her arm-chair even in the presence of the King and his children, " she was a very simple private person outside, always in the background, making way for women of title, and even for those of distinguished parts." Further, she was extremely disinterested ; she accepted nothing from the King but the estate of Maintenon, and was not even a duchess ; her household were all people of modest fortune, who remained in a more or less comfortable obscurity ;

her relatives received no conspicuous favours ; her brother, the Comte d'Aubigné, never succeeded in becoming either a duke or a Marshal of France. Pacific and scrupulous, she dreaded to disturb and harass the King her husband. . . . If she took part in affairs of State, it was from a sense of duty ; her confessors told her that Heaven had placed her beside Louis that she might be " the sentinel of God," and she believed herself to be bound in conscience to forward the salvation of her royal spouse. No doubt, when taking part in the government of the country, she turned to account the facilities thus afforded her to induce Louis to fill vacant posts with pious persons as far as possible, and her devout scruples counted for something, no doubt, as has been said, in the choice of ambassadors, generals, and ministers. But we must avoid exaggeration : it is evident that she had nothing to do with the Revocation of the Edict of Nantes, and Saint-Simon himself declares that she only "initiated herself " in religious politics in connection with " the affair of M. de Cambrai " (Fénelon) (1697). It would seem, then, that Mme. de Maintenon did in fact exercise more influence than the earlier favourites, whom the King had never allowed to interfere in the slightest degree in affairs of State ; but, save in the four or five closing years of his reign, that influence seems to have been less than that of Père de La Chaise himself, and that of Le Tellier.

In 1688 the Grand Dauphin was twenty-seven years old. Although his father had said grandiloquently, when dispatching **The Grand Dauphin.** him to command the Army of the Palatinate, " Go and show your merit to all Europe, so that when I come to die no one will notice that the King is dead," Monseigneur had not greatly distinguished himself in the course of this campaign, though he had behaved like a good soldier ; nor did he distinguish himself in the Councils when Louis XIV permitted him to be present. The truth was that " his mind was not brilliant in any respect." Sometimes he spent a whole day lying on his bed, holding a cane with which he slashed his boots, or seated in a corner of the reception-room, whistling, tapping on his snuff-box, staring wide-eyed at one and the other, and when he was absolutely obliged to hold a public

reception, answering the speeches addressed to him only " by
nods, and two or three halting words, so timidly pronounced
that they could scarcely be heard " (Spanheim). He was, in
fact, according to Saint-Simon, " an only son made expressly
for such a father," this prince who at the age of fifty " only
ventured upon what he was permitted to do." He was, however,
a good creature, kind to his servants and humane to the poor.

Like Louis XIV, the Grand Dauphin had his Maintenon
after the death of his wife in 1690. She was a big, sturdy
young woman, with a flat nose and a brown skin, " fresh, lively,
very plain, but gay, courageous, and witty," known as Mlle.
Choin. As she proved " right-minded, sensible, and reasonable "
(disinterested, in short), the King and Mme. de Maintenon
were indulgent to her, and wished her to come and settle at
Versailles, so that Monseigneur might be there more. But
Mlle. Choin preferred her *parvulo* at Meudon, where she received
the princesses seated in her arm-chair, offering the Duchess of
Burgundy herself nothing but a stool.

The Duke of Burgundy, Monseigneur's eldest son, born in
1682, was a richly endowed character. Proud, impetuous,
The Duke of subject to fits of blind rage, wild with joy when
Burgundy. pleased, mad with anger a moment after—
" fantastic," as Fénelon says in the portrait he has drawn of
him, a portrait to be preferred to the glowing picture of Saint-
Simon—but sincere and artless, lively, eloquent, subtle, and full
of new turns even in his " strangest and most senseless fury,"
showing in all things such vivacity of mind that he could not
concentrate it entirely on a single object, and that it was found
necessary, for instance, to let him occupy his eyes and fingers
with drawing when having a lesson—such was the Duc de
Bourgogne in early adolescence. The governor appointed for
him was the wise and pious Duc de Beauvilliers, and the tutor
the Abbé de Fénelon; of this violent and unequal but gifted
nature the two succeeded in making a man of perfect virtue and
deep religious feeling, scrupulous indeed to excess, and almost
to the point of indecision. For this conscientious and uneasy
soul the crown would have been a torture which he greatly
dreaded in anticipation. However, the young Duke had

prepared himself for his royal function with touching piety ; he had even renounced his scientific tastes that he might not steal a minute from his political instruction. When by the death of Monseigneur his father he became Dauphin, he worked more diligently than ever. He sought anxiously for some means of remedying the abuses he discovered, which filled him with despair. Moreover, he would have made Fénelon his Prime Minister, and Fénelon, who considered Louis XIV's " despotism " the " cause of all our woes," longed to relieve the masses, to renounce war entirely, to reconstitute the nobility as a real aristocracy, free to engage in trade and to enter the magistracy, to summon the States-General every three years, and to establish everywhere provincial States to control public finance, and report to the King upon everything. . . . This intelligent Duke of Burgundy, eager for the public good, and nourished on philosophy and morality, who wrote : " The rank of prince without that of upright man would only serve to make me more guilty at the tribunal of God, for the more favours we have received from His hand, the stricter will be the account we shall have to give Him "; and : " I ought only to make use of the greatness proper to my rank in order to rise to a more sublime degree of virtue, humiliating myself under the almighty hand of God, and doing all the good to others which they are entitled to expect from me "—this grandson of Louis XIV, who had perhaps the soul of a Marcus Aurelius or of a Saint Louis, guided by Fénelon might have been a great king, a pacific administrator, whose reign would have saved the monarchy.

At the age of fifteen, in 1697, the Duc de Bourgogne married his cousin Marie-Adelaide of Savoy, the daughter of Amadeo II **The Duchess** and Marie d'Orléans. The young girl had arrived **of Burgundy.** at Versailles a year earlier, delighting everybody by her youthful charm ; moreover the little creature was shrewd enough, in spite of her heedless ways, and it was evident from the deference she paid at once to Mme. de Maintenon that her father had thoroughly instructed her in the affairs of the Court of France. Her only critic was the portly Madame, who was always surly, and who was scandalized at her free-and-easy manners :

Good Heavens ! how badly they are bringing up the Duchess of Burgundy, to my mind ! [she exclaims on October 22, 1698]. It is pitiable to see the child. She begins to sing in the middle of dinner, jumps about on her chair, pretends to bow to the company, makes the most dreadful faces, tears chickens and partridges to pieces with her fingers, and dabbles in the sauces ; in short, it would be impossible to have worse manners, and those who stand behind her exclaim : " Ah ! how graceful and pretty she is ! " She treats her father-in-law (Monseigneur) most disrespectfully, and calls him " thou ! " He then imagines that he is in high favour and is quite delighted. . . .

As she grew older, the Duchess did not cease to romp about the King and the Marquise. They were delighted with her pranks : this spoilt child was the joy and brightness of their splendid, melancholy life. " Chattering, jumping, fluttering round them, now perching on the arms of their chairs, now upon their laps, she would throw her arms round their necks, embrace, kiss, and caress them, crumpling their attire, pulling them by the chin, and teasing them." All this in private, however, for before strangers she became " serious, reticent, respectful to the King, and timidly polite to Mme. de Maintenon, whom she always addressed as ' Aunt,' with a pretty confusion of rank and affection." Finally Louis could not be happy without her : when she was unable to be present at his supper " an additional cloud of gravity and silence " enveloped him.

She was not pretty, in spite of a regular face with " the most expressive and beautiful eyes in the world," marred, however, by a prominent forehead, pendant cheeks, an insignificant nose, and thick lips which disclosed defective teeth ; in compensation, she had " a long, rounded, slender, supple waist, perfectly moulded," a beautiful bust, a long flexible neck, and " the gait of a goddess upon clouds." Such as she was, her husband loved her with all the fervour of a temperament severely held in check in other directions—a fervour which Mme. de Maintenon, herself by no means subject to such ardours, considered as unpleasant for their object as for spectators. Deformed and lame (though not less active on this account), the young Duke of Burgundy was not handsome, in spite of an intelligent face, " so brilliant as to inspire brilliance in others." Nor was he very amiable ; while his wife, noisy and lively, dispelled the dullness of the Court, arranged riding-parties on horses or donkeys, and bathing-parties, delighted in acting, had a passion for dancing, spent the night at balls, and went to bed at dawn, he would shut himself up in his study working and praying, scrupulously avoiding pleasures to which he felt himself but too much inclined. But so much virtue inevitably gave him an air of constraint, and often an unintentional air of disapproval, " so that, in spite of himself, he seemed by his conduct to be reproving the King and every one else, which was not well received by the King or by any one. . . . However, as years passed, the Duchess sobered down, and the Duke, for his part, realized that his austerity and his devotion were exaggerated for one in the position of a prince destined to be a king and hold a Court, as Heaven had decreed ; thereupon, and especially after the death of Monseigneur, " he lent himself more to the world, and did so with so much grace and such a natural air that it was easy to understand his reason for having refrained therefrom, and his regret that he could only so lend himself." Once more, he was an admirable man.

Among the children of Louis XIV and Mme. de Montespan, the favourite was the Duc du Maine, who was club-footed. **The Duc du Maine.** Mme. Scarron had brought him up, as well as his brother and his two sisters, and she had retained " a nurse's tenderness " for him, says Saint-Simon, by reason of all the trouble the delicate childhood of the little prince had given her. Now M. du Maine had the most brilliant qualities of wit and intelligence, but he lacked a vice without which it is difficult to succeed—violence. Weakly of body, he was no more vigorous in character ; he lacked temperament, authority, that touch of brutality essential to a commanding nature. In spite of his intellectual gifts and his ambition, he was never able to overcome his timidity ; hence at Court he assumed the character of a religious person, a philosopher, and an unsociable being. In war he lost an opportunity of crushing the enemy one day because he could not take upon himself to order an attack, and this failure had dishonoured him as far as a favoured prince can be dishonoured.

But if he was deficient in health, he had the intelligence. " I will not say of an angel, but of a demon " (Saint-Simon). He excelled in deep manœuvres and " exquisite perfidy." Further, he could amuse, and charm, and fill the imagination. Finally, and above all, he played the part of " the good son, the loving son, tenderly contemplating a glorious father, and unable to be happy out of sight of him, doing violence to his own taste for seclusion in order to breathe the same air " (A. Barine). Thus he exercised a daily fascination over Louis XIV and Mme. de Maintenon.

His wife, by her force of character, succeeded in inspiring him with a little courage. Like all the Condés, Mme. du **The Duchesse** Maine was small and slender, remarkably intelli- **du Maine.** gent, and slightly cracked. The Prince, her father (Henri-Jules, son of the Great Condé), unfortunately discounted a delightful mind, an exquisite culture, and great refinement of manners by his capricious humours, his furious rages, and an avarice checkered by ostentation. As to M. du Maine, he trembled at the scenes caused by the violent little person he had married ; but urged on by her, he advanced yearly in the King's good graces, and finally obtained the principal prerogatives of the Regency to the detriment of the Duke of Orleans.

Until the death of Monsieur, his father (1701), the latter was known as the Duc de Chartres. His mother, the Princess-Palatine, was greatly attached to him ; in her correspondence she speaks of him with indulgence and even admiration, and this maternal sentiment in a great lady of that period, and even in this particular one, is very touching. Like the Duke of Burgundy, the Duc du Maine, the Condés, and many princes of the family of Louis XIV, the Duc de Chartres was highly gifted. He proved himself humane, brave in war, literary, a good judge of painting and music—altogether charming. Unfortunately he was by no means virtuous. He was licentious, dissipated, and weak. When in 1692 the King wished him to marry Mlle. de Blois, he dared not resist, in spite of the objurgations of Madame ; thus, on the morrow of the day when he had consented, as he approached his mother to kiss her hand, " Madame gave him such a sounding box on the ear that it was heard some paces off, covering the poor prince with confusion in the presence of the whole Court, and filling the numerous spectators, of whom I was one, with prodigious amazement," writes Saint-Simon, who, thirty years after this appetizing scandal, still rejoiced at having witnessed the scene.

DECLINE

Like her sister, Madame la Duchesse, the Duchesse de Chartres was far from well-behaved. Both were given to indulging in copious meals, after which the former would compose " very pretty verses," in which she spared " neither her dear papa, the King, nor the little Duke, her husband." At times they were surprised by Monseigneur " smoking pipes they had sent for from the guardroom of the Swiss Regiment," or they would be attacking their sister Conti, who was supposed to be over-susceptible. On the whole, none of these three princesses had as much intelligence in her whole person as the Duchesse du Maine in her minute little finger.

The Duchesse de Chartres.

III

On October 15, 1688, the Prince of Orange and his supporters landed at Torbay. Two months later James II was forced to fly from his kingdom. And on February 13, 1689, the Prince of Orange was proclaimed King of England under the title of William III.

The Prince of Orange King of England.

" To tell the truth," writes Madame, " our good King James is an excellent and worthy man, but the most foolish person I have ever encountered. Piety has positively stupefied him." But Louis XIV could not allow William, his bitterest foe, to take quiet possession of England in order to turn it against France, and overthrow a king who was the ally of France, and whose only crime was that he had wanted to restore Catholicism. He accordingly received James with great magnificence at Saint-Germain, and when on February 25, 1689, the latter set out to regain his kingdom, he was well provided with French money and protected by Château-Renault's fleet : " Monsieur, it grieves me to part with you, and yet I hope that I may never see you again," said the great king when taking leave of him. James II was not very quick in repartee ; it is not known what he replied ; but a month later he landed in Catholic and separatist Ireland, which rose and joined him. Alas ! on July 11, 1690, his Irish rabble was routed by William III at Drogheda, to the north of Dublin ; and he himself, saved by the little body of French troops he had brought with him, returned hastily to Versailles.

James II at Versailles.

THE SEVENTEENTH CENTURY

The following dialogue may be quoted as very characteristic of the Stuart King :

" Sire," said M. de la Rongère to him, " what became of the Frenchmen who were with Your Majesty [at Drogheda] ? "

" I don't know," replied James.

" What ! " exclaimed La Rongère, " Your Majesty does not know ! Were they not with you ? "

" You must forgive me," said the King ; " I am going to tell you : the Prince of Orange arrived with 40,000 men, I had only about half that number ; he had forty guns, I had only sixteen ; I saw that he was drawing out his left wing towards Dublin and that he would cut me off, so that I should not be able to return ; thereupon I came away, and here I am."

" But," said La Rongère, " there is some talk about a bridge which Your Majesty did not keep ; apparently you did not require it."

" Oh, as to the bridges," said the King, " I had ordered them to be well guarded, but guns and forces were brought up which threw back the troops I had placed at these points, and so the Prince of Orange got across."

On the very day when James II was defeated at Drogheda, Tourville, with seventy ships, routed the Anglo-Dutch fleet off Cape Bévéziers ; but this glorious victory of our sailors was useless, for shortly afterwards the only Irish town which had remained faithful to its lawful king, Limerick, was taken by William III in spite of a brave defence by the Frenchman Boisselau.

The subordinates of M. de Tourville admired him for his knowledge of " all departments of the navy," from that of carpenter to that of an excellent admiral " as much as they loved him for his gentleness, his equity, his courtesy, and his quiet valour. By his extraordinary skill this great sailor succeeded, throughout the campaign of 1691, in occupying the fleet of the allies, which was almost twice as strong as his own, and in preventing it from attacking the coasts of France ; this was the famous *campagne du large* (open sea campaign). In May, 1692, he set sail again from Brest to protect the landing of 30,000 men whom Louis XIV had once more confided to James II, and who were mustered at La Hougue, near Cherbourg. He encountered the fleet of the coalition, consisting of eighty-nine ships of the line, off Cape La Hague. He himself had only sixty ; but in spite of his numerical inferiority, he managed to fight for twelve hours and to sink two of the enemy's ships without losing any of his own. Then he tried to slip away under cover of night. Twenty-two of his vessels reached Naval battle of Saint Malo, thanks to a pilot who guided them La Hougue. through the passages of the Channel Islands. Seven others arrived at Brest. But three were burnt in the open roadstead of Cherbourg, and twelve in the roadstead of La Hougue, in the sight of the indifferent French troops (May 29–June 3, 1692). It was not this glorious defeat which ruined our navy; in 1693 Tourville again commanded a squadron of seventy-two ships and gained a fresh victory over the Anglo-Dutch fleet at Lagos. But as the expenses of the army increased, Louis showed increasing unwillingness to pay for the maintenance of his navy. Hence, after 1694, the Government abandoned the effort to maintain large fleets; this was the day of the corsairs, Jean Bart, Duguay-Trouin, Pointis, Forbin, etc., heroes whose incredible exploits form one of the most glorious pages of French history.

Meanwhile on the frontiers Louis XIV was resisting the attacks of the Empire, of the German Princes, of Savoy, Spain, and the United Provinces, which gradually leagued themselves together against him.

In order to check the advance of the enemy on the Rhine, Chamlay and Louvois harked back to the idea of devastating The Palatinate the Palatinate which had just been conquered by again the Dauphin's army (October–November, 1688). devastated. Louvois considered all atrocities permissible in war; already during the Dutch War he had caused whole districts to be burnt by Condé and Luxemburg; even Turenne had once before ravaged the Palatinate by his orders, but those earlier flames "were but sparks" compared with the new conflagration projected by the War Minister. In January, 1689, Tessé received orders to destroy the flourishing town of Heidelberg: on the 18th his soldiers blew up the castle of the Electors, the great tower of which is still to be seen, lying at the bottom of the ravine; then they deliberately destroyed the gardens, vineyards, and crops, cut the bridge, pulled down the houses of the city and carefully lighted fires among the ruins. By way of a civility to Madame, Tessé had saved several ancestral portraits for her, and he also sent a fine canvas to

Louvois to compensate for his first hesitation in obeying orders which he feared would cause him some distress " for a week to come." On the other hand, at Mannheim, Montclar had no such puerile scruples ; he was much surprised, indeed, to find that he could not induce the inhabitants to demolish their houses themselves " to prevent disorder " ; on the contrary, indeed, these *schnapans* (vagabonds) persisted in camping among the ruins. Louvois sent orders that they were " to be killed." Spires and Worms were entrusted to Duras ; like Tessé, he had scruples, but the fear of displeasing the powerful Minister soon overcame them, for Saint-Simon, who passed through Spires in 1694, tells us of " the few remaining inhabitants burrowing under the ruins, or living in cellars." Bingen and Oppenheim were similarly treated. At the same time the country was ravaged by the soldiery and even by the rascals of the district who were bribed to play the part of incendiaries. " Four hundred thousand persons were fleeing and sleeping on the ground. All the roads were covered with carts, and with terror-stricken families escaping they knew not whither," says Michelet, who for once exaggerates very little.

The French troops had merely to keep guard behind the Palatinate when it had been devastated in this fashion. The great effort was reserved for Flanders and the Alps.

Louvois hated Luxembourg ; he had therefore arranged at the beginning of the war that his enemy should remain at Versailles, unemployed. But after the army of Flanders had been compelled to beat a general retreat in 1689, the King appointed Luxembourg to command it.

M. de Luxembourg, the posthumous son of Montmorency-Boutteville the duellist, although he was so deformed that **Marshal de** Mme. de Grignan declared no one would have **Luxembourg.** noticed it if he had lost an arm or even a leg in battle, showed the same ardour in love and war as his father had displayed in single combat with an adversary. He was small, with a true hunchback's face, sharp and malevolent, and a hooked nose ; yet his deformity, " slight in front, but very marked and pointed behind," did not prevent him from finding favour with ladies, for more than one reason. In war he was an admirable general, whose genius resembled that of the Great

Condé in its rapid grasp of a situation, and power of prompt and ingenious decision.

Immediately on his arrival in Flanders he crossed the Sambre by surprise and turned the position of the old Prince of Waldeck with part of his forces while the rest attacked on the front. The allied English, Spanish, and German army, which was much more numerous than his, lost 6000 killed, 8000 prisoners, 106 standards, 49 guns, and almost the whole of its baggage : this was the splendid victory of Fleurus (July 1, 1690). The captured banners were hung in the cathedral of Paris, and gained for M. de Luxembourg the glorious sobriquet of the Upholsterer of Notre-Dame (*Tapissier de Notre-Dame*).

In 1691 and 1692 Luxembourg continued to hold the allies, while the King took Mons (April, 1691) with great pomp and circumstance, and then Namur (June–July, 1692), the conquest of which was celebrated by innumerable poets (we know to what flights of rhetoric it inspired the author of *Le Lutrin*).

But when the town was taken and Louis XIV had gone home, Luxembourg was left with some 60,000 men to oppose the greatly superior forces of the King of England. Weakened by illness, he relied more than was prudent on the counsels of one of his spies. William III caused him to be misled by false information, and succeeded in surprising him near the little town of Steinkerk, on broken ground where the redoubtable French cavalry was unable to charge. Happily for the French, an English column which might perhaps have overthrown them immediately in their disorder, was stopped by a misguided order of William III's, and Luxembourg was able to form his forces in order of battle. Nevertheless, hard pressed by the Duke of Würtemberg and Mackay's English division, his first two lines had been forced to retreat, abandoning their guns, and the battle seemed all but lost when he rallied all the infantry of the King's Household and sent them to retake the lost positions. Led by the Duke, the Prince de Conti, the Duke and the Grand Prior de Vendôme, Berwick, Villeroy, the three sons of Luxembourg, and the flower of the French nobility, the fine regiments of the Guards and the Swiss marched upon the enemy, shouldering their muskets and without firing a shot, as the Marshal had ordered

Battle of Steinkerk.

253

them; and as the English muskets were much better for firing than the old French weapon, "the whole business was done by cold steel." At the same time William's right wing fell back before the furious onslaught of the French, who drove his men "from garden to garden, from hedge to hedge, from ditch to ditch, striking them down with the butt-ends of their muskets when swords and bayonets were broken." Finally the King of England had to beat a retreat, abandoning a large number of prisoners, twelve cannon, and twelve standards (August 3, 1692). After this victory everything in France was for a time christened *à la Steinkerque*: "at this period men wore lace cravats, the arrangement of which cost considerable time and trouble; the French princes, dressing hastily for the fight, had wound their cravats carelessly round their necks; women wore adornments made in this fashion; they were called *Steinkerques*" (Voltaire); and M. de Luxembourg thus became the most fashionable of Marshals.

Unfortunately "all these famous victories procured a great deal of glory, but few solid advantages." Vanquished, but not crushed at Fleurus and at Steinkerk, the King of England had ever been able to retire in good order, "and a fortnight after a battle it was always necessary to fight another in order to become master of the district." In 1693 Louis XIV committed a serious blunder. William was not in a position to say, as the French king could, "I wish it" in order to be obeyed; jealousy, discouragement, and the distrust of his allies had prevented him from getting more than 75,000 men together, whereas Louis had assembled 110,000 near Namur. Entrenched not far from Louvain, William foresaw that he would inevitably be crushed, when he suddenly heard that Louis was sending half of his forces into Germany. At first he would not believe this news; yet it was true: Luxembourg had in vain opposed the incredible decision made by the King on Chamlay's advice.

With the 60,000 men he had left, Luxembourg marched on the enemy. Diminished by the detachment of various **Battle of** corps to protect certain towns, William's army had **Neerwinden.** dwindled to 50,000 men. But it was entrenched in an impregnable position, resting on a watercourse, the rugged banks of which defended it in the rear, its right in two good-sized market towns, Laer and Neerwinden, battlemented, barricaded, and surrounded with palisades and hedges, its left in two villages, Rumpsdorp and Neerlanden, similarly fortified; its front, about a league in extent, protected by a ravine, then by earthworks, a ditch, and redoubts, the whole raised and excavated in a night. Twice Luxembourg rushed his troops to the attack of Neerwinden, which commanded the entire position; twice the village was taken and lost again. Then, as at Steinkerk, the Marshal assembled all the infantry of the King's Household, placed himself at its head with the princes, and dashed forward to attack for the third time; very soon the Prince de Conti planted the standard of the Guards in the centre of the village. William at once detached part of the troops of his centre, sending them to the right to try to recapture Neerwinden; Luxembourg had expected this: by his orders the French cavalry approached the camp thus deprived of the main body of its defenders, and succeeded in entering it by surprise. At the same time the troops which had seized Rumpsdorp at the beginning of the action attacked the enemy's left. The Anglo-Dutch troops were forced to give way under the fury of the French onslaught (July 29, 1693). The young Duc de Chartres (who charged accompanied by his governor), the Prince de Conti, and Villeroy had covered themselves with glory; Luxembourg's son, the Duc de Montmorency, had been wounded by a bullet in the shoulder while covering his father with his body, and a few moments after the Marshal had seen his second son carried off on a litter, his own duty as a general making it impossible for him to quit the field. Indeed, French valour never showed itself in a more attractive light than at "Nerwinde." A stray bullet shattered M. de Rivarolle's wooden leg: "What fools they are!" cried he; "they don't know that I have two others in my valise!" At Rumpsdorp the French cavalry stood against the enemy's cannonade without stirring save to close up the ranks. William rode up to his batteries in a rage, accusing his pointers of lack of precision; when he had duly noted the effect of their fire, he turned away, exclaiming: "Oh! the insolent nation!" Neerwinden was the last victory of the glorious Upholsterer of

Notre-Dame: after a skilful defensive campaign against his eternal adversary William in 1694, he died almost suddenly on January 5, 1695.

The King's greatest effort had been made in Flanders from the outset of the war. While Luxembourg was fighting **Marshal** brilliantly there against the Anglo-Dutch, the **Catinat.** army commanded by Marshal de Lorge was holding its own precariously on the Rhine. In Catalonia, Marshal de Noailles had a certain measure of success. Finally, M. de Catinat gained the notable victory of Staffarde over the Duke Vittorio-Amadeo (August, 1690), and then took possession of Savoy and of the County of Nice (1691).

M. de Catinat, long, thin, and dark, with a pensive face and deliberate gestures, was a whilom barrister, who had left the bar in disgust at having lost a suit which he believed to be just, and having embraced the career of arms, proved himself so apt in his new calling that he had made his way by sheer merit. A good general, " instinct with precautions and all the talents which tend to economy," sparing of the lives of his men, he was looked upon somewhat contemptuously at Court because he was prudent, of obscure birth, modest, and unskilled in intrigue. After his disgrace he retired to his little country-house of Saint-Gatien, and lived the life of a philosopher, occupying himself in the cultivation of his garden, and, every year, in " receiving the first nightingale " there. He died at Saint-Gatien, poor and unmarried, in 1712.

In 1692 he had at his disposal only some 20,000 men, without provisions, and without enough horses for transport and artillery. Vittorio-Amadeo crossed the Alps with 40,000 men and took Gap and Embrun, but ravaged the province so mercilessly that the exasperated peasants armed themselves, and under the direction of an heroic young girl, Mlle. de La Tour du Pin, waged such a murderous war of ambuscades upon the invaders that Catinat had no difficulty in throwing them back across the Alps. The following year he beat them again at La Marsaille (October, 1693), and this victory gained him his Marshal's bâton.

But Louis XIV had come to the end of his soldiers and of his money. The Emperor, on his side, did not know how to meet the demands of the German princes, who were not accustomed to fight for nothing. And the English and Dutch merchants were tired of loosing their purse-strings. Hence the military operations languished on the Rhine, in Catalonia, and everywhere. In Flanders, the incapable Marshal de Villeroy,

> Villeroy, Villeroy
> Qui si bien servit le Roy
> Guillaume,

allowed the King of England to recapture Namur in 1695. Jean Bart and the corsairs continued their extraordinary exploits on the seas, but Louis XIV took away the soldiers of the royal navy to reinforce his armies on land. It seemed as if both France and her enemies were too weary to strike a decisive blow.

Throughout the war Louis XIV had worked continually to embroil the allies one with another. In 1691 those of his advisers who were in favour of peace, notably Beauvilliers and Chevreuse, had persuaded him to open negotiations with Vittore-Amadeo, and in 1693, not only Savoy, but the two maritime Powers were parleying with France. Everybody was agreed in principle on the necessity of terminating the conflict, but differed concerning the details of the treaty. . . . Finally, in 1696, French diplomacy gained a signal advantage by the defection of Vittorio-Amadeo. It was liberally paid for : the Duke recovered all his states, even Pignerol which had belonged to France since 1630, and his daughter married the Duc de Bourgogne (June–August, 1696).

Having thus become the ally of Louis XIV, Vittorio-Amadeo called upon the Emperor and the King of Spain, who hastened **Peace of** to treat with him (October, 1696), to evacuate **Ryswyck.** Italy. William III, angry and uneasy at this peace brought about without reference to him, pressed on his private negotiations with Louis XIV, unmoved in his turn by the knowledge that he was forcing the Emperor's hand, and the Anglo-Dutch and French plenipotentiaries met near Ryswyck, in a country-house belonging to the Orange family. Although Louis XIV had made it known beforehand that he would not abate anything of the claims he had made in the Treaty of Nimeguen, their discussions were very complicated. Moreover, the question William had most at heart, that of James II, was dealt with outside the Congress, by Lord Portland and Marshal Boufflers; but these two finally came to an agreement. Immediately after this, Pointis, with the help of the filibusters of the Tortugas, seized Cartagena, whence they returned with fabulous spoils; finally Vendôme entered Barcelona (August 9, 1697). All this facilitated the task of the French diplomatists. On September 20, 1697, Spain, England, and Holland signed the peace; and on October 30 following, the Emperor, who had been left in isolation, had to sign it in his turn.

By the Treaty of Ryswyck France gave back to Spain, to the Empire, and to the German princes all the fortresses "reunited" or conquered since the Peace of Nimeguen, with the exception of Strasburg, which Leopold definitively ceded to France; the Duke of Lorraine recovered his duchy (occupied by the French since 1633), save Marsal and Sarrelouis; the Palatinate was secured to the Elector in consideration of a yearly payment of 300,000 crowns to the Duchess of Orleans; the Dutch, pleased at the restitution to Spain of the fortresses of the Netherlands, obtained a commercial treaty; but returned Pondicherry, which they had taken from the French: finally, Louis XIV recognized William III as King of Great Britain, and abandoned the cause of James II. In short, the King renounced the profits of the "gnawing peace" except as regards Strasburg, lost Lorraine and Pignerol, which had belonged to France since the time of Richelieu, and humbled his pride before the Prince of Orange.

WORKS TO CONSULT: In addition to the volumes already mentioned, the *Memoirs* of Catinat, Villars, Berwick, and Tourville; E. de Broglie, *Catinat* (1902); Comte d'Haussonville, *La Duchesse de Bourgogne* (1898–1908); Legrelle, *Notes et Documents sur la Paix de Ryswick* (1894); Macaulay, *History of England*; Marquis de Ségur, *Le Tapissier de Notre-Dame* (1904); Marquis de Voguë, *Le Duc de Bourgogne et le Duc de Beauvilliers* (1900).

CHAPTER X

RELIGIOUS MATTERS

I. Protestantism.   II. Jansenism.   III. Gallicanism.   IV. Quietism.
V. Jansenism (sequel).

I

AT the time of Mazarin's death, Louis XIV was by no means devout. Not, indeed, that he was at all a free-thinker (*libertin*) ; the only part of his education which Anne of Austria had supervised was that of religion. Nevertheless, he had no knowledge of theology, for he had nothing of the **Orthodoxy of** metaphysical turn of thought. But he was regu-**Louis XIV.** lar and orthodox, fasted, and attended Mass daily—Saint-Simon tells us that he only missed a service once in his life—and devoutly accompanied the Holy Sacrament with torches, as in 1664, by virtue of which he confidently counted on winning Paradise. Indeed, he was not much occupied by thoughts of his salvation. " I dreamt you were mad ! " he replied to the Duc de Mazarin, who had exhorted him to repent and to leave La Vallière. In 1668 he did not make much difficulty about forgiving the fair Montespan her transactions with soothsayers. At the beginning of his reign the King thought only of his " glory " and his love-affairs ; and, if we may say so, it was only when he had ceased to love women that he began to love God.

Although by no means devout, the young Louis XIV was not at all tolerant. True, the " Libertines," who had been forced **Intolerance of** to lie low during the triumph of the Company of **the King.** the Holy Sacrament, from 1640 to 1660, came to the surface again in large numbers after the defeat of this pious cabal, and vigorously applauded Molière's *Tartuffe*, which His Majesty caused to be given in defiance of the sanctimonious.

259

For twenty years they flourished, and it was only after Louis' conversion that they again subsided—at least at Versailles, for " the strange thing is, that the same man who plays the part of an atheist in Paris, plays that of a saint at Versailles " (Madame, 1699). And in the eighteenth century they became " the philosophers." However, if he tolerated the " Libertines," the young King could not suffer Protestants. And, indeed, there was a great difference between them. The Libertines might, after all, be looked upon as believers who were holding aloof for the moment ; they were only bad Catholics, they did not dogmatize. But the Protestants had embraced, avowed, and proclaimed a religion hostile to that of the Prince ; their state of mind, their manners, their very costume, were peculiar—they were a discordant note in the harmony of the kingdom. And this discord was so shocking to every French soul of the seventeenth century, instinctively inclined to unity and harmony, that it became so even to the Protestants themselves. Further, it was a question whether, if the King were at war with a nation of the same faith as his Reformed subjects, they would be sure to desire the success of Catholic France and the defeat of their co-religionists ? In other words, were they more French than Protestant, or, as they had been under Louis XIII, more Huguenot than Royalist (or French ; for this was the same thing) ? The point was raised, and the Reformers were so conscious of it that in all their supplications they never ceased to protest their fidelity to the very Christian King. It must also be remembered that at the time of Louis XIV no one, either Huguenot or Papist, admired tolerance. From the Catholic point of view, tolerance is not a virtue, but a weakness, and Christian charity imperatively commands us to liberate other men from the greatest of misfortunes, which is heresy. On the other hand, the Dutch Calvinists were demanding precisely the same measures against the Papists which the King was one day to take against the French Reformers by revoking the Edict of Nantes. In short, in the seventeenth century nearly every one considered it a duty to use force and compulsion in order to bring back the erring, and looked upon liberty of conscience as an absolute scandal. Thus Louis XIV carried out the national will when he worked to procure for his people that religious unity which every one at that period held to be useful and even necessary.

The Assemblies of the clergy had long been demanding the abolition of the Edict of Nantes, or at least what they called its **Revocation of** " execution "—which was almost the same thing. **the Edict of** Henri IV has been unduly praised for this famous **Nantes.** edict, which was forced upon him, and satisfied neither the Huguenots nor the Papists. Strictly speaking, it was no more liberal than the other edicts granted to the Reformers by the last Valois kings ; its whole merit—considerable enough indeed—was that it had been applied, whereas this had not been possible in the case of those which had preceded it. Its text is obscure ; a literal interpretation thereof would have made it easy to deprive the Protestants of many privileges, and a subtle interpretation would have sanctioned the withdrawal of most of the rest. The Company of the Holy Sacrament, the Jesuits, and the Assemblies of the clergy were successful in achieving these results under Louis XIII, under Mazarin, and finally under Louis XIV.

In 1661 the King granted what his Catholic subjects had long been demanding : the appointment of Commissioners to " verify the Edict of Nantes " ; these Commissioners worked in couples—one very Catholic, the other a member of the R.P.R. (*Religion prétendue Réformée*, the so-called Reformed Religion) ; but care was taken to elect Protestants of humble birth, even if these were not bought over by the Catholics. Before these two judges the clergy appeared as prosecutors. The Commissioners decided, and when they could not agree, sent the affair on to the King's Council. Now the interpretation of the Edict by the clergy was singular : " the text nowhere declares that the burial of a member of the so-called Reformed Religion may be performed in the day-time ; it must therefore take place at night," maintained Père Meyneir, for instance. And the judges often decided, and finally always decided, after the manner of Père Meyneir.

Moreover, the Assemblies of the clergy periodically presented petitions against the Reformers to the King. The latter, it is true, retorted in like fashion, and Louis tried sincerely to be impartial : if in 1666, for instance, he granted most of the

261

demands of the Catholics, in 1669 he amended his first edict, the Protestants having remonstrated. Nevertheless, the **Measures against the Reformers.** Catholics, by dint of gaining lawsu'. on matters of detail, and also because the Assemblies which presented petitions against the R.P.R. were the very bodies which voted the ecclesiastical free-will offering (*don gratuit*) to His Majesty, a fact which naturally made them interesting, gradually obtained the suppression of an ever-increasing number of places where the exercise of Protestant worship was permitted, the demolition of a great many Protestant churches, partial interdiction of the provincial synods (the national synods had been suppressed in 1659), the abolition of the mixed courts (*Chambres mi-parties*) composed of Catholic and Protestant judges, before whom the Reformers might plead, etc. At the same time the Catholic controversialists redoubled their efforts ; the Jansenists and, above all, the great and magnanimous Bossuet fondly dreamed of giving the Protestants *proof* of their error, and bringing them back by reason ! Another and more efficacious means to this end was the " conversion fund " founded in 1676, but this indeed was too successful in some ways, for certain individuals abjured three or four times under different names or in different places, in order to receive the premium of from six to twelve *livres* on each occasion.

About 1680 the King began to show visible signs of his conversion. Mme. de Maintenon spoke to him of God at **The King's conversion.** every opportunity, but she was not yet in a position to exercise a direct influence on public affairs. On the other hand, Père de La Chaise, the King's confessor, was in high favour, and though M. de Colbert " thought only of his finances, and hardly ever of religion," M. de Louvois urged the King strongly to suppress the R.P.R., seeing in this a means of occupying the King and himself remaining " the indispensable man." Still, we must not exaggerate Louvois' action, nor even that of the confessor. Louis XIV was not easily influenced ; and the progress of his own conversion sufficiently explains his growing zeal against heresy. He, who in religion saw mainly observances and good works, no doubt appreciated " the pleasure of carrying out a facile repentance at the expense of others," as Saint-Simon says, and he must have thought that the Lord would certainly appreciate the suffering he would inflict upon the Protestants. Already, in a letter of 1679, Mme. de Maintenon had written : " The King confesses his weaknesses, he recognizes his faults " ; and she immediately adds : " He is thinking seriously of the conversion of the heretics, and very soon he will work at it in earnest." He was already working at it.

From 1680 onwards, indeed, a series of edicts made the situation intolerable for the Reformers. In the first place, **Severe treatment of the Huguenots.** children of seven years old were declared to be sufficiently reasonable to embrace the Catholic faith, and they were authorized to leave their heretic parents and demand a maintenance allowance from them. Further, the Protestant " academies " (universities) were suppressed ; the small schools were relegated to isolated and inaccessible places, and parents were forbidden to send their children abroad to be educated. All public offices, the professions of barrister, doctor, and midwife, and certain trades, were closed to Huguenots. Catholics were forbidden to marry Protestants, or to embrace the R.P.R. The royal functionaries were empowered to visit heretics on their death-beds to learn from their own lips whether they persisted in their errors. Nearly all the Protestant churches were closed on the most astonishing pretexts. And finally, there were the dragonnades.

The dragonnades were not invented for the Huguenots. It was an old custom to lodge troops in communes or with individuals by way of punishment. Marillac, the administrator of Poitou, was no innovator when in 1680 he distributed the dragoons at his disposal among the Protestants of his province. But he was careful to let the soldiers know that he would shut his eyes if the fervour of their faith and their apostolic zeal should lead them occasionally to commit some excusable violence on the persons of their heretic hosts. Hereupon these " booted missionaries " beat, wounded, robbed, pillaged, and ruined their hosts so conscientiously that they brought about a large number of conversions, which seemed miraculous to the Court, and delighted M. de Louvois. However, it seems to be clearly established that Louis XIV himself was not aware of these excesses ; when complaints reached him from Poitou, he caused Marillac to be reprimanded several times, and finally dismissed him. Nor did Louvois actually enjoin violence; but administrators were aware that the Minister would bear them no ill-will if they followed the example of Marillac, provided that **The Dragon-** no over-loud complaints reached the ears of His **nades.** Majesty. The dragonnades accordingly spread throughout a large part of France; it was terrible. As the King knew nothing, no one at Court did anything to inquire into the violence that was going on, and praises were lavished on the amazing success of " the provincial governors and magistrates, *supported by a few dragoons*," as Mme. de Sévigné says. She adds : " It is the greatest and finest thing which has ever been imagined and carried out." Meanwhile, towns such as Montpellier and Nîmes, and provinces such as Béarn, abjured wholesale. The King was at last made to believe that there were scarcely any heretics left in his kingdom. On October 17, 1685, Louis signed the revocation of the Edict of Nantes.

The act was approved in all quarters. The Pope sent a brief in which he declared that the revocation was indisputably " the finest thing His Majesty had ever done " ; he then granted plenary absolutions, and had the Vatican illuminated. France exulted : Bossuet, La Fontaine, Mme. de Sévigné, and La Bruyère all extolled the great King. Need we repeat that tolerance was considered no virtue, but a weakness ? However **Emigration of** several hundred thousand Huguenots fled from **the Huguenots.** the kingdom, in spite of the precautions taken to prevent them and the condemnation to the galleys of those who were caught. These Calvinists, who preferred the most terrible dangers, exile, and ruin to religious concession, sufficiently proved the quality of their energy ; their departure sensibly diminished the moral value of the State. They were for the most part artisans, humble folk, for the majority of the noble families had abandoned a religion which barred the way to *success*, and the members of the upper middle class who held royal offices had abjured in order to keep their posts. The refugees settled in England, in Holland, in Switzerland, and in Germany, more especially in Brandenburg, where the Elector did his best to attract them : in 1697 his dirty little capital, Berlin, contained 4292 Frenchmen among its 20,000 inhabitants.

Good workmen or worthy manufacturers for the most part, they made a valuable contribution to foreign trade, whereas their departure told unfavourably on French products. From many points of view the revocation of the Edict of Nantes impoverished France

And from the point of view of Catholicism it was futile enough. For it had the usual effect of religious persecutions; it gave a marked impetus to the persecuted faith.

Nearly all the N.C.'s (New Converts or New Catholics) had abjured only with their lips. In vain were priests sent to evangelize them; they had generally to confess what Fénelon wrote to the Duchesse de Beauvilliers, begging her to let M. de Seignelay read his words in secret: " We found in all minds an incredible persistence in heresy." The N.C.'s had resort to the device of folded arms, if I may venture to describe it thus; they refrained from public worship altogether. What was to be done? It was impossible to punish all the King's Catholic subjects who behaved in like fashion. Besides, the Edict of Revocation did not exactly order the Reformers to be converted; it merely deprived them of the right of performing their service **Oppressions** *publicly*; they were free to do so mentally, if **and cruelties.** indeed they had the courage to bear their situation, which had been made crueller than ever by fresh edicts, forbidding doctors to attend patients who refused the sacraments, annulling marriages celebrated without a Catholic priest, approving the abduction of the little children of Huguenot parents, ordering that the bodies of those who died without the sacraments should be dragged through the streets on hurdles (though this was hardly ever actually done), etc. The dragonnades were greatly multiplied; the soldiers hustled the recalcitrant into the churches, " where their enforced presence was reckoned as an act of abjuration " (true, it was a Protestant pastor who said this). For the rest, the penalties decreed against relapse and against pastors surprised in the kingdom, and the condemnations to the galleys were powerless to prevent secret gatherings for worship, " in the desert," as the Reformers said. They, for their part, kindled a civil war in the Cévennes. When, after the death of Père de La Chaise, an amiable and moderate Jesuit, the King took as his confessor the austere and ardent

Le Tellier, it was in vain that persecution revived; at the end of the reign Protestantism was still alive.

II

In the fifth century Saint Augustine, "the most subtle of dialecticians, and the most perturbed of men," agreed with Saint Paul that man, corrupted by original sin, cannot be saved by his own efforts, and that his own will is powerless to procure salvation; the souls to whom God does not grant His help and grace are damned to all eternity, whatever they may do. But if we are thus predestined, how can we exercise free will and deserve reward or punishment by our actions? How can we reconcile the omnipotence of God with our own liberty? Theologians have displayed prodigious ingenuity in their efforts to solve this insoluble question. The Church did not insist on any very definite doctrine; since the Council of Trent it had merely forbidden its members to go to extremes, i.e. either to believe that a man can procure his salvation "by works alone, accomplished by the power of human nature, and without the help of God," or, on the contrary, "that man's free will was lost and extinguished after the sin of Adam, that it is a word without meaning, a fiction introduced by Satan into the Church." Between these two extremes the faithful were free to adopt the tenet they preferred. The Jesuits had chosen and disseminated a theory which allowed considerable latitude, because this encouraged the faithful to perform good works, and also because the Calvinists upheld the doctrine of predestination. On the other hand, at the beginning of the seventeenth century, a Bishop of Ypres named Jansen or Jansenius, a professor at the University of Louvain (1585–1638) revived the theology of Saint Augustine, and accepted its extreme conclusions. His friend and disciple, Duvergier de Hauranne, Abbé of Saint-Cyran, became the apostle of his ideas in France.

Meanwhile, in the year 1599, a child of eight years old, Jacqueline Arnauld, the daughter of a famous advocate who had pleaded against the Jesuits, was appointed coadjutrix of the Abbess of Port-Royal. This Cistercian convent was situated in

Jansenism. (margin note)

the hollow of a retired and delightful valley, which in those days was described as a " frightful desert." As in all the con-

Port-Royal. vents of the period, the rule had been greatly relaxed there, and the nuns lived very freely, by no means isolated from the world. When she became Abbess, Jacqueline Arnauld (in religion, Mother Angélique) reformed her daughters by dint of energy and piety, and subsequently those of the neighbouring convent of Maubuisson (1609–1623). In 1626 the nuns of Port-Royal quitted their domicile, which had become too small for them, and was, moreover, damp and unhealthy, and removed to Paris, where they settled in the Faubourg Saint-Jacques (in the building which is now the Maternity Hospital). And in 1636 they obtained as their spiritual direc- tor the Abbé de Saint-Cyran (the friend of Mother Angélique for some ten years past), who won them over to his ideas, and made their community the centre of Jansenism.

Now from the year 1637 onwards, certain men touched by grace, who desired to work out their salvation apart from the world, yet without binding themselves by any vows, had estab- lished themselves in the deserted buildings of Port-Royal-des- Champs. " While some of them took the temporal affairs of the Abbey in hand, and endeavoured to put them on a solid footing, others were not too proud to till the soil like simple day-labourers ; they even repaired portions of the building which were falling into ruins, and raising those which were too low and subter- raneous, made the habitation of this desert much healthier and more comfortable than it had been " (Racine). Thus, when in 1648 the house in Paris had become too small for all the nuns who had entered the order, a considerable number of them returned to live at Port-Royal-des-Champs. Making way for the holy women, the anchorites accordingly retreated to the farm of Les Granges on the neighbouring hill-side. There they lived a humble, devout, and active life. In 1647 Messrs. Lance- lot, Nicole, Wallon de Beaupuis, and others gathered together a few pupils in Paris, in the Rue Saint-Dominique d'Enfer, close to the convent ; molested by the Jesuits, and harried by the Lieutenant of Police, they came and installed themselves with their children at Port-Royal, and by 1650 their little schools there had become famous. Those of the " Messieurs " who were learned gave instruction, or occupied themselves with works of erudition, or in replying to the attacks of the Jesuits. The rest undertook " the lowliest and most menial tasks," such as cooking, poultry-keeping, vine-dressing, and gardening.

In this " little Thebaid " at the gates of Versailles, there were some exquisite and admirable souls : M. Hamon, the learned **Eminent** physician of the community, who was to be met **Jansenists.** on the roads, mounted on his donkey, murmuring his orisons, his fingers busy with some knitting as he went to visit his patients ; M. Nicole, the author of that work which Mme. de Sévigné loved so dearly that " she would fain have made it into a broth and drunk it," and who, gentle though he was by nature, was always warring against the Jesuits, and then against the Huguenots that he might not disappoint his great friend, M. Arnauld ; M. Claude Lancelot, an excellent Hellenist, who taught Greek so successfully to Jean Racine, and took the classes of the younger children, to whom he was akin in his guilelessness and gaiety (" The abundance of the mercies which it pleased God to heap upon me, and the peace with which He filled my heart were so great that I could scarcely refrain from laughing continually," he wrote) ; M. Antoine Le Maistre, a famous advocate, who " at the age of twenty-nine had renounced the bar, and all the advantages which his great eloquence might have procured him, to retire to this desert," where, indeed, he occupied himself in a careful publication of all his speeches, into which, however, he inserted edifying passages ; and Blaise Pascal. . . . But the soul of the community was Antoine Arnauld.

Jansenism was an episode of the Catholic reaction of the seventeenth century against the religious anarchy, the heresy, and the pagan " libertinage " of the sixteenth. " The years of dissension and misery, which revived the energy of French souls, inclined them to evolve a hard, virile, and ascetic form of Catholicism, which, while asking much of man, gave him back much in depth of emotion and capacity for action " (Lanson). Jansenism, which prostrates man before a terrible God ; which fills him with despair by denying him even the assurance of salvation through his efforts ; which treats as a crime the love of art, science, and even of Nature, in short, preoccupation with anything tending to beautify life and distract the mind from the one thing needful : salvation ; which systematically stripped the churches of ornament ; which sought to replace pleasaunces by kitchen-gardens ; and which caused the *Pensées* to be rewritten before publishing them, that so Pascal's style might be that of the generality—this dreary and ardent creed was the antithesis of the amiable, facile, and worldly faith of the Jesuits. Moreover, the Company of Jesus felt itself to be menaced socially by the Jansenists, who competed with it successfully for the direction of souls and the education of children, and whom it considered the advance guard of its Gallican adversaries. This was why it attacked them from the outset. They retorted : Saint-Cyran published his *Petrus Aurelius* in 1632 ; but he had displeased Richelieu by his political and religious independence ; he was imprisoned at Vincennes in 1638, and released only in 1643, to die shortly afterwards.

That same year, 1643, Antoine Arnauld published his *Traité de la fréquente Communion*, to defend Saint-Cyran against Père **The Arnaulds.** de Sesmaisons. Like Mère Angélique, the great Arnauld was one of the twenty-two children of the advocate who had pleaded against the Jesuits in 1594, and Port-Royal was full of the members of his family ; his own mother, seven of his sisters, two of his brothers, five of his nieces (the daughters of his brother, Arnauld d'Antilly), three of his nephews (the sons of his sister, Mme. Le Maistre), Antoine Le Maistre, Le Maistre de Sacy, Le Maistre de Séricourt, entered the monastery, or lived like himself among the an-chorites. In his treatise Arnauld attacked the frequent use of the Sacrament enjoined by the Jesuits. The considerable success of his work made the Company more anxious than ever for the destruction of that Port-Royal " whence issued all those excellent works, so edifying for the Church, which caused them so much chagrin " (Racine).

The Jesuits replied effectively in 1649 : the syndic of the Faculty of Theology, Nicolas Cornet, who was devoted to them, extracted from the *Augustinus* (a book published in 1640, in which Jansenius had epitomized his doctrine), five propositions summing up Jansenism, which he begged the Faculty to examine.

Eighty-five bishops referred the question to the Pope. The Jansenists intrigued busily at the Papal Court, as did also their adversaries ; finally, on May 31, 1653, the Pope condemned the five propositions. But the Jansenists argued that the doctrine of Jansenius was in no wise affected by this condemnation, seeing that the five propositions submitted to the Holy See were not in the *Augustinus*. This was defensible, for the propositions were not textually in the book, but it was not equitable, for, as Bossuet declared, they were there in substance ; however, the Pope settled the question by declaring formally, on September 29, 1654, that he had condemned the doctrine of Jansenius together with the five propositions. The Jansenists were not yet beaten ; they maintained still more forcibly that the propositions were nowhere to be found in the *Augustinus* ; that in any case, in the sense in which Jansenius had understood them, they had not been condemned ; for the rest, that the question was one of historic fact, and that, though the Pope be infallible when he decides a question of *law*, he is not so when he decides a question of *fact*, and his decisions only demand " a respectful silence " on the part of the faithful. There is no doubt that these subtleties would have greatly irritated the author of the *Provinciales* if they had been put forward by the Jesuits ; was it not absurd to allow the Pope the faculty to determine a doctrine, but to refuse him that of deciding whether this doctrine was or was not in accordance with that of a given book ? The public deemed the Jansenists to be in the wrong, and Arnauld was censured by the Faculty of Theology. Pascal's campaign, and the prodigious success of his *Provinciales*, no less than the miracle of the Holy Thorn (the miraculous cure of a little girl called Marguerite Périer), which took place at Port-Royal, brought about a temporary reaction, it is true ; and the recluses came back to Les Granges, which they had been obliged to abandon. But the Jesuits obtained a fresh Bull, insisting that the five propositions were a correct summary of the *Augustinus*, and that they had been condemned even in the sense given to them by Jansenius (October 16, 1656).

The Jansenists were in very bad odour at Court, chiefly because the Jesuits were in high favour, but also for purely political reasons. Racine admits that they had relations " with many persons disgusted with the Court, or fallen into disgrace, who came to them to seek consolation, and sometimes even to devote themselves to penitence"; in other words, with the Frondeurs, certain of whom, such as the Prince de Conti and the Duchesse de Longueville, gave them a compromising support. At a later period Louis XIV stated in his memoirs : "Cardinal de Retz, Archbishop of Paris, who, for well-known reasons of State, was insufferable to me just then, favoured or was favoured by the whole of this infant sect." The young King, little inclined to piety, and Mazarin, who was quite indifferent to theology, pronounced themselves against the Jansenists.

On December 13, 1660, the King summoned the Presidents of the Clerical Assembly to the Louvre, and ordered them to **Jansenism** extirpate the Jansenist sect. As a result, the **condemned by** Assembly instructed all the clergy of the kingdom **the Church.** to sign a formulary declaring that the doctrine of the condemned propositions was certainly that of the *Augustinus*. And Louis XIV at once ordered all the bishops to see to the matter of this signature (April 13, 1661); then he forbade the nuns of Port-Royal to receive pupils or novices in the future, and caused the police to expel all the inhabitants of the convent.

The Grand Vicars who governed the diocese of Paris were favourable to Port-Royal, as was also Retz, their exiled Archbishop ; they attempted to evade the difficulty of the formulary by drawing up, in conjunction with Arnauld and the most acute intelligences of the party, a recommendation, the ambiguous arguments of which should enable the Jansenists to sign without stultifying themselves. But neither the King not the Pope would lend themselves to this casuistry (1661). Retz was obliged to resign his archbishopric, and was replaced by Marca, who in his turn was succeeded by Hardouin de Péréfixe (1662). The latter was kindly, but peremptory. As the nuns of Port-Royal had declined to accept the formulary unreservedly, he undertook to convince them; but they were better controversialists than he; he wasted his Latin on them, and this angered him.

In August he sent them a formal order to subscribe purely and simply ; they refused. Hereupon the prelate spoke of the venerable Mère Madeleine de Sainte-Agnès du Ligny as " a little prig " ; he then deprived the saintly women of the sacraments, telling them that " they were indeed pure as angels, but as proud as devils." (The Church has always condemned its rebels for their pride.) Five days later the Archbishop returned to Port-Royal with eight coaches full of police, and seized twelve of the nuns, whom he caused to be distributed in different convents. However, as they soon began to make proselytes in the very communities in which they had been placed, they were finally all brought back to Port-Royal (July, 1665).

They were not alone in their resistance. Four prelates : Choart de Buzenval, Bishop of Beauvais, Henri Arnauld (one **Resistance of** of Antoine's brothers), Bishop of Angers, Etienne-**the Four** François de Caulet, Bishop of Pamiers, and **Bishops.** notably Nicolas Pavillon, Bishop of Alet, declared that in drawing up the formulary the Clerical Assembly —an assembly without definite spiritual powers, irregular, and uncanonical—had exceeded its powers. Hoping to overcome their opposition, the King begged the Pope to compose a new formulary himself. But the nuns of Port-Royal and the four bishops were no more amenable to the formulary of the Holy Father than to that of the Clerical Assembly.

Greatly incensed, Louis XIV roundly demanded that the Pope should appoint commissaries to judge the rebellious prelates and abbey. It was a false step : such a trial would have been contrary to those famous " Gallican liberties " for which the French Church had been fighting against Rome for centuries. The Pope, highly delighted, hastened to choose the judges asked for by the King. But nineteen bishops, secretly supported by others, immediately made common cause with the revolting prelates to protest against the interference of Rome in the affairs of France.

Thus Jansenism was now linked with the Gallican question. The King considered the matter : after all, he was by no means inclined to forward the claims of the Holy Father at the expense of the prerogatives of his own kingdom. The Pope, whose Nuncio informed him that the agitation among the French clergy was immense, hesitated in his turn. It was known that Bishop Nicolas Pavillon would probably declare for schism rather than yield; he was a man of stern and austere virtue, who had the confidence of the heretic in his own logic, and the temperament of a Calvinist, so to speak. At this juncture, Alexander VII died and was succeeded by Clement IX; every one was longing for peace, even Arnauld; every one worked to bring it about.

The greatest obstacle in the path was the character of Pavillon: to effect a settlement it was necessary to imply **The " Peace** concessions, to foster compromise, to make use of **of the Church."** ambiguities and reticences; how was the rigid Bishop of Alet to be induced to accept such methods? By dint of importunity he was won over to a sort of adjustment; he and the three other prelates signed the formulary, at the same time writing a letter to the Pope in which they set forth their reservations, but in terms sufficiently ambiguous to enable the Holy Father (with a little goodwill) to see nothing reprehensible in it. Subsequently prodigies of tact were necessary to prevent the uncompromising Pavillon from indulging in some ebullition. Finally the controversy died out; this consummation is known as the *Peace of the Church* (1668).

III

On many points the relations and the reciprocal rights of Catholic France and the Holy See were not clearly defined, and **The Gallican** the King claimed on behalf of the French clergy **attitude.** privileges which the Pope by no means conceded. In 1639 an advocate of the Parliament, Pierre Piton, had codified these " rights " and " liberties of the Gallican Church," and though it had never been officially recognized, his work was accepted as law on the matter. The two principles laid down by him were: (1) that the Pope has no authority over temporal things in France; (2) that even in things spiritual his power is not absolute and indefinite, " but that it is limited by the canons and rules of the ancient Councils of the Church received in that kingdom." From these principles a host of other maxims were deduced, by virtue of which the King caused his Parliament to examine pontifical bulls, and the canons of Councils, and permitted or forbade their publication, etc., while the

French bishops admitted the superiority of the Œcumenical Council over the Pope, maintained that they had not been instituted by Saint Peter and his successors, but that they were the direct successors of the Apostles, just as much as His Holiness himself, and claimed consequently to be tried only by their colleagues, to judge themselves in matters of first instance even in questions of faith, to examine bulls before they were received in France, etc. In opposition to these doctrines, the Ultramontanes defended the authority of the Holy See both in the spiritual and in the temporal domain, and it was they who at the beginning of the century had openly upheld the theories of the Leaguers concerning the right of the Pope to excommunicate and depose the sovereign or release subjects from the duty of obedience. However, at the beginning of Louis XIV's reign they were not numerous; the Parliament, the Sorbonne, and all the clergy save certain of the regular religious orders were Gallicans, ready to support the King vigorously in his struggle with Rome.

By the Concordat of 1516 the Kings of France had obtained the right of nomination for important benefices, such as bishoprics, abbeys, priories, and in a large part of France they enjoyed the privilege of *régale*—that is to say, the right to draw the revenues of bishoprics and to appoint incumbents to all benefices in the diocese during such time as the see remained vacant. Now the King always presented to newly elected bishops the sums he had received as *régale* in their dioceses. Hence, when by two edicts, of 1673 and 1675 respectively, Louis XIV extended the *régale* throughout the kingdom, only two prelates protested against the decree, which in practice changed nothing. The dissidents were Nicolas Pavillon, Bishop of Alet, and François de Caulet, Bishop of Pamiers, the two Jansenists. They maintained obstinately that their churches had always been exempt from the *régale*, and that the second Council of Lyons had decreed that he who extended this claim to bishoprics hitherto exempt should be excommunicated; nothing could induce them to bow to the royal will. Pavillon died in December, 1677, but Caulet continued to resist. Deprived of his see and condemned by his Archbishop, he appealed to Rome.

The "Régale."

The combative Innocent XI had been Pope from 1676 onwards. In 1678, not only did he hasten to accept the appeal, but he congratulated Caulet, excommunicated the Archbishop of Toulouse, of which Pamiers was a dependency, and wrote to the King in a tone of pride no longer habitual to the Holy See.

Louis XIV replied very mildly. But in 1681 he convoked an extraordinary Assembly of the Clergy, which first of all declared him to be in the right, then wrote to the Pope, saying it approved the extension of the *régale* to the whole kingdom, and, finally, on March 19, 1682, voted a declaration in four articles, drawn up by Bossuet, in which the Gallican theories were plainly and clearly set forth. It stated: (1) That Saint Peter and his successors received their power from God only as regards spiritual things, and not as regards temporal matters, and that therefore the Church could not depose kings and princes, nor release their subjects from their vows of fidelity; (2) that Œcumenical Councils are above the Pope in authority; (3) that the "rules, customs, and constitutions" (somewhat vague terms) accepted in the kingdom of France are immutable; (4) that the Pope's decision is not "irreformable" even in matters of faith, unless it is in conformity with that of the Church (in other words, the Pope is not infallible). The King at once issued an edict, commanding that these maxims should be taught throughout the kingdom, and that all doctors or licentiates in theology and canon law should uphold them in one of their theses before being received by the faculty (March, 1682).

Innocent XI, for his part, bore this blow without any show of anger; but after declaring the decisions of the Assembly **Struggle for** null and void, he systematically refused canonical **Gallican** institution to all the new bishops who had approved **liberties.** and subscribed the four articles—that is to say, all those nominated by the King, for Louis would have no others. The struggle went on for years. The revocation of the Edict of Nantes failed to appease the Holy Father; in 1688, at the time of the franchise affair, thirty-five French dioceses were without bishops. Louis XIV, who had become devout, felt that his position was extremely embarrassing, for his sincere piety forbade a rupture with Rome, and the Curia, well aware of this, was by no means intimidated by his threats, nor by his military preparations, nor by the seizure of Avignon. The death of the "holy zealot" Innocent XI (1689), and subsequently that of Alexander VII (1691), made no difference in the situation. Finally the King, who needed the diplomatic support of the Holy See, decided to compromise. All the bishops presented themselves before the Nuncio and signed a disavowal of the four articles, in virtue of which they obtained their bulls of institution ; the Pope, on his side, recognized the right of *régale* throughout the kingdom (1693).

Nevertheless, the Church of France had not abandoned her claims ; in the eighteenth century we shall find the Parliament again fighting in the name of " Gallican liberties."

IV

Quietism has been known in all ages, and in the seventeenth century Falconi and Malaval or Desmarets de Saint-Sorlet **Quietism.** each revived it individually ; but Miguel Molinos expounded it more completely than they. This Spanish priest, who was living at Rome about 1670–1680, taught his penitents that there is a supreme state of divine love, in which the soul adores so ecstatically that, lost in the contemplation of the Creator, it becomes indifferent to all else, even to the hope of heaven and the dread of hell, the desire to do right and the fear of sin, and is without thought, feeling, or conscience. The Pope manifested little hostility to this mysticism, the consequences of which might certainly be far-reaching, but which was unlikely to attract any but souls of a high order. However, as the King of France fervidly denounced it, the Holy Office was obliged in 1687 to condemn Molinos' book, *The Spiritual Guide* (published in 1675).

Now at this period a certain Mme. Guyon, a widow of agreeable appearance, noble birth, and great wealth. the **Mme. Guyon.** mother-in-law of Fouquet's son, discovered in her turn the delights of " perfect," " passive," " infused " prayer, of " slumber-prayer," and " the deiform life."

Love left me not a moment of rest [she writes]. I said to it : " O Love, it is enough. Leave me ! " My prayers were entirely devoid of form, species, or images ; nothing took place in my brain, yet it was prayer, without action or speech. Sometimes, however, I was free to say a few words to my Well-Beloved ; but subsequently all was taken from me. . . . I had no vision of Jesus Christ or of His divine attributes ; all was absorbed into a delectable faith. . . . If any one asked me why I loved God, whether it was because of His mercy or His kindness, I did not know what they were talking about. . . . I had no thought of myself in loving Him. . . . Everything in the nature of self-interest or reward was irksome to my heart. . . .

Mme. Guyon had revealed the dreams of her agitated and ecstatic soul to many devout women of the aristocratic world to which she belonged. She believed she had power to transfuse into those she loved, by a sort of physical emanation, something of that " torrent " of divine grace which was " flowing " in herself, and even filled her to such an extent that one day her corset was rent. She begged those present to unlace her as quickly as possible, undertook miracles, and declared that she was, literally, the bride of Christ. She was first censured, but this had little effect, for this gentle, absurd, and rather indecent monomaniac was a fascinating creature, who continued to charm every one even after her condemnation, from the Abbé de Fénelon, so alert and subtle, but full of " sensibility " (already !) and imagination, to the prudent Mme. de Maintenon, who introduced her into Saint-Cyr.

There, as was her habit, Mme. Guyon turned all heads. But one day, in 1694, the Bishop of Chartres, Godet des Marais, who was the Superior of the community, intervened ; having interrogated some of the teachers and pupils, he raised the cry of heresy and warned the Marquise. Mme. Guyon was at once expelled. She asked for arbitration, which was not denied her ; Bossuet, Noailles (then Bishop of Châlons), and the Superior of Saint-Sulpice, M. Tronson, carefully examined and then condemned her numerous and interminable works. Fénelon, who had just been appointed Archbishop-Duke of Cambrai, had upheld Mme. Guyon to the end ; yet it was impossible for him to avoid signing with the three commissaries the thirty-four articles in which the errors of the visionary were condemned (1695). But he was the reverse of grateful to his old friend Bossuet for this condemnation.

Mme. Guyon, who had retired to a convent, escaped, resumed her speeches and her propaganda, and ended by getting herself interned at Vincennes (December, 1695). Bossuet then

prepared an *Instruction on the States of Prayer* to "crush the
false mystics of our day," and submitted the proof-sheets to
Noailles, Tronson, and Fénelon, who had signed the condemnation of Mme. Guyon with him. Now not only did Fénelon
refuse his approval this time, but he hastened to compose, in
Controversy refutation of Bossuet, an *Explanation of the*
between *Maxims of the Saints*, where he in his turn adopted
Bossuet and the thesis of "pure love." Then he appealed to
Fénelon. the Pope. Thus between the two prelates, one
of whom, upheld by the King and Mme. de Maintenon, represented the past, and the other, supported by the Duc de Bourgogne, the future, a duel began, the causes of which were perhaps
not purely theological, and in which the arguments were certainly not so. At Rome Bossuet, aided officially and energetically by the King, who demanded the condemnation of M. de
Fénelon, intrigued as ardently, but with less amenity than
Fénelon. In France the Bishop of Meaux took advantage of
Mme. Guyon's absurdities to discredit his adversary, and at the
same time the Government ostentatiously condemned certain
debauched priests who claimed to be Quietists. But the skilful
Fénelon, on his side, did not fail to turn the "persecution" to
which he was subjected to excellent account. Moreover, he
continued to defend Mme. Guyon obstinately, though he did
not accept her theories with all their logical conclusions.

At last the Pope pronounced the sentence invoked by the
King ; by a brief of March 12, 1699, he declared twenty-three
propositions presumptuous, erroneous, and pernicious, but
refrained from pronouncing the word heresy and from any
mention of Fénelon. The judgment was announced to M. de
Cambrai just as he was about to go up to the pulpit ; without
hesitation, the Archbishop communicated the adverse decision
to his flock ; he then published a pronouncement in which he
declared that he submitted humbly to the judgment of the Holy
Father, and presented a commemorative monstrance to his
cathedral.

Conduct so tactful attracted sympathy. Moreover, his
tender mysticism, which, after all, had not been nominally discredited, was more in harmony with the aspirations of the dawn-
ing century than the reasonable and practical faith of M. de

Meaux : this was, thinks M. Rebelliau, because he allowed more scope for that sensibility which was already making its appearance even in serious and Christian minds. Preachers were invited to win men through the heart and through tears, and Massillon succeeded Bourdaloue, as Fénelon succeeded Bossuet. When in 1699 *Télémaque* appeared, a work in which every one agreed to see a sort of satire on the Government, M. de Cambrai, whose friendship and correspondence with the Duke of Burgundy were well known, was acclaimed as the great doctrinaire of the opposition, and the master of to-morrow, a rôle by no means displeasing to him.

V

The " Peace of the Church " had not cured the King of his natural antipathy for those Jansenists in whom he saw **Jesuit influence** former Frondeurs protected by Retz or Mme. de **on the King.** Longueville, and whose austere morality, independence, proud candour, and contempt for luxury, art, " glory," whose whole spirit, in short, he felt to be the antithesis of that prevailing at Versailles. The vexations caused him by Pavillon and Caulet in the affair of the *régale* were not calculated to remove his prejudices. Further, as the King's conversion progressed, he came more and more under the influence of the Jesuits and their friends, who surrounded him. Finally the Jansenists, who were at least as combative as their adversaries (and much less adroit), broke the " Peace of the Church " perpetually by attacks such as that of the fiery Arnauld and his faithful Nicole in 1677, on the morality of the Jesuits.

Hence the persecution revived somewhat. A month after the death of the Duchesse de Longueville (April 15, 1679) M. de Harlay, the Archbishop of Paris who had succeeded Hardouin de Péréfixe in 1670, evicted from Port-Royal the pupils and the lay persons who had retired there, and forbade the nuns to receive any more novices ; this was virtually a decree of extinction. Hereupon, on June 17, Arnauld fled, disguised, with two friends to Flanders, where Nicole joined him ; he was sixty-eight years old. He acted prudently, for the Government began to commit Jansenists to the Bastille very freely ; the gentle M. Vuillard spent twelve years there, and was only released after the death of the King.

Nevertheless, Arnauld and his friends now had the Holy See on their side. Innocent XI (1676–1689) did not forget the assistance they had given him in the matter of the *régale*; Alexander VIII (1689–1691) did not attack them, nor did Innocent XII (1691–1700). Even in France, Bossuet and several other prelates, for the sake of peace, and also out of opposition to Jesuit Ultramontanism, occasionally supported them. And they were soon to find a very powerful ally in the new Archbishop of Paris.

In 1693 an Oratorian, Père Quesnel, who, after the death of Arnauld (1694) and of Nicole (1695), became the most prominent member and the leader of the party, had **Père Quesnel.** published a third and much enlarged edition of *A New Testament with Moral Reflections*, an incontestably Jansenist work, which the Bishop of Châlons, M. de Noailles, conceived it his duty to recommend warmly to the faithful of his diocese in June, 1695. This Noailles, a very saintly man, of a somewhat vacillating disposition, hostile to the Jesuits, not by reason of Jansenist leanings, but from Gallican sentiment, and who intended at least to remain impartial, was appointed Archbishop of Paris in 1695. Having on October 28, 1697, paid a visit to Port-Royal, he returned greatly edified by the piety of the nuns, and begged Louis to rescind the decree forbidding them to receive novices. But the King refused ; he hated Port-Royal worse than ever. In 1699 he struck the name of the Comtesse de Grammont off the visitors' list of Marly, because she had committed the crime of going into retreat at the Abbaye des Champs : " Those who go to Port-Royal must not come to Marly," he declared. And he was still in the same mind when the strife broke out again in 1702.

Either out of bravado or ineptitude, this question had been submitted in July, 1701, to forty doctors of the Sorbonne : Is it permissible to give absolution to an ecclesiastic who confesses on his death-bed that he condemns the five propositions, as the Church enjoins, but that, touching the fact of the presence of these propositions in the book of Jansenius, he has merely kept respectful silence ? Yes, replied the forty doctors. This

Case of Conscience was published. All the anti-Jansenist bishops at once attacked it in rescripts, and the Pope con-

The Bull "Vineam Domini." demned it in two successive briefs. But the briefs were not recognized by the Gallican Church. Importuned by the King, Clement XI was solicited and almost threatened for two years before consenting to confirm his brief by a bull ; but on July 15, 1705, he fulminated the bull *Vineam Domini*. In it he declared " respectful silence " to be insufficient, and demanded that the doctrine of the *Augustinus* as formulated in the five propositions should be whole-heartedly rejected. This was aiming beside the mark ; the Jansenists had long agreed to repudiate the doctrine of the five proposi- tions, whatever it might be ; they limited themselves to denying that the five propositions were to be found in the book of Jansenius, and it was solely on this question of *fact* that they maintained that the Pope's decision imposed no duty on the faithful beyond that of " respectful silence." And on this point the Gallicans were not far from agreeing with them, as soon became evident.

A clerical Assembly having met to receive the bull, the Cardinal de Noailles, the leader of the Gallicans, who presided, began by delivering a very skilful speech, the subtleties of which once more saved Jansenism theologically. Further, in order to safeguard the Gallican maxim according to which pontifical decisions could not be received in France until after they had been accepted by the bishops, the Assembly took care to vote a rescript approving the constitution *Vineam*, a sanction which greatly offended the Holy Father. Finally, in 1706, the Bishop of Saint-Pons published a pastoral instruction boldly defending the " respectful silence " in spite of Rome, and entered upon a controversy with Fénelon on the subject. Thus the bull would have entirely missed fire if it had not caused the downfall of Port-Royal.

As no novices had entered the community for seventeen years, only twenty-five nuns remained in 1705, the youngest of

Suppression of Port-Royal. them being sixty years old. Their opponents had not the patience to let them die in peace : they were ordered to sign a new formulary condemning " respectful silence." The proud yet humble women did not understand

the subtleties of the theologians very well ; at all hazards, and
to guard against pitfalls, they refused to sign without adding the
following reservation : " without prejudice to what took place
concerning us at the Peace of the Church under Clement IX."
Then Noailles, hard pressed by the Court, was obliged to sacrifice
them ; he forbade them to elect a new Abbess in place of Mère
Agnès de Sainte-Thècle (Racine's aunt), and deprived them
of the Sacraments (1707). At the same time the Paris Port-
Royal, which had become the worst enemy of the Jansenists,
demanded the suppression of the Abbaye des Champs. The King
begged for a papal bull, obtained it on March 27, 1708, and had it
registered in the following December. Cardinal de Noailles in
his turn issued a decree of abolition on July 11, 1709. In vain
did the nuns resist as best they could, and appeal to the Primate
of Lyons, and then to the Parliament; on the morning of October 29, d'Argenson, the Lieutenant of Police, presented himself
at the Abbey, produced a decree of the Council and twenty-two
lettres de cachet (one for each of the fifteen nuns of the choir and
the seven lay-sisters who still survived), seized all papers, put
everything under seal, and made the old nuns get into the
coaches he had brought, which took them to various convents,
guarded by mounted archers. A month later the Paris community took over the furniture and relics. But it was necessary
to destroy " what was still quivering " : in 1710 the King
ordered the convent to be razed to the ground ; in 1711 the two
graveyards were dug over, corpses were scandalously disinterred,
bones were heaped into a cart, and thrown ignominiously into
a common grave at Saint-Lambert ; in 1712 the Church was
demolished. Thus perished miserably Port-Royal-des-Champs.

The Jansenists had left it to its fate, for it was round the
Réflexions morales of Père Quesnel that the battle was now
raging. Having by force of circumstances become the defenders
of the liberty of the Church of France against the authority of
the Pope, they had rallied all the enemies of the Jesuits, so that
now the struggle appeared entirely as one between the Gallicans,
directed by Cardinal de Noailles, against the Ultramontanes,
directed by Père Le Tellier and Fénelon.

Noailles had again notified his approval of the *Réflexions
morales* in 1699, after certain slight corrections. On July 15,

1708, the Pope pronounced them Jansenistic and pernicious. Nevertheless, Noailles did not withdraw his approval. Then **The Bull** his opponents circulated in Paris, and insolently **"Unigenitus."** posted up on the doors of the Archbishop's palace, a rescript by the Bishops of Luçon and La Rochelle condemning Quesnel's book. Noailles, supported by his parish priests, retorted by forbidding the faithful to read the placard of the two bishops, and ended by disallowing the hearing of confessions by Jesuits in his diocese. Hereupon Louis XIV once more intervened : a decree of the Council prohibited the sale of the *Réflexions morales* (November 11, 1711), and the King begged the Pope to condemn it solemnly.

It was under these circumstances that on September 8, 1713, the famous bull *Unigenitus* was published, which condemned as false, captious, ill-sounding, calculated to wound the ears of the pious, scandalous, presumptuous, etc., 104 propositions of Père Quesnel. But the bull *Unigenitus* encountered the same difficulties as the bull *Vineam*. First, the clerical assembly, charged by the King to receive it, voted a rescript to confirm it, by way of reserving Gallican rights. But more than this : the Archbishop of Paris and fifteen prelates formally refused to accept it ; Noailles went so far as to interdict it in his diocese. And as on September 28 he had revoked the approval he had formerly given to the *Réflexions morales*, it was clear that he and his allies were rejecting the *Unigenitus* constitution, not in the name of Jansenism, but in the name of Gallican liberties. Now on this ground the objecting bishops found plenty of allies : primarily the Sorbonne and the Parliament, which the King only constrained by threats to register the pontifical decree, and, secondly, the general public, which considered the bull absurd.

For under Louis XIV religious questions interested the crowd much as do political questions to-day. They were discussed in the stage-coach, the ferry-boat, the inn. Ray, an English traveller, remarked at the beginning of the eighteenth century, that whereas in Italy it was considered impolite to ask strangers " what faith they professed, in France one has scarcely exchanged three words with one's neighbour before this question is put." Tatlers accordingly were of opinion that the bull *Uni-*

genitus was revolting to common sense, and they were not far wrong, perhaps, seeing that it condemned propositions such as those which merely recommended the study of the New Testament; hearing this, the Parisians laughingly asked if the Holy Father considered it an offence to read the Gospel.

In short, when Louis XIV died in September, 1715, the Gallican Jansenists were more vital than ever. And shortly afterwards the Regent was to appoint the rebel Noailles, whom the Great King had proposed to bring to trial, President of the Council of Conscience.

WORKS TO CONSULT : *Mémoires* of Arnauld d'Andilly, by G. Hermant ; *Journal* of Jean Migault ; Works of Bossuet and Fénelon ; *Mémoires des Évêques de France*, published by J. Lemoine ; Racine, *Abrégé de l'histoire de Port-Royal*, Gazier ed. ; *Bulletin de la Société de l'histoire du Protestantisme* (in course of publication); Et. Dejean, *Nicolas Pavillon* (1909) ; E. Faguet, *L'Anticléricalisme* (1906) ; A. Hallays, *Le Pèlerinage de Port-Royal* (1909) ; J. Lemaître, *Fénelon* (1910) ; Rebelliau, *Histoire de France*, published under the direction of E. Lavisse, vol. viii, 1 ; *Bossuet historien du Protestantisme* (1909) ; Sainte-Beuve, *Port-Royal* (1888–91) ; cf. Griselle in *Études*, May 20, 1907.

CHAPTER XI

SUNSET

I. The Spanish Succession. II. War. III. The end of the Great King.

I

WHEN in 1665 the late-born son of Philip IV ascended the throne of Spain, it seemed evident that he could not live long. At the age of four years, Charles II was a rickety child, consumed by scrofula and fever, a degenerate, as yet unweaned, who could speak very little, and could only **The Spanish** walk upheld by straps. Yet this abortion reigned **Succession.** for thirty-five years. He had a singularly long, thin face, a heavy nose, a hanging under-lip, a retreating forehead, and thin, dull, light hair; illiterate and restless, spending his days playing spillikins with his dwarfs, the victim of an intellectual anæmia which made him incapable of mental effort, the poor man was at least conscious of the great traditions he incarnated, and his pride, his gravity, and his piety gained the hearts of his people in spite of everything. His first wife, Maria-Luisa, having died suddenly in 1689, he married that same year Maria-Anna of Neuburg, the daughter of the Elector-Palatine. She was a fresh German girl of twenty-two, coquettish, ambitious, and violent. The weakly Charles II loved her with all his strength, which was very limited, and the various emotions induced by this passion brought him nearer to the grave each night.

Spain seemed almost as moribund as her King. At this period she possessed only from twenty to thirty thousand soldiers in rags, begging or stealing their daily bread, to guard the remnant of Flanders, the province of Milan, Naples, Sicily, Sardinia, the hulks of Africa, the Canaries, part of Oceania, the Antilles with Cuba, and, finally, the whole of South America save Brazil and Guiana. Nevertheless, there was no lack of princes who aspired to the possession of this vast empire in ruins and the twenty crowns of the Spanish sovereign, after the death of Charles II. Three among them outshone their competitors as much by their powers as by their rights.*

(1) The Dauphin claimed the succession through his mother, Marie-Thérèse, daughter of Philip IV and elder sister of **Candidates for** Charles II, and further through his grandmother, **the Spanish** Anne of Austria, sister of Philip IV; these two **Throne.** princesses had certainly renounced their claims to the throne of Spain on their marriage, but their renunciations might be considered null and void, for the law of succession to a throne cannot be altered by a mere convention, and moreover the dowry on which Marie-Thérèse's abnegation had been conditional had never been paid.

(2) Ferdinand-Joseph, Electoral Prince of Bavaria, claimed the throne in right of his mother, Maria-Antoinetta, daughter of Margaret-Theresa, and thus the granddaughter of Philip IV and niece of Charles II, just as the Dauphin was his nephew.

(3) Finally, the Emperor Leopold claimed the succession in right of his mother, Maria-Anna, and his wife, Margaret-Theresa, kinswomen of Charles II and Philip IV in the same degree as Anne of Austria and Marie-Thérèse, but the younger sisters of these princesses, and he promised, should the heritage fall to him, to make it over to the second son of his second marriage, the Archduke Charles.

In order to exclude Louis XIV and his family, the Emperor invoked the renunciations of Anne of Austria and Marie-Thérèse,

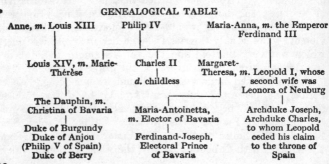

GENEALOGICAL TABLE

Anne, m. Louis XIII   Philip IV   Maria-Anna, m. the Emperor
                                    Ferdinand III

Louis XIV, m. Marie-   Charles II   Margaret-
Thérèse   d. childless Theresa, m. Leopold I, whose
                                      second wife was
                                      Leonora of Neuburg

The Dauphin, m.   Maria-Antoinetta,   Archduke Joseph,
Christina of Bavaria   m. Elector of Bavaria   Archduke Charles,
                                              to whom Leopold
Duke of Burgundy   Ferdinand-Joseph,   ceded his claim
Duke of Anjou   Electoral Prince   to the throne of
(Philip V of Spain)   of Bavaria   Spain
Duke of Berry

and alleged that Maria-Anna and Margaret-Theresa had not been disinherited as their elder sisters had been. To exclude his grandson, the Electoral Prince, he invoked a renunciation of the throne of Spain which he had dictated to his daughter on her marriage to the Elector. To which the Electoral Prince retorted that this document was valueless, since Leopold was not competent to modify the rights of succession to the throne of Spain, and that, moreover, Charles II had formally refused to ratify Maria-Antoinetta's renunciation. On the whole, the claim of the House of France seemed the most valid.

Every one felt that this question of the Spanish succession threatened to bring about a general war. Now neither France, **Secret Treaty** still hampered by her recent effort, nor commercial **of The Hague.** Holland, nor England, whose King was engaged in a struggle with his Parliament, desired war. Thus they tried at the outset to arrange the matter amicably, and this miracle came to pass : Louis XIV and William III agreed to sign a convention and impose it on the other nations ; by the Treaties of The Hague (September–October, 1698) the two naval Powers and France decided beforehand on the division of the heritage between the three aspirants. It was impossible to keep the convention secret ; Spanish patriotism was greatly incensed by it, and Charles II, to avoid the dismemberment of his kingdom, hastened to make a will in favour of the Electoral Prince (November, 1698). But three months later this child of seven years old died, and the signatories of The Hague thereupon concluded a fresh compact (March, 1700) : on the death of Charles II, France was to take over all the Italian possessions ; the Emperor was to have Spain, the Low Countries, and the Indies, and should he refuse the portion they assigned him without consulting him, it should be given to some other prince. Leopold protested.

What made him so recalcitrant was that he believed he could reckon upon the support of Charles II. His party, it is true, was predominant at the Court of Spain, where the Queen, his sister-in-law, who was omnipotent with her feeble and uxorious husband, pressed his claims vigorously. But Maria-Anna was herself surrounded by a clan of greedy Germans, indecently eager to make their fortunes ; she was governed by her confessor, a Tyrolese monk, Father Gabriel, and by a

lady-in-waiting called Gertrud-Maria-Josefa Wolff von Guttenberg, the widow of the Baron von Berlepsch; and this monk,
aided by this Baroness, put up everything saleable in the way
of offices and honours to auction. Moved by hatred of this
" Camarilla," the Spaniards gradually rallied to Louis XIV's
ambassador, the Marquis d'Harcourt, whose French cordiality
was skilfully opposed to the stiffness and rapacity of the Imperial
ambassador, Count von Harrach. At the same time Cardinal
Porto-Carrero, the leader of the nationalist party, and the Pope
himself pointed out to Charles II that the Emperor would never
be strong enough to protect the Spanish monarchy against the
combined forces of England, France, and Holland, and advised
him to save his kingdom by giving it to a French prince. Accordingly the poor King, patriotically overcoming his traditional
Death of hostility to the Bourbons, ended by choosing as
Charles II of his heir his grand-nephew, the Duc d'Anjou, on
Spain. condition that this prince should solemnly renounce
all claims to the crown of France. A month later he died
(November 1, 1700).

The news of his will and of his death reached Versailles on
November 9, and placed Louis in a most embarrassing position.
What should he do ? Repudiate the will ? Or, on the other
hand, break his covenant with England and Holland ? On the
very day of the arrival of the courier, at three o'clock, he held
a Council of his son and the Ministers of State in Mme. de
Maintenon's apartments. The Duc de Beauvilliers was for
adhering to the partition treaty, which secured certain solid
advantages for France, rather than undertake a war against
the whole of Europe for the sake of establishing in Spain a
dynasty which in a few generations might easily become hostile
to that of France, in spite of the ties of kinship. But Torcy
and Pontchartrain pointed out that war could not be avoided
in any case; if the will were set aside, war would have to be
waged against the Emperor, whose son, failing the Duc d'Anjou,
would become the universal legal heir of Charles II, and who
would certainly oppose any partition; on the other hand, since
from the time of Charles V nothing had succeeded in embroiling
the Hapsburgs of Vienna and those of Madrid, there was every
reason to suppose that such would also prove to be the case

with the Bourbons ; finally France would reap innumerable advantages of all sorts, and notably commercial advantages, from an intimate connection with Spain and her immense colonial empire. The Dauphin intervened in his turn, with a firmness that surprised his auditors, to claim the heritage of his son. On the following day Louis XIV decided to accept the will.

It was at Versailles, on November 16, that he made his decision officially known :

The King, when he came out from his *lever*, received the Spanish Ambassador in his cabinet, which M. le Duc d'Anjou had entered from behind. The King, presenting the Prince, said the Ambassador might salute him as his king. The Ambassador at once fell to his knees in the Spanish fashion, and made a rather long complimentary speech in that tongue. The King remarked that the Duke did not yet understand the language, and that it should be his business to reply for his grandson. Thereupon, contrary to all precedent, the King caused the two folds of the door of his cabinet to be thrown open, and ordered all the crowd assembled without to enter ; then, glancing majestically over the numerous company : " Gentlemen," said he, indicating the Duc d'Anjou, " this is the King of Spain. His birth has called him to the throne and also the deceased King by his will ; the whole nation desired his succession, and urged me to approve it ; it was the will of Heaven ; I agreed with pleasure." Then, turning to his grandson : " Be a good Spaniard, this is now your first duty, but remember that you were born a Frenchman to promote union between the two nations ; this is the way to make them happy and to preserve the peace of Europe." Then, pointing his finger at his grandson and turning to the Ambassador, he said : " If he takes my advice, you will be a great personage, and very soon ; he cannot do better than follow your counsels." When this first excitement of the courtiers was over, the two other royal princes arrived, and all three embraced each other affectionately, with tears in their eyes. (Saint-Simon.)

Louis accepts the throne for his grandson.

In thus accepting the Spanish succession for the Duc d'Anjou, Louis XIV apparently adopted the wisest course open to him ; but it was incumbent on him to employ all his diplomatic skill in reassuring England and Holland, his former allies. What they most dreaded was the union of France and Spain under his direction ; he should have clearly shown that Philip V was master in his own kingdom, that he could act as he chose, that the King of France would henceforth look upon him as a friend, perhaps an ally, but a foreigner. Louis XIV pursued a directly opposite course, and committed blunder after blunder.

In the first place, on February 1, 1701, he published letters patent in which he declared that the Duc d'Anjou and his descendants would retain all their rights to the crown of France; then, a few days later, on February 6, without any preliminary announcement, French troops suddenly entered the Spanish fortresses of the Netherlands in the name of the King of Spain, and took the Dutch garrisons they found there prisoners. No enterprise could have been more calculated to alarm the United Provinces, which for over thirty years had made considerable sacrifices in order to maintain this barrier of fortresses between themselves and too adventurous France. From this day forth they accordingly made up their minds to fight; their States-General shortly afterwards made an appeal to England which excited much emotion in that country.

Spanish fortresses seized by the French.

In Italy hostilities against the Emperor were already in progress. Leopold had secured the support of nearly all the German princes, notably that of the Elector of Brandenburg by recognizing him as King of Prussia. On September 7, 1701, he entered into an agreement with William III and Holland; this was the *Grand Alliance of The Hague.*

A final blunder on the part of the King cemented this coalition. James II died at Saint-Germain (September, 1701); the dethroned Queen of England implored Louis XIV to recognize her son, the Prince of Wales, as King of England: " You see, Sire," she said, " the state in which I am; shall I also lose my son, and shall the son of a king lapse into the condition of a private individual ? " Louis XIV replied that he would consult his Council, but the Queen's appeal had struck him. In vain his ministers reminded him that he had recognized William III by the Treaty of Ryswyck; Monseigneur was in favour of granting royal honours to the Prince of Wales, and this counsel prevailed. To his mind, perhaps, the title he accorded to the son of James II was a mere matter of courtesy, of no more practical importance than that of King of France assumed by the sovereigns of Great Britain ever since the Hundred Years' War. But the whole English nation, its susceptibilities deeply wounded, quivered with wrath; the last partisans of peace were reduced

Death of James II.

to silence in Parliament, the Commons voted the supplies necessary to begin hostilities (January), and William III delighted, recalled his ambassador. He was preparing his army for battle when he died on March 19, 1702, at the age of fifty-two.

His death did not check the movement which carried the English people on against the " Papist " king, and three persons were ready to replace him as leaders of the coalition : Heinsius,

Heinsius. Marlborough, and Prince Eugene. The Grand Pensionary of Holland, Heinsius, was a man of sixty who lived modestly in a little house, passed along the streets on foot, and worked ten hours a day ; this honest burgher had but one passion : hatred of France ; he could never forget how one day at Versailles, Louvois had threatened him, a diplomatic envoy, with imprisonment in the Bastille.

Marlborough. John Churchill, who became Duke of Marlborough, was both a skilful diplomatist and a great commander. His wife had complete ascendancy over Queen Anne, whose favourite she was, and he himself, abetted by Godolphin, the Minister of Finance, directed Parliament with unscrupulous political dexterity. In short, he could do what he liked, and could even please the ladies, for he was a handsome man. But he was so dishonest as to create a certain amount of prejudice ; he amassed a scandalous fortune in the army. As to Prince

Prince Eugene. Eugene, son of the turbulent and brilliant Olympia Mancini, Comtesse de Soissons and Duchesse de Savoie-Carignan, this ugly little man with a turned-up nose over an upper lip too short to conceal his teeth, had inherited from his great-uncle, Mazarin, indisputable diplomatic aptitudes, which, like Marlborough, he combined with the talents of an excellent general. Born a French subject, he had been taken into exile by his mother, who had been deeply compromised in the poisoning affairs, and out of pique at being unable to obtain a command from Louis XIV, he had entered the service of Austria, where he had lately won his spurs by defeating the army of the Grand Turk. He never forgave the King for having overlooked him.

Such were the " triumvirs of the League," as Torcy called them : having at their disposal the wealth and ships of Holland, the Imperial armies, trained by long years of warfare against

Turkey, and, above all, a kingdom in the hey-day of commercial prosperity, eager England, they all but compassed the ruin of Louis XIV. France had a few allies besides decrepit Spain : the Electors of Bavaria and of Cologne, the Duke of Savoy, and the King of Portugal, but the last two went over to the enemy in 1703, and the first two were very insignificant princes ; Louis XIV accordingly soon found himself alone against Europe. Now France was very weary ; her navy, her trade, and her finances had been half destroyed by the last war. And then she had lost her great Ministers. The incapable Chamillart had replaced Barbezieux, the successor of Louvois, as War Minister, and was in his turn replaced in 1709 by the deplorable Voysin. Torcy, fortunately, still presided over Foreign Affairs. And the King, of course, still had Marshals such as Boufflers, Vendôme, Berwick, and Villars, but they were not numerous enough for all the work on hand ; so it became necessary to employ a Villeroy, and even a La Feuillade.

II

The war opened badly for the French.

Immediately upon receipt of the news of Charles II's will, the Emperor had instructed Prince Eugene to occupy the province of Milan with an army corps. Louis XIV had secured the support of Savoy by the marriage of the Duke's second daughter, the sister of the Duchess of Burgundy, to the new King of Spain, Philip V. But the treacherous Vittore Emanuele played a double game, and Catinat, who commanded the French army, betrayed by him and discouraged, allowed himself to be outwitted by Eugene, and retired beyond the Oglio ; thus in the summer of 1701 the Austrians were already on the French frontier.

The King, highly displeased, determined to change his generalissimo, and replaced Catinat by Villeroy, the only man, **Villeroy.** says Saint-Simon, whom Louis himself ever called his " favourite." Unfortunately Villeroy, an attractive courtier and indeed a very gallant soldier, was a wretched general. Having received orders to give battle at all costs, he at once marched upon Chiari (between Milan and

Brescia), which he supposed to be held merely by a detachment ;
he found the entire hostile army awaiting him there, and had
to beat a precipitate retreat, leaving 2000 men on the field
(September 1). After this exploit he took up his winter
quarters at Cremona.

On February 1, 1702, at daybreak he was writing in his
room, fully dressed, when he heard cries and shots ; he went
down in all haste, and fell into the midst of a large body of
Austrians ; it was Prince Eugene, a few of whose soldiers had
entered the town by a drain, and opened one of the gates to
their comrades. A few hours later the Imperialists were
driven out of the town, but they took with them the unfortunate
Marshal, who was quite in the dark as to the whole business :

> Français, rendez grâce à Bellone,
> Votre bonheur est sans égal :
> Vous avez conservé Cremone
> Et perdu votre général.

The Duc de Vendôme was appointed Villeroy's successor.
Tall and big, with " a very noble countenance and a haughty
The Duc de air," this great-grandson of Henri IV was a
Vendôme. " Libertine " and a debauchee like his brother the
Grand Prior, who, according to Saint-Simon, always went to
bed dead drunk. We must not, however, take the written
caricature which the terrible Duke has left us quite literally ;
he declares that Vendôme often did not get up till four o'clock
from the bed where he lay among his dogs, and where his
bitches had their litters ; that waking late when with the army,
he gave his orders on his night-stool, considered riding very
fatiguing, and was more than once nearly captured by enemy
scouts as a result of lingering too long in comfortable quarters
too far from the camp. There is a good deal of exaggeration in
all this, but Vendôme's laziness was proverbial, and his men
loved him for his very disorders, and for his familiarity towards
them. His culpable negligence often imperilled the success of
operations. But on the day of battle he was a leader of quick
and sure perception and prompt and irresistible decisions,
somewhat akin to Condé and Luxembourg.

This mixture of activity and indolence enabled him in 1702
to gain an advantage over Prince Eugene at Santa-Vittoria and

at Luzzara, and force him to evacuate the Duchy of Mantua. In 1703, the Austrian army being diminished, and Prince Eugene having been recalled to Vienna, the campaign opened favourably for the French ; but unfortunately Vendôme had to stop and disarm his Piedmontese soldiers on receiving news of the definitive defection of the Duke of Savoy, who, having obtained from the Emperor the promise of Montferrat and other territories, had turned his coat unblushingly. A retreat before the combined forces of Austria and Savoy was inevitable : in 1705 the enemy recrossed the Adige. And in 1706 the King had to recall Vendôme and send him to the Netherlands to repair the disasters brought about by Villeroy's negligence. The army was placed under the nominal command of the young Duke of Orleans, and under the effective direction of " a man very small in person and in all else, active, lively, and extremely loquacious," who was known as Marshal de Marcin.

Meanwhile 25,000 French soldiers were besieging Turin under the direction of La Feuillade, Chamillart's son-in-law, and the **La Feuillade.** son of the courtier who in 1684 had bought the Hôtel de La Ferté-Sennecterre to lay out a square on its site for the famous monument celebrating the victories of Louis the Great.

The Duc d'Elbeuf [says Madame] one day surprised La Feuillade standing in front of his glass, and saying : " I am well made, the ladies love me. Come, Feuilladin, Feuilladin, La Feuillade." This was the origin of his nickname, Feuilladin.

This Feuilladin was a lunatic with a pretty wit. When Vauban offered to go and serve under him as a volunteer, he replied gracefully : " I shall then take Turin *à la Cohorn*." Alas ! . . . He began by allowing the Duke of Savoy to escape, then placed his lines in the most absurd manner ; finally, when the Duke of Orleans and Marcin, hard pressed by Prince Eugene, arrived before Turin, he refused to accept the sensible advice of the young Duke, who, judging his positions to be deplorable, urged him to quit them and give battle. Hereupon, on September 7, 1706, Prince Eugene attacked the French army and completely routed it. Marcin was taken prisoner and died of his wounds, while Feuilladin retreated precipitately to the Alps, abandoning his siege material, several hundred guns, his wounded, a quantity of standards, his baggage, etc. The French had to evacuate Italy (March, 1707). The enemy was very soon to besiege Toulon.

In Germany, war had been declared in May, 1702. It began by a failure. Catinat, who was in command on the Rhine, had only 21,000 men to oppose to the 50,000 soldiers of the Margrave Louis of Baden; he could not prevent his adversary from taking Landau, though it was heroically defended by Mélac (September, 1702), and it was thought at Versailles that there, as in Italy, he had been over-cautious. But the loss of Landau was made good by a marked advantage. The Elector of Bavaria had lately signed a fresh treaty of alliance with Louis XIV (June, 1702); a portion of Catinat's troops, under the command of Lieutenant-General de Villars, was sent to join the Bavarians. Deceiving the Prince of Baden by a feint in the direction of Neuburg, Villars succeeded in crossing the Rhine near Huningen (October, 1702), and then, in spite of the inferiority of his forces, he defeated his adversary at Friedlingen. He barely escaped defeat himself; surprised by a violent counter-attack, his hitherto victorious regiments began to waver when he received news that his cavalry had routed that of the Margrave; he at once ran along the ranks, shouting: " Come, friends, victory is ours. Long live the King ! " (Voltaire); in short, he put new heart into his infantry, which forced the enemy to retire. The troops, filled with enthusiasm, proclaimed him Marshal on the battlefield, and the King confirmed the well-earned honour.

The Marquis de Villars was a tall man of fifty, " who had become somewhat stout as he grew older, but not heavy; he **Marshal de** had a lively, open, *forthcoming (sortante)* counte-
Villars. nance, rather fleshy, with which his gestures and demeanour harmonized. He had made his way by his zeal, his goodwill, and his dexterity. " It seems as if this little fellow sprang out of the ground to be present wherever there is any firing," cried Louis XIV once at the siege of Maestricht. By dint of looking out for " opportunities," as he himself said, Villars ended by conquering fortune : he became a Marshal, a duke and a peer, and saved the kingdom. His luck as a general

was proverbial; when the weather was radiant during manœuvres, the soldiers called it " Villars' weather." Further, he was a fine soldier, a born leader of men after the manner of Napoleon's Marshals, but with something both noble and subtle in his character, which was peculiar to his century; he possessed audacity, gaiety, a strain of dramatic gallantry (*panache*): " a genius created for war and created to lead Frenchmen." For the rest, he was not very refined; the courtiers ridiculed his braggadocio and swagger, and Saint-Simon hated him.

Villars joined the Elector of Bavaria at Willingen in the Grand Duchy of Baden on May 6, 1703. But he could not persuade Max Emmanuel to march directly upon Vienna, which would perhaps have brought the war to an end; and while the Elector was vainly trying to join forces with Vendôme in the Tyrol, he was obliged to defend Bavaria with his 25,000 men against the 50,000 soldiers of Styrum and the Margrave. He defeated Styrum at Höchstädt on September 25; but he agreed so ill with Max Emanuel that he himself begged to be recalled. He was sent into the Cévennes against the Camisards, and Marcin took his place.

The allies resolved to concentrate their forces against the Elector and Marcin, whose advanced position was a continual menace to Vienna. Leaving his lieutenant, Stahrrenberg, and the Duke of Savoy to hold Vendôme in Italy, Prince Eugene proceeded to Germany. Marlborough, for his part, left the Low Countries with his troops, passed along the right bank of the Rhine, observed by Villeroy who was following the left bank, and then, suddenly parting company with the hero of Cremona, to the great bewilderment of the latter, and picking up on his way the remnants of the army of the Prince of Hesse which Tallart had just defeated near Spires, he joined the Margrave of Baden at Ulm, and devastated the Palatinate in a terrible fashion. The Elector was beginning to think of begging the Emperor for mercy when he learned that Tallart was coming to his assistance with his 30,000 men. This threw him back upon the French alliance.

The Franco-Bavarian troops took up their position near Höchstädt, on the very ground where Villars had gained his victory the year before. Tallart—a thin haggard person " with rather jealous eyes [i.e. a squint], full of fire and intelligence, but very short-sighted," commanded the right wing; as the village of Blindheim, on his own right, seemed to him the key **Battle of** of his positions, he posted half of his forces there **"Blenheim."** with orders not to stir until they received his express command. The left wing was under Marcin. The centre was composed of the Elector's troops. On August 13, 1704, towards eight o'clock in the morning, Marlborough deployed his Anglo-Dutch army before Tallart, while Prince Eugene with his Austrians took up a position in front of Marcin (the Margrave of Baden and his Germans were absent, detained by the siege of Ingolstadt). First of all, the English attacked Blindheim; they were vigorously repulsed. Marlborough did not persist; forgoing Blindheim, he threw himself on Tallart's left, which was composed mainly of cavalry, which, embarrassed by a sort of ravine or chasm, gave way, carrying with it a portion of the Elector's troops. M. de Tallart had himself been taken prisoner, in the plain, while galloping furiously across it in an attempt to reach Blindheim. The troops he had posted there, with orders not to move, receiving no instructions and finding themselves surrounded by Marlborough's army, laid down their arms instead of trying to rejoin Marcin: this "ignominy," this "horrible capitulation," was signed by all the corps-commanders, save that of the regiment of Navarre, whose veterans tore up and buried their colours. Meanwhile, the right wing was victoriously resisting Prince Eugene; but exposed on their right flank by the destruction of Tallart's troops, Marcin and the Elector had to retreat with the French army corps and what remained of the Bavarian troops; they retired into Alsace under the protection of Villeroy, who had at last approached. By these means they saved some 20,000 men out of an army of over 50,000; the enemy held their standards, their wounded, a vast number of prisoners, and several generals, as well as Marshal Tallart. The French had to quit Germany entirely, and the Elector was obliged to take refuge in Alsace. Thus France was now reduced to defending her frontier.

Villars, recalled from the Cévennes, was entrusted with the task, and fully justified the confidence the King had in him, and that which, as his conversation sufficiently proclaimed, he had in himself. He entrenched himself at Sierk and on the

297

Moselle. Marlborough—"that rascal of a Marlborough," as he called the Englishman—advanced against the French lines, but owing to the insubordination of his German and Dutch troops, who could not be induced to leave their homes too far behind them, he was obliged to fall back, first writing very politely to M. de Villars to say he was in despair at being unable to fight a splendid battle with him (June). Hereupon, the Marshal's boasts were redoubled, but at the same time he crossed the Rhine and with great adroitness surprised the Prince of Baden at Wissembourg. In 1706 he completed the liberation of Alsace. . . .

In the Low Countries the modest and worthy Marshal de Boufflers had been charged in 1701 to occupy the fortresses of the Barrier in the name of the King of Spain. **Marshal de Boufflers.** Saint-Simon has left us a noble eulogy of him : "He was a very short man, but all compact of honour and valour and probity, of gratitude and attachment to the King, and of love for his country." He had some successes at first, but lacking provisions, he was obliged to fall back ; then part of his army was sent to Catinat in Germany ; with the result that Marlborough, who was in command of the Anglo-Dutch forces, took Venloo, Ruremonde, and Liége (October, 1702). In 1703 Villeroy, whom the Emperor had released without ransom, came to direct operations in place of Boufflers ; but fortunately he had received orders to confine himself to the defensive, and as in the hostile army the Dutch absolutely refused to risk a decisive battle, Marlborough had to be content with completing the conquest of Guelderland, doing some damage to Cologne and Limburg, and then, in defiance of Villeroy, forcing the bridges of the Dyle (July, 1705). He would fain have profited by this success, pushed on, carried the war boldly into France ; once again the over-prudent generals of Holland held him back.

In 1706 he deployed his forces not far from Louvain to prevent the junction of Villeroy with Marcin, who was bringing up **French losses in the Low Countries.** reinforcements from Germany. The " favourite " took cover for his left behind some marshes which made it impossible for them to move ; it was the blunder of Höchstädt over again. Marlborough threw himself upon the French right with his whole force, broke it, and took the left in flank. Villeroy had to retreat to Louvain. So far he had lost only 2000 men ; he lost 6000, fifty-four cannon out of sixty, and a large number of standards in the rout which this retreat very soon became, after passing through the defile of Jardoigne. As a sequel to this disaster Louvain, Brussels, Ghent, Bruges, and Oudenarde fell into the hands of the enemy. The Prussians sang :

> " Varus, rends-moi mes légions ! "
> S'écriait autrefois Auguste.
> " Tallart, rends-moi mes bataillons ! "
> Dit Louis à titre plus juste.
> " Demandez-les à Villeroy,
> Il en a perdu plus que moi."

The King decided to disgrace his favourite, and Vendôme, hastily recalled from Italy, was charged to reconstruct the shattered army. But his absence was fatal to French fortunes in Piedmont. We have already spoken of the disaster of Turin. At the end of 1706 France was everywhere thrown back upon her frontiers.

Meanwhile, civil war had broken out in the kingdom.

The most serious of the popular outbreaks caused by the persecutions which followed the Revocation of the Edict of **Revolt in the** Nantes was that in the Cévennes. Lamoignon de **Cévennes.** Basville, the Intendant of Languedoc, a man of a mild countenance of almost feminine charm, was singularly successful in making life a burden to New Converts of ill repute. The War of the Spanish Succession was just beginning ; Huguenot refugees were passing secretly throughout the country, predicting that, with God's help, the Dutch, the English, and the Germans would shortly overcome the King's armies : inflamed by these speeches, and exasperated by Basville's agents, the hardy Cévennes mountaineers revolted. On July 24, 1702, a troop of armed ruffians massacred the arch-priest of the diocese of Mende ; other bands were at once formed. The war was peculiarly atrocious. The " Camisards " (so called from the white shirts they wore over their clothes) had some good leaders, such as Jean Cavalier, a baker's assistant aged twenty-three, Couderc, Roland, Ravenel, etc., and the royal troops, accustomed to fight in good order, had no stomach for this war against ferocious churls, whom it was impossible to get at among their rocks and precipices. Villars in 1704 succeeded better than his predecessors ; he employed relatively mild methods, and very intelligently made Cavalier a colonel, begging him to raise a regiment among his former comrades. When he left in January, 1705, the situation was better, but it was not until 1710 that the last bands of Camisards disappeared. Thus throughout the War of the Succession, France was obliged to keep troops to fight the Protestants of the Cévennes, troops which, as we shall see, were badly needed on the frontiers.

In Spain the young French prince had been very well received at first. Philip V was seventeen. "He was well made, fair **Philip V of** like the late King Charles and the Queen his **Spain.** grandmother, grave, silent, sedate, and reserved, just the person for the Spaniards." He was withal gentle, an easy master, with a just and honest mind ; he was capable of intrepidity upon occasion, but he spoilt his many fine qualities by irresolution, timidity, a piety quite Spanish in character, savouring more of superstition than of ardour ; also he was indolent—in short, " God had given him a docile, nay, more, a servile spirit " (Louville). He needed some one to govern him · he had his wife, Queen Maria-Luisa of Savoy, and the Princesse des Ursins (Orsini). The little Queen, who was barely fourteen at the time of her marriage (1701), was no less lively and intelligent than her sister, the Duchess of Burgundy ; however, she cared nothing for " music, or acting, or conversation, or walking, or hunting—in a word, for any of the pleasures of her age " ; her one preoccupation was " to rule the King her husband absolutely, and keep him always in leading-strings "—in other words, to govern Spain. She had excellent means at her disposal to attain her ends, the traditional means used by the Queen-Dowager, Maria-Anna of Neuburg, for Philip V was no less amorous, no less devout, and no less ardent than Charles II had been. And apparently she turned them to good account, for Philip V never resisted her will, which was also that of the Princesse des Ursins.

SUNSET

The Princesse des Ursins. Marie-Anne de la Trémoille, the widow, first of the Prince de Chalais (a Talleyrand), and, by her second marriage, of Prince Flavio Orsini (in French, des Ursins), Duke of Bracciano and grandee of Spain, was fifty-nine when she was appointed *camarera-mayor*, thanks to the patronage of her friend Mme. de Maintenon, of the Duchess of Burgundy, who was grateful for all the pains she had taken in connection with her sister's marriage, and of Cardinal Porto-Carrero, who remembered that he had once loved her.

She was tall rather than short, a brunette with blue eyes, which said whatever she wished them to say, with a perfect figure, a fine bust, and a face which, without being beautiful, was charming; a very aristocratic air, something majestic in her whole bearing, and in everything such natural and perpetual graces, even in the most trivial and unimportant things, that I have never seen any one to approach her either in person or in wit, of which she had a large share of every variety; flattering, caressing, insinuating, sedate, seeking to please for the sake of pleasing, with a charm which it was impossible to resist when she wanted to attract and fascinate; withal, an air which, albeit grand, attracted instead of alarming; her conversation was delicious, never-failing, and extremely amusing by reason of all the countries and persons she had known; her voice and speech were most agreeable, with an air of gentleness; she had also read a great deal, and she was a person who reflected much; she was, moreover, a greater adept in intrigue than any one in the world, and had spent her life in it by choice when in Rome; she had many vast ambitions, much above her sex and the ordinary ambitions of men, and a will to govern not inferior to her will to exist, etc. (Saint-Simon.)

This expert old lady, who when necessary had no difficulty in becoming a charming young woman, and who, in spite of her fifty-nine years, had renounced nothing, easily fascinated the Queen of fourteen and the King of seventeen who were about to govern Spain, and on whom her functions kept her in perpetual attendance.

I have the honour to take the King of Spain's dressing-gown when he gets into bed, and to hand it to him with his slippers when he gets up [she gaily confides to Mme. de Maintenon on November 12, 1701]. When the King comes to the Queen's room to go to bed, the Comte de Benavente hands me His Majesty's sword, a chamber-pot, and a lamp, which I generally upset over my clothes; it is too grotesque. The King would never get up if I did not go and draw his curtain.

Unfortunately the Spaniards soon began to murmur at the too apparent influence of the *camarera-mayor*, whose first fault

301

in their eyes was that she was a foreigner, which she could not help. Philip V and Maria-Luise indeed surrounded themselves with French people, and they, who considered the " hidalgos " perfectly ridiculous and, to sum up, provincial, could not refrain from making them feel the superiority of the culture of Versailles ; with the result that French impertinence daily made enemies for France, and that the nobles, kept outside the domain of State affairs and humiliated, gradually rallied to the Austrian party. Add to this, that from the moment when the people of Castille had declared enthusiastically for Philip V, those of Catalonia and Aragon had felt at once less repugnance to the Hapsburgs.

As the Spanish monarchy lacked every necessary, France had to undertake the task of defending it. Already, in October, 1703, the English had destroyed the galleons coming from America laden with gold in the actual roadstead of Vigo : a catastrophe for the public finances. In May, 1703, an event still more serious took place : the defection of Portugal, whose king turned traitor too suddenly for his future glory, when the Emperor promised him several Spanish towns. An English fleet came to Lisbon, bearing the Archduke Charles, to whom the Emperor Leopold, his father, had solemnly made over his claim to the crown of Spain in September, 1703 ; and very soon " Charles III " set out for Madrid at the head of an army of English, Dutch, and Portuguese soldiers. But on the way he met the French troops, commanded by the Duke of Berwick, the son of James II and Arabella Churchill, and thus the nephew of Marlborough (he became a naturalized Frenchman in 1703). This " tall English fellow," pious and rigid, narrow, taciturn, sententious, cold, and dry, was " the most exact and precise of men in his measures " (Dangeau) : he methodically annihilated the efforts of the allies, and vanquished his quondam compatriots by the most purely Anglo-Saxon qualities. On the other hand, by sea, Admiral Rooke surprised Gibraltar : this fortified rock was considered impregnable, and the English have since proved that it is so, but the Spanish soldiers who guarded it were so averse from fighting that they laid down their arms as soon as the Admiral began to disembark his troops (August 4, 1704).

The Archduke Charles in Spain.

However, this check was not taken to heart very seriously at Versailles, and was amply compensated for in the King's eyes by a slight advantage which the Comte de Toulouse obtained, in spite of the inferiority of his vessels, over Admiral Rooke.

Unhappily the great disasters were about to begin; the Spanish nobility became more and more estranged from Philip V; Berwick was recalled by Louis XIV at the request of the young Queen of Spain, who could not endure him; the Archduke Charles and Lord Peterborough embarked at Lisbon for the Mediterranean : as they passed along the coasts of Valencia, several towns proclaimed Charles III, and on August 25, 1705, Barcelona opened its gates to them, carrying with it all Catalonia and Valencia. In vain did Philip V attempt to recapture the great town the following year : on May 12, 1706, he was obliged to raise the siege, abandoning his munitions, his cannon, his wounded, while in order to return to his capital he was forced to cross the frontier and pass through Pau. Moreover, Madrid itself was not too safe, for the allies were approaching; Philip V had to transfer his Court to Burgos, and in the capital he had just quitted Charles III was proclaimed king.

At this moment, then, Louis XIV seemed to be vanquished in Spain, as everywhere else. He asked his grandson to **French recovery in Spain.** abdicate, but Philip V answered bravely that " he would shed the last drop of his blood rather than abandon his States." He was right. He had never ceased to be popular in Castille, and Madrid cordially hated the Portuguese, the Catalans, and the heretic English who supported Charles III. Massacred piecemeal by the people at the instigation of the clergy, the little army of the allies dwindled visibly. It was obliged to leave Madrid and fall back hastily, not upon the too distant frontier of Portugal, but upon the northern provinces. Philip V returned amidst acclamations to his capital, and on April 25, 1707, Berwick gained a brilliant victory at Almanza (to the north of Murcia), over Las Minas and the Protestant Frenchman Ruvigny, who had become Lord Galloway : thus Valencia, Aragon, and the greater part of Catalonia were regained. Finally, on October 10, 1707, the young Duke of Orleans took Lerida in a very brilliant manner,

THE SEVENTEENTH CENTURY

On every side the year 1707 was marked by similar French successes. Prince Eugene and the Duke of Savoy, who had invaded Provence, had to return to Italy after vainly besieging Toulon for five months (August). In the Low Countries, Vendôme held Marlborough in check. On the Rhine, Villars defied adversaries weaker than himself, carried the famous "lines of Stolhofen" by a celebrated manœuvre, occupied Heidelberg, Mannheim, and Stuttgart, and pushed on to Ulm and Nuremberg.

At this moment Charles XII of Sweden, who had just concluded the Peace of Altranstadt after a fabulous series of Charles XII of victories, insolently camped in the midst of Sweden. German territory. A new Gustavus Adolphus, it was open to him to take the coalition in the rear with his terrible army, bring the Emperor to his knees, and do what he pleased— and no one knew what this would be ; Villars was hopeful, the allies were uneasy. Marlborough, the commander-in-chief of the coalition, and a skilled diplomatist on occasion, went to Altranstadt to try to beguile the arbiter of Europe. He was received with disconcerting coldness, but he is said to have seen a map of Russia spread out on the King of Sweden's table, and to have thought this a reassuring omen. He was not mistaken : in September, 1707, Charles XII, after imposing humiliating conditions on the Emperor, recklessly set his army on the march towards Moscow. And with him the best hope of France disappeared.

Louis XIV had made up his mind that the whole effort of the campaign of 1708 should be concentrated in the Low Campaign in Countries, and that elsewhere, except in Spain, the Low the troops should simply remain on the defensive. Countries, By dint of an immense effort an army was 1708. mustered, "a splendid, complete, eager army, of great goodwill," under the effective command of Vendôme, and the nominal direction of the Duke of Burgundy. But, alas ! no more impossible collaboration could have been devised than that of the overbearing, lazy, and debauched Vendôme with the grandson of France, the most timorous and least military of men, and also the most easily scandalized of mortals. Vendôme

304

advanced with his habitual nonchalance ; not until July 6 did he recapture Bruges. Eugene hastily brought up 35,000 men from Germany to reinforce Marlborough, who already had 60,000 ; it was essential to prevent their junction. Instead of at once investing Oudenarde and there entrenching himself strongly, Vendôme wasted three days doing nothing, with the result that when the French army finally crossed the Scheldt, its advanced guard came into contact with that of Marlborough, who had come up by forced marches ; this happened on July 11, at two o'clock in the afternoon.

Taken by surprise, Vendôme directed the action very badly. He threw his troops forward at random, as they **Battle of** gradually came up to the field of battle ; his **Oudenarde.** breathless regiments were mauled by the enemy. Later, in his report to the King, he complained that the Duke of Burgundy, far from charging as he had begged him to do, had entrenched his troops, without even informing him : " I could not suppose," he said, " that fifty battalions and nearly a hundred and eighty squadrons of the best troops in this army would content themselves with seeing us fighting for six hours, and would look on at the spectacle as one looks on at the opera from the third row of boxes." Of course this was not the version given by the Prince's partisans. In any case, " night was falling ; a great deal of ground had been lost ; half of the army had not finished deploying. In this depressing situation the Princes consulted with M. de Vendôme as to the best course to adopt." Vendôme wished to resume the battle on the morrow, but his proposal found no supporters : " Oh, well ! " he exclaimed, " gentlemen, I see you are all of one mind, so we must retire. Moreover," he added, looking at the Duke of Burgundy, " you have wished this for a long time past " (Saint-Simon). According to Saint-Hilaire, Vendôme's opinion prevailed at the council of war, but a portion of the army, which had received neither orders nor ammunition, spontaneously retired the next day, entailing the disorganization of the rest. To put it briefly, the retreat took place in fearful disorder ; every one made for Ghent as fast as he could.

> Six mille tant morts que blessés,
> Trois autres mille désertés,

THE SEVENTEENTH CENTURY

Près de cinq mille prisonniers,
Et plus de neuf cents officiers
Immortalisent la besogne
De M. le Duc de Bourgogne.

While the dissensions between the leaders redoubled, and even the soldiers, divided into parties, quarrelled violently, and **Capture of** sought to fix responsibility on each other, Marl-**Lille.** borough and Eugene quietly laid siege to Lille. In spite of the splendid defence made by the aged Boufflers, the town was taken in October, and the citadel in December, 1708. Then Louis XIV disgraced Vendôme, and made Boufflers a duke and a peer; but it was said that the Duke of Burgundy was playing tennis when the news of the capitulation of Lille reached him, and that he did not interrupt his game for such a trifle. . . . This disastrous campaign left France in the most terrible distress.

And the year 1709 was that of the famous winter. The cold began on the eve of the Epiphany; the rivers were soon frozen **Terrible winter** over down to their mouths. The thaw came at **of 1709.** the end of two months, but " was followed by a frost as hard as the first, which lasted for three weeks more." Wine and strong waters burst the bottles, and the bread hardened on the table. In the vast, draughty rooms at Versailles in vain did the fireplaces devour perfect forests of trees; Mme. de Maintenon felt paralysis coming on; the King alone, imperturbable and solar, continued his walks in the gardens; he only interrupted them out of pity for those in attendance, who were obliged to accompany him. Hares and partridges were found lifeless in the fields, and travellers on the high roads; others perished in their beds; nearly all the new-born infants died. Madame declares that 24,000 persons succumbed from January 5 to February 2; " the common people are dying of cold like flies," she adds. She exaggerated. But, nevertheless, the wolves were ravening in the country; the fruit-trees and the early sowings were frozen; the water-mills could not work; corn and flour were lacking. But the Parisians, pale with hunger and pinched with cold, managed to laugh at the thought that the Maintenon was eating oatmeal bread, and they chanted the following *Paternoster*:

SUNSET

Our Father which art at Versailles, thy name is no longer hallowed, thy kingdom is no longer so great, thy will is no longer done either on earth or on the waters. Give us our bread which on every side we lack. Forgive our enemies who have beaten us, and not thy generals who allowed them to do so. Do not succumb to all the temptations of the Maintenon, but deliver us from Chamillart.

At Versailles " the King himself heard some rude home-truths from his windows." The Court murmured, feeling little gratitude to the aged Louis for having " reduced his table at Marly," sent his gold plate to the Mint, and tried to pawn his jewels. " He is reproached for all his expenditure," confessed Mme. de Maintenon at this crisis ; " the journeys to Marly have caused the ruin of the State ; they would like to take away his horses, his dogs, his servants. . . . There are murmurs at his very door ; they would like to stone me because they imagine that I never tell him anything unpleasant, for fear of grieving him." Of course the taxes had ceased to come in ; how were the troops to be maintained ? Soldiers and even officers sold their arms, their clothes, and their linen to buy bread : " It is now impossible to serve in the army without swindling right and left," wrote Fénelon. France seemed to be in her death-throes.

Then Louis' pride had to give way, and the King resigned himself to ask for peace. Ever since 1705 he had been in **Peace** communication with the allies ; in March, 1709, **negotiations.** President de Bouillé was sent secretly to Holland to ask definitely what conditions could be made the basis of peace ; they were such that he expected to be recalled immediately, but nothing of the sort happened. The King called his Council. " The Duc de Beauvilliers painted such a touching picture of the state to which France was reduced that the Duke of Burgundy shed tears ; the Ministers of War and Finance confessed that they were without resources " (Voltaire). Torcy went off to The Hague under a false name. But the demands of the allies had become still more humiliating. The United Provinces insisted on a new " Barrier," but this time it was to consist of French fortresses such as Lille and Tournai ; the English claimed the destruction of Dunkirk, recognition of their Queen, Anne, the expulsion of the Pretender, and the cession of

Newfoundland; the Empire asked for Alsace and Strasburg; finally, the Spanish crown was to be taken from Philip V without compensation, and the Very Christian King was to combine with the allies to fight against his grandson, if, as seemed probable, the latter should resist; if all these conditions were granted, France should enjoy a truce of two months, after which the allies would reconsider the matter!

On June 12, 1709, the aged Louis made known to his people the shame it was proposed to inflict upon him:

> Although my affection for my people is no whit less than that I feel for my own children [he added], although I share all the sufferings inflicted by the war on my faithful subjects, and have plainly shown all Europe that I sincerely desire to let them enjoy peace, I am convinced that they themselves would refuse to receive it on conditions so opposed to justice and to the honour of the French name.

This noble letter, which was read aloud in all the churches by the parish priests, raised the whole kingdom, and, reinforced by the prevailing destitution, caused the peasantry to enlist *en masse*. The army thus recruited lacked everything: horses, provisions, munitions, money; but it was commanded by Marshal de Villars.

With such raw troops, the Marshal deemed it prudent to remain on the defensive in his entrenchments, and to let the **Magnetic leadership of Villars.** allies take Tournai and invest Mons. But every day his good-humoured raillery enlivened the ranks; he went about " caressing the soldier," as he said; he mocked at " Monsieur de Malbrouck," amazed the men by his braggadocio, talked of the millions which were shortly coming from India as a loan, read aloud the beautiful and noble letters he received from the King; the soldiers laughed, rubbed their hands, joked: " M. le Maréchal is right; one must suffer sometimes." Then they would shout at the top of their voices: " Long live the King ! " One fine day the hero of Lille, M. de Boufflers, arrived to join the army; he came to fight for France as a simple volunteer under the command of his junior. . . . Then Villars asked permission to march against the enemy.

The troops were massed to the south of Quiévrain; they decamped quietly; then, masked by the curtain of woods which cuts the plain of Mons in two, they defiled unperceived all along the enemy's front, and debouched unexpectedly on their left, on September 9, 1709, by the gap of Malplaquet, between the woods of Sars and La Lanière. The majority of the Dutch and Austrian soldiers were off marauding; Eugene and Marlborough were some distance away, at the mill of Sars, with only a few troops; the French might perhaps have suddenly overthrown the surprised and scattered enemy, but Villars halted. Why? We know not. He had only from 90,000 to 100,000 men, for the most part recruits, to oppose to 120,000 soldiers accustomed to victory; he had to remember, too, that his army was the last which was left to France.

But while the French army lay firmly entrenched in the Gap of Malplaquet, the troops of the coalition took up their **Battle of** position at their leisure. On the morning of the **Malplaquet.** 11th Eugene threw himself upon the French left, and Marlborough on the right, which Villars had entrusted to Boufflers. It was about eight o'clock. Boufflers, who was well entrenched, repulsed Marlborough vigorously, but, embarrassed by his own fortifications, he was unable to follow up his advantage. Meanwhile, the left had been turned, and was falling back step by step through the wood of Sars on which it rested. It reformed on the plateau of Malplaquet, behind the reserves, which threw back the enemy by an admirable bayonet charge. Villars had received a bullet just above the knee; he had to be carried to the rear lines, in a swoon, on a litter made of standards taken from the foe. At this moment Marlborough threw his fresh troops upon the centre, the ranks of which had been depleted to strengthen the left, and broke through. Boufflers had taken over the command: six times he hurled all his cavalry upon the enemy, and thanks to these magnificent charges, the French right retired quietly towards Le Quesnoy, and the left on Valenciennes, the troops of the coalition not daring to pursue them. The French got away their cannon, thirty-two standards captured as against nine which they left in the enemy's hands; they had lost 11,000 men, but they had killed or wounded 22,939. "If God be pleased to let us lose another such battle," wrote M. de Villars to the King, in his usual somewhat swaggering strain, "Your Majesty may take it that your enemies are destroyed."

Hereupon negotiations were again begun at Gertruydenberg. But the Allies had not moderated their demands : indeed, it was now proposed that Louis XIV should undertake to dethrone his grandson, "*with his own unaided forces*, within a term of two months ! " " Since I must make war, I would rather make it on my enemies than on my children," said the old King sadly, and the Abbé de Polignac, when he asked the States-General for his passports, remarked wittily : " It is plain, gentlemen, that you are not accustomed to conquer ! " (March–July, 1710).

In Spain the Castillians, still devoted to their Bourbon King, waged that war on the Imperialists which was afterwards to save their country from the hands of Napoleon ; one by one the foreign soldiers were assassinated or poisoned, and the allied army gradually melted away. Louis XIV sent a few troops under Vendôme to his grandson, and on December 10, 1710, Stahrenberg was completely defeated at Villaviciosa ; it was all he could do to bring back a handful of his men to Barcelona, the only town now remaining to the Hapsburg.

Was fortune about to turn ? In January, 1711, a secret agent, the Abbé Gaultier, arrived at Versailles, bearing proposals **England pro-** of peace from Queen Anne. This was due to **poses peace,** certain changes that had taken place in England : **1711.** Marlborough and his duchess had been disgraced, and in their fall had dragged down the Whig Ministry, which was in favour of war. Then, on April 17, 1711, the Emperor Joseph I died, leaving no heir but his brother, the Archduke Charles, the aspirant to the throne of Spain. Could the Powers allow the might of Charles V to be reconstituted ? . . . On October 8, 1711, France and England signed the preliminaries in London, and Queen Anne threatened to retire from the coalition if the allies would not reopen negotiations.

Thus a conference began again at Utrecht in January, 1712. It was a pure comedy : Eugene already saw himself in Paris. The departure of the British forces scarcely weakened him at all : they consisted of 12,000 Englishmen and 50,000 auxiliaries ; when the first had left, Holland bought the second, and it was an army of about 145,000 men, confident, well paid, and well fed, which had to be met by the 70,000 miserable soldiers under

Villars, who constituted the last defence of the kingdom of France.

The final struggle was to take place on the single line of fortresses which still protected the valley of the Oise : Arras, Cambrai, and Landrecies. In July, 1712, after taking Le Quesnoy, Eugene invested Landrecies. Villars received orders to make every possible effort to save the town. He hesitated a little under the fearful responsibility laid upon him : he lost **Battle of** several days, and it seems probable that it was **Denain, 1712.** the Court which gave him the strategic idea on which his glory rests ; but at least, when once this plan was decided upon, he carried it out with extreme resolution and skill. Prince Eugene's commissariat base was at Marchiennes, and he communicated with it by the fortified camp of Denain, and by a line of entrenchments which his soldiers had insolently christened the " road to Paris." Villars marched upon Landrecies and seemed to be preparing to attack the besiegers on the side nearest to the Sambre ; throughout the day of July 23 the French troops mustered in order of battle on the banks of the river, ostensibly preparing bridges for the morrow. But suddenly in the night of July 23–24, the royal army decamped without sound of drum or trumpet, in spite of the dissatisfaction of the soldiers, who supposed they were beating a retreat ; by a flanking movement they skirted the besieging forces of Landrecies at a distance, followed the left bank of the Selle, crossed the Scheldt beyond Bouchain, and about eleven o'clock in the morning, spent with fatigue, but full of enthusiasm, they threw themselves with the bayonet upon the entrenched camp of Denain, and captured it. At this moment Eugene, informed of what was happening in his rear, arrived in hot haste from Landrecies. Too late ! He stopped, biting his gloves with rage (July 24, 1712).

And it was this little battle of Denain that saved France. His communications being cut, Eugene was obliged to raise the siege of Landrecies. Then Saint-Amand, Douai, Le Quesnoy, and Bouchain, which had cost him so many efforts, opened again to the French. Finally Holland became weary of an interminable war, which was doing great damage to trade. . . . In April–July, 1713, and June, 1714, the treaties so long debated were signed at Utrecht by France and Spain on the one hand, and by Prussia, Savoy, England (final peace), and Holland on the other. There was still the Emperor to deal with; but Prince Eugene, deprived of his English and Dutch soldiers, was too much weakened to continue the campaign, and Villars seized Landau and Freiburg (September, 1713). Negotiations were set on foot at Rastadt, and lasted for two months and a half, between the Prince, who was a very skilful diplomatist, and Villars, who was not quite his equal in this domain; **Peace of** fortunately Louis XIV was watching over all; on **Rastadt, 1714.** March 6, 1714, the honourable Peace of Rastadt was concluded with the Empire.

It was on Spain that the main cost of the war fell. In the first place, Philip V explicitly renounced his claims to the throne of France, a solemn engagement which was ratified by the Cortes. If she retained the Indies, Spain was to lose all her European possessions, including Gibraltar and Minorca, which were to remain in the hands of the English; she had to give up the Low Countries and her Italian possessions to the Emperor, with the exception of Sicily, which came to the Duke of Savoy, together with the royal title. France, for her part, ceded Newfoundland to England (reserving only her fishery rights there), and, further, Acadia, Hudson Bay and Strait, and the island of Saint Christopher in the Antilles; moreover, Louis XIV formally recognized the Protestant House of Hanover, and promised to expel the Pretender, James Stuart, from France; finally, he undertook to raze the fortifications of Dunkirk. To Holland the King made over the Low Countries in trust, to be transmitted to the Emperor Charles VI when they had come to an agreement with him concerning the famous Barrier. With Vittorio-Amedeo, Louis exchanged a part of Dauphiné, situated on the Piedmont slopes, for the Barcelonnette valley, situated on the French slope; he further restored Nice and Savoy to him, and recognized his title of King of Sicily.

The Emperor obtained the reconstruction of the frontier as determined by the Treaty of Ryswyck, and the King of Prussia recognition of his new dignity. The Archbishop of Cologne and the Elector of Bavaria, the faithful allies of France, retained their respective States.

SUNSET

III

"The King remarked with pleasure," says Dangeau in August, 1695, "that the Duke of Burgundy would be of age in six days, that we need not fear a minority in France, and that ever since the foundation of the monarchy there had been no other instance of a grandfather, a father, and a grandson, all of an age to govern the kingdom." Before the troubles due to the Spanish Succession, Louis XIV, secure in the support of his family and his people, might consider himself the most mighty monarch on earth. Twelve years later, humiliated in his glory, and stricken in his race, he had only a little child of two years old to assume the heavy burden of the crown after him.

Portrait of Louis XIV at sixty-four. Students of history should study the astounding medallion in which Antoine Benoist recorded the appearance of the King in 1702, at the age of sixty-four. "The royal countenance, modelled in a coloured wax which is extraordinarily lifelike, shows, under the luxuriant and severe wig, the proud and senile profile, with the haughty nose and heavy pendulous under-lip. This is indeed the aged Louis, arrogant and fanatical, petrified by fifty years of power, still great, in spite of the decline of his strength and of his star ; he whose despotic presence yet fills the huge palace he built, the palace his glorious and taciturn shade still seems to haunt" (H. de Régnier).

In 1701 Monsieur, the King's brother, had died of apoplexy, being old, worn out with debauchery, and short in the neck. **Death of the Duke of Orleans.** Louis was greatly attached to his brother; nevertheless, Monsieur was "still warm" when the King ordered the card-tables to be set out as usual at Marly. So also in 1702, on the morrow of the naval defeat at Vigo, Madame wrote : "One sees nothing but long faces here ; only the King seems quite serene." Thus did Louis XIV bear with equal courage the disasters of France and the losses of his family. To tell the truth, so much stoicism is rather disquieting, and we should be tempted to call the Great King's firmness by the less flattering names of selfishness and insensibility, had not Saint-Simon himself borne witness that Louis XIV "felt the culmination of so many misfortunes

313

THE SEVENTEENTH CENTURY

deeply " ; that " his ministers saw his tears flow " ; that " his closest personal attendant beheld his grief." Moreover, the seventeenth century knew nothing of that " sensibility " of which the eighteenth and nineteenth made such deplorable use : what seemed praiseworthy to the contemporaries of the aged Louis was, not the display of a " tender " soul and a parade of lofty sorrow, but a manly and Christian mastery of grief. Again, Saint-Simon, the Great King's worst enemy, could not refrain from writing :

Stoicism of the King.

> Under adversities so prolonged, so repeated, and so intimately poignant, his firmness, nay, more, his immutability, remained unshaken ; the same face, the same bearing, the same graciousness, the same occupations, the same journeys, the same course of years and days. . . . Let us declare with all the cordiality of a true Frenchman, naturally well pleased when truth does not check his praises, that it was out of the depths of this abyss of sorrows of every kind that Louis XIV contrived to deserve, in the opinion of all Europe, the epithet of *Great* which his flatterers had prematurely bestowed upon him. The title *Great* became in these later years a title justly acquired, a real name, the fitting name for this prince who showed, with simplicity, the greatness of his soul, his firmness, his stability, his evenness of temper, a courage undaunted by the most terrible reverses and the keenest griefs, a strength of mind which concealed nothing from itself, which dissimulated nothing, which saw things as they were, and so, leading him to humble himself under the hand of God, preserved the even tenor of his external life with a steadiness so simple and unaffected that the admiration aroused in all who saw him both in public and in private was daily renewed.

In August, 1704, the Court had received the news of the defeat at Höchstädt so sadly that it had composed no songs upon M. de Tallart, which was unprecedented. As to the King, when Père de La Chaise sought to console him by referring to the reverses of King David, he asked simply " if David took his revenge ; for his part, he meant to do so." And Primi, again, noted (in his correspondence) this answer of Louis to the Great Dauphin and Chamillart, when they announced the disaster of Ramillies : " We must think of retrieving it, we must hope for all help from God. It is not the Marshal's fault, but mine." Nevertheless, Mme. de Maintenon wrote : " I confess that the pain of seeing the King suffer is great."

In April, 1705, the little Duc de Bretagne, the King's great-grandson (the first, long-expected child of the Duchess of

314

SUNSET

Burgundy), died before he was a year old. On April 14, 1711, Monseigneur, his grandfather, died suddenly of smallpox. The **Deaths of the King's Heirs.** King " spoke kindly to every one," gave his orders calmly, but every moment " his eyes filled with tears," says Madame ; " I pity him with all my heart. By the death of Monseigneur, the Duke and Duchess of Burgundy became Dauphin and Dauphiness. On February 12, 1712, the new Dauphiness, the darling of the King and Mme. de Maintenon, died. Seven days later, on February 19, the Dauphin died. And on the 8th of March following, their son, the second Duc de Bretagne, followed them.

At this moment the enemy was preparing to march upon Paris. A few days before the triple obsequies of his children, the old King sent for the man to whom he had confided his last army, and addressed him in these magnanimous words :

There are few examples of such disasters as have fallen upon me, as the loss in one week of a grandson, a granddaughter-in-law, and their son, all of great promise and most dearly loved. God is punishing me. I deserve it. I shall suffer the less in the next world. . . . This is what I think ; you shall tell me your opinion afterwards. I know all the arguments of my courtiers ; nearly all of them wish me to retire to Blois, and not to wait until the enemy approaches Paris, which would be quite possible were my army defeated. As to me, I know that armies so considerable are never so utterly defeated as to prevent the main body of my troops from retiring upon the Somme. I know that river ; it is difficult to cross ; there are fortresses, and I have thoughts of going to Péronne or Saint-Quentin, mustering all the troops left to me there, making a last effort with you, and perishing together or saving the State, for I will never consent to allow the enemy to approach my capital. This is my plan ; now give me your opinion. (Villars.)

We have just seen how Villars saved France at Denain by carrying out the plan suggested to him by the King and Voysin ; but Louis was to suffer yet another loss. As the Duc d'Anjou, who had become Philip V, had definitively renounced his claim to the throne of France, only two direct heirs to the crown were now living : the little Dauphin, the future Louis XV, the King's **The Duc de Berry.** great-grandson, who was four years old, and his uncle, the Duc de Berry, the King's third grandson. " M. le Duc de Berry was of medium height, rather stout everywhere, fair-haired, with a fresh, good-looking face, indicating perfect health." By nature lively, gay and undisciplined, he had been subjected, like his father, the Great Dauphin, to a crushing education, which had disgusted him also for ever with all intellectual work, and had made him absurdly diffident by having convinced him that he was but " a fool and a simpleton, fit for nothing." For the rest, he was "a good, round Prince," an ardent sportsman, a hardy pedestrian, and a brilliant horseman. He died suddenly, on May 4, 1714, without issue, thus leaving the eventual Regency and his claims to the throne to his cousin-german, the King's nephew, the Duke of Orleans.

The Duke of Orleans was thoroughly unpopular : public opinion, indeed, did not hesitate to accuse him of having **The Duc d'Orléans.** poisoned all the princes who had stood between him and the throne. The King, for his part, certainly believed in none of these abominations, any more than in the current rumours concerning the incestuous loves of the Duc d'Orléans and the Duchesse de Berry. He understood his nephew's character. " He is one who brags of crimes," he said. But the profligate Philip was notoriously " Libertine," and, on the other hand, the Protestants counted upon him, no less than the adversaries of the devout, and the enemies of Mme. de Maintenon ; in short, every one felt that his accession would be that of a policy diametrically opposed to that of the Great King. It is not to be wondered at, therefore, if Louis did his best to bar the Duke's way to the throne ; by an edict of July, 1714, he appointed the Duc du Maine, the Comte de Toulouse, and their posterity heirs to the throne failing legitimate descendants of the King, and then, by a will of the following August 2, he instituted a Council of Regency, of which the Duc d'Orléans was to be merely the President, and confided the charge of the royal child to the Duc du Maine. In his heart Louis was not very firmly convinced that his last wishes would be more effectually respected than those of his grandfather and his father : " You wished to have it thus," he wrote to the Duc du Maine, " but know that, however great I make you, you will be nothing after me, and it will be your business to turn all that I have done for you to account—if you can." And it was very soon evident that the Duc du Maine could not.

SUNSET

At this time the King's health was visibly failing. Louis, who had always had bad teeth, had always been "a prodigious eater," and he ate no less prodigiously after he had lost them all: it was not until the close of his life that he began to have a poor appetite. Now on August 9, 1715, it was noticed that he seemed very much exhausted after following a stag in a little carriage which he drove himself. A few days later he complained of sciatica in his leg; black marks soon appeared; it was gangrene. Louis was seventy-six; having lived very nobly, he did not fail to die nobly, and to remain a great king to the end. On August 24 he supped in his dressing-gown, for the last time in public: "I noticed," says Saint-Simon, "that he could only swallow liquids, *and that it distressed him to be looked at.*" On August 25 he dictated to the Chancellor a codicil by which he added to M. du Maine's other prerogatives that of the direction of the King's Household. Then he received the last sacraments; but death could not subdue this temperament; he lived for six days more, which he employed very tranquilly in regulating his conscience, the affairs of his family and those of the State, and in making a little speech, very noble and regal in tone, to all about him. To the courtiers he said:

Gentlemen, I ask your pardon for the bad example I have set you. I have to thank you sincerely for the manner in which you have served me, and the fidelity you have always shown to me. I ask you to give the same zeal and the same devotion to my grandson which you have given to me. He is a child who may have to suffer much. I hope you will all work for union, and that should any one fail in this, you will seek to call him back to his duty. I feel that I am allowing my feelings to overcome me, and am causing you to do the same. I ask your pardon for this. Farewell, gentlemen, I trust that you will sometimes remember me.

Having heard the princesses lamenting in his cabinet, he summoned them to his bedroom, told them they must not weep so noisily, and bade them farewell in terms which Madame, the shy Liselotte, to whom he spoke very gently, confessed had nearly made her faint. He exhorted Condé and Conti to be submissive and united. He talked for a long time alone with the Duc du Maine and the Comte de Toulouse. He was friendly to the Duc d'Orléans. He advised that the little Dauphin

should be taken to Vincennes, the air of which he considere
favourable to the health ; and, " shortly after, he remembere
that Cavoye, the Quartermaster of his Household, had neve
arranged for the lodging of the Court at Vincennes, as the Cour
had not been there for fifty years ; he showed a casket in whic.
a plan of the castle would be found."

Finally, having asked Mme. de Ventadour to bring th
future Louis XV to him, he gave his great-grandson certair
Louis XIV's counsels which were afterwards reproduced on a
counsel to his placard and hung up in the child's bedroom :
successor. My dear child, you are going to be the greatest king
on earth. Never forget what you owe to God. Do not imitate me by
making war, try to keep the peace with your neighbours, to comfor
your people as far as possible, which I have unfortunately not beer
able to do, by reason of necessities of State. Always follow good advice
and remember that you owe all you are to God. I give you Père L.
Tellier as your confessor, follow his counsels, and always remember you
obligations to Mme. de Ventadour.*

Death did not seem terrible to his great character. Madame
heard him say to Mme. de Maintenon : " I thought it would
be harder to die than this ; I assure you it is not a very terrible
business ; it does not seem to me difficult at all." He spoke
of his funeral and gave instructions as if he had merely been
going on a journey ; and in speaking of the Dauphin he even
said : " the young King."

Finally, on August 30, he lost consciousness. Then, towards
five o'clock in the evening, Mme. de Maintenon withdrew ;
Death of he had begged her to retire, because her presence
Louis XIV. moved him, and she did not wish to be a spectacle
for the Court at the moment when the death of the King would
throw her back " into nonentity." She therefore went to her
own apartments, divided her furniture among her attendants,
and left for Saint-Cyr, never to leave it again. On the 31st,
about eleven o'clock in the evening, " the remedy of the late
Abbé Aignan," which had been applied at all hazards, recalled
the King to consciousness ; he repeated the prayers for the
dying in such a strong voice that it was heard above those of
the numerous ecclesiastics and all those who had come into the

---

* This last clause seems to indicate that it was Mme. de Ventadour,
the child's governess, who took down the King's last words.

SUNSET

room. At the end of the prayers he recognized the Cardinal de Rohan and said to him : " These are the last benefactions of the Church." Rohan was the last person to whom the King spoke. He repeated several times : *Nunc et in hora mortis*, and then said : " O my God, come to my help, haste Thee to help me ! " These were his last words. He again became unconscious, lay in his death agony all night, and expired on Sunday, September 1, 1715, at eight o'clock in the morning, aged seventy-seven years less three days, after a reign of sixty-three years.

WORKS TO CONSULT. Baudrillart, *Philippe V et la Cour de France*, vol. i (1890) ; Boislisle, *Le Grand Hiver et la Disette de* 1709, in the *Revue des questions historiques* (1903) ; Marquis de Courcy, *La Coalition de* 1701 *contre la France* (1886) ; Fortescue, *History of the British Army*, vol. i (1899) ; E. Hubert, *Les Pays Bas espagnols et la République des Provinces-Unies depuis la Paix de Münster jusqu'au Traite d'Utretcht*, 1648–1713 (1907) ; Legrelle, *La Diplomatie française et la Succession d'Espagne* (1895–1900) ; Marquis de Vogüé, *Villars* (1888), and the article in the *Correspondant* (1904) ; *Malplaquet et Denain* (1892) ; O. Weber, *Die Friede von Utrecht* (1891).

CHAPTER XII

THE KINGDOM UNDER LOUIS XIV

I. Central Government. II. Colbert. III. Colbert and finance; Fouquet. IV. Colbert and industry, commerce, and the Colonies. V. Colbert and the Navy; Seignelay. VI. Provincial administration. VII. Estimate of Colbert. VIII. "Colbertism" after Colbert. IX. The Clergy; The Nobility; The Officials; The People.

I

THEORETICALLY—for in practice it was far from being the case—the power of Louis XIV was absolute. In law, the King of France was the sole source of all authority, and everything had to be done in his name. The only dispenser of justice, the judges were merely his repre-**Powers of the** sentatives and delegates; he caused whom he **Monarchy.** would to be judged by whom he pleased, increased the sentence if he felt so inclined (Fouquet) or condemned without a sentence (Lauzun, Matthioli, Rohan). The sole proprietor, all the possessions of his subjects belong to him; this was the opinion of the Sorbonne. Thus he had all rights, like God Himself, of Whom he was the "living image" and the delegate on earth, and to Whom alone he owed an account of his actions; to disobey him was a sin; such was the doctrine universally admitted, and adopted even by the Church; in 1677, Bossuet wrote his *Politique tirée de l'Écriture Sainte* (Polity derived from Holy Scripture) to establish it. Louis XIV governed with the help of various Councils and Secretaries of State.

The first was the *Conseil d'État, Conseil d'en haut,* or *Conseil* (Council of State, Higher Council, or simply Council), which at the beginning of the reign was held on Sundays, Wednesdays, and Thursdays, and, in addition, on two Mondays in the month, from ten to twelve approximately, in the King's apartments. Those who had seats at this Council were called **The King's** Ministers of State: they were usually the Secre- **Councils.** taries of State and the Controller-General of Finance, but not necessarily so: Barbezieux, for instance, appointed Minister for War on the death of his father, Louvois, was never admitted to it, whereas Beauvilliers and Pomponne (after 1691) were included without being Secretaries of State. The Council decided great political affairs, diplomacy, war; it was somewhat like the Council of Ministers of to-day. On the other hand, in the *Conseil des Dépêches* (Council of Dispatches), only questions of administration were considered; the Secre- taries of State, standing, reported on the principal affairs of their respective departments; it was a sort of Council of the Interior. The *Conseil royal des Finances* (Royal Council of Finance), where the business was taxation, was generally held on Tuesday and Saturday mornings. It was composed of the Chancellor, the head of the Council of Finance (Villeroy, and then Beauvilliers), of the Controller-General, and the two Coun- cillors of State.

These were the Councils at which the King was regularly present. At the *Conseil Privé* (Privy Council), or *des Parties*, or *Grand Conseil*—which played much the same part as our Council of State and our Court of Appeal, but also gave a first hearing to all the cases "evoked" by the Sovereign—his great red arm-chair generally remained empty in front of the table covered with a cloth of purple velvet, embroidered with golden fleurs-de-lis, round which the Councillors, in black robes with wide sleeves, sat on folding seats of black morocco leather, presided over by the Chancellor, who sat to the left of the royal chair. The Council was composed (after 1673) of thirty Coun- cillors who judged, and of over eighty Masters of Requests who reported, a function much coveted, for the King often chose his Intendants among these officials.

In addition to these four principal Councils, there were others, in the nature of temporary commissions, like the War Council, the Council of Commerce, the Council of Conscience, which dealt with ecclesiastical affairs, etc.

However, the King was by no means bound to act upon the

advice of these Councils, and we must not suppose that Louis XIV's government worked with the regularity of a modern government. The Higher Council, for instance, was held less and less frequently, and finally Louis decided matters of moment in a *tête-à-tête* with the respective Secretaries of State.

These were still, as in the Middle Ages, hardly more than the "servants" of the sovereign. At the beginning of the **Secretaries of** reign their names figured in the household accounts **State.** side by side with those of the food controllers and the castle attendants, and at Fontainebleau, for instance, they had a right to the *ordinary*: two loaves, a quart of wine, on non-fast days a piece of game and a pound of bacon, and on fast days six carp and three pounds of butter. Thus it seemed natural to every one that Louis XIV should treat them as simple secretaries on occasion, and should demand services of a private nature from Colbert or some other minister. Moreover, as we know from the famous ebullitions of Saint-Simon and many others, the King never employed the nobles in the Government, the Duc de Beauvilliers being almost the sole exception to this rule.

There was no systematic division of affairs between the Controller-General of Finances and the four Secretaries of State. In the first place, one of them sometimes held several Secretary-ships of State, as did Colbert, Louvois, and Chamillart. Besides, several of them were to some extent co-Ministers of the Interior; in 1689 Poitou, Lyonnais, Roussillon, Lorraine, the Three Bishoprics, and the conquered districts were under the jurisdiction of Louvois, the Ile-de-France, "Soissonnais as far as Noyon," Orléanais, and Touraine under that of Seignelay, and so on. Finally they divided the various services more or less according to their predilections; Colbert, the Minister of Finance, for instance, undertook Commerce, Industry, the Colonies, the Navy, Public Works, Education, the Fine Arts, and the Postal Service, to say nothing of several provinces with their fortifications, and even the special war credits, which should logically have fallen on Louvois. But he accepted these overwhelming labours with joy.

THE KINGDOM UNDER LOUIS XIV

II

Colbert. Jean-Baptiste Colbert was born at Reims on August 29, 1619, of a tradesman's family. One day his father left his sign of the *Long-Vêtu* and the sale of serge and camlet to take up a modest function at the Hôtel de Ville of Paris ; thanks to this circumstance, and to the kinship of his mother, Marie Pussort, with the Secretary of State, Le Tellier, Jean-Baptiste entered the offices of the Ministry of War at the age of twenty, about the year 1640. In 1648 he made a very suitable marriage with Marie Charon, daughter of one of the Conservators of the Loire (*intendant des turcies et levées*, i.e. the piers and dikes). As Le Tellier's secretary he did not conceal from his patron that he had "no esteem " for Mazarin. But when in 1651 he became Mazarin's man, he seems to have ceased to feel any regard for Le Tellier. He was a model steward ; he applied the same impassioned skill to increase the scandalous wealth of that " poor M. le Cardinal," his master, which he was to employ some years later in administering the kingdom of Louis XIV. Hence the grateful Cardinal inserted in his will a bequest in the following terms : " To Colbert the house in which he lives, without the obligation of rendering any account, those who would demand any such account from him to be disinherited ; and I beg the King to make use of his services, as he is very faithful." This advice Louis XIV did not neglect.

Colbert had a naturally sour countenance, hollow eyes, thick black eyebrows, an austere appearance, and " savage and negative " manners. He was by no means amiable ; Mme. de Sévigné calls him " The North," or " the surly Minister," and Mme. Cornuel, having one day obtained an interview with him with great difficulty, was so exasperated by his silence that she could not help exclaiming : " Monseigneur, at least make a sign that you hear what I am saying. " Yet this " man of marble " had a weakness; he wanted at any price to be accepted as a descendant of the ancient Kings of Scotland, and he had accordingly arranged for the discovery by accident in one of the churches of Reims of a tombstone, bearing this inscription in half-effaced Gothic characters : " Here lies the valiant knight, Richard Colbert called the Scot . . . 1300."

To this he took occasion to bring the Dukes of Chevreuse and
Beauvilliers, the husbands of his daughters, to kneel with him,
" repeating psalms and making his sons-in-law repeat them
very devoutly " ; in like manner he became furiously angry with
those who gave him to understand that, out of consideration
for him, his son would not be required to prove the quarterings
necessary for admission to the order of the Knights of Malta.
But in spite of his Scottish nobility, Colbert was ready for a
great many tasks, for, though not devoid of prejudices, neither
was he hampered by scruples. His wife was secretly engaged
to bring up the children of La Vallière—which occasioned the
Great King to write to his Controller-General of Finances :
" My daughter de Blois has asked my leave to discard her bibs ;
I have consented "—and there was nothing undignified in such
an employment in those days.   But Colbert readily made use of
Colbert's his authority in a thousand different ways, such
nepotism. as that of intimidating the judges who had to
pronounce in his own suits or those of his relatives, and he took
advantage of the facilities it offered him to amass a fortune, which
was estimated at over ten millions ; then he made one of his
sons, Seignelay, a Secretary of State for the Navy, and the
other, Ormoy-Blainville, a Superintendent of Buildings, of the
third a coadjutor of the Bishop of Rouen, of the fourth the
General of the Galleys at Malta, of the fifth the Abbé of Bonport,
of the sixth a Colonel ; of his three daughters, three Duchesses ;
of his three brothers, a Bishop, a Secretary of State, and a
Lieutenant-General ; and no doubt this was just the way in
which Mazarin, Richelieu, Luynes, and Concini had behaved
before him ; but they had not made such a repellent parade of
honesty, nor had they adopted such treacherous means to hunt
down a Nicolas Fouquet, guilty of having enriched himself
precisely as they had done.

Thus Colbert had not a noble character, but he had a noble
passion ; he loved his work profoundly. He laboured for
fourteen hours a day with joy, to realize certain projects which
would, he thought, make the King, his master, the mightiest
monarch in the world ; and (if we except his own fortune)
nothing interested or touched him save in its bearing on this
enterprise. He encouraged art and letters, for instance, not

because he cared for them, but because he thought it seemly
that art and letters should flourish under the sway of a great
prince. So too, he was a believer and a good Catholic, but he
instructed one of his agents in Japan to " say, concerning
religion, that the French have two sorts, one the same as that
of the Spaniards, the other the same as that of the Dutch; " for
nothing, not even religion, was so close to his heart as the
trade of the kingdom. And since his impassioned efforts
tended to promote the greatness of France, it is only just that
Colbert, who was harsh to all, hated by the people, detested
by the courtiers, a dishonest financier who amassed a
scandalous fortune, should be praised by historians.

Methodical and rationalistic like his contemporaries, he had
conceived, starting from certain *à priori* ideas on the wealth of
Colbert's States (which, however, were false), a programme
theory of he laboured to carry out in France in spite of
wealth. opposition. It is certain that the King's extravagance caused his attempt to fail to some extent; and as it is
evident that if Louis XIV had listened to Colbert he would have
sought to rule the world, not so much by force of arms as by that
of money, and that he would have laboured, either by economy
in finance or by the protection accorded to agriculture, trade, and
industry, to possess the richest kingdom, and so the most powerful kingdom in the world, it seems lamentable that Louis XIV
should not have followed the principles of his Minister more
assiduously, and thus worked for order and economy. But it is
unjust to overwhelm him (as his detractors have always done)
by holding him alone responsible for Colbert's comparative
failure. And it is also an unsound method of decrying the Great
King, to compare the glorious and ruined France of 1715 to the
rich, commercial France of Colbert's dreams, for that France
never existed, after all, and we do not even know if it was
possible in those days. There is, in fact, nothing to prove that
even if Colbert had been free to carry out his projects just as he
wished, he would have succeeded; indeed, it seems more probable that he would have failed. Throughout the country he
met with unanimous opposition, perhaps because his projects
on the Dutch model were ill suited to the France of his time,
and that he claimed power to regulate arbitrarily too many

325

things which among us Frenchmen will only flourish in liberty. As to the Dutch war which ruined so many of his plans, was it not he himself who desired, invited, and provoked it ? Finally, if Colbert failed, it was to a great extent his own fault ; and it was not so much the King as the entire kingdom, nobles, magistrates, citizens, tradesmen, workmen, and peasants who resisted his great effort.

III

" If out of one hundred crowns spent by the King, forty were effectively used in his service, he might consider himself well served," wrote the Venetian ambassador, Angelo Correr, about the year 1642.   Richelieu had died leaving the finances in a deplorable condition.   Mazarin aggravated their disorder by confiding them to an over-amiable financier, who could refuse nothing to any one (and least of all to himself).

This Nicolas Fouquet, born in 1615, came of a good legal family.   An advocate at sixteen, a Councillor in the Parliament of Metz at nineteen, Master of Requests, Intendant of the Army of the North, then in Dauphiné, then in Catalonia, then in the Army of Flanders, then in Paris (1648), he remained faithful throughout the first Fronde to Mazarin, who authorized him to purchase the office of Solicitor-General to the Parliament of Paris.   He supported the Court ably during the troubles, and employed himself very successfully in safeguarding the little profits of " poor M. le Cardinal " during Mazarin's exile at Bruhl.   As a reward for his services, after the death of La Vieuville in January, 1653, he was appointed Superintendent of Finances jointly with Servien (February), and he at once distinguished himself in his office by his extreme dexterity in filling the Government coffers , this was the most essential duty of the moment, and it was a difficult matter, for no one would risk lending money to the King, even at an exorbitant rate of interest.   But Fouquet had imagination, and he manœuvred wonderfully ; he generally acted in his own name, so that at the end he no longer kept the accounts of his private fortune and the budget of the State apart.

Fouquet.

He was very rich personally and by his second marriage in

February, 1651, with Marie-Madeleine de Castille, who belonged to one of the wealthiest financial families of France, allied to the great names of the nobility and the magistrature. But Fouquet was one of those sumptuous individuals who always spend more money than they possess. He was an attractive person, with a nervous, intelligent face, " a friend of the arts, a friend of letters, a friend of women." He wrote occasional verses; protected Scarron, La Fontaine, Benserade, Boisrobert, Bombault, Charles Pérrault, and Corneille. For his estate of Vaux-le-Vicomte, which was already in progress in 1640, but which dates mainly from 1656, he wisely chose Le Vau as architect, Le Nôtre as gardener, and Le Brun as painter and decorator. His cook was called Vatel. He was interested in manuscripts and medals, marbles and tapestries, pictures and jewels. He had a collection of orange-trees which the King appropriated for Versailles after his condemnation. In short, everybody was attracted by his gracious manners, his liberality, his cordiality, his " smiling and intelligent aspect," and he encountered as few obdurate beauties as a Minister of Finance witty enough to delight Mme. de Sévigné was likely to encounter.

Colbert envied him for all these things; as early as 1659 he denounced him to Mazarin in a secret note; but at that time **Colbert's** Fouquet was not much afraid of the Sieur Colbert. **enmity to** On the death of the Cardinal, however, he did not **Fouquet.** take the young King seriously, and this gross error of psychology caused his ruin; he failed to see that his luxury, his successes, his brilliance were insupportable to one who aspired to be the only star; on the contrary, he expected to be called to office. The cunning Colbert, for his part, purposely exaggerated his rôle of humble clerk, dressed himselt modestly as a simple citizen in a black cloak, a black doublet, a point lace collar, and a plain hat. Mme. de Sévigné called him " Little One." But daily after the Council " Little One " spoke to the King of the Minister's fantastic accounts.

Moreover, Fouquet was very maladroit. By his efforts to win the good graces of La Vallière, he caused it to be supposed that he was the lover of the King's mistress, though he was not, and did not desire to be. Then he sold his office of Attorney-General, which had ensured the support of the Parliament.

327

Finally, in August, he tried to pay court to the King by receiving him at Vaux with unprecedented splendour ; when Louis saw this domain which had cost eighteen millions, to make room for which three villages had been razed, the marvels of which Mlle. de Scudéry described in *Clélie*, and beside which the royal castles, Fontainebleau and Saint-Germain, seemed mere shanties, the King was so outraged that he had thoughts of arresting his Superintendent on the spot. But Colbert had depicted Fouquet's conspiracy in terrible colours : " He intended to make himself Duke of Brittany and lord of the adjacent isles," declared th young Louis subsequently, " he won over every one by his pr fusion ; I had no one left whom I could trust." And it is true, indeed, that the Minister had tried to make a party of his own by pensioning a great many people, including Hugo de Lionne, that he had, further, fortified Belle-Isle which belonged to him, and finally, that he had drawn up a plan of campaign which was found, corrected by his own hand, and that consequently he had proposed to offer armed resistance and provoke some new Fronde should he be disgraced. But it was above all necessary, to satisfy Colbert's hate, that the King should think the most minute precautions necessary for the arrest of Fouquet; he went so far as to send battleships to cruise about in view of Belle-Isle. Finally, when all was ready, on September 5, 1661, d'Artagnan, the Captain of the Musketeers, suddenly seized the Superintendent at Nantes, put him into a coach, and escorted by one hundred soldiers took him to Angers, where he shut him up in the castle.

Adopting Richelieu's methods, the King had the prisoner tried, not by his legal judges, but by special commissaries. The Trial of Court of Justice formed to inquire into the Fouquet. " abuses and malversations committed in the finances since the year 1635 " was not very severe to farmers of revenue, provided they had stolen enough to enrich themselves, and were able to pay ransom ; and thus over 100 millions returned to the exchequer. But the suit they brought against Fouquet lasted three years. The accused made an admirable defence ; he affected to consider himself " the prey of the Sieur Colbert," to whom he obstinately referred as " my prosecutor," and he was warmly supported by his family and his friends, many of whom remained very faithful to him. But his offences were undeniable, and then Colbert caused the judges who seemed favourable to the man whose death he desired to be changed and disgraced, after which he calmly falsified the documents bearing on the case. In spite of everything, the Superintendent was not condemned to pay the capital penalty, but only to banishment; it was the King himself who commuted this punishment, which he thought too mild, into that of life-long detention at Pignerol (December, 1664).

The Superintendent had been replaced in the State by Council of Finance in which Colbert sat with the title of Intendar of Finances until 1665, when he became Controller-General. Fouquet had sometimes been obliged to borrow at the rate of from 15 to 18 per cent.; to liquidate the situation, Colbert simply suppressed a good share of the Government securities. To tell the truth, the victims of this iniquitous measure were not very interesting; they were chiefly financiers, shady speculators; but there were some honest folk among them. Some raised an outcry; they were sent to the Bastille; this calmed the others.

The principal tax at this period was the *taille*, from which not only the clergy and the nobility, but a large number of **The " Taille."** officers of justice, finance, and municipalities—in short, a host of privileged persons, all of considerable means—were exempt. In the districts where the States which voted the taxes had been retained, the sum total of the *taille* was less than in the regions of the Elections; moreover, the *taille* was often *real* there—that is to say, assessed on real estate; finally, it was the States themselves which distributed it as equitably as possible among the parishes, and collected it. The regions of the Elections were not so fortunate; as they were taxed directly by the King, they had always to pay a much larger sum; and, further, here the *taille* was *personal*—that is to say, it was assessed on the approximate income of the tax-payers as arbitrarily computed by the authorities. The manner in which the personal *taille* was collected was as follows: each Finance Office divided the sum it was its duty to recover between the Elections within its jurisdiction (just as now the *Conseil Général* divides it among the *arrondissements*); the Elections, in their turn, made a further distribution among the parishes (somewhat after the manner of our modern *Conseil d'arrondisse-ment* (District Council)); finally, in each parish certain inhabitants in rotation, the *collectors*, taxed each individual inhabitant. The collectors, detested by the whole village, were further responsible for their parishes, and were obliged to pay for the insolvent—in other words, ruin themselves or go to prison (sometimes both). This explains why each peasant awaited with terror the moment when it would be his turn to perform this dangerous duty.*

The *gabelle* was the tax on salt. In most of the provinces the State had a monopoly of salt, which it sold at an exorbitant price (as it now sells matches), while compelling its subjects to purchase a minimum quantity, which was called *duty-salt*. Like the *taille*, this tax was unequally imposed, for all France did not pay the same price for salt : the districts of the *grandes gamelles*, lying approximately between the Somme and the Loire, paid from 35 to 40 *livres* for a " peck " of 100 pounds ; those of the *petites gamelles* (the basin of the Mediterranean) from 6 to 30 *livres* ; the regions between the Loire and the Garonne had bought themselves off (*rédimé*) once for all ; those of the north, of the basin of the Garonne, of Brittany, and of Alsace, were exempt. The King did not himself exploit his monopoly ; he farmed it out to a syndicate of financiers, and the people hated these *farmers* and their employees, the *gâpians*, as these excisemen were then called, from the name of a small bird of prey. No one was allowed, for instance, to salt pork or cod-fish with the *duty-salt*, which the law restricted to use in the kitchen, nor might the salt destined

The **"Gabelle."**

---

* The personal *taille* had at least this advantage, that the farmers of the nobles and the clergy paid it ; it was probably for this reason that the *Encyclopædia* of the eighteenth century, compiled by persons of the privileged classes, attacked it so bitterly. Now, in default of adequate monographs, too often even now all discussion of the finances of the *ancien régime* is based upon information given by the *Encyclopædia*. It would seem that the injustice of the incidence of the *taille* has been greatly exaggerated ; the Intendant was there to check fraud, and as he had no local attachments he could do so freely ; further, as the collectors were taken by roster, the assertions as to their venality and vindictiveness seem *a priori* excessive.

to preserve meat or fish be used in cooking, nor salt water be given to cattle to drink ; this gave occasion for endless petty vexations ; on the pretext of inspecting, the hated *gâpian* would have the bread-bin and the salt-box opened, and often took advantage of the peasant's simplicity. On the other hand, salt-smuggling (*faux-saunage*) was comparatively easy, and the penalties by which it was repressed were lighter than those by which other smuggling was punished : the salt-smugglers, indeed, were not condemned to death unless they were old offenders or were taken with arms in their hands. Salt accordingly passed secretly in large quantities from the exempted or redeemed districts unto those of the *gabelle*, and thus smuggling sensibly modified the rigour of the law.

The customs (*traites*) were not paid only at the frontiers of the State. The kingdom was divided into districts where the **Customs.** excise duties (*aides*) were in force—these districts formed a kernel the shell of which comprised Normandy, Picardy, Champagne, Nivernais, Lyonnais, Bourbonnais, Berry, Poitou, Aunis and Saintonge, Anjou and Maine—and the districts not subject to them, from which the King derived dues analogous to the excise duties, and varying according to the region. In the provinces subject to excise the dues were no more uniform than in the districts not so subject, and thus the kingdom was intersected by lines of customs the tariffs of which varied infinitely, and studded with local toll-systems ; there were the *droit de Septembre*, the great and small *pied fourché*, the *vingtain de caresme*, the *chemins obliques*, the *trop bu*, the *traité d'Arzac*, the *droit de Manicault*, the *trépas de la Loire* ; in Languedoc, the *patente du Languedoc* and the *denier de Saint-André* ; in Guyenne, the *branche de cyprès* and the *guillage* ; at Arles, the *liard du Baron* ; at Marseilles, the *table de mer* ; in Roussillon, the *tarif catalan*, etc. In short, goods were held up incessantly, to the great injury of trade.

The *aides* (excise duties) were indirect taxes, chiefly dues upon drink. Like the customs, they varied greatly.

" Aides " and Finally, the last legal revenue of the Treasury **" Domaine."** was that of the *domaine* ; this was the name given to the King's estates and his feudal and seignorial rights. In 1661 the *domaine* was mortgaged, sold, and alienated to a great extent.

Like many others before him (Fouquet, for instance), Colbert was alive to the imperfection and injustice of this financial system. But he had not the tender and Utopian spirit of a Vauban, and he never dreamt of transforming it ; he merely undertook to organize it practically as well as he could.

The *gabelles*, *traites*, *aides*, and the *domaine* were farmed by companies of financiers. It seems evident that if the taxes had **Farming of** been collected directly by the royal agents, the **the revenues.** King and his subjects would have benefited by the enormous sums which enriched the farmers. But we must remember that the administration of the farms was very superior to that of the State ; the farmers made very careful tours of inspection, and the modern system of indirect taxation and of State property has retained the greater part of their technical organization. Colbert therefore did not attempt to abolish the farming of revenue ; he merely endeavoured to concentrate as many leases as possible in the hands of a single company, because he hoped that the more important the company became, the less it would steal ; that, further, it might act as the banker of the State, and that it would have a more stable, better paid, and more carefully graded staff, one in every respect superior. Moreover, Colbert struggled with all his strength against abuses in detail, exhorting the Intendants unceasingly to repress the frequently dishonest practices of the farmers' clerks. Then he tried to codify the financial regulations, to simplify them, and make them uniform. He made some improvement in the disorder of the excise. He had a dream of suppressing the customs (but it was only a dream). Finally, he reconstituted the *domaine* to a great extent by arbitrary purchase at low prices to the detriment of the holders of the alienated portions, and he reformed the administration of the rivers and forests by an admirable decree. Unfortunately many of his plans were stopped by the Dutch war (which he furthered) and by the vast increase in public expenditure resulting therefrom.

Louis XIV was less interested in finance than in war or politics ; in his heart he was of opinion that money is not a matter for a gentleman. True, he answered " Yes " courageously when Colbert asked if he should send him some wearisome detailed report ; but this was because he meant to be master, and to appear so in everything, over Colbert as over others : in practice he relied a good deal on his Controller-General of Finances. " As you think best," he would frequently write on the margin of reports, or " I order you to do what you think will be most advantageous." And he was very grateful to his great Colbert. He remunerated him by an annual salary of over 100,000 *livres*, equal perhaps to from 400,000 to 500,000 francs of modern money, by 400,000 *livres* of gratuities, by 1,400,000 *livres* of dowry to his daughter Mortemart. He encouraged and thanked him incessantly with a charming and unvarying grace. But he treated him rather like one of those devoted and clever old servants, who grumble a good deal, and whose lamentations need not be taken too seriously.

Colbert, indeed, dared to tell the King some very plain truths. He disapproved of the ruinous reviews of troops to **Colbert's** which Louis XIV loved to invite ladies ; in this **admonitions** connection he wrote boldly : " Your Majesty **to the King.** ought to know . . . that a lampoon has been placarded in Paris containing these words : ' Louis XIV will present the great puppet-show in the plains of Moret.' " And again, in reference to the building at Versailles, which he could not endure : " This house will tend far more to the pleasure and amusement of Your Majesty than to your glory " (1663) ; and : "It has seemed to me that Your Majesty was beginning to prefer your pleasures and amusements to everything " (1666). He writes in the same strain on July 22, 1666 :

It is well to save fivepence on unnecessary things and to pour out millions when it is a question of your glory. I declare to Your Majesty that, for my own part, a useless meal which costs one thousand crowns distresses me beyond measure ; yet, when it is a question of millions of gold for Poland, I would sell all I have ; I would mortgage my wife and my children ; I would go on foot all my life to provide it, were this necessary.

Your Majesty must please excuse this little outburst.

All these letters date from the first years of the reign, but a memorandum of 1680 and later notes show that to the end of his life the Minister addressed these necessary remonstrances to his master with praiseworthy frankness.

As to Louis XIV, he bore Colbert's insinuations patiently,

and replied with grace and civility, or with one of those delicate flatteries of which he was a past-master ; but afterwards he pressed his demands inexorably ; some of these were occasioned by the war, and these were the most considerable ; but others were in connection with the expenses of the Court. It has been calculated (very approximately) that the annual budget of expenditure under Louis XIV amounted on an average to about 600 million francs of the present day ; 150 being used for the war and the navy, and ninety perhaps for secret expenses, for the King's Household, for buildings, for entertainments (these last items, which were moderate at the beginning of the reign, increased steadily). In 1670 Colbert was already complaining that the expenditure exceeded the revenue by five millions ; in spite of which, Mme. de Montespan lost 4,000,000 *livres* at the gaming-table on March 6 ; it is true that she won back five the same night. The war with Holland increased the deficit, and the distracted Minister was obliged to have recourse to all the deplorable expedients of his predecessors : loans, creation of offices, new taxes, sale of the *domaine*, etc. In spite of everything, the deficit in 1680 was nearly forty-eight millions. And Bussy-Rabutin relates that in January, 1680, at the marriage of the Prince de Conti and Mlle. de Blois "there were seven hundred dishes at one table alone, which were served as five courses—that is to say, 140 dishes for each course." This prodigality on the part of the King was not the sole cause of Colbert's (comparative) failure ; but it must be admitted that it contributed thereto.

IV

Colbert believed that a State enriches itself (and so becomes powerful) by keeping its own money and attracting that of **Colbert's** others, and that to this end it is necessary : (1) **financial** That the State should manufacture all it requires **system.** itself, without buying anything abroad, so that it may not allow its current coin to leave the country ; (2) That it should manufacture surplus products in order to exchange them for the gold of other nations. In consequence, Colbert's system was to tax all imports heavily, and at the same time to stimulate French industrial activity, perfecting it by the means he approved, means which were traditional in France—that is to say, by tyrannical regulations. At first the results of this system were very good. Unfortunately Colbert at once exaggerated it. And his successors, by further exaggerating Colbertism, injured industry, trade, and agriculture almost as much as did war.

In the beginning, as he did not consider French industry sufficiently strong to be self-supporting as yet, Colbert favoured a certain measure of Free Trade. But as soon as he was able to record the "establishment of various manufactories in the kingdom," he caused an edict to be issued fixing such a high tariff that he practically closed France to foreign imports (1667). Holland retorted by putting high duties on French products, and the tariff-war which ensued brought about the war of 1672, which initiated the ruin of French finance. At the Peace of Nimeguen, Louis XIV was obliged to renounce the tariff of 1667, and this clause, which drove Colbert to despair, was apparently of happy augury for France.

Colbert's Protection policy inflicted the gravest injury upon agriculture, which was on the whole the most important industry of the kingdom. True, the Minister endeavoured to encourage certain branches, such as the culture of the mulberry-tree ; he had pines planted in Gascony ; he established horse-breeding centres. But in 1664 he had imposed a heavy export duty on corn, in the hope of averting famines ; and thus, deprived of any outlet, corn remained at a very low price, save in certain years when the crops were bad, a consummation the peasant finally wished for with his whole heart. Further, in response to the tariff of 1667, all agricultural products, notably wine and spirits, which were the principal exports of France, were heavily taxed abroad.

In the towns, the majority of crafts were not *free*, but *close*— that is to say, that nearly all artisans and tradesmen belonged to **The Guilds.** *corporations* composed of masters, journeymen, and apprentices in fixed numbers. The drawback to these privileged corporations was that they encouraged routine and prevented improvement. For instance, as the number of drapers was fixed, and as the public could not buy cloth anywhere but in their shops, there was no reason why the drapers should have tried to make cloth better and cheaper. On the other hand, the corporations had one great advantage : they ensured the perfection of French workmanship and French taste. Moreover, the monarchy had circumvented the difficulty by the invention of *royal factories* : the manufacturer who had the right to inscribe this title over his door escaped the juris-diction of his corporation, and henceforth was controlled only by the requisitions of the Hôtel.

Colbert, reviving the efforts of Henri IV and Sully with increased ardour, subsidized hundreds of factories, lavished the title of royal factories upon them, granted them temporary monopolies, found customers for them, and bought their products. In 1662 he installed the famous factory for the manufacture of Crown furniture in the Hôtel des Gobelins, under the direction of Le Brun. In 1664 a citizen of Paris, Hinard, founded, with his help, the Beau-vais tapestry factory. In 1665 Josse van Robais of Middel-burg, invited to France by him, created the manufacture of cloth at Abbeville. At Aubusson, he encouraged the corpora-tion of carpet-makers. At Chaillot, he reorganized the factory of La Savonnerie. At Alençon, Chantilly, Sedan, Gisors, Aurillac, privileged lace workshops, at Saint-Gobain and Cirey, looking-glass factories, at Saint-Etienne, a gun-foundry, were established. For the Minister intended that France should learn to make all the most renowned products of other nations : the fine cloths of Holland, the laces and mirrors of Venice, the tapestries of Flanders, the steel of England, the tar of Sweden, the tin of Germany. To this end he caused the French ambassadors to recruit the most skilful workpeople in foreign countries ; he established them in the kingdom, and facilitated their naturaliza-tion ; thus he attracted the artisans of Faenza, who founded the potteries at Nevers ; the six Venetian and the twenty-two Flemish women who taught the women of Reims to make Venetian and Flemish point ; the workmen from Murano, who taught French workmen to blow glass artistically, etc. Finally, he worked successfully, as we may imagine, to " disgust " those subjects of the King who persisted in placing their orders beyond the frontiers, instead of supporting national industry.

Industries created by Colbert.

THE KINGDOM UNDER LOUIS XIV

It would be unjust to say that Colbert's splendid effort was unsuccessful; the prestige of French industry in the eighteenth century sufficiently proves the contrary. But its success was partial. And this was primarily the fault of the kingdom: the peasants, conservative and distrustful, refused to enrol themselves in the factories, nor would the municipalities concern themselves with the fate of the new industries which the Minister was creating among them. But it was also the fault of Colbert himself, who wished to make the people happy logically and in their own despite. He intervened despotically in private enterprises, and imposed prescriptions contrary to the taste and habits of the population by force. Thus at Chevreuse, where, thinking the ribbon factory did not flourish because the workpeople did not work enough, he prohibited publicans from selling food and drink to them, save for one hour during the day. His regulations of output would have been beneficial in ensuring the quality of work, but their harassing minuteness tended to check production; an edict of August, 1669, for instance, on the preparation of stuffs, laid it down that shearers were not to use any grease but lard, and that they were not "to use teasels to tease the said cloths and serges, nor to keep them in their houses," but only "thistles, under penalty of a fine of 12 *livres* for each infringement." In vain did sellers and buyers claim more liberty and ask for changes; Colbert dealt severely with "products which did not conform to regulations," as he said, regardless of remonstrances, and his tyranny was only tempered by the fact that three-quarters of the magistrates would not carry out the excessively harsh measures he promulgated.

He laboured for trade as for industry with admirable zeal and unfortunate dogmatism.

The trading companies founded by his predecessors, Sully and Richelieu, had failed disastrously. But he had before his eyes the example of the flourishing Dutch East India Company, and, further, he dwelt with delight on the idea of all French traders duly enrolled in great societies, each of which should methodically exploit its special region of the world, and all of which should be dependent on the

337

(margin notes: Arbitrary restrictions on industry. Trading Companies.)

King and his Minister. Accordingly, in 1664, he created and
very skilfully floated the French East India Company, which
was privileged to traffic on the ocean from the Cape of Good
Hope to the Straits of Magellan, with the island of Madagascar
as its centre ; an Academician, François Charpentier, composed
the prospectus, and the crowd was informed with great circumstance that the King, the Queen, the Dauphin, the Princes of
the Blood, and the sovereign Courts were eagerly competing for
the shares. The advertisement fell flat ; the public thought the
Government was preparing some new snare akin to the many it
had already seen ; the recent reduction in Government securities
was not calculated to inspire confidence—as a whole, it prudently refrained from purchase. Even at this period French
capital was timid ; the peaceful ambition of the citizen was to
retire from business as soon as he had gained a small competence,
and to buy some municipal or other post, which would entitle
him to the respect of his neighbours. To find the capital
necessary for the working of the Company, it became necessary
to exact subscriptions from the great parliamentary capitalists.
Naturally these proceedings did not increase the popularity of
the French East India Company. It was in vain that Colbert
caused a fictitious dividend to be paid in 1675. Seven years
later he had to confess himself beaten ; the King withdrew its
charter from the moribund enterprise.

All the great trading companies Colbert persisted in founding
failed in like manner. The West India Company succumbed
in 1674, after having swallowed up 3,523,000 *livres* in ten years.
The Companies of Senegal, Guinea, the Levant, the Pyrenees,
and the North had no better success. It was perhaps because
they prevented all private initiative ; the French have never
taken kindly to this system. But the too logical Colbert could
not believe that what was successful in Holland might not be
suitable for his own country.

Nevertheless, here again his effort was not altogether sterile.
He greatly improved the roads and waterways of the kingdom :
Improvement the canal from Orleans to Montargis, that from
of Trade Saint-Omer to Calais, and, above all, the Canal du
Routes. Midi (Southern Canal), constructed by Riquet from
1666 to 1681. The rivers, which were made navigable and freed

from a large number of tolls, bore to Marseilles, Nantes, Le Havre, and Dieppe the cloth, wines, and silks of France, and there French merchant vessels, which had increased in numbers, were loaded to take them to Spain, England, Holland, and Sweden. Then, in March, 1673, the great commercial ordinance appeared, the code which was law until the end of the *ancien régime*. Finally, Colbert was passionately interested in the development of the colonies.

Until the Treaty of Utrecht, in 1713, they were immense, embracing nearly the whole of North America (Newfoundland,
The French Colonies. Canada, Acadia, Louisiana, discovered by the heroic Cavelier de la Salle from 1673 to 1683), a good share of the Antilles, Guiana, Senegal, Madagascar, Hindustan. The two Companies of the Indies had received sovereign powers in their domains ; they governed, judged, and declared war on the natives at their pleasure. After their failure the King took over the direct administration, and Colbert unfortunately set up a system modelled on that of the metropolis, with governors and intendants who were not allowed to decide any thing of importance without consulting him. But he did his best to foster the development of the colonies, their commercial prosperity, and their population. " We are getting ready the 150 girls, the brood mares, stallions, and sheep to be sent to Canada," he wrote one day ; and after the arrival of such a cargo soldiers were given a week in which to get married ; finally, those who had no children were fined.

V

Louis XIV took little interest in naval operations. In spite of Colbert's entreaties, it was not until July, 1680, that he made
The Navy. up his mind to go to Dunkirk ; he came back filled with wondering admiration after seeing one of his battleships manœuvre. But : " I considered that, as the interest of the State forbids a king to expose himself to the chances of the sea, I should be obliged to entrust my lieutenants with the entire care of my effectives, and should be unable to a on my own initiative," he wrote on one occasion ; and it is evident that the expenses necessitated by the upkeep of this fleet that he could never command, never see in action, and

never pass in review before a crowd of ladies, after the manner of Louvois' splendid regiments, were very irksome to him. One day in 1666 Colbert urged on the King the necessity of constructing six new ships : " At the very time when Your Majesty was telling me that this was so essential to your glory that we ought to take the very bread out of our mouths to provide the funds," he adds, " Your Majesty spent 200,000 *livres* of ready money on the journey to Versailles—that is to say, 13,000 pistoles for the gambling expenses of yourself and the Queen, and 50,000 *livres* on banquets." This lack of interest on the King's part makes the Minister's energy all the more creditable.

At the time of Louis XIV's accession the ports were in a deplorable condition and the arsenals empty ; the fleet created by Richelieu had disappeared, and the disbanded crews were serving foreign governments : a third of Admiral de Ruyter's effectives were Frenchmen. Colbert set to work in 1665, and after 1669 he had the help of his son Seignelay. At first the young man, who was eighteen, seemed only anxious to get as much pleasure as his father's position enabled him to enjoy ; but M. Colbert senior was not the man to put up with such a manner of living ; Seignelay was taken to task severely, and began to work in earnest. In temperament Colbert's son was no less strongly individual than his rival, the son of Le Tellier ; presumptuous and violent as Louvois himself, " audacious in the extreme," " he dared everything " (Voltaire), and even " showed civility haughtily." But " he had all the qualities of a great Minister of State," and after the death of his father he carried on Colbert's work worthily ; it was during his ministry that Louis XIV's navy was at its apogee, and the French squadrons and ports were the first in Europe.

Ships of the line were classified according to the number of their guns ; if they carried from 74 to 120, they were of the first **Types of** class, and so on down to the fifth class. The fast **vessels.** frigates had rarely more than forty guns. Merchant vessels such as transport-boats, corvettes, schooners, and the large brigs might be equipped for war. Bomb-ketches were first used in 1682, at the bombardment of Algiers ; before the time of their inventor, Renaud d'Eliçagaray, known as " little Renaud," no one had supposed that mortars could be
340

established anywhere but on land. Indeed, these vessels, built for two or three rows of guns, too round and too massive, with some imposing figure in gilded wood at the bowsprit, and a three-decked poop loaded with rich and heavy carving, were cumbrous and slow, in spite of their complicated rig. Their names were the *Terrible*, the *Mutine*, the *Capricieux*, and the *Royal-Louis*.

For the recruiting of crews Colbert organized naval enlistment (*inscription maritime*) (1669 and 1673). But seafaring **Naval** folk detested this kind of regular military service, **enlistment.** and had recourse to every kind of trick to avoid it. Indeed, to secure the required number of sailors it became necessary to revert to the ancient press-gang system—that is to say, to blockade some port from time to time, and ship by force all the sailors surprised there.

The galleys formed but an insignificant section of the fleet, and were used chiefly in the Mediterranean. Flat, and drawing **The Galleys.** but little water, they could travel two leagues to the hour; they could take advantage of a strong wind by hoisting their two triangular sails, and rely on their oars in perfectly calm weather. On their prows rose a sort of platform bearing big guns; in the stern was the cabin, where the officers lived. Between stern and bows were the wooden benches where the convicts rowed, ate, slept, and lived in chains. Whip in hand, the warder and the under-warders ran along the *coursie*, a passage which separated the right-hand from the left-hand benches lengthwise. Above the rowers, on a platform that extended all along the bulwarks, and was called the *couroir*, the soldiers were stationed. Below, in the hold, were store-rooms and cabins for the officers. As we see, the space was limited, and the galleys, in spite of their large staffs of soldiers, sailors, and convicts, could carry but a small stock of provisions; this was one of their disadvantages.

The recruiting of the oarsmen was always a difficult business. Colbert enjoined the tribunals to condemn as many prisoners as possible to forced labour. But certain magistrates ventured to have scruples. In 1662 the Intendant of Poitou announced to his Minister: "I have at present in my department twenty convicts condemned to the galleys, who are strong, vigorous fellows; whenever you like you can send off a commissary with a chain to take them, and the sooner the better, that they may not deteriorate." But shortly afterwards the same Intendant apologized for having only five convicts to send : " One has no real hold on the magistrates," he complains regretfully.

The convicts were taken to the galleys by easy stages, chained together in gangs of a hundred ; they lived on food given them **Galley slaves.** by the charitable on the way. On their arrival hair, beards, and eyebrows were shaved ; they were given two shirts, two pairs of drawers, a jacket, a cap, and an overcoat, and sent on board. But there were never enough of them. After the Revocation of the Edict of Nantes, Calvanist ministers who had been caught preaching, and Protestant citizens and gentlemen guilty of attempting to leave the kingdom, came to row in the King's galleys. Yet still the effectives were insufficient. It was in vain that raids were made on vagabonds and beggars ; in vain that convicts were kept in the gang sometimes " for fifteen and twenty years after their sentences had expired " ; convicts were sometimes bought from the Duke of Savoy, who had no navy himself ; but the supply was mainly kept up by the purchase of Barbary slaves in the markets of Leghorn, Genoa, and Malta, and of captive Slavs sold by the Tatars at Constantinople. The Turkish slaves, fatalistic and vigorous, were the most prized ; the average price of one was from 400 to 450 *livres*. The negroes of Senegal and Guinea had the inconvenient habit of dying of despair ; the Redskins were tried : the Marquis de Denonville lured some Iroquois chiefs into an ambuscade, and sent them to His Majesty ; but the Indians rose, and carried out reprisals so terrible that four years later it was thought prudent to restore their chiefs to them. Finally volunteers were engaged, known as the *bonne-voglie*—for there were miserable creatures who agreed, in return for a pittance, to pass a part of their lives, crouching in filth, and goaded by the lash, at the task of " writing on the water with a pen fifteen feet long." But in France the *bonnevoglie*, unlike their Italian *confrères*, refused to be chained ; and then they had to be paid wages.

The galleys on the whole spent more time in port than cruising on the seas, and the crews were more on land than in their floating prison : at Toulon the convicts wandered about the streets, dragging their chains, and selling passers-by purses, shoulder-knots, and little pieces of handwork ; some of the more wretched among them found the life bearable, and asked to be taken on again at the end of their term. But at sea their existence was horrible in the extreme. Naked as a rule, beneath their loose red jackets, shaven and shorn—many had had their ears and noses cut off as a punishment for attempted escape—swarming with vermin, and fed on beans, black bread, and a little salt pork, the convicts lived chained to their benches in gangs of seven, six, or five, according to the size of the galley. Each gang worked an oar, the strongest man, called the *passe-avant*, directing the handle, while the others, the *apostice*, the *tercers*, etc., down to the puny *cague-rageole*, pulled the rings. The overseer or warder marked the rhythm of the stroke by blowing on a whistle, and the under-warders, running along the *coursie*, stimulated the efforts of the galley-slaves by slashing at them with whips. Sometimes the poor wretches would row thus for twenty-four hours ; on these occasions they were given biscuit soaked in wine, which the under-warders would thrust into their mouths, so that they might not have to loose their hold of the oar. If the enemy came in sight the order was given : *Tap en bouche* (Stoppers in), and the convicts had to take between their teeth a piece of cork which was hung round their necks by a cord and prevented them from screaming at blows or wounds. Life was a grim business on the King's galleys.

VI

In the domain of provincial administration Louis XIV and Colbert continued the work of centralization inaugurated by Richelieu.

The States of Normandy, Berry, Maine, Anjou, Touraine, Auvergne, etc., were suppressed, and to nullify the freedom of **Administrative** the others the usual traditional expedients were **centralization.** employed : official candidature, the corruption of deputies, and intimidation. The Intendant and his subordinates presented to the electors candidates " devoted to the King's service " ; at the Assembly of the States, votes were bought ;

finally, the deputies, always very few in number, who persisted in their independence, were subjected to a thousand annoyances, which deterred others from imitating them. After a time these precautions became unnecessary : the Intendant had merely to state the sum of the tax the King proposed to lay on the province, and the States at once voted it.

In like manner in the towns the municipal elections became a farce : the Governor or the Intendant proposed the candidates who were to be chosen, and they were elected. As to the communal budget, the Intendant revised it, and at need drew it up himself ; as their municipalities robbed them, the towns were no worse off for this supervision. In 1692 an edict suppressed even the simulacrum of elections, and transformed the functions of mayors into offices which the King sold like any others.

All the authority which was withdrawn from the Governors of provinces, the sovereign Courts of Justice and Finance, the States, and the Municipalities, passed to the Intendant, who was henceforth a permanent official. This representative of the central Government was also the judge of the cases he " evoked " (save when there was an appeal to the Council) ; he had to organize and superintend the collection of the taxes, either officially or semi-officially ; to inspect and regulate trade and industry ; to direct public education ; to control the police, the administration of the troops, and the municipalities. Subject to dismissal, of modest birth, without personal relations in the province, and directly dependent upon his Minister, t e Intendant was an ideal instrument of centralization.

VII

Colbert remained gruff and surly to the end.

It is said that M. Colbert died ill-content, that, the King having written to him a few days before his death desiring him to eat and to take care of himself, he said not a word when the letter was read to him. Hereupon, they brought him some broth, which he refused. Mme. Colbert said to him : " Will you not answer the King ? " He replied : " Is this the time for such things ? What I have to think of is how to answer to the King of kings." When on another occasion she said something of the same sort to him, he

Death of Colbert.

replied : " Madame, when I was in this cabinet working at the King's business, neither you nor any one else dared to enter ; and now that I have to work at the business of my salvation, you will not leave me in peace." (Racine.)

Finally, after having made a will in favour of his son Seignelay and arranged his affairs like the able man he was, he died on September 6, 1683, in his magnificent house in the Rue Neuve-des-Petits-Champs. " The hatred of the Parisians for him was so great that it was considered unsafe to have him buried by day ; and even at night the funeral procession was escorted by the archers of the watch." They could not forgive his harshness and his scandalous wealth, nor the fact that he had begun his administration by a bankruptcy of Government stock, and finished by tampering with the currency. Nevertheless, it was greatly against the grain that he had increased taxation, and he died in despair at the ruin of the public Treasury ; but though he succeeded in introducing more order into State finance, he had not carried out any of the essential reforms. He had seen the downfall of his commercial creations and his colonial imperialism. He had been more successful in developing industry, but here again the results he had obtained were inferior to those he had expected.

On the whole, if Colbert failed partially, it was mainly because of his theories ; his economic ideas seem to have stopped short at those of Montchrestien (and, consequently, those of Richelieu). Perhaps his greatest achievement in the domain of administration, was to have " codified " (like Napoleon) his noble ordinances touching justice * (notably the Civil Code of 1667 and the Criminal Code of 1669), on the rivers and forests, on accountancy (1669), on criminal procedure (1670), on the Paris police (1672, still in force), on trade (1673), on indirect taxes and the salt tax (1680),

Colbert's Life-work.

* It has been stated that these great edicts of reform in procedure were never carried out ; but, in fact, in the absence of adequate monographs on the subject, we know nothing about this, and isolated cases prove nothing. M. Maurice Besnier, the archivist of the Eure Department, has, for his part, recognized that in Normandy order certainly was very much greater after the famous ordinance of 1667 ; seignorial cases were tried by advocates and royal officers ; a notary acted as registrar, and kept the registers regularly.

on the farming of revenues, on the navy (1681), on the negroes (the " black code " of 1685), to which we must add the military regulations of Le Tellier and Louvois—all these codes had long the force of laws, and served as a basis for ultimate legislation. We repeat, Colbert's failure was relative : the reconstruction of the navy, and of a great number of highways, the making of the Languedoc Canal, the saving of the forests, the reinforcement of industry ; and then the valiant remonstrances of the Minister to his prodigal King, his noble passion for public welfare, and, finally, his conception, then a novel one, that the greatest strength of a nation is in its wealth—nearly every one of these achievements of Colbert's would suffice to make a statesman illustrious.

VIII

War, which broke off the economic relations of France with other nations, did not, perhaps, inflict greater injury on trade and industry than Colbert's system as exaggerated by his successors. In vain did Ministers protest with all their power against " Colbertism " ; the Government had seemed to listen to them after the Treaty of Ryswyck (1697); but the War of the Spanish Succession made it impossible to conclude commercial treaties, and from 1713 onwards its Protectionism increased in stringency.

"**Colbertism.**"

The duties upon foreign goods became indeed prohibitive. The English and the Dutch retorted by analogous taxes on French products, and took their custom elsewhere. These Protectionist measures, which were taken solely with a view to the encouragement of manufactures, continued to affect agriculture, and notably the cultivation of the vine, very unfavourably ; moreover, in many districts the peasants were compelled to dig up their vines in order to plant corn, which was less profitable, because it was supposed that this would avert scarcity, which would have been much more effectively dealt with by allowing the free circulation of corn. While agriculturists were discouraged by such measures, the tyrannical regulation of production did not encourage manufacturers, for the State now prescribed even the number of strands in the warp of cloths. Finally, the large number of commercial companies still existing were very detrimental to maritime traffic ; enjoying privileges which made them indifferent to competition, they dozed comfortably, and considered it prudent to restrict rather than to increase their business, indemnifying themselves by increasing prices, which they fixed to suit themselves.

At the close of the reign the public finances were in a deplorable state of disorder. At the time of Colbert's death **Disorder of** the deficit in the budget was already sixteen **Public** millions, although every financial expedient had **Finance.** been tried. In 1697 expenditure had risen to nearly 219 millions, while the regular receipts amounted only to 81 millions ; the requisite 138 millions had therefore to be procured by the pitiful device of " transactions extraordinary." Not only were new offices created and sold by the thousand, but the King also granted patents of nobility for cash, issued bonds to meet which he had not a halfpenny at his disposal, evaded State creditors by bankruptcy, borrowed money at ever-increasing rates of interest, organized lotteries, mortgaged the revenues of future years, and, above all, altered the currency. To crown all, he astounded the courtiers by himself doing the honours of his gardens at Marly to the Sieur Samuel Bernard " with all the grace he knew so well how to display when he was minded to dazzle," and squeezing the enormous sum of money he required out of the banker " by this species of prostitution."

In 1695 a new and nominally temporary tax was levied, which lasted until the Revolution (save for a brief interval of time, from 1698 to 1701) : the poll-tax. All Frenchmen, from the Princes of the Blood to the lowliest workman, were divided into twenty-two classes, the first of which paid 2000 *livres*, the second less, and so on to the last, which was taxed at one *livre*. But in reality the clergy bought exemption with a comparatively moderate sum, various provinces obtained leave to become " subscribers "—that is to say, to follow the example of the clergy—and the great and powerful generally managed, either by traffic, influence, or adroitness, to pay very little, so that it was mainly the least wealthy—workmen, citizens of the middle classes, and country nobles—who continued to pay. Moreover, after 1701 the character of the poll-tax was modified : those liable to be taxed were assessed at a mark in the *livre* of the *taille*, whereas the exempt, according as they were nobles, officials, or citizens of free cities, were taxed arbitrarily or by certain special tariffs.

Finally, from 1710 onwards to the poll-tax was added the *tenth*. This was also a tax on income, but it was based on the revenue of Government securities, offices, and industry, and therefore affected the privileged classes as well as the masses. But the former bought exemption from the *tenth* as they had done from the poll-tax ; and the middle classes were almost the sole contributors.

IX

Under Louis XIV the clergy were more docile than they had ever been, and had occasion offered they would probably **The Clergy under Louis XIV.** have supported their sovereign against Rome even to the point of schism. The clerical assemblies voted as the King wished. Even the Jesuits appear to have greatly modified their traditional Ultramontanism, and they taught the Gallican articles of 1682 in their colleges without raising any objections. The priests brought up the children of the nation in religious respect for the monarchy and the worship of Louis XIV. Finally, the inferior clergy were actually a wheel in the State machine ; the parish priest presided regularly over the parochial assembly, where the affairs of the commune were arranged : the incidence of taxation, the upkeep of the roads, State relief, etc. ; moreover, he was empowered to receive testamentary dispositions, to read edicts after preaching, to communicate agricultural instruction ; it was through him alone that the illiterate people of the rural districts communicated with the rest of the world.

As to the nobles, under Louis XIV they had already lost all recollection of their feudal independence ; if they revolted at **The Nobles.** all, it was only to extort money from the sovereign. Still less did any prince or grandee make any claim to the smallest effective power under Louis XIV ; the Governors of provinces, for instance, were splendidly paid and

lavishly honoured, but they could not transfer a company of
soldiers or raise a farthing without the sanction of the Intendant.
The long reign of the great King witnessed but one aristocratic
conspiracy, if indeed this be not too grandiloquent a word to
apply to the crazy enterprise of the Chevalier de Rohan; in
common with a certain Mme. de Villers, two Norman gentlemen named Préaux and Le Tréaumont, and Van den Enden, a
schoolmaster of the United Provinces, this great nobleman, a
discredited person, deeply in debt and disowned by his family,
had plotted to hand over Quillebœuf to the Dutch for a sum of
money (1674); both he and his accomplices paid for their
treason on the scaffold.

And yet Louis XIV, like Richelieu, distrusted the nobles as
a body. He kept them out of politics, the administration, and,
as far as possible, out of the ranks of the superior clergy; he
left them no outlet but the army—and the military calling, far
from being lucrative, is generally very costly. Further, the
King considered it the duty of every gentleman to come and
pay court to him, and he bestowed favours only on those
personally known to him. In order to succeed, therefore, it
was essential to be a courtier—and Court life was ruinous.

The household of a man of quality had to consist of at least
seventy-five persons, reckons the Sieur Audiger in 1692; the
Ruinous cost stables could not decently contain less than four-
of Court life. teen carriage-horses, making two teams, sixteen
saddle-horses for Monsieur, seven carriage-horses and four
saddle-horses for Madame; the whole costing about 63,632
livres, equal to some 200,000 francs of modern money (apparently,
for this valuation is extremely uncertain), and exclusive of the
expenditure for the children, who had seven servants allotted
to them, and that of the country-houses. Thirteen years
earlier, Mme. de Maintenon, like the careful housekeeper she
was, drew up a strictly economical budget for her sister-in-law,
who was not rich; she considered the following essential for
service: three women, four lackeys, two men-servants, two
coachmen, the whole representing 12,000 *livres* (50,000 francs
approximately), exclusive of the upkeep of two coaches. A
simple Councillor, in 1675, kept a secretary, a master of the
horse, two men-servants, a porter, a house-steward, a pantler, a

cook, two pages, six lackeys, two coachmen, two postillions two footmen, four grooms, and in addition, to wait on his wife. two maids, a lady's maid, and four women-servants. We cannot therefore be surprised to learn that M. de Pontchartrain kept 113 servants, and that no less than 146 were lodged in the Hôtel de Nevers; for a great noble, it was a sort of social obligation to keep a veritable army of " people." And even with this huge staff he was very ill served, for nothing would induce a valet, for instance, to bring in a meal, nor a lady's maid to light a fire; in the absence of the house-steward, M. le Marquis would have to go without his dinner, and we know how one of Mme. de Sévigné's staff preferred to be turned out of the house rather than help in the haymaking when he had not been engaged to do so. Nevertheless, as a rule, servants succeeded each other from father to son in the service of the master and of his children. The master signed their contracts, employed their boys and gave dowries to their daughters; they grew old and died, as they had been born, under his roof, for he would have blushed to turn away aged and invalid servants; to spare them the humiliation of receiving alms, some sinecure was found for them, as, for instance, the task of carrying the Mass-book to church. But we must bear in mind that though these retainers were paid hardly anything (even when they were supposed to receive wages), such households were very costly. Even a gentleman who was determined to live quietly in Paris in 1692 could not spend less than from five to six thousand *livres* a year, if we may believe Audiger, the authority quoted above. Much more then, as may be supposed, was a large fortune necessary for Court life, and as no means of acquiring wealth was open to a gentleman save some profitable *mésalliance* or the favour of the King, the country nobility, who could hope for neither one nor the other, were always more or less dying of hunger.

For the nobility consisted not only of the luxurious aristocracy which shone at Versailles, but also of that multitude **The Provincial** of country squires whose manors—half farms, half **Nobility.** mansions—cover the soil of France. Their lot was as a rule far from enviable. Lacking the privileges of persons in favour at Court, they paid the poll-tax from 1701 onwards, and the *tenth* from 1710 ; from time immemorial they had paid the tithe, and even the *taille* in the districts where the real *taille* existed—that is to say, where this tax was levied not on persons, but on property. Now since the time of Louis XIII, the income from land had diminished ; many squires could no longer find tenant-farmers to keep up the value of their properties (and, further, they lacked capital to procure the necessary materials). How were they to bring up "nobly" the families of from fifteen to eighteen children they often had, to send their sons to the army and marry their daughters ? Some were reduced to working their fields themselves, and went off to the market to sell their poultry and vegetables, a sword at their side and a basket on their arm ; and for nearly all the rest there was no escape, if not from destitution, at least from debt, the struggle against the bailiffs, who now proceeded against the noble with no more fear of a cudgelling than in an action against a churl, and a poverty it was a point of honour to conceal : the farm-girl was promoted to the office of chambermaid when a visitor arrived, the little herd became a lackey, the skinny fowls were described as capons, the plough-horse played the part of a Spanish cob. There was nothing more ridiculous than a provincial baron in the eyes of the gentlemen of Versailles ; the vanity of the Sotenvilles, the Pourceaugnacs, the La Crasses, and the Escarbagnas, their garments " of the time of my grandmother," their country-houses through which all the winds of heaven whistled, their absurd meals—the memoirs and literature of the period are full of these things. And in the State the country squire was hardly more than the most prominent inhabitant of his village.

It was from the ranks of the upper magistracy, the *noblesse de robe* (legal nobility), that the old hereditary caste (*noblesse d'épée*) was reinforced when threatened with extinction.

The caste of " officials " had been, as a fact, consolidated since the time of Louis XIII. Colbert and the King had first **The Legal** planned to destroy it, the Minister because the **Nobility.** venality of office seemed to him as to every one a crying abuse, and Louis XIV for the same reason, but also because he remembered, as he says in his Memoirs, that " the elevation of Parliaments in general had been dangerous to the whole kingdom during his minority." Edicts were accordingly issued in 1665, 1669 and 1671, which reduced the price of offices, and were therefore apparently designed to prepare the way for their redemption by the State. But hereupon, the war with Holland broke out, and instead of suppressing offices, it became necessary to create new ones in order to raise money.

There were always people ready to buy them. The dream of every Frenchman thenceforth was to make enough money to enjoy a modest competence, and to acquire some office which would ensure consideration for his person ; every merchant hoped that his son would some day abandon trade to become a functionary of some sort, and so rise in the social scale. For officials formed a veritable order, a class superior to that of the citizens ; a President of the Parliament and a little country sheriff's officer belonged, indeed, to the same caste, in spite of the difference of rank, in like manner as an archbishop and a parish priest.

Several of the great functions of the sovereign Courts conferred personal nobility on their possessors, some, indeed, hereditary nobility (here we have the legal aristocracy) the *noblesse de robe*). Thus the office of *Président à Mortier* (Chief Justice) of the Parliament of Paris was worth 350,000 *livres* in 1665, 500,000 in 1684 (1,500,000 or 2,000,000 francs of our money, perhaps) ; the same office at the Rouen Parliament was worth about 150,000 *livres* ; at that of Bordeaux, Rennes, or Dijon, 120,000 *livres*. The post of Councillor was valued at 100,000 or 90,000 *livres* at the Parliament of Paris ; at 52,000 at that of Dijon ; at 48,000 at that of Rouen ; at 22,000 at that of Bordeaux. The office of First President of the Court of Accounts of Paris was worth 400,000 *livres* ; that of the Court of Accounts of Rouen, 150,000 ; that of Dijon, 130,000. At the Châtelet in Paris the office of Civil Lieutenant was worth 400,000 *livres* ; that of Criminal Lieutenant 200,000 *livres*. A man had, therefore, to be wealthy in order to buy one of these important offices—if, indeed, the opportunity ever presented itself, for as a rule they were kept in the same families—and the more so as the incomes attached to them were very small ; but the social prestige they conferred was immense. In the provinces, the First President of the Parliament made a solemn entry, like a prince, to the roar of cannon, passing under triumphal arches adorned with his coat of arms; he took precedence of the greatest personages; when he died, all the bells tolled. . . . True, the sovereign Courts had changed a good deal in character since the Fronde; they could no longer dare to oppose the monarch boldly; in 1673 the King reduced their famous right of remonstrance to insignificance; and even in judicial matters the authority of the Parliaments was greatly diminished by the power arrogated to himself by the Intendant, who was always supported by the higher powers, to " evoke " any particular case, in order either to decide it himself or submit it to the Council. But the moral influence, the social position of the officials, continued to be considerable. Holding their office for life, and owning it themselves, knowing that their promotion depended only on their own wealth, and that they could rise from Councillor to President or from sheriff's officer to Registrar if their means allowed, without the intervention of the Minister, the Government had scarcely any hold over them. Hence the most difficult thing imaginable for Louis XIV, the " absolute " monarch, was to command the obedience of those who judged and administered in his name.

At the beginning of the seventeenth century the masses inspired no interest whatever. When in the States-General of 1614 Savaron uttered this eloquent apostrophe: " What would you say, Sire, if you could see your people in the provinces of Guyenne and Auvergne eating grass like the beasts of the field ? " the magistrates his colleagues, admirers of lofty harangues in the Roman style, applauded his rhetorical outburst. As a fact, the villein seemed to them a sort of domestic animal, much as the negro seemed to the planter of former days. Richelieu said terrible things in this connection, such as this : " All politicians are agreed that if the people were too comfortable, it would be impossible to keep them within the bounds of duty." In *Héraclius*, Corneille at first made the woman who saves the Emperor's son by sacrificing her own child, a simple nurse ; but on reflection, such heroism seemed to him too exalted for a woman of the people : and the nurse

The lower Orders.

353

was transformed into a governess. And in *Phèdre*, no one even commented on the blind devotion of Œnone to her mistress ; it was only natural, Œnone being a common person, and Phèdre a princess. The villein was not pitiful : he was ridiculous. How gracefully the good Sévigné rallies the Bas-Bretons, those " simpletons " who are sent to the war :

> They cannot understand their drill, nor what they are forbidden to do ! When they had their muskets on their shoulders, and M. de Chaulnes appeared, if they tried to salute him, the weapon fell on one side and the hat on the other ; they were told they must not salute under such conditions ; presently, when they were disarmed, if they saw M. de Chaulnes pass, they pulled their hats down on their heads with both hands, and took care not to salute. They were told that when they were in the ranks, they were not to go either to the right or the left ; they allowed M. de Chaulnes' coach to drive through them the other day, and would not give way an inch, whatever was said to them.

Yet La Bruyère, who had witnessed the most terrible year of the reign of Louis XIV in one of the most poverty-stricken **The misery of** regions of France, wrote the following pathetic **the poor.** lines for posterity :

> One sees certain sullen animals, male and female, scattered about the country, dark, livid, scorched by the sun, attached to the earth they dig up and turn over with invincible persistence ; they have a kind of articulate speech, and when they rise to their feet, they show a human face, and, indeed, they are men. At night they retire to dens, where they live on black bread, water, and roots ; they save others the toil of sowing, ploughing, and garnering in order to live, and thus deserve not to lack the bread they have sown.

And during the last years of Louis XIV, Vauban, Fénelon, and many others expressed their emotion after the manner of La Bruyère. For the Great Century did not last as long as the Great King ; by their tearful prose, their novel tenderness and pity, the latest writers of the reign heralded the triumph of " sensibility " and of Jean-Jacques Rousseau.

In the mediæval Corporations there was an intimate connection between employer and workman, between the *master* **Constitution of** and the quondam apprentice who had become a **the Guilds.** *journeyman*. The journeyman was often a member of the confraternity ; he might even become one of the *jurors* who governed the *craft* ; in case of illness or unemployment he might claim help from the *box*, or charitable fund of the corporation. But the gulf between masters and journeymen widened from century to century. Gradually excluded from the association of the employers, the workmen began to combine in secret societies which were reprobated by the Church and harassed by the Company of the Holy Sacrament, because the rites of initiation and the oath to reveal nothing to the workman's confessor were pronounced sacrilegious. We know little still of these occult associations, a species of workmen's syndicate, formed in opposition to the employers' syndicate into which the Corporation had developed : the *Compagnons du Devoir* (Journeymen of Duty), for instance, had signs of recognition, a rallying word, a common fund kept up by the contributions of its adherents ; on occasions they would proclaim a strike to obtain an increase of wages or the reintegration of a comrade, or to impose a certain condition upon an employer.

The workman was a nomad, who engaged himself for a short term only, sometimes for a single day, and wandered gaily through France. He worked in the shop, at the back of the dark, narrow, malodorous street, as did his master, for six, eight, twelve, or fourteen hours, according to the length of the day. Unless, indeed, he preferred to take a place in a factory (that of the Van Robais gave work to 1500 men in 1715), or to work at home, in defiance of prohibitions, in a bare room, furnished with a chest, a few saucepans, a palliasse and a mattress covered with green serge or black-and-white drugget, and, very rarely, adorned with an old piece of stuff by way of window-curtain, where the *chambreland* (home-worker), as he was called, lodged with his wife and children.

In 1700 workers in the serge-factories in the region of Amiens earned at most six *sous* a day ; the miners of Saint-Etienne got fifteen or sixteen *sous*. Vauban calculated that the artisans in large towns earned on an average twelve *sous* a day. And bread cost a *sou* per pound (Sagnac).

The peasant had less freedom than the nomad workman, his contemporary, who was not bound to the soil as he was. But, on the whole, he was not more heavily taxed than he is now. He paid his dues to his lord, the King's tax, and the tithe to the Church, which was his heaviest burden ; nor was it so heavy as might be supposed, for it did

The Peasantry.

not correspond to the tenth part of the crop, and was generally confined to the eleventh or the sixteenth sheaf. True, passing troops might requisition his provisions, steal his fowls or ravage his field, or he might be taken from plough or harvest and sent to a distance for forced labour, such as repairing a road or constructing fortifications. But troops rarely passed except in the frontier provinces, and forced labour was not frequent under Louis XIV. What harassed the peasant was not so much the tax as the manner in which it was collected ; also, the low prices he received for his corn and wine, and finally, in some cases, fear of the black band of business folk : the village usurer, the sheriff's officer, the agent of the farmer-general, the archers who were always pitilessly ready to seize his cattle, his furniture, and his agricultural implements.

It is usual enough to carry executions so far as to take away the doors of houses after selling everything inside them ; houses are even demolished to take the beams and rafters and planks, which are sold at sums five or six times less than their value, with the *taille* deducted. (Vauban, 1707.)

And then there were the years of crisis, such as 1698 and, above all, 1709, when famine was added to war : and at such periods the destitution in certain districts was heart-breaking. In 1698, in La Beauce, " although it is the best country in the world for the production of wheat," the peasant contented himself with bread made of barley or rye mixed with a little wheat, and sold the rest of his crop to pay his taxes ; only the rich ones were able to salt a little meat after the harvest. In the district of Rouen, out of 700,000 peasants there were not 50,000 " who could eat their fill of bread, or who slept on anything but straw." Those of La Marche, " dark, livid, and almost all hideous," fled to Catalonia, " and when they returned, came back again to their chestnuts and beetroot on which they lived themselves like their cattle." Those in Auvergne lived in their stables that they might not die of cold. Those of Riom fed on nut-oil, " and this is almost the only food, which is astonishing, seeing how fertile the country is ; but the taxes which oppress the people are so heavy that they are unable to enjoy the natural wealth of their native land." Again, in 1698 the Intendant of Berry wrote these poignant words :

There is no nation more wild than these people ; one sometimes comes upon troops of them in the country, seated in a circle in the middle of a ploughed field, and always a long way from the road ; but if one approaches, the band scatters at once.

" Your people are dying of hunger," said Fénelon to Louis XIV in 1709. " Instead of extorting money from these poor creatures, we ought to give them alms and feed them. All France is nothing but a vast, desolate hospital without provisions."

Nevertheless, we must remember that these testimonies, which have been used to furnish materials for the blackest pictures, refer to years of *exceptional* poverty and famine ; even the most heavily taxed districts presented a different appearance at other times, much more so those where the real *taille* existed, or where exemption had been bought (cf. Marolles and various **Peasant** accounts of travels). Peasants might still be seen **costumes.** dressed in those beautiful garments which, with the furniture of the house, the cattle, and the land then constituted the entire fortune (for there was little ready money in country districts, and stocks and shares were unknown). The woman wore a handsome head-dress of some sort, a braided bodice with coloured sleeves, a skirt trimmed with velvet, a ring on her finger, and a half-girdle round her waist, from which her keys hung. The man had a large hat, stockings and shoes, and a good cloak to keep him warm ; he baked his own bread, gathered his own vegetables, milked his cow or his goat, fattened his fowls and salted his pork ; he was not unhappy ; sometimes he was much better off than his lord, the country noble. In Normandy contemporary documents do not bear witness to any great destitution, except in those years of famine mentioned above, and yet this province is generally quoted as the one most severely tried—at any rate, as the one which paid the heaviest dues : personal *taille*, utensils for the army, and the *gabelle* as a tax (which was even more irksome than when it was a duty).

And, then, in the midst of the poorest districts there was sometimes found standing among flowery meadows, well culti- **Model** vated fields, and fat pastures, some fine, solid **estates.** farm-house, whose inhabitants seemed to breathe comfort and peace ; it was the property of some influential noble, who protected his tenant-farmers out of self-interest, to a certain

357

extent, and to increase his income, but also out of pride, and even charity, because they " belonged " to him, and because it was the traditional duty of the gentleman to protect his vassals as he protected his servants, his " people," his household.

In short, if at the end of the reign the rural population was wretched here and there, on the other hand there were instances of unprecedented prosperity. At Honfleur, for instance, the great shipbuilding firms became doubly important. Saint-Malo, thanks to the traffic of the gold galleons, and the trade of the South Seas (South America, Peru, etc.), open to France since the Spanish Succession had fallen to the Bourbons, was magnificently rebuilt ; it fitted out the fleet with which Duguay-Trouin went off to bombard Rio de Janeiro, lent the King fifty million *livres*, and maintained a swarm of corsairs.

Thus a few years of peace and tranquillity sufficed to restore plenty and prosperity in the weary kingdom ; never perhaps did the French nation expand with more vitality than during the first years of the Regency ; could it have done so if the country had been so utterly exhausted as it is said to have been in 1715 ?

The France of Louis XIV, sternly tempered by Catholic discipline, bore the trials which left her so great and glorious with as much stoicism as her King himself.

WORKS TO CONSULT. A. Babeau, *Voyageurs en France* (1885) ; *La Ville . . . La Province . . . La Vie rurale sous l'ancien Régime* (1882–94) ; Baudrillart, *Les populations agricoles de la France* (1880–93) ; A. Berton, *L'impôt de la Capitation* (1907) ; Bonnassieux, *Les grandes Compagnies de Commerce* (1892) ; Th. Chapais, *Jean Talon* (1904), see the bibliography ; Clamageran, *Histoire de l'impôt en France* (1867–76) ; P. Clément, *Histoire de Colbert* (1892) ; Depping, *Correspondance administrative sous le règne de Louis XIV* (unpublished documents) ; F. Dumas, in *Mémoires de l'Academie de Toulouse* (1908) ; Fléchier, *Mémoires sur les grands Jours d'Auvergne* (ed. of 1856) ; Glasson, *Histoire du Droit et des Institutions en France*, vol. viii (1903) ; Hauser, *Les Compagnonnages d'Arts et Métiers à Dijon* (1907) ; cf. *Revue d'Histoire moderne* (1908) ; Lardi, *La Capitation dans les pays de taille personnelle* (1906) ; Lavisse, in the *Revue de Paris* (1896, 1897, 1901) ; and *Histoire de France*, already quoted ; Martin Saint-Léon, *Histoire des Corporations et Métiers* (1897) ; *Le Compagnonnage* (1902) ; Sagnac, *Histoire de France*, edited by E. Lavisse, vol. vii, 1 (1908) ; Ph. Sagnac, *La Politique commerciale de la France* (1697–1713), in the *Revue historique*, July–August, 1910, p. 265 *et seq.*

CHAPTER XIII

THE GREAT AGE

I. The King's taste and influence. **II.** The Fine Arts. **III.** Music.
IV. Literature. **V.** Conclusion.

I

L OUIS XIV loved music passionately. The first operas
he heard enchanted him; in 1673 he declared that "if
he were in Paris when opera was being given, he would
go every day;" this speech, adds Mme. de Sévigné, who
records it, "will be worth 100,000 francs to Baptiste (Lulli)."
The King's As a young man the King played the hapsichord,
musical taste. the lute, and the guitar fairly well, and sang
agreeably; in his old age, Mme. de Maintenon arranged
concerts for his amusement. Moreover, when he visited Vauban's fortifications, he was struck, not only by their strength,
but by their beauty: "The bridge-head of the suburb at
Péronne is one of the finest things possible; it surprises one by
its air of magnificence," he remarked. As to the harmony of
stones, trees, flowers, and water, he clearly showed his sense of it
at Versailles and at Marly. He drew up with his own hand a
sort of guide for the use of visitors: *The Method for showing the
Gardens at Versailles*, for he was proud of the beauty he had
created:

Mme. de La Fayette was at Versailles yesterday. She was well, nay,
very well received, that is to say, the King made her get into a carriage
with the ladies, and took pleasure in showing her all the beauties of
Versailles, just like a private person one might be visiting in his country-
house. (Sévigné.)

"I am prepared," wrote Louis in agreeable anticipation,
"to feel some pleasure when I arrive [at Versailles]. It will not
be for some time. I expect to find a great many flowers, both

359

late and early ; my brother told me that the garden was not so full of them as usual, and that Le Bouteux was keeping some in reserve. I suppose this was the reason. Just find out about this " (October, 1673). It may be that he could not discourse learnedly on the cadence of a sonnet, the glow of a picture, the action of a statue ; but his great natural taste caused him to protect Racine and Molière against every one, to make Lulli the fashion, to ennoble him as well as Mansart, Le Nôtre, and Le Brun ; in short, it enabled him to feel that architects, musicians, painters, and writers are no less essential to the " glory " of a French King than conquests. And this was why, as early as 1662, Chapelain was ordered to draw up a list of the authors and scientists of every land, for a great King felt that he owed it to himself to pension them.

Colbert, Superintendent of Building (Minister of Fine Arts) from 1664 onwards, worked at encouraging the production of Encourage- the beautiful as strenuously as he had worked at ment of the the production of cloth, and sought to improve Fine Arts. science, art, and letters by methods akin to those he had applied to trade and industry. In other words, he regulated them as rigorously as possible. Chapelain was entrusted with the task of superintending the manufacture of literature, so to speak, and encouraging good producers by prizes and bounties. Le Brun directed the manufacture of art in the same manner. Finally, academies more or less privileged were established to determine the rules to be followed and the models to imitate, and Colbert would not allow them to be inactive any more than his factories, for he meant the King to have value for his money. Fortunately, artists and, more pre-eminently, writers were so great at this period that Colbert's solicitude was not so detrimental to them as might have been expected.

In 1663 the Académie des Inscriptions et Belles-Lettres was founded ; in 1666 the Académie des Sciences. The Académie Academies of française had hastened to invite the powerful Inscriptions Minister to " honour it by becoming one of its and Science. members " and in 1671 it conferred on him the title of Vice-Protector. Two years later Colbert invented the system of attendance-counters, stipulating that they should only be assigned to those who arrived at the sittings before the hour of opening and remained till after their close; in spite of this wise precaution, the Dictionary did not appear till 1694.

Under Louis XIII the Masters of the Arts of Painting and Sculpture still formed a corporation, and claimed to forbid those **Academy of Painting and Sculpture.** who were not affiliated to their guild to practise their profession. But the most famous painters and sculptors of the day did not belong to the confraternity, and as they lived at the Court, they gave little heed to the protests of the past-masters of their crafts. In 1648 Mazarin grouped them in an Academy which Colbert reorganized in 1664, appointing Le Brun Director for life. This new Academy of Painting and Sculpture was chartered: artists not included among its forty members were forbidden to take pupils.

As it was generally admitted that the masterpieces of art were all in Italy, Colbert founded the French Academy in Rome **French Academy in Rome.** in 1666. The twelve young painters, sculptors, and architects who composed it under the direction of one of the King's painters, had to be up at five o'clock in summer and six in winter, to study arithmetic, geometry, perspective, and anatomy, to pray in common, to go to bed at ten o'clock, and in the intervals to " copy all the beautiful things in Rome: " their college was thus both a school and a manufactory of models. When they had good reports, the King took them into his service under the superintendence of Le Brun.

Finally the Council of Buildings, formed in 1665, became in 1671 the Academy of Architecture, with quarters in the Palais Royal.

And now, what influence was exercised by the King, the Court, and all these establishments upon artists and writers?

It is true that painters, sculptors, and architects were influenced by the Court for this potent reason: that as long as he **Court influence on the Arts.** was not completely ruined, the King remained their principal patron, and that the princes, great nobles, and very rich magistrates or financiers who made up the rest of their *clientèle*, modelled their taste on that of His Majesty.

Throughout the greater part of the reign, the artists were nearly all employed in building and ornamenting the King's palaces and gardens, representing his actions, and reproducing his image and that of his courtiers. The whole Gobelins factory worked for the King. They wove his tapestries there, engraved his prints, composed his decorative panels, chased his silver and bronzes, carved his vases, capitals, and statues. The versatile Le Brun, " the King's first painter " (who died in 1690 and whose place was but poorly filled by Mignard), directed everything, superintended everything, inspired everything, gave ideas to every one, even sketching designs for locks and bolts. Coysevox, Girardon, Caffieri, Audran, and Sébastien Leclerc worked from his drawings, and the master tapestry-weavers from his cartoons. Van der Meulen painted the landscapes of pictures sketched by him, and others put in the figures. The Louis XIV style was elaborated under the inspiration of Le Brun, according to the indications given by the King, who followed the work with interest, at Versailles, and in that art-factory of the Gobelins, where sixty children were educated in the prevailing taste, to be afterwards dispersed throughout the kingdom. And thus it may be said, with no disparaging intention, that the seventeenth century witnessed the triumph of official art.

But during the early years of the eighteenth century great disasters and financial ruin forced Louis XIV to restrict his orders considerably, and his influence on artists waned in proportion. Moreover, the *clientèle* of these changed completely ; collectors of all sorts, and amateurs began to appear ; their tastes differed, they bought easel-pictures, statuettes—and this was the beginning of liberty for artists.

As to letters, the King, Colbert, and the Court combined apparently exercised less influence on them than the Hôtel de Rambouillet, for instance, had done. True, Colbert one day threatened the historian Mézeray that his pension of 4000 *livres* should be withdrawn if he persisted in speaking as he did of the *taille* and the *gabelle* ; and he actually reduced it by one-half. It is also a fact that the French Academy invariably gave a eulogy of the King as the subject for its competitions in eloquence and poetry, and authors, even the scientists themselves, never wrote the

Literary flattery of the King.

radiant name of Louis without encircling it with ridiculous hyperboles. " All the words of the language," declared Racine, " all the syllables seem precious to us, because we look upon them as so many instruments which may serve for the glory of our august protector."

> On ne peut trop louer trois sortes de personnes :
> Ses dieux, sa maîtresse, et son Roi,

sang La Fontaine. Every one is familiar with Boileau's odes and Molière's gross compliments. La Bruyère added the chapter on the sovereign to his *Caractères*. But what is proved by all these praises, more or less sincere, forced, or interested ? When we find that the greatest intellectual event of this period was the triumph of that Cartesianism which was proscribed by the State, it would seem that we ought to be careful not to imagine all the great intellects of the Great Century gravitating like stars about the *Roi Soleil*.

II

Before the dawn of Romanticism, what we call " the charm of the past " was almost unknown. Rationalistic and Cartesian, **Indifference to** the men of the seventeenth century lacked the **historic** sense of history. They were as certain that their **interest.** beauty was Beauty, and their taste Good Taste, as Descartes was sure that mathematical truth is Truth. Ancient things did not appeal to them, and the patina of age was merely dirt to them. With Molière they deplored " the insipid taste for Gothic monuments—those odious monstrosities of the ignorant centuries, which barbarism produced in torrents ; " but they looked upon the monuments of the Renaissance as Gothic buildings ; and if they did not destroy all the old stones which we think touching and they considered ugly, to replace them by constructions in their own manner, it was merely owing to the impossibility of raising the huge sums necessary for such an operation. However, they did their best, when they could, to make these ancient monuments less barbarous and uncouth ; thus, in 1699, for instance, at Notre-Dame, Robert de Cotte destroyed the rood-screen and the pierced screens round the choir, burnt the carved stalls, took away the memorial

stones, and replaced the coloured glass by white panes; in
like manner at Blois, François Mansart pulled down part of
Francis I's castle in order to raise a new building, admirable in
itself, but which would have been more acceptable had it been
built beside the rest; so, too, Le Vau put a quadrangular dome
on the central pavilion of Philibert Delorme's Tuileries; and yet
Le Vau was a great artist, as he showed in the Château de Vaux,
and also in the Louvre.

When in 1624 the worthy Louis XIII undertook to finish the
palace of his fathers, the Louvre consisted only of two wings
Completion of (besides the gallery along the bank of the river
the Louvre. which extended as far as the Tuileries), namely :
about half of the present south wing (parallel with the Seine)
and half of the west wing, as far as the central Pavilion of the
Clock ; between the Louvre and the Tuileries, as also between
the Louvre and Saint-Germain-l'Auxerrois, there was an entire
quarter of houses. Louis XIII wished his architects to carry
out the plans made by Lescot, and these, as has recently been
proved, provided for a courtyard quite as spacious as the actual
Cour du Louvre. Consequently, Le Mercier, after rebuilding
the Pavillon de l'Horloge, continued the west wing to the end,
and then built the ground floor of the north wing (that parallel
with the present Rue de Rivoli), to about half its present length.
Le Vau, who succeeded him, finished the north wing, recon-
structed the exterior façade of the south wing, and had laid the
foundations of the east wing (that opposite to Saint-Germain-
l'Auxerrois), when Colbert became superintendent. Unhappily
Colbert condemned the aged Lescot's plan as insignificant,
stopped the works, invited competitors to submit plans for the
east front, and finally, to evade the resulting difficulties, had
recourse to the most famous architect of the day, the Pope's
protégé, the Neapolitan Cavaliere Bernini.

This lordly personage was lent by the Pope, and graciously
undertook the task. He passed through France amidst ovations,
and was received most graciously by the King.
Bernini. He was a good-looking little man, boastful and
self-satisfied, naïve, eloquent, and astute, like many of his race.
He began in Paris by an ostentatious display of his contempt for

everything that was not Italian, and even proposed to send to
Rome for *muratori*, alleging that the Parisian masons did not
understand building. Further, as an architect " he ignored all
details, thought only of making great rooms for banquets and
dramatic performances, and did not trouble his head about
comfort and convenience, and the lodging of the inmates." The
practical Colbert, on the other hand, insisted upon knowing
"where and how the King would be housed, how the service
could be most conveniently performed," and a thousand details
of the same kind, and he overwhelmed the Italian with letters and
memoranda. Their disputes must have been comic to a degree :
" The Cavaliere understood nothing and did not want to understand anything of all these details, considering it unworthy of a
great architect like himself to descend to such minutiæ." " M.
Colbert," he complained, "treats me like a little boy with all his
idle talk about privies and underground conduits." Finally,
one fine day " he brought a plan which he held against his breast,
and addressing M. Colbert, he told him he was convinced that
the angel who presided over the fortunes of France had inspired
him, that he honestly acknowledged that he was incapable of
inventing anything so magnificent, so great, and so happy as the
design which had come into his mind," etc. (it would be amusing
to quote the whole of Perrault's malicious account) ; every one
exclaimed in admiration, and, on October 17, 1665, the King
himself laid the foundation-stone of Bernini's proposed palace
with great pomp. But a few days later the Cavaliere departed
for Italy, loaded with money and honours, on the pretext that
he was afraid of a winter in Paris. And a year afterwards his
plans were laid aside in favour of those of the Sieur Perrault.

The dismal colonnade stuck on to the Louvre by this doctor
was begun in 1667 and finished in 1674. Its pediment is kept
Perrault's up by means of clamps and bars of iron. It had no
Colonnade. windows on the first floor ! One hundred and
seventy-six metres long, it extended beyond the south front,
making it necessary to rebuild the charming façade of Lescot
and Le Vau, which was replaced by a dull wall. As the colonnade
was higher than the north wing, it was further necessary to over-
load this with an additional story, which spoilt its beautiful
proportions. Fortunately Louis XIV's lack of interest in the

Louvre saved the rest of the palace, by stopping short Colbert's embellishments about the year 1672.

Jules Hardouin Mansart (great-nephew of François), who became first architect to the King on the death of Le Vau in 1670, was consequently not called upon to work at **Mansart.** the Louvre ; but he built Versailles. He was the King of building, as was Le Brun of decoration. It was Libéral Bruant who built the Invalides, but Mansart added the graceful, harmonious dome which is perhaps his finest work. His pupil Prétot would never have constructed the Place des Victoires if he had not first constructed the Place Vendôme. France is full of his country-houses : he built Clagny for Mme. de Montespan, and for the King, not only Versailles and Trianon, but Marly. He fixed the character of the Louis XIV style ! Henceforth, no more unexpected details, gay improvisations and caprices, pointed roofs, picturesque alternations of brick and stone ; but simple, grandiose lines ; for roofs, Italian terraces, whose balustrades, decorated with statues, crowned the walls ; around the building, Le Nôtre's gardens, prolonging them agreeably and linking them to Nature ; everything harmoniously arranged ; white statuary and dark groups of trees, marble vases and flower-beds, green bronzes and yellow porphyry, the slender jets of fountains and the calm surface of pools, the regular or *baroque* figures of the ornamental waters ; in general, a complete subordination of parts to the whole ; Mansart's work is an admirable symbol of the classic spirit.

Under Louis XIII and Mazarin painting was a mediocre art. True, Jacques Callot engraved his *Miseries of War*, his *Travelling Gipsies*, his *Beggars*, his *Tortures*, and his **Painting.** *Temptation of St. Anthony*. But the fashionable painter was the rhetorical Simon Vouet. The three brothers Le Nain painted their heavy and joyless peasant scenes (very interesting as documents). The skilful Le Sueur produced a rapid succession of intolerably wearisome canvases (1616–1655). Philippe de Champaigne the Jansenist (1602–1675) painted his austere and glacial portraits with a brush that was always sincere and conscientious, producing excellent works in his portraits of the sisters of Port-Royal. But there was Nicolas Poussin.

THE GREAT AGE

Poussin was born in Normandy of very poor parents in 1593 or 1594, and led a laborious, honest, regular, and happy life.

Poussin. After studying optics, perspective, and anatomy, he succeeded, thanks to the Cavaliere Marini, his patron, in going to Rome, where he settled in 1624. Sixteen years later, when he had become famous, he returned very unwillingly to France at the express order of Louis XIII, who gave him a magnificent reception and appointed him his first painter-in-ordinary. But he returned to his little house on the Pincio as soon as he could (1642), and died there in 1665, two years after his excellent wife, Marie-Anne Dughet. He had come to Rome at the period of the great Italian decadence. Caravaggio, who died in 1609, had sought to bring about a reaction against the conventional idealism of the Carracci, and a return to realism ; he had merely achieved melodrama. The school of the Carracci was therefore triumphant in 1624, and Poussin did not altogether escape the influence of their declamation in colour, but his sincerity, his conscience, and his intelligence saved him from facile painting, as did also his reverence for the antique, which he studied ardently. Poussin felt as a sculptor perhaps no less than as a painter ; when, for instance, he portrays the emotions of his personages, he translates them rather by gestures than by the expression of their somewhat inanimate faces. Intellectually, he thought out his pictures as poems ; he gave them a fable and a moral ; he wanted them to tell a story, to translate sentiments and ideas. To this end, he chose in Nature the phenomena which seemed to him expressive, and thus Nature to him was not merely a model to copy, but a repertory of means of expression : of him it might truly be said that his landscapes are states of the soul. But his ideology is a small matter, since he equals the greatest of those who have made line and colour sing. He has the most appealing sense of values, light, and shade; like Racine or Mansart, he organizes all the parts of his work strongly and poetically, in view of the impression he desires to produce. " My disposition constrains me to seek well-ordered things, avoiding the confusion which is as hostile and repellent to me as is light to darkness," he once wrote. This painter, who spent his life in Rome, is the most French of artists and the most classical of Frenchmen.

THE SEVENTEENTH CENTURY

His art sums up all the painting of his day, and the great Poussin was the initiator of academic art in France. His pictures were greatly admired in the time of Louis XIV, and have never lacked admirers since, though their admiration has been based on very varied, and even contradictory, grounds. The Academy of Painting and Sculpture, encouraged by Colbert, who hoped by its intermediary to regulate the fine arts some day like all the rest, endeavoured to build up a theory of æsthetics from his works (for the artists of the seventeenth century believed in "rules," as did the authors). At one of its meetings Philippe de Champaigne, discoursing upon *Eleazar and Rebecca*, regretted that M. Poussin "had not treated the subject of his picture with all the fidelity of history, since he had suppressed the camels mentioned in the Scriptures "; to which Le Brun replied peremptorily that "M. Poussin . . . had omitted strange objects which might seduce the eye of the spectator, and amuse it by details." It was thus the painters of the day talked of painting. Intellectual and bookish, like Poussin himself, they looked upon objects as means for the expression of sentiments and ideas, arranged Nature in accordance with reason (as Le Nôtre so admirably did in his gardens), remained spell-bound by antiquity, and produced pictures which were " painted bas-reliefs." What they wished to do was merely to make

> Le grande choix du vrai beau, de la belle nature
> Sur les restes exquis de l'ancienne sculpture ;

to translate the state of mind of " the heroes of the picture " by means of appropriate action :

> Par les gestes puisés dans la passion même
> Bien marqués pour parler, appuyés, forts et nets,
> Imitant en vigueur les gestes des muets
> Qui veulent réparer la voix que la nature
> Leur a voulu nier, ainsi qu'à la peinture.

(Never has total insensibility to painting as such been so perfectly revealed as by Molière in these lines.)

But what the academic artists of the seventeenth century lacked to make them equal to their leader was the meditative and poetic soul, the conscience of the profound and exquisite master who wrote one day : " The beautiful girls you saw at

Poussin the initiator of academic Art.

868

THE GREAT AGE

Nîmes cannot, I am sure, have delighted you less than the sight of the beautiful columns of the Maison Carrée, seeing that the latter are only old copies of the former;" and again: "I feel I have done a great deal when I have done a head in a day, provided it produces its true effect."

Le Brun. The decorator Le Brun seems to have been mainly a skilful stage-manager. To reconstruct the costumes and combine the theatrical attitudes of his personages, to direct the work of his assistants, to make, as he talked, sketches for a piece of furniture or a figure, to improvise the decoration of a gallery (the Galerie d'Apollon in the Louvre is his work, save the present ceiling painted by Delacroix)—all this amused him, for he had invention and draughtsmanship, but the laying on of colour wearied him; in the end, he left this tiresome business to his pupils. And he is less admirable in his *Battles of Alexander* than in his portraits.

Portraiture. Indeed, it is in portraiture that the art of the seventeenth century excels, though the portrait-painters tried to generalize, so to speak, and to paint "Man" in the individual —an ideal alien to their art, but characteristic of their age; they painted in the grand style, like Mignard (1610–1695), who succeeded Le Brun as the president of the Academy, and more especially Largillière (1656–1746), or Hyacinthe Rigault (1659–1743).

Claude Lorrain. We must give a place apart to Claude Gellée, called Le Lorrain (1600–1682), who, born in the Vosges, spent his whole life in Italy, and thus hardly belongs to French art. He felt, more deeply than any Italian, the grandeur and poetry of the Roman Campagna, and rendered them in artificial and cunningly concocted landscapes, invariably animated by some mythological or scriptural episode in the taste of the times, and altogether delicious. Anticipating the moderns, Claude Lorrain worshipped and painted sunlight more exquisitely than Turner.

Le Brun apportioned tasks to his sculptors as to his painters, and the former obediently carried out the decoration of Versailles from his designs. All this sculpture is cold, empty, and

369

so impersonal that it is not always easy to tell from an examination what was the portion of each; but it forms an **Decorative Sculpture.** admirable whole, which harmonizes perfectly with the groves and fountains of Le Nôtre, as with the walls of Mansart and the ornament of Le Brun. It further produced very spirited decorative compositions, like the Horses of Marly (now at the entrance to the Champs Elysées), by Guillaume Coustou (1678–1746). Nevertheless, like painting, its chief triumphs were won in portraiture : Coysevox (1640–1720) is as elegant as Girardon (1628–1715) when he models some nymph or allegory in the grand style, but there is no line of such portraits as his bust of Condé or his statue of the Duchess of Burgundy which does not quiver with emotion.

Pierre Puget (1622–1694) was far from being the neglected genius he has been called. Colbert employed him to decorate **Puget.** the galleys ; he then worked for the Court. If he lived an independent life, apart from Le Brun, it was because he had both a passion for his art and a deplorable temper. Like Bernini, with whom he had much in common (though he had less genius), he was lamentably lacking in taste, but he was gifted with an admirable temperament as a sculptor. " I am in my element among great things : I soar when I work at them, and the marble trembles before me, however great it may be."

III

At the close of the sixteenth century the Italians had discovered opera. The new music at once aroused frantic enthu-**Invention of Opera.** siasm among these susceptible people : at the first representation of Monteverde's *Ariadne* the six thousand listeners burst into sobs.

Under Louis XIII (who loved music as passionately as did his son) France knew nothing of dramatic music beyond ballets. **Ballets.** These " masquerades " were danced in costume by lords and ladies, and often by the King himself, in presence of the whole Court : the framework was very loose ; each performer had the words he sang composed to suit his own taste or improvised them himself ; only the orchestra which accompanied was composed of professionals ; typical examples of such performances were the comic ballet of *Les Andouilles* in 1628, and that of *La Prosperité des Armes de France* in 1641. It was Mazarin who revealed Italian opera to the French; he introduced several companies from his native land. But many connoisseurs preferred the traditional ballet to Italian opera, and among them was the Florentine, Jean-Baptiste Lulli (1633–1687).

This former servant of the Grande Mademoiselle was a very diverting person. After finding favour, while he was quite young, with his mistress, who spoke Italian with him, he was received among the King's violins, and in this position succeeded in attracting the notice of Louis XIV, who created the band known as the *little violins*, in order to appoint him its conductor, and then made him superintendent of the King's music. As such, he presented or composed a great number of ballets, for which Benserade generally wrote libretti, and also several ballet-comedies in collaboration with Molière, among them the *Princesse d'Élide* (1664), *L'Amour Médecin* (1665), *M. de Pourceaugnac* (1669), *Le Bourgeois Gentilhomme* (1670). He declared at this time that it would be impossible to execute an opera in French, or " to write an elegant score to French words."

Lulli.

At this period a host of persons took part in the Court ballets: princes, great ladies, citizens, professional singers, musicians, dancers, and the King himself, who always loved to figure, if but before the footlights, as Jupiter or Apollo. But after 1669 Louis ceased definitively to appear in these masquerades, perhaps because he had been impressed by these two lines in *Britannicus*: Nero, said Racine, excelled

> A se donner lui-même en spectacle aux Romains,
> A venir prodiguer sa voix sur un théâtre.

In this same year, on June 28, 1669, a certain Abbé Perrin—an industrious writer of verses for cantatas, and the joint author with the musician Cambert of a *Pastorale*, successfully acted in 1659, which was almost a musical comedy—obtained letters patent granting him the privilege of representing tragedies sung in French. In 1671 *Pomone*, by Cambert and Perrin, the first French

Royal Academy of Music.

opera, was given with immense success. It sufficed to convert Lulli to the new dramatic music; as the two partners could not agree, this astute person bought their charter, got the King to extend its scope, in 1672, and founded the Royal " Academy " (in the Italian sense) of Music.

Thus, in spite of the raillery of Saint-Evrémont, opera became the passion of the day. From 1673 to 1687 Lulli composed, with the help of Quinault, thirteen "lyrical tragedies," ranging from *Cadmus* and *Alceste* to *Armide*, and his Academy drew crowds to it. It displayed beautiful scenery and amazing " machines "; its frequenters listened to languorous and erotic verse sung to delicious music; the opera at this period was a very delightful spectacle. Love is the theme of all Lulli's and Quinault's lyrical tragedies : Love, say verses and music; be not cruel ! . . . In vain Boileau, who thought Quinault insipid, and did not care for music, launched his thunderbolts; neither Mme. de Montespan's royal lover, his Court, nor the Town agreed with M. Despréaux !

Lulli did not only write operas; he composed cantatas, religious songs, notably (according to a dubious tradition) a "God save sort of hymn, *Dieu sauve le Roi*, adopted by the the King." English as *God save the King*. Nor must we forget to mention together with him Lalande, the Master of the King's Chapel, who in conjunction with Molière and La Fontaine wrote the opera *Mélicerte*, in addition to many sacred airs.

IV

There is perhaps a certain analogy between the fate of the Revolutionists after the Revolution and that of the Frondeurs The Decline after the Fronde : both suddenly appeared to of Romantic belong to another age. In 1660 the Grande Literature. Mademoiselle, describing her ideal of life to Mme. de Motteville, still could not conceive of it without heroes and heroines of various kinds. But the Grande Mademoiselle found herself prodigiously old-fashioned at the Court of the youthful King; the dreams and tastes of her generation were no longer those of the day; for the accession of Louis XIV marks an important date in the history of the sentiments. In 1661 Bossuet and Molière had been living in Paris for two years, Boileau was beginning to publish his satires, La Fontaine brought out *Joconde*, his first tale, Racine was about to produce the *Thébaïde*; and with this new generation moral observation and a taste for truth was to triumph over heroic and amorous romanticism. It was the end of a literature designed for women; they never held intellectual sway again until the rise of modern romanticism. Under Louis XIII and the Fronde they had become intoxicated with politics and action, and they had imagined themselves the heroines of Corneille; under Louis XIV they were reduced to occupying themselves with the sentiments natural to their sex, and following the King's example, men asked from them no more than what it required no great heroism to give. Louis XIV was, indeed, if we may say so, by no means feminist. He was certainly fond of women, but his feeling for them was a kind of fascinated contempt, and with the exception of Mme. de Maintenon—who swayed him when he had grown old and pious —there was no woman among those he distinguished to whom he ever looked for guidance. Was it not because of the poor opinion he had of their brains that he forgave the Frondeuses more readily than the Frondeurs? As to the latter, they remained branded, during his reign, with an indelible stain, a stigma no less fatal than that which marked the regicides at the beginning of the nineteenth century. We may cite the history of the unhappy Fargues in the pages of Saint-Simon. The majority of them, though pardoned, were never received into the royal favour again, and they had perforce to stifle all political ambition in their breasts, after the fashion of Cardinal de Retz and the Duc de La Rochefoucauld.

For La Rochefoucauld, too, had plotted furiously under Louis XIII and the Regency, and had dreamt of heroism, of glory, and of lofty sentiments in general. Only he had by no means the temperament of his ideal personage. Contemplative, and so timid that he could never utter a sentence in public, " habitually irresolute," brave indeed, but with the bravery of determination and not that of constitution, we cannot wonder that one of his character should have

La Rochefoucauld.

failed in everything. Seriously wounded at the Porte Saint-Antoine, and recognizing that his cause was lost, he withdrew from politics, sore of heart, and feeling that he had failed in life. "There was always an unknown quantity in all M. de La Roche-foucauld," wrote Retz maliciously. What there was is shown by the *Maximes*. It must indeed have been embarrassing for a Frondeur to read his own heart and that of others so clearly.

When he had retired into private life, La Rochefoucauld no longer tried to be anything but an honest man, in which he succeeded perfectly. The old age of this bitter, delicate, and graceful patrician, always shy and somewhat reserved, but gentle and witty, was brightened by feminine affection, and we know that he inspired in the ironical Mme. de La Fayette an attachment which endured till death. In Mme. de Sablé's salon, which was still a trifle " precious," and in which he was a constant visitor, a favourite amusement was the composition of aphorisms, just as in that of Mademoiselle and elsewhere the pastime was written portraiture, and the subtle Duke took great pleasure in this game ; it was in this way that for the space of five years, in conjunction with the mistress of the house and its *habitués*, he composed, polished, and pointed his *Maximes*, which he decided to print in 1665, when he knew that copies of them were being circulated. Nothing of the sort had ever appeared before ; the first incomplete edition of the *Pensées* was published in 1669, and the *Caractères* not until 1688. The " lively, precise, and delicate " style of the *Maximes* was so much admired that five editions appeared before 1678, and nothing contributed more powerfully to cast ridicule upon the chivalrous ideals of the preceding generation than this disillusioned little book. Let us avoid the pedantry of treating La Rochefoucauld's pessimism as a system of philosophy. The charming author of the *Maximes* was too excellent a man to insist that personal interest and self-love are the springs of *all* our actions ; he only said that they inspired *nearly* all of them ; and no one, I think, will deny that " what we take for virtues are often nothing but a concatenation of varied interests which fortune or our own industry enables us to arrange," nor even that " the love of justice is *very often* merely a lively dread that others may deprive us of what we have."

Among the friends of La Rochefoucauld was a little fair,
plump, exuberant lady called the Marquise de Sévigné. She,
Mme. for her part, had an over-witty cousin, M. de
de Sévigné. Bussy-Rabutin, who, one day when she had
refused to lend him a large sum of money, composed a sketch
of her, which had every reason to be, and even had a superficial appearance of being, unflattering, but in which, nevertheless, the painter finds little to record against his model, save that
she allowed herself to be too easily dazzled by the splendours of
the Court (that she was, in short, a bit of a snob), and that she
" tried to be too amusing " in conversation. What injustice !
This Mme. de Sévigné read Virgil, Tacitus, and Saint Augustine (in Latin), spoke Spanish and Italian, had a smattering of
theology, was as well acquainted with the historians of antiquity
as with the philosophers of her own time, and would have been
capable of holding forth on literary subjects like the most
inexorable of *Précieuses* ; how lucky it was that, knowing all
she did, she should have had that over-merry temperament
reprobated by M. de Bussy ! Let us further add that, being
very practical, she managed her business matters extremely
well, and that when far from the Court she could (as Mlle.
de Scudéry admiringly tells her) " amuse herself in the
country as calmly as if she had been born in the woods."
Had she never written a line we must all have loved this
Mme. de Sévigné.

An orphan at seven years old, the widow at twenty-five of a
roué who had never loved her, she was always so judicious that
she had the best reputation in the world, and all her ardour was
concentrated in her passionate affection for that dry, pedantic
person her daughter. The letters she wrote to this Mme. de
Grignan, who lived at the other end of France, being the wife
of the Lieutenant-General of Provence, form the greater part of
the famous Correspondence.

We must not look to her for profound and original views :
Mme. de Sévigné was no thinker, but a *reporter* of genius ;
she has given us, with incomparable talent, " the chronicles of
the Court, of the Town, of literature and the drama, of the provinces, of the country, of the watering-place, of war, of famous
crimes, of fashion, a familiar chronicle, and personal confi-

dences "; she is "the charming patron-saint of our society journalists " (J. Lemaître).

And now we come to the less charming patron-saint of critics.

Fils d'un père greffier et d'aïeux avocats,

Nicolas Boileau, called Despréaux, was born on November 1, 1636. After a half-hearted trial of theology and law (to please his family), he abandoned all else to devote himself to literature, which was not as yet considered a career. He was a terrible person; from 1660 to 1674 he scarified Chapelain, Scudéry, Quinault, and other successful writers in the name of the young realistic school; after which, having dealt faithfully with those he denounced as bad writers, he proceeded to teach the art of writing well : his *Art poétique*, which appeared in 1674, is the manifesto of the new triumphant Pleiad. He was then thirty-four; thenceforth, as if his pre-destined work had been accomplished, he did very little. Appointed historiographer to the King in 1677 together with Racine, and admitted to the Academy only in 1683, he bought in 1687 the little house at Auteuil in which he was to live for twenty years, perfectly insensible to the beauty of the country, and no doubt quite capable of composing his *Ode sur la Prise de Namur* on some fine spring morning, but enjoying good company, good cheer, and a game of skittles, full of vivacity, a clever mimic, kind-hearted though a trifle avaricious, and on the whole the most honest fellow in the world.

As an artist Boileau had taste, and that tireless patience which makes masterpieces possible, a sense of the picturesque value of words, a most admirable conciseness, the robust syntax which Flaubert lacked, and he shows continually in his poems that he might have been a great prose writer. But he was quite without sensibility ; he could not feel any essential difference between prose and poetry ; to him verse was merely a more distinguished kind of prose, and a few fine but isolated alexandrines which might be quoted prove nothing to the contrary. Then he had no psychological insight (an exceptional case in his days). But he was a keen observer of the superficial aspects of man, and he has given us, in a kind of rhymed and rhythmic prose, social pictures which are slightly conventional, but full of vigour. His gift was purely critical, and it is his glory to have helped La Fontaine, Molière, and Racine, not only to triumph, but to feel confidence in their own strength.

As his system of æsthetics was that of the great French classical writers, it will be well to examine it briefly. In a general way his criticism enjoins a return to realism, and we shall see that Racine's first tragedies seemed almost as crude and outrageous to spectators as did the first " naturalistic " novels of the nineteenth century to the "romantic" public. *Nature*, observed by *reason*, and expressed in the forms of *antiquity*, was the sum of Boileau's teaching.

Boileau's System of Æsthetics.

"Nothing but truth is beautiful, only truth is worthy to be loved," but it is not well to tell the whole truth. There are, indeed, in real life strange, exceptional, and grotesque cases which appear incredible and outrageous to good sense or good taste (which are identical); "the true may sometimes seem incredible ; " such incidents are no fit subjects for art ; "never offer the spectator anything incredible." And there is also in realities a considerable element of vulgarity and triviality, which the artist should ignore. The subject should be " agreeable," just as the language should be seemly ; even in treating the comic the writer should " jest with dignity," and it was a weakness in Molière, for instance, to have written for " the masses," and too often to have " forsaken the refined and agreeable for the absurd." Thus Art is indeed Truth, but selected Truth. Let us seek in real life general and universal traits ; let us paint in the individual Man himself, with his great immutable passions, and not those historical, physical, and moral peculiarities which constitute the sole value of what Louis XIV called Teniers' " apes " and of our modern novels. This is why, when a seventeenth-century writer says of one of his characters that he was " very well made " or " very good-looking," he considers that he has sufficiently distinguished him as an individual, and goes on to show the movements of the human heart in him. Two results followed from this system : in the first place, absolute reliance on considered observation and good sense excludes fancy, pure imagination ; and to make the interpretation of Man in general and of reality only in its

377

universal and objective aspects the sole aim of art is to exclude poetic enthusiasm, which is essentially personal and subjective; on the other hand, the great eternal sentiments do not offer an infinite material, and artists who treat of them are in danger of repeating themselves. This is of no importance; the old themes may be used perpetually; originality will manifest itself sufficiently in the different expression various writers will give to the same subject; the classic author aims at novelty, not in invention, but in expression.

Finally, Boileau prescribes the imitation of antiquity. Antiquity, indeed, teaches us to express Nature, and by means **The Imitation** of its masterpieces, which are the masterpieces **of the** of humanity, it gives us lessons in Art. From **Antique.** another point of view, as antiquity is " noble " (like the East, for it would seem that distance, in space as in time, gives majesty to a theme), antiquity (or the East) should be drawn upon for the right names, costumes, accessories, and scenery. Therefore let us borrow from the ancients lessons of technique on the one hand, and of scenery on the other, but not modes of thought or feeling. The Christian characters of Racine, La Fontaine, Molière, and La Bruyère have absolutely nothing essentially Greek or Roman. And it is necessary to insist upon this, for many have deplored this " imitation of the antique " which is supposed to have distorted French genius; could not our great classic writers, it has been asked, have found in the past of their own nation heroes as splendid as those of Homer, wars as noble as that of Troy, legends more moving than those of mythology? Yes, no doubt; but everything seems to show that under other names and costumes their characters would have been much the same; it is merely a question of clothing.

The principles here laid down were to Boileau the Rules of Art. For Boileau and the classic writers believed that there are one Beauty, one Art, one set of Rules. They could not admit that man's idea of these things may differ according to race, period, and soul. They had no historic sense. They were perfect Cartesians.

The reign of Louis XIV, indeed, witnessed the triumph of Descartes, in spite of Louis XIV. The most religious minds of the day—the Jansenists even—might be, and were, Cartesian.

And yet rationalism was dangerous to Catholicism : when the aged Malebranche, abandoning the distinction his master **Triumph of** had carefully established between the domain of **Descartes.** philosophy and that of religion, insisted that all dogmas should be subjected to the examination of reason, when he boasted of being " a reasonable theologian," he opened up the road which the *philosophers* of the eighteenth century were to follow to the end. But the contemporaries of Louis XIV (with the exception of Bossuet) did not foresee this danger. Only the Jesuits opposed Descartes; and this, not because they thought his rationalism dangerous to the Church, but because their enemies, the Oratorians and Jansenists, supported him. At their instigation the Courts of Rome and Versailles forbade the propagation of the new theories. And, as might have been expected, these interdicts were useless, for Cartesianism was the fashion. Society crowded to lectures on metaphysics (of which, indeed, it understood nothing, but this was of little moment) ; great ladies were to be found in the humble cell of the insignificant Malebranche ; the Academy of Sciences was Cartesian ; in 1686 Fontenelle published his *Entretiens sur la pluralité des Mondes.* In the end the old Aristotelian systems were discredited even among babes; at the bare phrase: "Nature abhors a vacuum," schoolboys began to laugh. The new theories had to be tolerated.

Cartesianism and the doctrine of Boileau have much in common. Both postulate the knowledge of " man " in general, take their stand on pure reason, and exclude poetic enthusiasm, erudition, and history. But Cartesianism absolutely confounds art and mathematics, and, as M. Lanson has shown, it could only have evolved " a scientific literature, without æsthetic character, reducing expression to the algebraic notation, so to speak, of the idea." The contribution of the classical doctrine to Cartesianism was a principle which modifies it considerably : that of the imitation of the ancients. Our great writers admired and desired absolute truth, but they admired and desired antique art no less warmly. In them the influence of Descartes and that of Greek and Roman æsthetics met and amalgamated so perfectly that on the whole their doctrine ended by differing very notably from Cartesianism. This was clearly demonstrated by the quarrel touching Ancients and Moderns, which was, in fact, that of the Classicists and the pure Cartesians.

It had long been smouldering, but it burst into flames at last on January 27, 1687, at a meeting of the Academy, and was **Ancients v.** prolonged for nearly ten years. Fontenelle, in his **Moderns.** *Digression sur les Anciens et les Modernes* (1688), and Perrault, in his *Parallèle des Anciens et des Modernes* (1688 *et seq.*), argued approximately as follows : It does not appear that Nature creates fewer men of genius now than formerly ; now humanity has progressed since the days of antiquity ; hence it is reasonable to conclude that the great men of modern times, who enjoy the results of this progress, should produce works superior to those of the great men of antiquity. As we see, literature was for them a mere product of reason, not essentially different from science, and susceptible of increasing perfection. This was the pure Cartesian theory : Malebranche necessarily supported the Moderns. But the great artists of the period, Racine, La Fontaine, and La Bruyère, whose sense of beauty was offended thereby, defended the Ancients. As to Boileau, without going to the root of the matter, he contented himself at first by launching a series of somewhat heavy and brutal epigrams against Perrault and his friends, which did not increase his reputation either for wit or politeness ; not until 1694 did he publish his *Réflexions sur Longin.* . . . In reality he found it very difficult to maintain the theory of the complete inferiority of his great contemporaries—notably Racine—to the Ancients. When he had been reconciled to Perrault he admitted with a certain relief that the Moderns had surpassed the Ancients in some respects.

Jean-Baptiste Poquelin (in theatrical circles Molière) had already made a name as an author and actor in the provinces **Molière.** when he made his first appearance before the King at the Louvre, on October 24, 1658, in the tragedy of *Nicodème*, in which he failed to please, and in a farce written by himself. In this he had such a brilliant success that the King allotted him the theatre of the Petit-Bourbon (on the site now occupied by the Colonnade of the Louvre), and later, in 1661; that which Richelieu had built in the Palais-Royal. It was here that Molière for thirteen years (from 1659 to 1673) presented and acted in twenty-five plays of his own composition, and died in harness.

At the time of his first great success (*L'École des Femmes*, December, 1662) the theatrical quarrel which absorbed his contemporaries and those of Racine was at its height. His triumph marked him out for attack by the sanctimonious of all persuasions (but rather the Brethren of the Holy Sacrament and the Jansenists than the Jesuits), who were endeavouring to secure the suppression of dramatic performances, and they at once began a campaign against him which lasted all his life.

Supported by Boileau, he was also protected by the King. Louis XIV was at that time ill-disposed towards the devout, who disapproved of his " disorders "—in short, bored him to death—and on May 12, 1664, he went so far as to sanction the performance at Versailles of a comedy which Molière had composed as a retort to the pious adversaries who had dragged him through the mud. It was called *Tartuffe*. However, the devout raised such a clamour at this assault that the young King yielded, and forbade the representation of the piece. The Prince de Conti, lately notorious for his misconduct and atheism, a great lover of the theatre, and the protector of Molière, whose schoolfellow he had been, but converted about 1655–1656, and finally, in 1657, a member of the Cabale des Dévots, was one of those who were most zealous in protesting against *Tartuffe* and against the author he had formerly encouraged. Molière had him in his mind when he drew the hypocritical hero of his romantic drama *Don Juan* (February, 1665).

Meanwhile the battle raged round *Tartuffe*, the representation of which was not finally authorized till 1669, after a mass of petitions, libels, and passionate intrigues for and against. Each of Molière's plays was attacked in the same fashion. During the dispute concerning *Tartuffe* he brought out *Le Misanthrope* (in 1666) and *Amphitryon* and *L'Avare* (in 1668). In 1669, after his victory, he produced *Monsieur de Pourceaugnac*, which enabled the Court nobility to laugh once more at the provincial nobility, and the Rabelaisian lyricism of which delighted the Court ladies and the King at Chambord;

in 1670 the *Amants magnifiques*, perhaps an allusion to the story of Lauzun and the Grande Mademoiselle, and the *Bourgeois Gentilhomme*, where he ridiculed the manuals of etiquette which differed very little from the lessons given to M. Jourdain by his masters, and also those *Turqueries* which the solemn reception of the envoy of the Grand Signor on November 1, 1669, had made fashionable. In 1671 came the ballet-tragedy of *Psyché*, produced in collaboration with Lulli, Quinault, and Corneille, who was deeply attached to Molière's wife, Armande Béjart ; then *Les Fourberies de Scapin* and *La Comtesse d'Es carbagnas*. *Les Femmes Savantes* was played without much success in March, 1672 ; the unfortunate Abbé Cotin gained a reputation from this piece which he was far from deserving. Molière's last work was *Le Malade Imaginaire*. It was at the close of the fourth representation of this immortal comedy, on Friday, February 17, 1673, in the Rue de Richelieu about ten o'clock in the evening, that he died. By reason of his profession he was denied the obsequies of an honourable citizen ; he was buried shamefully at night, on February 21.

With the exception of La Fontaine, the great writers of the age of Louis XIV praised him with considerable reservations ; this was because in those days no one dreamed that comedy could have the same value as tragedy, and a writer who makes us laugh as much merit as one who makes us weep ; and then Molière was reprobated for his commonness, his farces, his familiar style, and, lastly, his profession. To-day little remains to be said concerning his genius, the most popular, the most universally known in French literature, and there is no need to break a lance with Edmond Schérer, who accused the author of *Le Bourgeois Gentilhomme* of writing badly.

Jean de La Fontaine, the son of a modest finance official (1621–1695), performed very negligently the duties of the little post of master of rivers and forests at Château-
La Fontaine. Thierry, where he had succeeded his father, deserted his wife and son, dissipated his small patrimony, and lived a very irregular life in Paris as the dependent of Fouquet, the Vendômes, Mme. de La Sablière, Mme. de Bouillon, M. d'Hervaȑt, and others. All this was not very edifying ! But

he did it all so gracefully! For if this ingenuous roué knew nothing of morality, at least, like the Milanese dear to Stendhal, he was governed by his inclinations and not by self-interest, and this entire abandonment of the reason and will to the impulses of the heart, this sentimental egotism of La Fontaine's, is one of the most sympathetic of vices. Jean was absent-minded enough to fall into a well like the astrologer of whom he sang, because he remarked only what touched him. Out of pure voluptuousness he loved faithfully and well those whom he loved. He gave way to his enthusiasms with an adorable spontaneity. When he opened a Bible he was all ardour, he wanted to enter a monastery at once. After hearing an ode by Malherbe he set to work incontinently to write poetry. One day he discovered Spinoza ; he at once began to run about crying : "Baruch! Do you know this Baruch ? You must read Baruch." His friend Canon Maucroix revealed the ancients to him : he devoured them all—Homer, Virgil, Terence, and, after these, Voiture, Rabelais, Marot, and even the mediæval writers, which was astonishing in his times.

> J'aime le jeu, l'amour, les livres, la musique,
> La ville et la campagne, enfin tout ; il n'est rien
> Qui ne me soit souverain bien,
> Jusqu'aux sombres plaisirs d'un cœur mélancolique.

Being a year older than Molière, fifteen years older than Boileau, and almost nineteen older than Racine, "Polyphile" was the eldest of the four friends. But he commenced author only at the age of thirty-three, with a translation of Terence ; and the three collections of his *Fables* were published respectively when he was forty-seven, fifty-seven, and seventy-one years old, for he wrote with extraordinary labour. Thus the art of the *bonhomme* is conscientious and mature in the extreme ; his work reveals a continuous progress ; the *Contes* are no more than a miracle of style, the perfectly conventional personages of which bear the same relation to the more vital characters of the *Fables* as do the personages of Italian comedy to those of Molière's comedy ; and the licentious poet of the *Contes* must have felt the influence of Boileau before creating his "ample comedy with its hundred different acts." So that the evolution of La Fontaine under the action of classical realism demonstrates the benefits of the discipline of the Great Age, and is an example of the perfection to which it brought French genius.

A few well-worn words, barely reinforced by very ordinary adjectives, the whole in the simplest order, but arranged by La Fontaine—and we have the most picturesque painting, the most touching music. All art seems coarse, almost unseemly, so to speak, beside his, and only minds alien to our race, such as Rousseau and Lamartine, have been capable of misunderstanding and outraging the beauty of the truest and most exquisite verse a French ear has ever been privileged to hear.

In 1652, after the failure of *Pertharite*, the great Corneille, deeply offended, retired to sulk in his tent ; his wrath lasted for **Thomas** seven years, during which he kept silence. His **Corneille and** brother Thomas and Quinault took his place **Quinault.** successfully. Both were skilful manipulators of the romantic sentiment and superhuman gallantry which were in vogue ; their characters refine upon heroism and work up to a given point by a series of dramatic incidents arranged with much art and situations of the most unusual and unprecedented kind. Moreover, in the midst of political discussions, conspiracies, and murders, love fills an important place in their tragedies, a polite and languid love, which Quinault more especially excelled in singing in liquid verse that delighted the young King and his Court for a while. When Corneille returned to the theatre in 1659 with his *Œdipe*, he tried to adapt himself to the taste of the new generation, and thenceforth his supermen were clothed *à la Quinault*. Compared with these dandies of the sublime, Racine's characters seemed to many persons the creations of an ignoble and cynical realism.

On becoming his own master at the age of twenty-two (he was an orphan) Jean Racine formed a close friendship with **Racine.** La Fontaine, Furetière, Boileau, and, above all, Molière, his senior by eighteen years, already famous, and the manager of a theatre which produced the young man's first two pieces—*La Thébaïde ou Les Frères ennemis* (1664) and *Alexandre le Grand* (1665). He was then a handsome fellow of twenty-five, passionate, enthusiastic, susceptible, and very much a man of letters. His success turned his head. He withdrew his *Alexandre* abruptly from Molière, on the pretext that it had been badly acted, and took it to the Hôtel de Bourgogne. Then, thinking that a phrase of Nicole's concerning dramatic authors was aimed at him—the quarrel of the drama was then at its height—he published a witty and cruel epistle attacking his former masters, who were in despair at the impious calling their child had adopted. Only Boileau's intervention prevented him from following this up by a second, though later he confessed that he would gladly have atoned for his ingratitude by twelve or fifteen years of his life.

After the success of *Andromaque* (1667)—comparable, says Perrault, to that of the *Cid*—and *Les Plaideurs* (1669), many people agreed that no doubt this young Racine showed a certain talent in the treatment of love, but that he was incapable of composing a great political Roman drama in the manner of Corneille : *Britannicus* was written to show them they were wrong. Then in 1670 he triumphed again with *Bérénice*, but his enemies were not disarmed. When *Bajazet* appeared (1672) they objected that it was not sufficiently Turkish. *Mithridate*, it is true, had a success. But *Iphigénie* (1674) was met by the *Iphigénie* of Leclerc and Coras, and *Phèdre* (1677) by the puerile *Phèdre et Hippolyte* of Pradon, which was acclaimed by a cabal.

What was the cause of all these violent attacks upon Racine ? His enemies accused him of degrading tragedy. Moreover, to his contemporaries he was by no means the " noble, harmonious Racine," and they were far from recognizing in him that " inimitable elegance " · praised by Marivaux. They reprobated what they considered the brutal and even coarse realism of his works. The Corneilles and Quinault had accustomed them to the idea that tragedy should evoke admiration ; and here was this Racine appealing only to pity ! In the place of heroes of superhuman greatness of soul, he represented persons who were exceptional only in the violence of their passions, and gave them the sentiments natural to men and women in the terrible moral crises he imagined, caring nothing whether these sentiments were " lofty " or not. Nor did it seem to him necessary that there should be blood and murders in his plays, or politico-historical speeches, or even any intrigue at all sometimes. And love—not the intellectual and platonic love (desire for per-

Racine's "Realism."

fection) nor the romantic and gallant love of Quinault—but the love-frenzy, " Venus tout entière à sa proie attachée," seemed to him a subject worthy of tragedy. Thus in his hands tragedy became merely a picture of the play of common passions in the state of paroxysm, among persons who differed from the generality of mankind only by their exalted station. To many his Pyrrhus seemed a ruffian, his Nero a monster of iniquity, Phèdre a monomaniac, the feverish Hermione a creature half distraught. What could those critics who had found fault with Chimène's lack of virtue have thought of this strange young girl ? And what must they have said when they read, in the preface to *Phèdre*, this delicious detail : " I thought it necessary to give Hippolyte a certain weakness which would make him somewhat guilty towards his father " ? Further, Racine's style seemed to them here and there outrageously familiar, and in general wanting in elevation. This was why the partisans of Corneille could not endure the popularity of the author of *Andromaque*. And they abhorred it also because it made them conscious that their modes of thought and feeling were cruelly out of date, and that they themselves were all elderly gentlemen and mature ladies.

Racine's early Jansenist education had left a profound impression on his mind. Arnauld admired *Phèdre*, the heroine of **Racine's** which, powerless in spite of all her efforts to con-**Jansenism.** quer the passion which consumes and damns her, has been called " a Christian to whom grace was denied." And *Phèdre* was therefore perhaps " the first stage in Racine's conversion " (J. Lemaître), for at the age of thirty-seven Racine suddenly became converted. He conceived a horror of his works, which he imagined to be corrupting and diabolical, burned all his sketches and plans, and then, after thinking for a time of embracing a religious life, married (by way of penance, as his son Louis tells us), a middle-class wife without beauty by whom he had two sons and five daughters, charming and ardent souls, to the rearing of whom in the fear of the Lord he henceforth devoted all his powers.

The King loved him and he loved the King with all his heart. In 1689, at the request of Mme. de Maintenon who wished to combine " amusement with instruction " for her young girls, he consented to write *Esther* for the young ladies of Saint-Cyr, and *Esther* was played six times before the whole Court with great magnificence. But *Athalie* (1691) was given only in the Marquise's bedroom, and without costumes ; in spite of the care taken to make the young actresses repeat the *Veni Creator* before their appearance on the stage, it seems that the applause of the courtiers inspired worldly thoughts in them. Moreover, the Jansenist Racine began to lose favour. He died on April 21, 1699, cut to the heart by the coldness with which the King treated him.

To include Bossuet—" the last of the Fathers of the Church " (La Bruyère)—among men of letters would be an impertinence.

Bossuet. He was the great voice by which the Catholic, Apostolic, and Roman religion expressed itself in seventeenth-century France in all its strength, its harmony, and its cohesion. All his works were occasional, and composed, not for art, but for action. There is no philosophy to be derived from the immense sum of his work, but integral Catholicism (save for certain opinions peculiar to Gallicanism). His very biography is merged in that of the Church. If this great athlete of the faith is one of the two or three pre-eminent masters of French prose, he became so by the force of native genius, and not through any desire for profane glory.

At the age of thirty-two, in 1659, he was already famous for his eloquence when he came to Paris, where he preached for ten years, in the town and at Court, sermons of all kinds, and his first funeral orations, notably those on Anne of Austria (1667, not preserved), Henriette of France (1669), and Henriette of England, Duchess of Orleans (1670). We do not possess Bossuet's sermons as they were delivered to his contemporaries. He wrote them all beforehand ; but in the pulpit his eloquence carried him away, and the recollection of what he had written merely served to co-ordinate the movement of his ideas.

In 1670 Bossuet, then Bishop of Condom, was appointed tutor to the Dauphin, and he undertook to compose with his own hand all the works he considered necessary for the instruction of the royal child, among others the *Traité de la connaissance de Dieu et de soi-même* ; *La Politique tirée de l'Écriture Sainte*, in which he explained that kings are absolute rulers, answerable for their conduct only to God ; and the *Discours sur l'Histoire universelle*, which is a summary of general history, followed by a demonstration of the Divine Providence working throughout the ages.

As a recompense for the ten years of his life he had devoted to the education of the Dauphin, Bossuet received in 1681 the bishopric of Meaux, and thenceforth, though only a bishop, he was the real head of the Church in France. In 1688 he published his *Histoire des variations de l'Église protestante*, the principal effort of the war he waged throughout his life against the Reformation. From 1695 to 1699 he wrote some thirty works directed against Quietism and Fénelon. In 1702 he published the *Défense de la Tradition et des Saints-Pères* in refutation of the rationalistic Oratorian, Richard Simon. Nor must we omit his long correspondence with Leibnitz, in giving a slight idea of his leading works. He died on April 12, 1704.

Official speeches, philosophical manuals for the use of a child, theological polemics, historical treatises long out of date, occasional writings—in all our literature there is nothing less " actual " or more admirable than these works of vigour and warfare in which all the genius of Catholicism expresses itself with all the art of antiquity. Nourished on the Latin writers and Balzac, Bossuet wrote in the " Louis XIII style," which was that of the period when he was formed, but he gives it the contemporary clarity of Boileau. It is in his works that the French language takes on its fullest sonority, its noblest movement, its most succulent, most vital form. And even in the simplest portions of his works, where he is concerned only to say what he has to say without any subtlety, everything lives and palpitates, transfigured by an imagination akin to that of Chateaubriand.

As an orator he was never so popular in his day as the Jesuit Bourdaloue (1632–1704). The latter preached from memory, with half-closed eyes and in a kind of chant, **Bourdaloue.** almost without gesture, solid, logical, and closely reasoned sermons, very accurate in their psychology, which aimed at convincing rather than at moving a congregation addicted to " reason." His success was amazing. We know with what enthusiasm Mme. de Sévigné speaks of Père Bourdaloue : " He always strikes like a deaf man," she wrote one day, "uttering truths at full speed. . . . Look out for yourselves ! he always goes straight ahead."

Fénelon, on the other hand, did not admire him : to his mind these demonstrations learnt by heart were not eloquence ;
Fénelon. his own sermons were extempore, and none of them have survived, but we may form some idea of their subtlety and emotion from the letters of François de Salignac de La Mothe-Fénelon (1651–1715). His theological writings are innumerable, and he wrote, in addition to the *Fables*, the *Dialogues des Morts* and *Télémaque*, composed for the instruction of the Duke of Burgundy, the *Traité de l'Éducation des Filles*, which set forth principles very novel in 1687, and the *Lettre sur les Occupations de l'Académie*, the charming lecture of a delightful old man. But it is in his letters, and in works written without literary preoccupations, and directly expressing his nature, that he is most enjoyable, as, for instance, in his *Manuel de Piété*—" a delicious book, worthy to be placed beside the *Imitation* " (J. Lemaître). Fénelon's feminine and emotional mind hardly belongs to the age of Louis XIV. His ideas of education are those of Jean-Jacques ; in politics he grants more than was demanded by the States-General of 1789 ; his religion, which asks everything from the heart and almost nothing from reason, differs as much from that of Bossuet as his criticism, subjective and careless of rules, differs from that of Boileau. Fénelon was the precursor of Rousseau and his progeny, as La Bruyère was the precursor of our modern men of letters.

Jean de La Bruyère (1645–1696), a citizen of Paris, at the age of thirty-eight bought the office of treasurer-general of the
La Bruyère. bureau of finance in the district of Caen, which did not prevent him from living in Paris, and this is about all we know of the first forty years of his life. In 1684 he was appointed tutor to the grandson of the Great Condé. Neither comely of face nor nimble of wit, he was entirely

deficient in worldly graces, and did not shine in the Court of the Condés ; why was it, then, that when, at the end of twenty-eight months, his pupil's education was pronounced finished, he asked and obtained permission to remain in it ? We can guess, and must deplore the reason : the great La Bruyère suffered because of his lack of charm and seduction ; he would have given all his intelligence to be one of those agreeable lordlings who fascinated the ladies of his circle. Accordingly he jested, alas ! (see his letter to Pontchartrain of July 16, 1695) ; then " he would suddenly set about dancing and singing very unpleasantly." Boileau wrote to Racine : " He is a very excellent man, who would lack nothing if Nature had made him as agreeable as he would like to be." And Valincourt tells us : "He was a good creature at bottom, but the dread of seeming pedantic had driven him to an opposite extreme of absurdity impossible to describe."

In March, 1688, after the publication of his *Caractères*, La Bruyère became famous. The first three editions appeared in a year ; six others followed, gradually expanded, corrected, and improved with touching care. Elected to the Academy in 1693, not without difficulty, he made (whether deliberately or not) an unfortunate speech ; and it was after this incident that it became customary to submit the speeches of newly elected members to a commission charged to make sure that they contained nothing offensive. Three years later he died of apoplexy, leaving an unfinished series of *Dialogues sur le Quiétisme*, which a certain Abbé Du Pin published in 1698 after having recast them.

Vauvenargues has said : " La Bruyère was a great painter, and not perhaps a great philosopher ; the Duc de La Rochefoucauld was a philosopher and no painter " It is true ; and La Bruyère himself claimed to be an artist rather than a thinker. (" All has been said during the seven thousand years that there have been men and that they have thought.") La Rochefoucauld had proposed to explain the human heart in general—the Cartesian Man ; the author of the *Caractères* wished to compose a gallery of sketches from Nature and studies of individuals. It was a very novel essay : hitherto all that had been attempted in the name of portraiture had been psychological descriptions ;

in those he painted he was less concerned to expound the sentiments themselves than to note the physical movements by
which the individual reveals them. It was because of this, no
doubt, that the *Caractères* raised an outcry, and passed for a
book with a key without being more or less so than our contemporary novels. In this sense La Bruyère was the first of the
Moderns.

He was also a modern in virtue of his style. The short
phrase had certainly been used by others before him (*see* Sévigné,
Racine in the *Abrégé*, Fontenelle, etc.); but this was a familiar,
unpretentious style, which proposed only to express a thought
directly; the ceremonious style was periodic prose. Now La
Bruyère used this prose also (for his book is an epitome of all
forms of French); but his originality lay herein, that he made
the short phrase " an artistic style," so to speak, which proposed
above all to paint. He preferred the picturesque and precise
epithet to the vague, sonorous moral epithet as used by Bossuet ;
and yet he wrought his phrases in a rhythm more subtle than that
of verse. On the whole, he was perhaps the first French writer
who looked upon prose as an art equal to that of poetry, and
hence Jean de La Bruyère may be considered the first of our
" Stylists."

As a master of style he had no equal among his contemporaries. As a portrait-painter he is not superior to Saint-
Saint-Simon. Simon (1675–1755). After waiting for fifteen
years, consumed by hatred and impatience, for
the death of the King and the end of " the reign of the vile
middle class," this little surly dog—puny, yellow, and irritable
—at last came into power with the Regent, who was his friend ;
but after a few years, having made himself intolerable to
every one, he was obliged to retire. Then, in the quiet of his
town house or his country estates, where he lived for another
twenty-two years, he assuaged his passion by reviewing his
past life, and describing the scenes which still blazed before
his eyes as vividly as when he lived them, trembling with
pleasure or with rage. And out of the struggle of this ignoramus
of genius, obsessed with the desire of giving utterance to his
visions, with the language he had neither the art nor the

patience to woo, with words which escape him, which he seizes nervously, which he compels, and from which he wins unrivalled accents, arose the incorrect, the palpitating, the admirable *Memoirs* of Saint-Simon.

V

By its moderation, its clarity, and its perfection, our happily named classic literature was pre-eminently fitted to become universal, and did, in fact, become so, as is well known. Our language, our manners, and our authors conquered Europe, and from the end of the seventeenth century our country exercised an intellectual and moral influence greater than that exercised by any country since the days of antiquity. It was in the reign of Louis XIV that the French acquired the true sense of their national superiority which they have retained to the present day. By his very faults, his lofty pride, this king was an admirable inspirer of the French spirit.

French classical Literature

He demanded exhausting material efforts of his kingdom, and caused it sufferings, some of which were vain and useless. What would have happened if he had listened to Colbert ? Colbert's conception of the glory of a sovereign differed essentially from that of Louis XIV : he dreamed of an austere, equitable, economical king, the director of a commercial State on the pattern of Venice or Holland, encouraging art and letters, work and workers. But it is hardly just to judge kings by comparing what they accomplished with what their ministers dreamed of doing, or to heap opprobrium on Louis XIV while glorifying Colbert, since there is nothing at all to prove that the kingdom would have been better off under Colbertism. Moreover, if the Duke of Burgundy had not been cut off at the age of thirty, the conqueror Louis XIV would have been succeeded by a peaceful sovereign, an intelligent, virtuous, liberal, and reforming prince, with Fénelon as his adviser. And Fénelon had a programme much finer even than Colbert's—on paper. To what heights might not the monarchy have risen under these conditions ! But we must turn away from the land of dreams.

392

THE GREAT AGE

In 1715 France was very weary, but a few years of repose were to enable her to arise more lively and vigorous than ever. Materially greater, she was enriched—through the successive efforts of Louis XIII and Richelieu, Mazarin and Louis XIV—by the acquisition of Roussillon, Franche-Comté, Alsace, Flanders and Artois, provided with a vast colonial domain, and protected by a solid and stately girdle of fortresses. Intellectually, she shed her radiance throughout the world. The age in which our national patrimony was enriched by so many provinces, by so much glory, and so much beauty is justly known as The Great Age.

WORKS TO CONSULT: See the bibliography of Chapter V. Bonaffé, *Les Collectionneurs de l'ancienne France* (1873); Choisy, *Histoire de l'architecture* (n.d.); P. Desjardins, *Poussin* (n.d.); Jouin, *Le Brun et les arts sous Louis XIV* (1889); Maurice Donnay, *Cours sur Molière*, in the *Revue hebdomadaire*, 1911; A. Lefranc, *Cours sur Molière*, in the *Revue des Cours et Conférences*, 1906–1910; J. Lemaître, *Jean Racine* (1908); *Fénelon* (1910), etc.; Masson-Forestier, *Racine ignoré* (1911), to be corrected by the articles of A. Halleys, in the *Journal des Débats*, December, 1910, January, 1911; Lavoix, *Histoire de la Musique* (n.d.); S. Reinach, *Apollo* (1907); R. Rolland, *Histoire de l'Opéra en Europe*.

INDEX

ABBAYE DES CHAMPS, 280, 282
Abbeville, cloth factory at, 336
Académie Française, origin of, 125
Académie des Inscriptions, 360
Académie des Sciences, 360
Academy, Dictionary of the, 125–7
Academy of Architecture, 361
Academy of Fine Arts, 361
Academy in Rome, French, 361
Acadia, ceded to England, 309, 339
Agnès de Sainte Thècle, Mère, 282
Aides (tax), 331–2
Aignan, Abbé, 318
Aix, Parliament of, 88
Aix-la-Chapelle, 223
Alais, captured by Louis XIII, 55
Alais, Peace of, 56
d'Albert, Charles, 18; *see also* Luynes
Albi, Bishop of, 100
d'Albret, Jeanne, 24
d'Albret, Maréchale, 194
Alençon, lace-making at, 336
Alexander VII, Pope, 219, 220, 273, 276, 280
Algeria, 98
Algiers bombarded, 237
Allerheim, taken by Turenne, 140, 141
Almanza, Battle of, 303
Alsace, 63, 69, 70, 75, 76; ceded to France, 149; invaded, 231, 308, 393
Altkirchen, skirmish at, 231
Altranstadt, Peace of, 304
Amadeo II of Savoy, 245
Ambassadors, quarrel of the, 219
America, 63
Amiens, 44, 45, 83; factories at, 355
Amsterdam, 210, 226, 228; saved by inundation, 228
Anarchy during Fronde, 165
Ancients *versus* Moderns, 380
d'Ancre, Concini as Marquis, 4; his autocratic power, 16, 17; deprived of governorship, 14; *see also* Concini
Angélique, Mère, *see* Arnauld, Jacqueline
d'Angennes, Julie, *see* Rambouillet, Mlle. de
Angers, Peace of, 22

Angoulême, Treaty of, 22, 27
Anjou, 343
d'Anjou, Duc, birth of, 193; becomes King of Spain, 288, 289; his claims to French throne maintained, 290; *see also* Philip V of Spain
Anne of Austria, marries Louis XIII, 7; relations with Richelieu, 34; her faction at Court, 43, 44; hostility of Queen-Mother to, 43, 45; relations with Buckingham, 45; complicity in intrigues, 48; reconciled to her husband, 57; and Marie d'Hautefort, 77; secret correspondence with Spain, 80–82; appointed Regent, 87; *quoted*, 115; her appearance and character, 137, 138; as Regent, 136–141; fury with the Frondeurs, 156; as mother, 172, 173, 259
Anne of England, 291, 307, 310
Antilles, the, 339
d'Antin, Duc, *quoted*, 240
Appartement, the, 205, 240
d'Argenson, Lieut. of Police, 282
Army under Louis XIII, 71–74; constitution of the, 215, 218
Arnauld, Antoine, 128, 129, 212, 268, 269; flees to Flanders, 279; supported by the Pope, 280, 286
Arnauld (d'Andilly), 58, 269
Arnauld, Henri, 269, 272
Arnauld, Jacqueline, 267
Arnoux, Père, 26
Arras, 142, 311
d'Artagnan, Captain of Musketeers, 328
Artillery Corps created, 217
Artois, ceded to France, 169; captures in, 76, 393
Arts, the Fine, 360; Court influence on the, 361–3
Astrée, 112, 113
d'Aubigné, Agrippa, 194
d'Aubigné, Comte, 243
d'Aubigné, Françoise, *see* Maintenon and Scarron
Aubuisson, factory at, 336
d'Auchy, Mme., 119

INDEX

Audiger, **349, 350**
Audran, 362
Augsburg, League of, **237, 239**
Augustine, St., 266
Augustinus, the, 269, 270
d'Aumont, Duc, 203
Aurillac, lace-making at, 336
Austria, 63 ; House of, 62, 64, 71, 77, 96 ;
  see also Hapsburg
Auvergne, 343, 356
d'Avenel, *quoted*, 105, 201
Avignon, 238 ; seized, 275

BADEN, MARGRAVE OF, 295, 296
Balagny, 108
Ballets, 370
Baltic Provinces, 68
Balzac, J. L. Guez de, 124, 388
Barbezieux, War Minister, 292, 321
Barbin, Claude, 15, 31
Barcelona, taken by the English, 303, 310
Barcelonnette, 312
Barine, Arvède, *quoted*, 195, 248
Barradas, 18, 94
Barreaux, *see* Vallée
" Barrier " fortresses, 298, 307, 312
Bart, Jean, 257
Bassompierre, 13, 58, 87, 200
Bastille, treasure in the, 7 ; prisoners in
  the, 74, 81, 84, 87
Bavaria, Duke of, becomes Elector
  Palatine, 39
Bavaria, Elector of, 292, 295, 296
Bavaria, Electoral Prince of, 286, 287, 312
Bavaria, Prince Clement of, 238
Bayeux, revolt in, 97
Béarn, Church property in, 24
Beauce, 356
Beaufort, Duc de, 136 ; imprisoned at
  Vincennes, 142, 160, 163 ; exiled, 166
Beaupuis, Wallon de (Jansenist), 267
Beauvilliers, Duc de, 203, 244, 257, 288,
  307, 321, 322, 324
Béjart, Armande, 382
Belfort, 231
Bellegarde, M. de, 200
Belle-Isle, 328
Benoist, Antoine, his bust of Louis XIV,
  313
Benserade, 124, 182, 327, 371
Berlepsch, Baroness von, 288
Bernard, Samuel, 347
Bernhard of Weimar, 75, 145
Bernini, 364, 365, 370
Berry, 343, 356
Berry, Duc de, birth, 193 ; death, 315,
  316
Berry, Duchesse de, 316
Bérulle, 23, 102

Berwick, Duke of, **239, 292, 302** ; his
  victory at Almanza, 303
Besançon, 230
Besnier, Maurice, 345 *note*
Beuvron, 109
Bidassoa (river), 168
Bingen destroyed, 252
Bishoprics, the Three, ceded to France,
  149, 322
Blancmesnil (Frondeur), 155, 157
Bleneau, 164
Blenheim (Blindheim), Battle of, 297
Blindheim, *see* Blenheim
Blois, 83 ; Castle of, 19, 21, 364
Blois, Mlle. de, 192, 248, 324 ; marriage
  of, 334
Bohemia, 63
Boileau, 183 ; *quoted*, 227, 363, 372, 373,
  376-8 ; his system of æsthetics, 377,
  379, 381
Boisrobert, 102, 125, 327
Boisselau, 250
Bombay, 221
Bombault, 327
Bordeaux, a centre of the Fronde, 166 ;
  Parliament of, 88, 92
Bosse, Abraham, 72
Bossuet, 116 ; *quoted*, 143-4 ; procures
  dismissal of Mme. de Montespan, 189 ;
  tutor to the Grand Dauphin, 193 ;
  attitude to Huguenots, 262, 264 ;
  attitude to Mme. Guyon, 277, 278 ;
  controversy with Fénelon, 278, 373 ;
  funeral orations of, 387, 388, 391
Bouchain, ceded to France, 234, 311
Bouchavannes, Mme. de, 119
Boufflers, Maréchal de, 239, 258, 292 ;
  occupies the " Barrier " fortresses, 298 ;
  defends Lille, 306 ; a volunteer under
  Villars, 308 ; at Malplaquet, 309
Bouillé, President de, 307
Bouillon, Duc de, 4, 7 ; leagued with
  Condé, 8, 83, 85, 105, 203
Bouillon, Duchesse de, 150, 160, 170
Bourbons, the, 288, 289
Bourdaloue, *quoted*, 240, 279, 288, 289
Bourgogne, Duc de, birth of, 193 ;
  education of, 205 ; becomes Dauphin,
  244-5 ; character, 244-7 ; Fénelon on
  character of, 244 ; marriage of, 245 ;
  upholds Fénelon, 278-9 ; commands
  army in Low Countries, 304-6 ; death
  of, 315 ; mentioned, 389 ; his probable
  development had he come to the
  throne, 392
Bourgogne, Duchesse de, and Mlle. Choin,
  244 ; her marriage, 245 ; her affection
  for the King and Mme. de Maintenon,
  245, 246 ; appearance and character,

246; mentioned, 300, 301; death of, 315

Bourgogne, Hôtel de, 385

Bouthelier, 38, 58, 87

Boutteville, Comte de, 107–9, 252

Brandenburg, 234, 236; Elector of, 229, 290

Breda, Peace of, 222

Breisgau, 63

Breitenfeld, Battle of, 69

Brice, Don Gregorio, 147–8

Brienne, *quoted*, 25

Brissac, Duchesse de, 9

Broc, Bishop of, 102

Broussel (Frondeur), 155–7

Bruant, Libéral, 366

Brûlart de Léon, 56, 66

Brûlart de Silléry, 27, 28, 41

Brûlarts, the, 40

Brunetière, *quoted*, 123

Brussels, 61

Buckingham, Duke of, accompanies Prince of Wales, 39; romantic attachment to Anne of Austria, 44, 45; his expedition to the Isle of Ré, 52

Bullion, 35, 95

Bulls, Papal, 281–4

Buquet, 109

Burgos, Philip V at, 303

Burgundy, 76

Burgundy, Duke of, and Duchess of, *see* Bourgogne, Duc de, *and* Duchesse de

Bussy d'Amboise, 109

Bussy Rabutin, *quoted*, 107, 186, 190, 334, 375

Buzenval, Choart de, 272

Cabale des Dévots, 103

Cabale des Importants, 141

Caen, revolt at, 97

Caffieri, 362

Callot, Jacques, 72, 366

Cambert (musician), 371

Cambrai, taken, 233; ceded to France, 234, 311

Camisards, the, 296, 299

Canada, 99, 339

Canals, construction of, 338, 346

Caravaggio, 367

Carinthia, 63

Carniola, 63

Carracci, the, 367

Cartesianism, *see* Descartes

Casale, relieved by Louis XIII, 55; invested by Spinola, 56; occupied by the French, 66, 76, 235

Cassel, taken by the French, 147; Battle of, 233; ceded to France, 234

Castelnaudary, Battle of, 60

Castille, Marie-Madeleine de, 327

Castres, 55

Catalonia, 256

Catholic Revival, 23

Catinat, Marshal, 216; in retirement, 256; death of, *ib.*; disgrace of, 292; in command on the Rhine, 295

Caulet, Etienne de (Bishop), 272, 274, 275

Caussin, Père, 82, 83

Cavalier, Jean, 299

Cavoye, 108, 318

Centralization of government, 343

Cerdagne, 169

Cévennes, the, 55; revolt in the, 296, 299

Chalais, Comte de, conspiracy of the, 45–47; barbarous execution of the, 48; mentioned, 93, 108, 134

Chambord, the Court at, 381

Chamillart (Minister), 239, 292, 314, 322

Chamlay (Minister), 251, 254

Champaigne, Philippe de, 366, 368

Chantilly, 232; lace-making at, 336

Chapelain, Jean, 116, 132, 360, 376

Chapelles, Des, 109

Charleroi, 230, 233

Charles, Archduke, 286; invades Spain, 302; enters Madrid, 303, 310; *see also* Charles VI, Emperor

Charles I of England, 54; *see also* Wales, Prince of

Charles II of England, at Compiègne, 205; his French sympathies, 210; compared with Louis XIV, 211; yields precedence to Louis XIV, 219; his marriage with the Infanta of Portugal, 220–1; subsidized by France, 225; becomes the ally of Louis XIV, 226; makes peace with William of Orange, 233

Charles II of Spain, degeneracy of, 285; his attitude respecting the Spanish succession, 287–8; death of, 288

"Charles III of Spain," *see* Charles, Archduke

Charles IV of Lorraine, 84

Charles V, Emperor, 62, 218, 310

Charles VI, Emperor, 312

Charles XII of Sweden, 304

Charon, Marie, 323

Charpentier, François, 338

Chartres, Duc de, 248, 255

Chartres, Duchesse de, 248, 249

Châteauneuf, Marquis de, 60; appointed Keeper of the Seals, 78; beguiled by Mme. de Chevreuse, 78; arrested and imprisoned, 79, 93, 95

Château-Trompette, 194

Châtillon, Maréchal de, 74, 84, 101

Chavigny, 87, 304

INDEX

Cherasco, Treaties of, 67

Chevreuse, factory at, 337

Chevreuse, Duc de, marries the widow of Duc de Luynes, 26, 44; adviser of Louis XIV, 257; husband of Colbert's daughter, 324

Chevreuse, Duchesse de, marriages of, 26, 44; friendship with Anne of Austria, 44; her intrigues and banishment, 45–8, 78; beauty and intelligence, 77; exile in Touraine, 79; character, 80; escapes to Spain, 82; hint to Gondi, 138; and Mazarin, 141–2; again banished, 142; quarrels with Condé, 163

Chiari, 292

Chiavenna, 41

Chigi, Cardinal, 220

Choisy, *quoted*, 181, 190, 213

Choin, Mlle., 244

Christina of Savoy, 168

Christina of Sweden, 21, 76, 127

Churchill, Arabella, 302

Churchill, John, *see* Marlborough

Cinq-Mars, Marquis de, mentioned, 18, 73; the favourite of Louis XIII, 84; plots against Richelieu, 85; disgraced and executed, 86

Cirey, factory at, 336

Clagny, 189, 198, 366

Classical Style, evolution of, 121

Clement IX, Pope, 273

Clement XI, Pope, 281

Clement, Jacques, 11

Clergy, under Louis XIII, 100–1; under Louis XIV, 348

Clergy, Assembly of the, 104, 261, 271

Coalition against France, 229

Coblenz, 70

Colbert, as agent of Mazarin, 169; his love of Paris, 197; and Poland, 210; and Pomponne, 212; and the Dutch War, 223; his protectionist tariff, 234; mentioned, 235; his indifference to religion 262; plurality of offices held by, 322; birth and parentage, 323; marriage, 323; appearance and manners, 323; services to Mazarin, 323; character, 324; his nepotism, 324; his political conceptions, 325; his enmity to Fouquet, 327, 328; his unscrupulous finance, 329; his reproofs to the King, 333; his financial system, 334–5; industries created by, 336; death of, 344; failure of his policy, 345; his legislative achievement, 345; his conception of the State, 392

Colbert de Croissy, 212

Colbert de Seignelay, 212; *see also* Seignelay

Colbert de Torcy, 212

"Colbertism," 335, 346

Coligny, 220

Colletet, F., *quoted*, 154

Colmar, 231

Cologne, Elector of, 292, 312

Colonies, French, 339

Combalet, Mme. de, 34 *note*, 57

Commendams, 100

Comminges (Lieut. of the Guard), 156

Companies, trading, 337–8

Company, French East India, 338–9; French West India, *ib.*; of the Holy Sacrament, 102–3, 259

Compiègne, 74

Concordat of 1516, 274

Concini, Concino, 3; enriches himself through his wife's influence, 4, 15; hated by the French, 14, 17; his appreciation of Richelieu, 15; his power and arrogance, 16, 17; resentment of Louis XIII against, 18; assassination of, 19, 94

Concini, Leonora, her influence over Marie de' Medici, 3, 4, 15; trial and execution of, 9, 20

Condé ceded to France, 234

Condé, Prince Henri de (father of the Grand Condé), his position as Prince of the Blood, 4, 5, 104; revolts against the Regent, 8; intervenes in Gallican controversy, 12; intrigues with Protestants, 13; character and popularity of, 14; arrogance of, 16; imprisoned in Bastille, 16; liberated, 22; retires to Italy, 27; opposes marriage of Gaston d'Orleans, 45; his severities against the Huguenots, 55; raids Franche-Comté, 74; mentioned, 104; his squalid habits, 106; quarrels with Beaufort, 136; death of, 147

Condé, Prince de (the Great Condé), as a youthful commander, 142–4; gains Battle of Rocroy, 87, 144; leader of the Fronde, 154; rivalry with Gaston d'Orleans, *ib.*; reconciled to Mazarin, 158; leads royal troops against Paris, 159; goes over again to Fronde, 161; arrested, *ib.*; released by Mazarin, 163; intrigues with Spain, 167; in old age, 192; death of, 193; as diplomatist, 212; his campaign in Holland, 226–8, 229–30; *see also* d'Enghien, Duc

Condé, Prince Henri Jules de (son of the Great Condé), 248

Condé, Princesse de, 155; *see also* Montmorency, Charlotte de

INDEX

Conrart, M., 125

Conti, Prince de, active as Frondeur, 160; arrested, 161; released by Mazarin, 163; marriage to Mlle. de Blois, 192, 334; at Battle of Neerwinden, 255; supports Jansenists, 271; leads attacks upon Molière, 381

Conti, Princesse de (Frondeuse), 58

Conti, Princesse de (niece of Mazarin), 170

Coras (dramatist), 385

"Corbie Year," 74, 75, 143

Corneille, Pierre, at the Hôtel de Rambouillet, 116; birth and manners, 131; production of his Cid, 131–3; his exaltation of the will, 133; his influence on the Frondeurs, 134; his Galerie du Palais, 152; protected by Fouquet, 327; ethics of, 353; collaborates with Molière, 382; temporary eclipse of, 384; relation to Racine, 385

Corneille, Thomas, 384, 385

Cornet, Nicolas, 269

Cornuel, Mme. de, quoted, 323, 232

Correr, Venetian envoy, 326

Corsican Guard, affair of the, 219–20

Cotin, Abbé, 116, 382

Coton, Père, 4

Cotte, Robert de, 363

Coudere (Camisard), 300

Councils, the King's, 151, 321

Cours-la-Reine, 153, 158

Court life, discomfort of, 206, 240

Courtrai, 147, 230, 233

Coussay, Priory of, 31, 32

Coustou, Guillaume, 370

Coysevox, 362

Cramail, Comte de, 84

Cremona, 293

Créqui, Duc de, 219, 220, 233

Dangeau, at Court, 203, 240; quoted, 241, 302, 313

Daquin (physician), 203

Dauphin, 207, 315, 317–8; see also Bourgogne, Duc de, and Dauphin, Grand

Dauphin, Grand, his severe education, 193; marriage, ib.; mediocrity of, 243–4; and his daughter-in-law, 246; and the Spanish Succession, 286, 289; death of, 315

Dauphine, Place, 152–3, 155

Dauphine, wife of Grand Dauphin, 193; wife of Duc de Bourgogne, afterwards Dauphine, 315

"Day of Dupes," 58, 59, 62, 77

Déageant, 18, 19

"Declarations," royal, 42

Delacroix, 369

Delorme, Philibert, 364

Denbigh, Lord, 53

Denmark, 65, 67, 210, 221, 234, 236

Denain, Battle of, 311, 315

Denonville, Marquis de, 342

Descartes, René, 127–8, 378–80; in Holland, 210

Desmarets de Saint-Sorlet, 276

Despréaux, see Boileau

Desportes, 123

Devolution, Law of, 221–2

Dijon, Parliament of, 88

Dixmude, 236

Dôle, 230

Domaine (Crown lands), 331–2

Douai, 311

Dover, battle off, 76; Treaty of, 225

Dragonnades, 263–4

Drogheda, Battle of, 249

Duelling in France, 107–9, 252

Dughet, Marie Anne, 367

Duguay-Trouin, 358

Dunkirk, Spanish fleet sails for, 76; taken by the Duc d'Enghien, 147; sold to France, 221; Louis XIV at, 339; English demand dismantlement of, 307; fortifications razed, 312

Duquesne, Abraham, 233, 236–7

Duras, 252

Edict of Nantes, 24, 49, 50, 56, 324; ambiguity of, 261; revocation of, 237, 260–2, 264–5, 299

Edict of Restitution, 64, 65; rescinded, 71

d'Effiat, 84, 95; see also Cinq-Mars

d'Elbeuf, Duc, 160, 294; Duchesse, 9, 58

"Elections," the, 97

Electors of the Empire, 63

d'Eliçagaray, Renaud, 340

Elisabeth of France marries Philip IV of Spain, 14

Embrun, 256

d'Emery, 104

Enden, Van den, 349

d'Enghien, Duc, victor at Rocroy, 87, 142–146; becomes Prince de Condé, 147; see also Condé (the Great)

d'Epernon, 4, 21, 22

Estates, the, 97

Estrade, Comte, 219

d'Estrées, 236; Gabrielle, 136

État de la France, 203–4

Eugène, Prince, origin and aptitudes, 291; occupies Milan, 292; in Germany, 296–7; in the Low Countries, 306, 309; at Malplaquet, 309; at Denain, 311; negotiates Peace of Rastadt, 312

Faenza, 336

Fagon (Court surgeon), 202–3

2 c

INDEX

Faguet, M., *quoted*, 135
Falaise, revolt at, 97
Falconi (Quietist), 276
Fancan, 35
Fargues, 373
Farmers of revenue, 332
Favre, *see* Vaugelas
Fayt, Battle of, 243
Fénelon, and Mme. de Maintenon, 243; his influence on the Duke of Burgundy, 245, 392; his philanthropic outlook, 245; and the Quietists, 277–9; and Bossuet, 278; submission to the Pope, 278; his *Télémaque*, 279; and Père Le Tellier, 282; as precursor of Rousseau, 354; *quoted*, 307, 357; as man of letters, 389
Ferdinand II, Emperor, 56, 64–7, 74
Ferdinand-Joseph of Bavaria, 286
Fernando, Cardinal-Infante, 74, 75, 80
Ferrier, Jérémie, 49
Finance under Louis XIII, 93; under Louis XIV, 347
Flanders, 393
Fleurus, Battle of, 253–4
Fontainebleau, 197, 201, 328
Fontaines, Comte de, 144
Fontanges, Mlle. de, 190, 192, 193, 195
Fontenay-Mareuil (ambassador), *quoted*, 26, 78
Fontenelle, 380
Fontrailles, M. de, 102
Fortresses seized, Dutch, 290
Fortune-tellers, 191–2
Fouquet, Nicolas, character and career of, 326–329; mentioned, 324, 332, 382
Franche-Comté, Spanish possession, 63; attack on, 74; restored to Spain, 223; taken by Louis XIV, 230; ceded to France, 233, 393
Francion, *quoted*, 102
Freiburg, 234, 312
Friedlingen, Battle of, 295
Fronde, the, 13, 150–66; origin of the term, 155; revival of the, 163; end of the, 166; survivors of the, 372–3
Frondeurs, 150, 271, 279, 373
Frondeuses, 373
Fuensaldaña (Spanish commander), 167
Fürstenberg, Cardinal von, 238

Gabelle, the (salt-tax), 330–2, 357
Gabriel, Père, 287
Galen, Bernhard von, 221
Galigai, Leonora, *see* Concini
Gallas, General, 70
Galleys, the, 341–3; slaves of, 342–3

Gallicanism, 272–3
Gallicans, 11, 12
Galloway, Lord, 206
Gambling at Court, 206, 240, 334, 340
Gangnières, General, 216
Gap, 256
Gassendi, 128
Gassion, 144
Gaultier, Abbé, 310
Gellée, Claude, 369
Genoa bombarded, 237
Germany, campaign in, 295
Gertruydenberg, 310
Gesvres. Duc de, 9, 203
Ghent, 233
Gibraltar, 302; ceded to English, 312
Girardon, 362, 370
Gisors, lace-making at, 336
Glapion, Mme. de, 195
Gobelins, Les (factory), 362, 386
Godeau (Bishop), 101
Godet des Marais (Bishop), 277
Godolphin, 291
Gombard, 124
Gondi, 138, 156, 161–3; *see also* Retz, Cardinal de
Gonzaga, Anna di, 163
Gonzaga, Maria di, 55
Gonzaga, Vincenzo di, 54, 55
Goulas, *quoted*, 58
Gourgues, M. de, 92
Gourville, *quoted*, 213
Grammont, Comte de, 101; Comtesse de, 280; Maréchal de, 110, 158
Grand alliance, 290
Grand Cyrus, Le, 113, 134, 150
Grand Condé, *see* Condé
Grande Mademoiselle, *see* Mademoiselle
Gravelines, 147
"Greybeards," the, 6, 15, 21
Grève, Place de, 165
Grignan, Mme. de, *quoted*, 252; mentioned, 375
Grisons, the, 40
Grotius, 210
Guastalla, Duke of, 55
Guébriant, Maréchal de, 76, 84, 145
Guéménée, Mme. de, 141
Guiana, 339
Guiche, Duc de, 201
Guilds, 335, 354–5
Guise, Chevalier de, 108
Guise, Duc de, 58, 94, 105
Guise, Duchesse de, 101
Guiton, Jean, 53–4
Gustavus-Adolphus of Sweden, 67, 69, 70
Guttenberg, *see* Berlepsch
Guyon, Mme., 276–8

INDEX

HAGUE, secret treaty of The, 287

Hamilton, Anthony, *quoted* on siege of Lerida, 147–8

Hamon (Jansenist), 268

Hanotaux, M., *quoted*, 36

Hapsburgs, the, 62, 64, 65, 288

d'Harcourt, Comte, 76 ; Marquis, 288

Harlay, M. de (Archbishop), 279

Haro, Don Luis de, 168

Harrach, Count, 288

Hauranne, *see* Saint-Cyran

Haussmann, Baron, 156

Hautefort, Marie de, 79–80

Heidelberg destroyed by Tessé, 251 ; occupied by Villars, 304

Heinsius, 291

Henri III, 11, 112

Henri IV, assassination of, 1, 11, 23 ; and Marie de' Medici, 2 ; and restoration of Church property, 24 ; Louis XIII's cult of, 37 ; unceremonious Court of, 112 ; statue of, 153 ; familiar manners of, 200 ; and the Edict of Nantes, 261 ; mentioned, 336

Henrietta Stuart, 201 ; *see also* Madame (Henriette) *and* d'Orléans, Duchesse

Henriette-Marie, marriage to Prince of Wales, 41, 44

Hérouet, 115

d'Hervart, M., 382

Hesse, Prince of, 296

Hinard, founder of Beauvais factory, 336

Hindustan, 339

Höchstädt, 296, 314

d'Hocquincourt, Maréchal, 108, 164

Holland, 210 ; war between England and, 221 ; peace with, 234 ; *see also* United Provinces

Holland, Earl of, 44, 78

Honfleur, 358

Hôtel-de-Ville, Paris, sack of, 165

Hudson Bay ceded to England, 312

Huguenots, seditious attitude of the, 23–5, 260 ; revolts of, 41, 48–54 ; ecclesiastical hierarchy of the, 51 ; emigration of the, 264–5 ; persecution of the, 264–5

d'Humières (General), 233

Hundred Years' War, 290

Hungary, 63, 220

Huygens, 210

ILE-DE-FRANCE, 322

Industry, restrictions on, 337

Infanta, the, 39

Innocent XI, Pope, 238, 274, 280

Innocent XII, Pope, 280

Intolerance, religious, 49, 260, 264

Invalides, the, 366

Italy, 209 ; campaign in, 292–5

JAMES II of England, deposed, 238 ; defeated at Drogheda, 249-50 ; forsaken by Louis XIV, 258 ; death at Saint-Germain, 290

James Stuart (Old Pretender), 207, 290, 312

Jansenism, 212, 266–273

Jansenists, eminent, 267–8 · support Descartes, 379

Jansenius, 266, 269–70

Jars, Chevalier de, 78, 140

Jarzé, de (*protégé* of Condé), 138, 161

Jesuits, 23, 98, 261, 266, 269

Joseph I, Emperor, 310

Joseph (Le Clerc du Tremblay) Père, the "Grey Cardinal," 35–6 ; envoy at Diet of Ratisbon, 56, 65–6 ; intercedes for Richelieu, 58 ; opposes annexation of Alsace, 69–70 ; admonishes Richelieu, 75 ; insensibility of, 100

Justice, administration of, under Louis XIII, 88–91 ; under Louis XIV, 344–5

KEMPEN, Battle of, 84

Koeprilü (Grand Vizier), 220

LA BERTHE (duellist), 109

La Bruyère, on Corneille, 131 ; on Lauzun, 185 ; on the cult of Louis XIV, 202 ; on the devout courtier, 239 ; attitude to the Huguenots, 264 ; on the misery of the peasantry, 354 ; as a classical writer, 378, 380 ; personality and career, 389–91 ; his *Caractères*, 363, 390–1

La Chaise, Père de, 240, 243, 262, 265, 314

Ladenburg, 231

Laer, 255

La Fare, *quoted*, 185, 230

La Fayette, Mme. de, on Philippe d'Orléans, 180 ; on Madame (Henriette), 181 ; at Versailles, 359 ; her friendship with La Rochefoucauld, 374

La Fayette, Mlle. de, 79–80, 82, 84

La Feuillade, Duc de (senior), constructs Place des Victoires, 202, 294

La Feuillade, Duc de (junior), *quoted*, 141 ; at the King's *lever*, 203 ; commands expedition against the Turks, 220 ; mentioned, 239, 292 ; routed by Eugène, 294

Laffemas, 94

La Fontaine, Jean, as minor poet under Louis XIII, 124 ; on the fortune-tellers, 191 ; and the Huguenots, 264 ; protected by Fouquet, 327 ; his

INDEX

flattery of Louis XIV, 363; collaborates in *Mélicerte*, 372; publishes first tale, 373; encouraged by Boileau, 377; upholds the classical ideal, 378, 380; his appreciation of Molière, 382; character and career, 382–4

La Force, Maréchal de, 25, 75

La Frette, Marquis de, 109

La Hague, Cape, 250

La Hougue, Battle of, 250

Lagos, Battle of, 251

Lalande (composer), 372

La Marfée, Battle of, 84, 85

Lamboy (Spanish General), 84

La Meilleraie, Mme. de, 170

Lamoignon de Basville, 299

La Mothe-Fénelon, 389

La Motte-Argencourt, Mlle. de, 168

La Motte-Houdancourt, Mlle. de, 201

Lancelot, Claude (Jansenist), 267–8

Landau, 295, 312

Landrecies, 311

Languedoc, 55

Lanson, M., *quoted*, 121, 268, 379

La Porte (Louis XIV's valet), 80, 170, 173

La Porte, Suzanne de, 30

Largillière, 369

La Rochefoucauld, Duc de, on Duke of Buckingham, 44; abets Mme. de Chevreuse, 80; on Duc de Beaufort, 136; as leader of the Frondeurs, 160; exiled, 166; at the King's *lever*, 203; character and career, 373–5; his *Maxims*, 374

La Rochelle, Huguenot Assembly at, 24–5; Peace of, 42; Huguenot stronghold, 51–2; siege of, 52–4

La Rongère, M. de, 250

La Sablière, Mme. de, 382

La Salle, Cavelier de, 339

La Tour du Pin, Mlle. de, 256

La Trémoille, Duc de, 203

Lauzun, Duc de, his extraordinary personality, 185; marries La Grande Mademoiselle, 186; imprisoned at Pignerol, *ib.*; restored to favour, *ib.*; mentioned, 382

La Valette, Cardinal, 35, 100

La Vallière, Louise de, mentioned, 175; distinguished by the King, 182; created a duchess, 183; supplanted by Mme. de Montespan, 184; takes the veil, 188; the Duc de Guiche and, 201; the Queen and, 201; mentioned, 259; her children by the King, 324; Fouquet and, 327

Lavardin, Bishop, 102

Lavardin, Marquis de, 238

La Vieuville, 28, 29, 39, 326

Le Bouteux, 360

Le Brun, his decorations for Marly, 199; and at Vaux, 197, 327; director of Les Gobelins, 336; ennobled, 360; director of Academy of Painting and Sculpture, 161; elaborates Louis XIV Style, 362; the art of, 369–70

Leclerc (dramatist), 385

Leclerc, Sébastien (artist), 362

Le Clerc du Tremblay, *see* Joseph, Père

Leipzig, 69

Le Maistre, Antoine, 268

Le Maistre de Sacy, 269

Le Maistre de Séricourt, 269

Lemaître, Jules, *quoted*, 133, 376, 386

Le Mercier, 364

Le Nain, the brothers, 366

Lenglée (milliner), 189

Le Nôtre, work at Vaux, 197, 327; ennobled, 360; work at Versailles, 197, 366, 368, 370

Lens, victory at, 155

Leopold, Archduke, 148, 160, 167

Leopold I, Emperor, insecurity of his tenure, 209; contrasted with Louis XIV, 211; accepts French aid against the Turks, 220; helplessness of, 221; his alliance with United Provinces, 229; accepts Peace of Nimeguen, 234; advances claim to Spanish crown, 286–7; a party to the Grand Alliance, 290

Le Quesnoy, 30; taken by Eugene, recovered by French, 311

Lérida, siege of, 147–8; taken, 303

Lescot, Pierre, 364–5

Lesdiguières, 4, 5, 27, 58

Les Granges, 267, 270

Le Tellier, Michel (War Minister), 212–3, 225, 323, 340

Le Tellier, Père (the King's Confessor), 243, 266, 282

Le Tréaumont, 349

Le Vau (architect), his work at Vaux, 197, 327; at Versailles, 197–8; in the Louvre, 364–6

Leyden, 210

l'Hermite, Tristan, 124

l'Hôpital, Maréchal de, 143–4

l'Hospital, Nicolas de, *see* Vitry

"Libertines," 99, 102, 259–60

Liége, taken by Marlborough, 298

Lille, fortress, 306–8

Limerick, 250

Lionne, Hugues de, 211, 218, 220, 225, 328

"Liselotte," *see* d'Orléans, Duchesse

Lizza, Andrea di, 4

Locatelli, describes the Queen's *lever*, 207; and a review by the King, 214

Longueville, Duc de, 8, 22, 134, 227

INDEX

Longueville, Mme. de, as Frondeuse, 150, 159-60; at Bordeaux, 161; mentioned, 191; supports the Jansenists, 271, 279

Lorges, De, 232

Lorme, Marion de, 84

Lorrain, Le, see Gellée, Claude

Lorraine, 76; portion ceded to France, 169; restored to Duke of Lorraine, 258; administered by Louvois, 322

Lorraine, Chevalier de, 180

Lorraine, Duke of, 164, 169, 234

Louis XIII, accession of, 1; childhood of, 3; at sixteen, 17; conspires against Concini, 17-19; his relations with Richelieu, 36, 77; at twenty-three, 37; character of, 37-38; military achievements of, 77; and the Parliaments, 92; death of, 136; at Versailles, 197; friendly relations with his courtiers, 200-1; and the completion of the Louvre, 364

Louis XIV, birth of, 83; majority of, 163; marriage of, 167, 169, 171, 179-80; youthful love-affairs of, 168; memoirs of, 172, 177; neglected education of, 173; asserts his power, 172-3; appearance and physique, 174; gigantic appetite, 175; character of, 176; polished manners of, 176; his belief in divine right, 178; intellect of, 178; inordinate vanity of, 179; as a young man, 201; etiquette of his Court, 202-7; conversion of, 202, 239; statues of, 202; his lever, 203-4; his coucher, 207; as diplomatist, 212; ambitions of, 218; invades Franche-Comté in person, 222; his imperturbability in misfortune, 306, 313; his will, 316; last days of, 317, 318; death, 319; his relations with Colbert, 332-4; his ruinous expenditure, 333-4, 340, 346

Louis XV, 315, 318

Louis-Philippe, 156

Louvain, University of, 266

Louvigny, Comte de, 47, 108

Louville, quoted, 300

Louvois, his hostility to Mme. de Montespan, 184, 192; his rivalry with Pomponne, 212; Secretary of State for War, 212-14; as disciplinarian, 216; prepares for war with Holland, 225; and the "Reunions," 235; death of, 241; devastation of the Palatinate ordered by, 251; severity to Huguenots urged by, 262; his arrogance, 340

Louvre, Louis XIII at the, 83; in the time of Louis XIII, 152; completion of the, 364-6

Low Countries, 63; ceded to the Emperor, 312

Loye, Maréchal de, 256

Lude, Comte de, 18

Lulli, Jean-Baptiste, 359, 371-2, 382

Lutter, Battle of, 65

Lützen, Battle of, 70

Luxembourg, Duc de, 105

Luxembourg, Maréchal de, commands in Holland, 226, 229-30; created Marshal, 232; at Battle of Cassel, 233; repulses William of Orange near Mons, 234; mentioned, 239; as a general, 252; death of, 256

Luxemburg (province), 236

Luynes, Charles d'Albert de, appointed Falconer to Louis XIII, 18; created Marquis d'Albert, 20; marries Mlle. de Rohan, ib.; his political nullity, ib.; as favourite of the King, 20-1; created Constable of France, 20, 25; decline of, 26; death of, ib.; mentioned, 324

Luynes, Duchesse de, 20; see also Chevreuse, Duchesse de

Luzzara, Vendôme at, 294

Lyonnais, the, 322

Lyons, Richelieu at, 86

MADAGASCAR, 98, 339

Madame, first wife of Philippe, Duc d'Orléans, 181-2, 184-5, 225; see also Henrietta Stuart

Madame, second wife of Philippe, Duc d'Orleans, quoted on Mlle. de Fontanges, 190; on manners at table, 205; on the discomforts of the Court, 206, 207; on the Duchess of Burgundy, 245; on the winter of 1709, 306; on death of Louis XIV, 318-9; see also d'Orléans, Duchesse

Madeleine, Mère (of Port-Royal), 272

Mademoiselle, La Grande, as Frondeuse, 134, 150; her quarrels with the Princesse de Condé, 155; commands troops in Orléans, 164; banished to the country, 166; her proposed marriage to Philippe d'Orléans, 185; her flattery of Louis XIV, 202; mentioned, 371; her romantic ideals, 372; mentioned, 382

Maestricht taken by Louis XIV, 229; restored to Holland, 234; siege of, 295

Magdeburg, Archbishopric of, 64; sack of, 69

Maine, 343; Duc du, 247-8; 316-7; Duchesse du, 248-9

INDEX

Maintenon, hostility of the Duchesse d'Orléans to Madame de, 187; character and career, 193-6; governess to children of Mme. de Montespan, 194; religious influence on the King, 195; founds Saint-Cyr, 196; marriage to Louis XIV; *quoted* on the emptiness of realized ambitions, 195; mentioned, 201, 208; on the King's religious attitude, 239; her life as the King's wife, 241-3; her political influence, 242-3; indulgent to Mlle. Choin, 244; her affection for the Duchesse de Bourgogne, 246; encourages severities against the Huguenots, 262-3; and Mme. Guyon, 277; her friendship with the Princesse des Ursins, 301; in 1709, 306; on murmurs against the King, 307; *quoted*, 314; retires to Saint-Cyr, 318; domestic budget of, 349; arranges concerts for the King, 359; ascendency of, 373; patroness of Racine, 386

Malaval, 276
Malherbe, 116, 122-3
Malebranche, 128, 379, 380
Malplaquet, Battle of, 309
Man in the Iron Mask, *see* Matthioli
Mancini, Filippo, 170
Mancini, Maria, 168, 170-1, 175
Mancini, Olympia, 168, 291; *see also* Soissons, Comtesse de
Mangot, 15
Mannheim occupied by Villars, 304
Mansart, François, 364
Mansart, Jules Hardouin, 189, 360, 366
Mantua, 65
Manuguet (jester), 57
Marca, Archbishop, 271
Marche, La, 356
Marciennes, 311
Marcilly, Siege of, 113, 150
Marcin, Maréchal de, 294, 296
Mardick, taken by the French, 147; sold to France, 221
Margaret-Theresa, Empress, 286-7
Maria-Anna, Empress, 286-7
Maria-Anna of Neuburg, 285, 287, 300
Maria-Antoinetta of Bavaria, 286-7
Maria (of Savoy), 168
Maria Christina (of Savoy), *see* Christina
Maria-Luisa, Queen of Spain, 285
Maria-Luisa (of Savoy), 300
Maria-Theresa, Infanta, 167; *see also* Marie-Thérèse, Queen
Mariana, Father, 12
Marie, Princess (of Mantua), 85
Marie de' Medici, on the death of Henri IV, 1; character and appearance, 2; as Regent, 4-8; dominated by the Concini, 15-16; banished to Blois, 19; her intrigues with Richelieu, 21; escapes from Blois, 21; appointed Governor of Anjou, 22; heads a rebellion, 22; hostile to Anne of Austria, 43; subservience of Richelieu to, 45, 57; her rupture with Richelieu, 57-8; checkmated by Richelieu, 58; exile and death, 59, 105
Marie-Thérèse, Queen, 179-80; and Mlle. de La Vallière, 188; at marriage of Mlle. d'Orléans, 190; and Mme. de Maintenon, 195; death of, 180, 195; and Charles II of England, 205; her *lever*, 207; non-payment of her dowry, 220; her claim to the Spanish throne, 222, 286
Marienthal, Turenne at, 146
Marillac, Maréchal de, 58, 59, 61, 78, 264
Marino, Cavaliere, 367
Marivaux, 385
Marlborough, Duchess of, 291
Marlborough, Duke of, 291; at Blenheim, 297; in the Netherlands, 298; and Charles XII of Sweden, 304; at Malplaquet, 309; disgrace of, 310
Marly, 199, 200, 213, 280, 307, 359, 366
Marolles, *quoted*, 357
Marsaille, La, 256
Marsal, 258
Martin, Jean, 196
Mary, of England, Princess, marries Prince of Orange, 233
Massillon, 279
Matha, M. de, 102
Matthioli, 212, 235
Maubeuge ceded to France, 234
Maubuisson, Convent of, 267
Maucroix, Canon, 383
Maugars (violinist), 101
Mayence, 146
Mayenne, leagued with Condé, 8
Maynard (writer), 123
Mazarin (Mazarini, Giulio), first appearance of, 56; envoy of the Pope, 67; Richelieu's agent, 76; appointed a member of the Supreme Council, 87; origin, character, and career, 138-142; unpopularity of, 149; and the Fronde, 149-166; at Bruhl, 163; returns to France, 163; makes alliance with Cromwell, 167; foreign policy of, 168-9; magnificence of, 169; death and will of, 171-2; superintendent of Louis XIV's education, 173; trained Hugues de Lionne, 211; mentioned, 259, 291, 324, 326; creates Academy of Fine Arts, 361

INDEX

Mazarin, Duc de, 170, 259
Mélac, 295
Melo, Don Francisco de, 142–4
Ménage, 116
Mercœur, Duchesse de, 170
Mercure Français, 42
Mercy (German General), 145–6
Méré, Chevalier de, 129
Mersenne, Père, 102
Meulen, Van der, 362
Meudon, 244
Michelet, *quoted*, 252
Mignard, 362, 369
Milan, 63, 76
Minorca ceded to the English, 312
Modena, Duchess of, 170
Molé, President, 160
Molière, *quoted*, on fashionable magic, 191;
    protected by Louis XIV, 360; his
    flattery of the King, 363; *quoted* on the
    art of painting, 368; collaborates in
    Mélicerte, 372; encouraged by Boileau,
    377; his career and works, 380–2;
    the controversy touching his *Tartuffe*,
    103, 259, 381; death of, 382
Molinos, Miguel, 276
Monçon, Treaty of, 42
Monheurt, siege of, 26
Mons, 234, 253, 308
Monseigneur, *see* Dauphin, Grand
Monsieur, 45–8, 104; *see also* d'Orléans,
    Gaston, Duc
Monsieur, 180; *see also* d'Orléans,
    Philippe, Duc
Montalto (physician), 3
Montauban, siege of, 25–27, 55
Montausier, Duc de, 193, 203
Montausier, Marquis de, 119
Montchrestien, 345
Montclar destroys Mannheim, 252
Montdidier, 4
Montecuculli, Imperialist General, 220,
    232
Montespan, Mme. de, her beauty and
    charm, 183; supplants Mlle. de La
    Vallière, 184, 189; supplanted by
    Mlle. de Fontanges, 192, 195; her
    dealings in magic, 191–2; chooses
    gifts for Dauphine, 193; children of,
    194, 247; her gambling, 334; Clagny
    built for, 366
Monteverde, 370
Montferrat, 294
Montmorency, Charlotte de, 14
Montmorency, Henri, Duc de, friendship
    with Anne of Austria, 44; joins Gaston
    d'Orléans in revolt, 60; taken prisoner,
    tried and executed, 60, 78
Montmorency-Boutteville, *see* Boutteville

Montmorency, Duc de, son of Marshal
    Luxembourg, 255
Montpellier, Treaty of, 27; Peace of, 40
Montpensier, Mme. de, 1
Montpensier, Mlle. de, 45–7
Moors in Spain, 63
Moravia, 63
Motteville, Mme. de, 78, 372
Muiden, 228
Mulhouse, 23
Münster, Congress of, 148
Music, 359

Namur captured, 253; retaken by the
    English, 257
Naples, kingdom of, 63
Napoleon, 227, 310
Nassau, Maurice of, 127
National Anthem, English, 372
Naval enlistment, 341
Navy, creation of the, 98, 99; under
    Louis XIV, 339–43
N.C.'s, the (New Catholics), 265
Neerwinden, Battle of, 254–5
Nègrepelisse captured, 27
Nemours, Duc de, 105
Nevers, Duc de, 4, 54, 56, 105, 170
Nevers, potteries at, 336
Newfoundland, 308, 312, 339
Newspapers, the first, 42–3
Nice taken by the French, 256; restored
    to Savoy, 312
Nicole (Jansenist), 267–8, 279, 385
Nietzsche, 134
Nimeguen, Peace of, 233, 235, 257, 258
Nîmes, 55, 369
Noailles, Bishop, 277–8; becomes Arch-
    bishop of Paris, 280; and Cardinal,
    281; leader of the Gallican party,
    280–1; agrees to suppression of Port
    Royal, 282; supports Père Quesnel,
    282–3; honoured by the Regent, 284
Noailles, Maréchal de, 256
Nobility, centralization of the, 207–8;
    provincial, 106
Nobles, the "great," 4–6, 83, 104–6;
    under Louis XIV, 348–51
Noblesse d'épée (patrician nobility), 351;
    de robe (legal nobility), 351–3
Nogaret, M. de, 216
Noirmoutiers, M. de, 150
Nordlingen, Battle of, 71, 146–7
Normandy, 343, 357
Notre Dame, Paris, 155, 253, 363
Noyon, 322

Oléron, captured by Huguenots, 41
Olier, 102
Oppenheim destroyed, 252

407

INDEX

Oratorians, 379

Orders founded, religious, 102–3

Orders, lower, 353–4

Orléanais, 322

d'Orléans, Gaston, Duc, brother of Louis XIII, 3; his good looks and despicable character, 45–48; marriage to Mlle. de Montpensier, 47; cause of rupture between Marie de' Medici and Richelieu, 57; raises a revolt, 59; marries his second wife, Marguerite of Lorraine, 60; servile submission to Richelieu, 61; mentioned, 70; in Lorraine and at Brussels, 78; plans assassination of Richelieu, 83; makes secret treaty with Spain, 85; Lieutenant-General of the Kingdom, 87; mentioned, 142; as leader of the Fronde, 154; mentioned, 156; won over by Mazarin, 157–8; negotiates with Condé, 164; concerned in the "Straw Sedition," 165; pardoned, 166

d'Orléans, Philippe, Duc, brother of Louis XIV, childhood, 173; character and appearance, 180–1; marriage to Henrietta Stuart, 180–1; at the Battle of Cassel, 233; unwilling to marry the Grande Mademoiselle, 185; marries the Princess Palatine, 186; death of, 313

d'Orléans, Philippe Duc, nephew of Louis XIV, commands troops in Italy, 294; unpopularity of, 316; at the King's death-bed, 317; see also Chartres, Duc de

d'Orléans, Elisabeth Charlotte, Duchesse, second wife of Philippe (I) d'Orléans, appearance and manners, 186–7; Louis XIV claims Palatinate on her behalf, 238; quoted on the King's conversion, 240; her affection for the Duc de Chartres, 248; quoted on James II of England, 249; Tessé sends her portraits from Heidelberg, 251; pension paid her by the Elector Palatine, 258; quoted on the death of the King's heirs, 315; at the death-bed of Louis XIV, 317

d'Orléans, Henriette, Duchesse, first wife of Philippe (I) d'Orléans, 180–2; death of, 184–5; her mission to England, 225

d'Orléans, Mlle., married to King of Spain, 190

d'Ormesson, quoted, 149, 182, 212

Ormoy-Blainville, 324

d'Ornano, Maréchal, Governor of Gaston d'Orléans, 46; imprisoned, ib.; death in prison, 48; mentioned, 93

Orsini, see Ursins

Osnabrück, Duchess of, 190–1, 206

Oudenarde, 168, 233, 236; Battle of, 305

Paix de grâce, 56

Palais de Justice, 152

Palais Royal, 140, 156

Palaiseau, 197

Palatinate, misery in the, 76; ravaged by Turenne, 231; conquest of the, 238; again ravaged, 251; pays indemnity, 258; devastated by Marlborough, 296

Palatine, Elector, 186, 238, 258

Palatine, Princess, 248; see also d'Orléans, Duchesse

Paris, centre of the Fronde, 156–161, 164–6; Louis XIV's dislike of, 197; Parliament of, 13, 90, 91, 151, 155–159

Parliaments, the ten French (Aix, Bordeaux, Dijon, Grenoble, Metz, Paris, Pau, Rennes, Rouen, Toulouse), 88, 91, 92

Pascal, Blaise, 128–31, 268; his Lettres Provinciales, 129–30, 270; his Pensées, 128, 130, 131, 269

Pascal, Jacqueline, 129

Paulet (financier), 10

Paulet, Mlle. 116

Paulette, the (tax), 10, 13

Pavia, Treaty of, 21

Pavillon, Nicolas (Bishop), 272–4

Peasantry under Louis XIV, 355

"Peace of the Church," 273, 282

Peace negotiations in 1709, 307–8, 310

Péréfixe, Hardouin de, 271, 279

Périer, Mme., 129

Périer, Marguerite, 270

Péroges, see Vaugelas

Péronne, 4, 315, 359

Perpignan, 77

Perrault, Charles, 327, 365, 380

Perrin, the Abbé, 371

Perron, Du, 12

Peterborough, Lord, 303

Petit-Renaud, 237

Philip II of Spain, 223

Philip IV of Spain, 55, 167, 209, 211, 219, 221, 285–6

Philip V of Spain, accepts throne, 289; his reception in Spain, 300; alienates Spanish nobility, 302; defeated by the Allies, 303; removes Court to Burgos, ib.; recovers Madrid, ib.; proposed abdication of, 303, 310; renounces claim to French crown, 312, 315

Philippsburg, 70, 146

INDEX

Piedmont, 77

Pignerol, occupied by the French, 67, 76; ceded to France, 149; Lauzun imprisoned at, 186; Fouquet imprisoned at, 329; restored to Savoy, 257

Pin, Abbé du, 390

Pirates, 98

Plessis, Du, 95

Pluvinel, Sieur de, 30

Pointis, 258

Poisoning scandals, 191–2, 316

Poitou, 264, 322

Poland, 68, 210, 225, 333

Polignac, Abbé de, 310

Polignac, Cardinal de, 200

Poll-tax, 347–8

Pomponne, Arnauld de, 211–2, 225, 235, 321

Pondicherry, 258

Pontchartrain (Minister), 239, 288, 350

Pontgibault, 108

Pont-Neuf, 42, 152–4; quacks of the, 151; ponts-neufs (pasquinades), 154

Ponts-de-Cé, Battle of the, 22

Poquelin, see Molière

Portes, Marquis des, 108

Portland, Lord, 258

Porto-Carrera, Cardinal, 288, 301

Port-Royal, reorganization of, 266–7; a centre of Jansenism, 267–8; the King's hostility to, 271, 280; severe measures against, 271–2; suppression of, 281–2

Portugal, 63, 73, 222; King of, 302

Poussin, Nicolas, 366–9

Pradon, 385

Praslin, M. de, 1

Préaux (conspirator), 349

Précieuses, the, 114, 118, 119, 375

Prétot, architect, 366

Primi, quoted, 176, 187, 314

Puget, Pierre, 370

Puisieux, 27, 28

Pussort, Marie, 323

Puy, Du, 25

Puylaurens, 61

Puymorin, 108

Pyrenees, Treaty of the, 108, 211, 218

Quercy, 27

Quesnel, Père, 280; his New Testament with Moral Reflections, 280, 282–3

Quietism, 276

Quiévrain, 308

Quillebœuf, 349

Quinault, 183, 372, 382, 384, 385

Racan, Marquis de, 123

Racine, Jean, admirer of L'Astrée, 114;
his Bérénice quoted, 170; his relations with Port-Royal, 267–70; protected by Louis XIV, 360; his Britannicus quoted, 371; début of, 373; encouraged by Boileau, 377; characters of, 378; declares for Ancients versus Moderns, 380; character and career, 384; his quarrel with Port-Royal, 385; converted to Jansenism, 387; death, ib.

Racine, Louis, 386

Rambouillet, Hôtel de, 115–121, 211, 362

Rambouillet, Madame de, 113–120

Rambouillet, Mlle. de, 119, 193

Ramillies, Battle of, 314

Rancé, 102

Rastadt, Peace of, 312

Ratisbon, Diet of, 65–6; Truce of, 236

Ravaillac, 11, 12

Ravenel (Camisard), 300

Ray (English traveller), 283

Ré, Isle of, 51–2

Recruiting, 214

Regale, the, 236–7, 274–6

Regency, of Anne of Austria, 136, 141; of Marie de' Medici, 2–8, 17–18; of the Duke of Orléans, 391

Regnier, H. de, quoted, 313

Regnier, Mathurin, 124

Reims, lace-making at, 336

Religious matters, 259–84

Renaudot, Theophraste, 42

Requests, Masters of, 321

Rethel, Battle of, 161

Retz, Cardinal de, quoted, on Richelieu, 32; a " Libertine," 99; as Frondeur, 94; quoted on Duc de Beaufort, 136; on Mazarin, 141–2; imprisoned, 166; favours the Jansenists, 271, 279; lasting disgrace of, 373; quoted, on La Rochefoucauld, 374

Retz, Maréchal de, 196

" Reunions," the, 235

Reviews, military, 215, 340

Rhine, League of the, 169, 209, 211, 220

Rhine, Passage of the, 226–7

Richelieu, Alphonse de, 30

Richelieu, Armand du Plessis de, quoted, on Condé's manifesto, 8; as Bishop of Luçon, 10, 12, 15; delegate to Third Estate, 10, 12; shares disgrace of the Concini, 21; banished to Avignon, ib.; recalled, 22; his influence over Marie de' Medici, 21, 22, 27; created a Cardinal, 28; becomes first Minister, ib.; birth, parentage, and early career, 30–2; Philippe de Champaigne's portrait of, 31; Retz' description of, 32; his nepotism, 33–4; character, 33–5;

INDEX

and Father Joseph, 35, 36 ; deference
to Louis XIII, 38 ; and Marie de'
Medici at the Court, 43 ; overreaches
the Emperor Ferdinand, 66–7 ; bar-
gains for alliance with Sweden, 68 ;
humiliates Anne of Austria, 82 ; death
of, 87 ; his special commissions of
justice, 93–4 ; his political ideals, 110,
111 ; institutes Académie Française,
125 ; persecution of Anne of Austria,
141 ; mentioned, 324 ; disorder in his
finances, 326 ; his insensibility, 353

Richelieu, Duc de, 208
Richelieu, Duchesse de, 9
Riez, Isle of, 27, 38
Rigault, Hyacinthe, 369
Rio di Janeiro, 358
Riom, 256
Riva, 41
Rivalta, Peace of, 56, 66
Rivarolle, M. de, 255
Robais, Josse van, 336, 355
Rocroy, Battle of, 87, 143
Rohan, Cardinal de, 318
Rohan, Chevalier de, 349
Rohan, Duc de, defends fortress of Mon-
taubon, 25 ; defends Montpellier, 27 ;
incites Huguenot revolt in the south,
41, 50 ; leads Huguenot insurgents, 55 ;
makes peace with Louis XIII, 55–6 ;
in the Valtellina campaign, 76
Rohan, Mme. de, 84
Rohan, Marie de, 20 ; see also Chevreuse,
Mme. de
Roland (Camisard), 300
Romanticism, 134
Ronsard, 123
Rooke, Admiral, 302–3
Rothweil, siege of, 145
Rouen, revolt in, 97 ; poverty in district
of, 356
Rouen, Archbishop of, 172
Rousseau, J. J., 114, 134, 354
Roussillon taken, 77 ; ceded to France,
169, 322, 393
Royan, 27
Roye, 4
"R.P.R." the, 261–3
Rueil, the Court at, 157 ; agreement of,
158, 161
Ruremonde, 298
Russia, 68, 210
Ruvigny, see Galloway, 303
Ruyter, Admiral de, 222, 233, 240
Ryswyck, Peace of, 257, 258, 290, 312, 346

Sablé, Mme. de, 114, 115, 119, 374
Sagnac, quoted, 355
Saint-Aignan, Duc de, 203

Saint-Amand, 311
Saint-Amant, 123
Saint-Antoine, fighting in the Faubourg,
164, 197
Saint-Antonin captured, 27
Saint-Christopher ceded to England, 312
Saint-Cloud, 201
Saint-Cyr, school at, 277, 318, 387
Saint-Cyran, Abbé de, 266, 267, 269
Saint-Etienne, foundry at, 336, 355
Saint-Evrémont, 372
Saint François de Sales, 23
Saint-Germain, Château de, 2, 84–5, 136,
159, 201, 231, 238
Saint-Gobain, factory at, 336
Saint-Hilaire, quoted, on Louvois, 213 ;
and on Battle of Oudenarde, 305 ;
wounded at Salzbach, 232
Saint-Louis-des-Français, Rome, 238
Saint-Malo, 251, 358
Saint-Omer ceded to France, 234
Saint-Pons, Bishop of, 281
Saint-Preuil (Captain of the Guard), 201
Saint-Simon, on Louis XIV's diet, 175 ;
on his self-control, 176 ; on Mme. de
Montespan, 183 ; on the second Duchess
of Orléans, 186 ; on the King's lever,
203 ; on Michel Le Tellier, 213 ; on
Mme. de Maintenon's political influence,
242–3 ; on Madame's violence to the
Duc de Chartres, 248 ; on the King's
conversion, 262 ; on the offer of the
Spanish crown to the Duc d'Anjou,
289 ; on the Vendôme brothers, 293 ;
on the character of Boufflers, 298 ; on
the Princesse des Ursins, 301 ; on the
Battle of Oudenarde, 305 ; on the
King's fortitude, 313–4 ; on Louis
XIV's exclusion of the nobles from
office, 322 ; his character and career,
391 ; his Memoirs, 391
Saint Vincent de Paul, 23, 102
Sainte-Beuve, quoted, 134
Sainte-Menehould, Peace of, 8, 14
Salzbach, 232
Samaritaine, La (pumping machine), 153
Sambre, the, 253
Santa-Vittoria, 293
Sarrelouis, 258
Saumur, Assembly of, 7
Savaron (deputy of the Third Estate),
10, 11, 353
Savonnerie, factory, 336
Savoy, 256, 257 ; Duke of, 54, 55, 292,
294, 296
Scarron, Paul, 123, 194–5, 327
Scarron, Mme., quoted, 179 ; see also
Maintenon, Mme. de
Schérer, Edmond, 382

INDEX

Schomberg, Duc de, 52, 59, 60

Scudéry, Abbé de, 116

Scudéry, Mlle. de, *quoted*, on Mme. de Rambouillet, 115; at the Hôtel de Rambouillet, 116; her own receptions, 119; her *Grand Cyrus*, 134, 150, on Mme. de Maintenon, 194; her novel, *Clélie*, 328; on Mme. de Sévigné, 375; attacked by Boileau, 376

Secretaries of State, 321–2

Sedan, Comte de Soissons at, 83; lace-making at, 336

Séguier, Chancellor, 81, 87

Seignelay, Colbert de, 237, 322, 324, 340, 345

Seneffe, Battle of, 230

Senegal, 339

Sens, Archbishop of, 104

Servien, Abel, 35, 211, 326

Sévigné, Mme. de, admirer of *L'Astrée*, 114; on Pascal's *Pensées*, 131; on Mme. de Montespan, 183–4; on the marriage of Lauzun and the Grande Mademoiselle, 186; on Mme. de Montespan in 1675, 190; on Mme. de Maintenon, 194; correspondence with Pomponne, 212; on Louvois as disciplinarian, 216; approves dragonnades and revocation of Edict of Nantes, 264; on Nicole, 268; on the Breton recruits, 354; on Mme. de La Fayette's visit to Versailles, 359; her character and literary gifts, 375; her *Letters*, *ib.*; *quoted*, on Bourdaloue, 389

Sicily united to Savoy, 312

Silesia, 63

Sillery, 6, 15

Simon, Richard, 388

Sinzheim, Battle of, 231

Siri, *quoted*, on Louvois, 213

Sirot, Baron de, 144

Smuggling, 331

Sobieski, John, 236

"Society," evolution of, 112

Soissonnais, 322

Soissons, Comte de, leagued with Marie de' Medici, 22; opposes marriage of Gaston d'Orléans, 45; implicated in Chalais' conspiracy, 48; joins in plot to assassinate Richelieu, 83; killed in the battle of La Marfée, 84, 106; mentioned, 104

Soissons, Comtesse de, 170; *see also* Mancini, Olympia

Sorbonne, 12, 280, 283

Soubise, Duc de, 27, 41

Sourdis (Archbishop), 35, 100

Sourdis, Marquis de, 58

Spain, possessions of, 63, 285; war between France and, 71, 236; defeated in sea-fight, 76; and revolt in France, 84; shorn of foreign possessions, 312; peace concluded with, 167–9; decadence of, 209; Louis XIV contemplates measures against, 221; claimants to throne of, 286

Spanheim, *quoted*, on Le Tellier, 212; and on Louvois, 213

Spanish marriages, the, 7, 14

Spanish Succession, 286–90, 313; War of the, 299, 302–3, 310–12

Spinola, 56

Spinoza, La Fontaine and, 383

Spires, 146, 252

Splügen Pass, 40

Staffarde, Battle of, 256

Stahrenberg, General, 296, 310

States-General convoked, 8; dissolved,13

Steinkerk, Battle of, 253–4

Stendhal, *quoted*, 208, 383

Stolhofen, 304

Strasburg, 231; occupied by the French, 235; ceded to France, 258; its restitution demanded, 308

"Straw Sedition," 165

Stuttgart, 304

Styria, 63

Styrum, 296

Suffren, Père, 58

Sully, 7, 101, 336

Susa, Pass of, 55

Sweden, 67; alliance of France and, 68; leagued against France, 222; bought over, 225; the ally of France, 234; deserts France and allies herself with Holland, 236

Sygognes, M. de, 123

Taille, the, 329, 357

Tallart, Maréchal de, defeated and taken prisoner at Blenheim, 296, 297

Tallemant des Réaux, *quoted*, on Leonora Concini, 3; on the death of Richelieu, 87; on Valençay's duel with Cavoye,108

Tangiers, 221

Tapissier de Notre-Dame, 253, 255; *see also* Luxembourg, Maréchal de

Tarascon, 80

Taxation, 196–7, 217, 329–32, 347–8

Teniers, 148, 377

Tessé, destroys Heidelberg, 251

Theatres, 380, 384–5

Théophile (poet), 123

Thionville, 145

Third Estate, 9

Thorigny, 109

Thou, François Auguste de, 86, 134

411

INDEX

Three Estates, struggle between the, 10–13

Tilly, 64, 68, 69

Tixier, Father, 141, 205

Toiras, 51, 52, 56

Torcy, 239, 288, 291–2, 307

Torstenson (Swedish General), 148

Tortuga, La, 98, 258

Toulon, Siege of, 295, 304

Toulouse, Comte de, 303, 316, 317

Tour d'Auvergne, *see* Turenne

Touraine, 343

Tournai, 307–8

Tourville, M. de, 250

Traites (duties), 331–2

Trent, Council of, 14

Treves, Elector of, 70

Tréville (Commander of Musketeers), 87

Trianon, 188, 199, 366

Triple Alliance, 222

Tripoli bombarded, 237

"Triumvirs of the League," 291

Tronson, Superior of St. Sulpice, 277–8

Tuileries, 364

Turenne, Vicomte de, succeeds Maréchal de Guébriant as commander, 145; appearance and character, *ib.*; takes over Enghien's command in Germany, 146; at Battle of Nordlingen, 147; subdues Bavaria, 148; leads troops against the Frondeurs, 165–6; takes Mardick and defeats Spaniards in Battle of the Dunes, 167; as diplomatist, 212; in Holland, 226; in Lorraine, 231; on the Rhine, 229; death at Salzbach, 232

Turin besieged, 294; French defeat at, *ib.*, 295, 299

Turks invest Vienna, 236

Turner, W. M., 369

Tyrol, 63

ULTRAMONTANES, 11, 12, 280, 282

Unigenitus, the Bull, 283–4

United Provinces, 210, 222–4

d'Urfé, Honoré, 113–14

Ursins, Princesse des, 300–1

Utrecht, 229, 310; Peace of, 312

VAIR, GUILLAUME DU, 15

Valençay, Cardinal de, 108

Valenciennes, 233–4, 309

Val-de-Grâce, 81

Valentinois, Prince of Monaco, 105

Vallée, Jacques, 124

Valtellina, the, 28, 40–2, 65, 76

Van Tromp, 76

Va-nu-pieds, revolt of the, 97

Vardes, *quoted*, 208

Vauban, Sébastien Le Prestre de, his genius, 216; his humanity, 217, 354–5; supports military reforms, 217; with the King at siege of Maestricht, 229; volunteers to serve under La Feuillade, 294; *quoted*, on evictions, 356; his bridge-head at Péronne, 359

Vaubrun (General), 232

Vaugelas, 116, 125–7

Vauvenargues, *quoted*, 390

Vaux-le-Vicomte, 197, 327–8

Vendôme, Duc de, leagued with Condé, 8; opposes marriage of Gaston d'Orléans, 45; plots to murder Richelieu, 46; arrested, 47; returns to Court, 87; mentioned, 136; Mazarin and, 140; mentioned, 239; enters Barcelona, 258; supersedes Villeroy in Italy, 293, 299; sent to the Netherlands, 294; his campaign in 1708, 304–5; in Spain, 310; patron of La Fontaine, 382

Vendôme, Grand Prieur de, 45–48, 87, 293, 382

Venloo, taken by Marlborough, 298

Ventadour, Duc de, 102

Ventadour, Duchesse de, 318

Verneuil, Duchesse de, 9

Verneuil, Mlle. de, 44

Versailles a modest country-house, 182, 196–7; fêtes at, *ib.*, 183, 188–9, 197; Mansart rebuilds, 198; Court installed at, *ib.*; splendour of, 206; gardens of, 359–60; a perfect expression of Louis XIV style, 366; sculpture at, 369

Viau, Théophile de, 102

Victoires, Place des, Paris, 202, 237, 294

Vigneul-Marville, *quoted*, 131

Vigo, sinking of galleons off, 302; naval battle off, 313

Villars, Maréchal de, mentioned, 239, 292; his appearance and character, 295–6; liberates Alsace, 298; Marlborough and, *ib.*; quells the revolt in the Cévennes, 300; his inspiring leadership, 308; at Malplaquet, 309; at Denain, 315

Villaviciosa, 310

Villeroy (Minister), 6, 15

Villeroy, Maréchal de, Governor to Louis XIV, 137, 173; Richelieu and, 169; mentioned, 239; at Battle of Neerwinden, 255; military incapacity of, 257, 292; defeated at Chiari, and taken prisoner at Cremona, 293; in Germany, 296; released, and succeeds Boufflers in Low Countries, 298; defeated and disgraced, 299; as President of Council of Finance, 321

INDEX

Villers, Mme. de, 349

Vincennes, 61, 318

Vineam Domini, the Bull, 281

Vitry, Maréchal de, 84, 87

Vitry, Marquis de, 19

Vittorio-Amadeo, Duke of Savoy, 67, 256, 257 ; becomes King of the Sicilies, 312

Vivonne, Catherine de, *see* Rambouillet, Mme. de

Voisin, fortune-teller, 191

Voiture, 70, 116, 119, 124

Voltaire, *quoted*, on abuses of church patronage, 101 ; on Corneille, 131 ; on Cardinal Mazarin, 168 ; on Louis XIV's majestic bearing, 176 ; on Cardinal Chigi's mission, 176 ; on the Passage of the Rhine, 227 ; on the French retreat in Holland, 230 ; on Turenne, 231 ; on Louis XIV's glory, 234 ; on Villars at Friedlingen, 295

Vossius, 210

Vouet, Simon, 366

Voysin, 292, 315

Vuillard (Jansenist), 279

Wales, Charles, Prince of, 39–40

Wales, Prince of, Old Pretender recognized as, 290

Wallenstein, 64, 65, 67, 70

Watteville, Baron de, 219

Werth (German General), 146

Westphalia, Treaty of, 149, 211, 235

William III of Orange, leader of the opposition in Holland, 224–5 ; appointed Captain-General, 226 ; becomes *Stathouder*, 229 ; marries Mary of England, 233 ; becomes King of England, 238, 249 ; at Battle of Steinkerk, 253–4 ; at Neerwinden, 255 ; recognized by France as King of Great Britain, 258 ; makes a pact with Louis XIV, 287 ; allies himself with Emperor Leopold, 290 ; death of, 291

Winter of 1709, 306

Witt, Cornelis de, 229

Witt, Jan de, 224, 229

Worms, 146, 252

Wrangel (Swedish General), 148

York, Duke of, 233 ; *see also* James II of England

Ypres taken by Condé, 148, 168, 233, 266 ; ceded to France, 234

Zuider Zee, 228

Zweibrücken, 236